'I share with Mark Latham th[...]
the task, from Opposition, [...]
Australian government—a go[...]
and then realise, a role within a contemporary society for
which past practices leave it ill-prepared.

The canvas Latham paints upon is very broad indeed.
May all his readers be able to appreciate it in its full
breadth, as I have, as my colleagues have and as, in time,
will a great many Australians.'

Kim Beazley

'The crisis facing the nation state in globalisation and the
power of footloose capital cannot be resolved by appealing to traditional left or right wing solutions. We need
new thinking that transcends historic differences.

This book arises from a Labor tradition, but honestly
analyses the limits and opportunities of that political
source. It is an impressive piece of thinking and a
thoughtful perspective on the dilemma of governance in
a global world.'

Tim Costello

'Advocates of the creation of a more competent and more
compassionate Australia in the post-industrial era will find
an abundance of policy ideas to ponder in this volume.'

Bernie Fraser

'Mark Latham shows that the Howard government's divisive policies of "downward envy" and the "Back to the
Future" policies of the New Right, the Old Right and
the Old Left will not and cannot deal with present
problems, let alone shape our future.'

Elaine Thompson

'Mark Latham's exploration of the dilemmas presented
for Labor by globalisation is an incisive and thought-
provoking contribution to the continuing debate on the
future of social democratic and left politics.'

Lindsay Tanner

'Mark Latham's analysis of the effect of the globalisation
of capital on ordinary people, and on our national culture,
couldn't be more timely.'

Moira Rayner

CIVILISING GLOBAL CAPITAL

New thinking for Australian Labor

MARK LATHAM

ALLEN & UNWIN

To my parents, Lorraine and Don Latham

First publisher in 1998
Allen & Unwin
9 Atchison Street, St Leonards 2065 Australia
Phone: (61 2) 9901 4408
Fax: (61 2) 9906 2218
E-mail: frontdesk@allen-unwin.com.au
Web: http://www.allen-unwin.com.au

National Library of Australia
Cataloguing-in-Publication entry:

Latham, Mark.
    Civilising global capital: new thinking for Australian Labor.

    Includes index.
    ISBN 1 86448 668 6.

    1. Australian Labor Party—Platforms. 2. Macroeconomics.
    3. Capital movements—Australia. 4. International finance.
    I. Title.

339.0994

Set in 10.5/12.5 pt Janson Text by DOCUPRO, Sydney

Printed and bound by Australian Print Group

10 9 8 7 6 5 4 3 2

CONTENTS

PART III   MANAGING THE COMMONS

FOREWORD

In Australian politics it always seems to be left to Labor to advance the nation's agenda. Since the March 1996 Federal election it has been remarkable to watch the speed with which the Coalition has run out of ideas and answers on each of the key issues of national concern—our place in the world, the growth of our economy, the strength and cohesiveness of our society. Even though the Howard Government has a large majority in the House of Representatives, it has only a small mandate and ambition for change.

Now, much faster than any of us could have expected, the pendulum has swung back to the ALP. The Australian people are again looking to Labor for the next generation of public policy ideas and reforms. This is why Mark Latham's contribution in this book is so valuable. It is a fresh and thoughtful assessment of the means by which Labor might renew its program for social democracy.

It is, of course, possible for the Party to revise and remake its policies in just one term of the Parliament. A heavy election defeat should not be taken as an excuse for too much introspection or caution. Nor should it be used as a way of reviving policies from the past. It must be used as a time for renewal, for bold steps and policy reform, for placing items on the national agenda that expose the inaction and inability of the Howard Government.

In my contribution to the cause of Labor, whatever may now be said about the many achievements and frustrations of the Whitlam Government 1972–75, the thing that mattered most was the renewal of policy and, with it, the renewal of the Party's relevance during the term of the Parliament after our electoral collapse in 1966. We were able to use those three years to set the agenda for the nation. Each month that passed made our program—for cities, for schools, for health, for regional development—more relevant to the needs and demands of all the people in Australia. By 1969, all the elements of policy had been defined and developed to the degree needed for a fully workable program for a national government. Our election victory in 1972 was founded on the agenda first devised and policies first proclaimed in the aftermath of our heaviest defeat.

Federal Labor now has a similar timetable and task. I have no doubt that many of the ideas and proposals set out in this book will form the basis of the next Federal Labor Government's agenda. Mark Latham has been able to deal constructively with each of the issues confronting social democracy and left-of-centre parties worldwide. He understands, most of all, that a nation's best response to economic globalisation lies in the development of its people, their skills and education system. He also understands, and describes persuasively, the need for major reform to Australia's welfare and health systems. His thoughts on the debate about social capital and civil society are likely to fashion for Labor an effective agenda for local issues of community and place.

I have known Mark Latham since 1978 and our interests and activities have overlapped considerably through these past two decades. He grew up in my old constituency and now represents it diligently and creatively in the House of Representatives. His time on my staff between 1982 and 1987 coincided with the preparation and publication of *The Whitlam Government 1972–1975*. He has the background, skills and tenacity needed to make a substantial contribution to the Party and the Parliament for quite a considerable period to come.

This book will ensure that his ideas have an enduring impact on the debate about social democracy's role and prospects during an era of globalisation and significant social change.

GOUGH WHITLAM

ACKNOWLEDGEMENTS

This book had its origins in Federal Labor's heavy defeat at the March 1996 election. After thirteen years in government implementing policy—often relying, as governments do, on the bureaucracy and, as this government certainly did, on the dominant talents of Paul Keating—it seemed a good time to be thinking about policy. In the logic of the electoral cycle, the public was virtually imposing its belief that Labor needed to reassess its values and policies from first principles. The hardest part of public life, however, probably lies in having to start again: to review all that has gone before; to revise the reasons for lost support; to regain the habits of policy research and commitment; to reassert the Party's relevance as a cause for reform and social progress.

Through its long history, Australian Labor has been a remarkably effective and resilient political cause. In each of its transitions—from agrarian Labor, to industrial Labor, to social democratic Labor—it has always been able to adapt successfully to changed economic and social circumstances. Acts of political adaptation and relevance, however, cannot be turned on and off like a tap. They have to be earned. This is what makes the current era of change—with the spread of internationalisation, massive technological advances impacting on the nature of work and society and seemingly, the evidence of community unease and insecurity all round—both so impressive and intimidating. There are no guarantees for any political movement or party, no matter how old and enduring. They have to be earned.

Internationally, social democratic parties appear to be struggling more than most. The post-war certainties of the nation and welfare states have gone forever. Even the core premise of social democracy, the expanding scale and scope of government activities, appear to have not only reached their limit but everywhere to be in retreat. Not withstanding what feels like the perpetuity of election campaigning in Australia, Labor needs to confront and debate these issues. We would be a fragile outfit indeed, especially during a term of Opposition, not to engage in the lifeblood of an active political cause: debate, disagreement and an enhanced plane of policy development. This is not the time or place for the preservation of sacred cows.

This book was originally proposed as a collaborative endeavour with Peter Baldwin MHR but over time, as its scale grew and the material assembled by each of us became too big for just one volume, we moved into separate projects. It originated as a suggestion and in a challenge to our thinking from Ric Sissons, a good friend and erstwhile publisher. In April 1996 the Leader of the Federal Parliamentary Labor Party, Kim Beazley, gave his support to such an endeavour, aimed at rethinking and reassessing Labor policy. In July 1997 Allen & Unwin took over the publication of the work, a decision and level of support, particularly from Joshua Dowse and Rebecca Kaiser, for which I am most grateful.

I also wish to thank my staff, Idalina Guerreiro and Gail Hazell, for their preparation of the manuscript up to the point at which, well over time, I discovered the joys of keyboard literacy. Michelle Rowland and the Federal Parliamentary Library assisted with the preparation of valuable research material.

My parliamentary colleagues Peter Baldwin, Jenny Macklin and Lindsay Tanner each helped to sharpen my thinking on various issues. Percy Allan provided a range of valuable suggestions for the introductory chapter. The Centre for Independent Studies provided useful and timely forums at which the material presented in Parts IV and V was initially presented. I also acknowledge the cooperation of Ian Hinckfuss from The University of Queensland in giving permission for the reproduction in Appendix III of parts of his paper advocating the introduction of a Kaldor tax in Australia. Throughout the book, of course, any errors and misinterpretations remain my responsibility.

Writing a book such as this, in addition to the other commitments of a Member of the House of Representatives, has not been easy. Without the support and advice of Gabrielle Latham all aspects of this project would have been much diminished. In ways that only we might properly understand, this book is as much her achievement as mine.

MARK LATHAM
Sydney, December 1997

Abbreviations

ABS	Australian Bureau of Statistics
ACTU	Australian Council of Trade Unions
AGPS	Australian Government Publishing Service
ALP	Australian Labor Party
AMA	Australian Medical Association
ANU	Australian National University
APEC	Asia-Pacific Economic Cooperation [Forum]
AURDR	The Australian Urban and Regional Development Review
CAD	current account deficit
CEDA	Committee for Economic Development of Australia
CEP	Community Employment Program
CPI	Consumer Price Index
DEETYA	Department of Employment, Education, Training and Youth Affairs
DSS	Department of Social Security
DVA	Department of Veterans' Affairs
ECUR	externally constrained unemployment rate
EMTR	effective marginal tax rates
EPAC	Economic Planning Advisory Council
GATT	General Agreement on Tariffs and Trade
GDP	Gross Domestic Product
GNE	Gross National Expenditure
GST	goods and services tax
HECS	Higher Education Contribution Scheme
I	national investment
IMF	International Monetary Fund
ISA	income security account
LGA	local government area
MP	Member of Parliament

NAFTA	North American Free Trade Agreement
NESB	non-English-speaking backgrounds
NWO	New Work Opportunities
OECD	Organization for Economic Cooperation and Development
QALYs	quality adjusted life years
PAYE	pay-as-you-earn
PET	progressive expenditure tax
RED	Regional Employment Development
S	national savings
WSROC	Western Sydney Regional Organisation of Councils

INTRODUCTION: TOWARDS SOCIAL CAPABILITY

> The Labor Party had developed naturally out of trade unionism. By 1891 unions were an integral social institution, with the vital task of maintaining and improving the quality of life, the living standards and the industrial conditions of the working class . . . Society's problem was not simply to restrain capitalism but to civilise it. The needs of the times demanded direct parliamentary intervention by Labor.
>
> Bede Nairn, *Civilising Capitalism: The Beginnings of the Australian Labor Party*, 1989

The aftermath of a lopsided election result can be a frightening time for the losers. Defeat in a democracy takes away not just political power but the moral authority of office. One of the fashions in political commentary since March 1996 has been to suggest that Australian Labor now lacks core values and, as a political cause, is confused about the things it believes in. It is, of course, not unusual for a grand old party like Labor to renew its agenda and to do so from Opposition. Political movements throughout the Western world are, likewise, struggling with the challenges of globalisation: how to reassert the sovereignty of the nation state; how to deal with new layers of economic insecurity and social inequality; how to rejuvenate the public standing of government and make welfare work. For parties interested in a fairer society, these challenges are particularly acute in both their moral and intellectual form.

In the title of his work on the origins of the Australian Labor Party, Bede Nairn identified a two-word summary of the historic cause of Labor: civilising capitalism. That is, Labor has always been a pragmatic, reformist party, setting its policies to suit the limits of parliamentary politics. Its purpose has never been to replace capital with some other economic and social system, but to ameliorate or civilise its impact on people and places marginalised by the profit system. For a century or more the cause of Labor, and the Party's goals and purpose, have barely altered. Its methods and programs, however, in response to an epoch of economic and social change, have had to be transformed. At a time when the sphere of capital has moved decisively to the international arena, Australian Labor—like parties everywhere engaged in the social democratic project—is being called on to civilise global capital.

This is a book about transition: the changing role of government as society shifts from the industrial to the information age; the changing role of Labor as it adapts its methods to the global sphere of capital; and the challenges faced by social democracy in dealing with the changing nature of work, welfare and society. In the extemporary work of a political cause, however, nothing is more threatening or turbulent than acts of policy transition. Particularly for parties of the Left, there is a powerful tendency to appeal to the perceived triumphs and legends of the past to guide the thinking and identity of the present. In the tribalism of these things, tradition can take on a contemporary life of its own. The collective interpretation of history becomes something more than a shared celebration of struggles past. It can become a cause in itself.

Acts of policy transition are also made problematic by the sheer weight of conformity among the institutions of public life. In any large organisation, socialisation always plays a role. In a political party this can often mean, for the sake of group harmony, that orthodoxy is allowed to survive well after its political use and relevance have expired. This reflects the comfort of conformity: that most conservative of instincts in the political arena holding people short of reasoned change. The momentum gained in the running of the herd becomes more important than the direction in which the herd is headed. Inevitably, given the way in which our society is in a steadfast state of change and evolution, this leads to the folly of persistence in error.[1]

These trends can be doubly dangerous for parties of reform: allowing tradition to become an excuse for inaction; allowing orthodoxy to march unchallenged down the path of folly. Modernisation becomes impossible if political means, expressed through the weight of history and conformity, are allowed to substitute for political ends. Hence Labor's strong sense of tradition needs to be celebrated, not as an end in itself, but as a remarkable expression of the Party's continuity of purpose. If, as seems certain, the rate of economic and social change continues apace in Australia, then

Labor can only keep this purpose alive through the politics of transition. In an era of permanent change the greatest threat to the historic cause of Labor, properly understood and pursued, lies in policy inertia.

The ALP has never been a socialist party in the sense of pursuing Marxist doctrines aimed at the state ownership of the means of production. It has always embraced the merit of a mixed economy: the primacy of the market as a means of generating income and wealth; and the primacy of public sector intervention as a means of ameliorating the market's treatment of the weak and vulnerable. Moreover, as the sphere of capital and market forces have altered over time, so too has Labor changed its policy methods. This reflects a rolling cycle of policy transition: from Labor's origins as a party defending the interests of agrarian labour, to the emergence of an industrial Labor Party in the 1940s, to the development of social democratic programs in the 1960s and more recently, Labor's embrace of internationalism in economic policy.

In this fashion, a regular pattern of initiative and resistance has characterised the making of ALP policy. At each turn of the cycle, reforms have been resisted by those pointing to a golden age of principle and Labor values. The Party's parliamentarians are seen to be out of step with extra-parliamentary views and the designation of tradition. Remarkably, transition after transition, Labor has managed to update its relevance, adapting its policy framework to changed economic, social and electoral circumstance. No matter the intensity of the debate and importance of the issues, the Party has kept the policy wheel turning. As, over time, the contingencies and inequities of the profit system have altered, Labor has been able to modernise the countervailing functions of government aimed at a fairer society. Acts of political transition, no matter how threatening or disruptive in their day, need to be seen as the most useful and enduring part of the construction of Labor tradition.

So too, history tells us that whenever Federal Labor has lost heavily at the polls it has had to fundamentally reinvent itself to regain office. The Party which won the 1972 election was very different to that which lost in 1966. Likewise, the Party which regained power in 1983 had remade itself out of the lessons of 1975. Accordingly, this is not a time for letting our pride about the past—the remarkable record of the Hawke and Keating Governments—blind Labor to the changes which need to be made post–1996. Yet history also shows that Labor, in attempting to deal with changed circumstance, has never actively pursued the resurrection of lapsed policies. While policy change has often been resisted in the name of tradition, Labor has seen little use in making new policies through the prism of eras past. It has always managed to find an abiding sense of policy progress, meeting fresh challenges with a new generation of idealism and reform.

Often in politics some seek to respond to adversity by returning to solutions which gave the appearance of working well in the past. The politics of nostalgia, however, has never been able to provide a lasting solution to the challenge of dynamic economic and social change. If events and circumstance were not in the habit of changing, then applying the methods of the 1960s to the problems of the 1990s might be a satisfactory technique. Rather, Labor faces a task of fundamental reconstruction: returning its thinking to first principles and reformulating the active tools of governance in response to the globalisation of capital and social conditions.

This task accepts the inevitability of movement and change in public policy. The economic restructuring of the 1980s in Australia has produced social and political restructuring, from which the ALP must devise a new political framework. This not only requires bold thinking and creative ideas, but a thoroughness of method. Much like Max Weber's description of democratic politics, it calls for slow boring through hard boards. Labor has no way back to the past, back to the slogans and certainties of an Australia now past: national economic controls, tariff walls, state paternalism and White Australia. As ever, Labor must rely on the politics of transition—new circumstance, new thinking, new policies—to guide its future constructively. This is the path to party modernisation.

POLITICS IN TRANSITION

This book examines the means by which left-of-centre thinking might respond to the changing nature of political events and ideology in a post-industrial society. In the industrial age economy, ideology was positioned around a clear dichotomy: capital versus labour, freedom versus equality, market forces versus state planning, individualism versus collectivism, liberalism versus socialism. The ownership features of industrial production promoted the polarisation of ideology and its attendant political contests. Questions of governance this century have focused on little else. At various times, especially during the Great Depression and the Second World War, the good society was thought to rely on the subservience of the market to state collectivism. At other times, particularly with the global collapse of communism, the state was deemed to be doing few things well and needed to make way for the enhancement of market freedoms. At all times this oscillation across the ideological divide has failed to provide lasting gains in the problem-solving capacities of government. In the fatalism of Manning Clark, 'we are like a herd of cows waiting for two tired old bulls—capital and labour—to decide which is the stronger'.[2]

While technological progress has transformed so many aspects of society this century, the prevailing techniques of governance barely seem to have progressed at all. Despite talk for a decade or more of the reinvention of government, the results have not been impressive. The choice on either side of the ideological divide appears limited. Globalisation, the accelerated movement of capital and information internationally, has left parties and politicians across the spectrum struggling for solutions. The small government policies of the political Right have not been able to show, once the active role of government is withdrawn, how individual liberty alone can answer the insecurity and remorseless inequity of an open economy. Equally, the Left has found it difficult to sustain the conventional functions and fixed structures of government as a workable response to new sources of social and economic exclusion. The choice between market freedom, with its army of the working poor in the United States, and unreconstructed public provision, with the failings and unsustainable costs of the welfare state in Western Europe, barely offers a choice at all. It simply points to the need for a third way.

In response to the failings of this political binary, the techniques of governance are in need of renewal. Systems of public administration, state and non-state, founded through the course of this century no longer seem suited to the demands of the new economy and dynamics of an open society. In Australia, as across the Western world, these trends abound in the public arena. The struggle between economic nationalism and internationalism, the re-emergence of social populism, the fragmentation of social values and connectedness, and the widespread public cynicism with parliamentary government represent much more than an aftershock from the reforms of the 1980s. They reflect a basic realignment in the role of the state and the way in which issues, values and policies now sit across the political divide. The work of the public sector is in transition.

The politics of the late twentieth century reflects an era of perpetual change and uncertainty. The enhanced mobility of capital, the emergence of an information society, changes in the nature of work, and the transformation of social institutions have fractured the effectiveness of the old ideological divide. The dichotomy constructed last century between capital and labour has gradually lost its pertinence through the course of this century. Far from reflecting the end of ideology, this process points to the need for the reconstruction of left-of-centre thinking. It is no longer sufficient to assume, as Marxists might, that the failings of the profit system will ultimately produce a vacuum within which the political Left can then unveil some new social structure. Functionalism of this kind leads to an unacceptable hardness in reformist techniques: the folly of waiting for social change to match the prescriptions of an outdated social theory.

Similarly, it is not sufficient for social democrats to assume, as they did with confidence in the decades following the Second World War, that the answer to every social problem simply lies in more public ownership, Keynesian economics and welfare statism. Traditions of this kind, if taken as a cause in themselves, are ultimately self-defeating. The relevance of a political cause does not lie in the application of fixed methods to the freshly formed issues of social change. It comes from the skillful anticipation of change and adaptation of policy methods. In the reconstruction of left-of-centre thinking and ideology, the current era of change offers widespread opportunities for this reformist ethos of political adaptation.

A defining feature of the new economy is the international mobility of large holdings of capital. The seamless movement of information and finance between nations, and the enhanced mobility of commodity production, have aided the integration of economic markets. The tendency in all Western nations is towards internationalisation—not necessarily the creation of a single global market, but a definite trend by which the cross-national interests of capital are breaking down the traditional economic controls and barriers of the nation state. In this sense, economic globalisation does not represent a completed process of market integration on an international scale. Rather, it signifies a transition in the sphere of capital from predominantly national to multinational features of ownership, control and mobility.

The transformation of capital—in finance, production and commodity trade—is impacting profoundly on the geography of public governance. Political jurisdictions, anchored in the nation state and politics of localism, have felt compelled to engage in the chase for capital across the globe. The upward shift of capital to the global arena has left politicians everywhere struggling to establish the new tools of national economic sovereignty. The tension between the multinational sphere of capital and local sphere of electoralism is fundamentally altering the politics of the nation state. As the geographer, Peter Dicken, has written:

> The tendency towards an increasingly interconnected and interdependent global economy will intensify. The fortunes of nations, regions, cities, neighbourhoods, families and individuals will con-

tinue to be strongly influenced by their position in the [international] network. In a rapidly shrinking and interconnected world there is no hiding place.[3]

So too, the shift in society's economic base from industrial age production to an information age is realigning questions of ideology and political partisanship. Throughout this century the system of economic production and value creation has moved from machines and manpower to the use of information and brain power. Increasingly, economic value is being generated by knowledge and the skillful manipulation of information and symbols. The OECD, for instance, has estimated that more than one-half of the output of the world's advanced economies now relies on knowledge-based processes.[4] Knowledge has joined capital and labour as a core factor of production.

The transformation of the economic base has had a profound impact on the nature of work and social organisation. The rise of knowledge work has broken the standardisation of production skills. It has also lifted the level of skills required for workforce participation, producing for some citizens the problem of long term economic exclusion. Moreover, the change in the economy's employment base, from manufacturing output to services production, has been associated with the growth in part-time and casual work, plus higher rates of female labour force participation. These new patterns of work are challenging conventional notions of income support. The design features of the post-war welfare state—built around an expectation that male workers could hold down jobs for life, earning a wage sufficient to support the nuclear family unit—have now become redundant. Policy makers everywhere are being forced to deal with a loss of economic certainty, the demands of reskilling and multi-skilling the workforce, the growth of two- and zero-income families and, in aggregate, the overload of the income support capacities of the state. Governments have been forced into a heavy rationing role in the distribution of public entitlements. With the spread of economic insecurity and the demand for public sector support and entitlements all round, the social legitimacy of the post-war welfare state is in decline.

As ever, changing economic events have produced social change. Vast gains in information technology this century have given the citizenry access to communication networks well beyond the walls of the family home and geographically defined communities. The diversification of work and social values has also loosened the glue of social cohesiveness. The strength of the family as a social institution and the connectedness of civil society appear to be waning. To give just one statistic: whereas at the 1947 census, one in thirteen Australian households featured an adult living alone, by 1991 the proportion home alone had risen to one in five. The growing spread of life's responsibilities—as more people work, travel and communicate in international areas—seems to have weakened society's sense of community and place. In this fashion, quality of life issues have returned to the centre of the political agenda. Importantly, however, this has not been a product of public demands for a new generation of personal freedoms and services, but concerns about the freedom of other citizens to cause social disorder and lawlessness.

Knowledge and information skills have now emerged as critical determinants of opportunities and outcomes in our society. Whereas in feudal times access to land was the fulcrum on which social outcomes rested, just as in the industrial age access to industrial technology and capital determined the spread of wealth and opportunity, the information age demands highly refined cognitive skills to unlock the full virtues of citizenship. Whether in the labour market, the pursuit of recreational interests or fashioning of social values, a knowledge-based society deals favourably with the information rich and less favourably with those citizens deprived of information and cognitive prowess. As the American writer, Larry Letich, has explained:

> It is possible that over the last 100 years, and especially the last 40, we may have created a society that demands more brain power than most people are able to give. One of the major reasons, in fact, our political system is breaking down, our social fabric is frayed, may be that we are expecting from people a level of cognitive sophistication—a level of abstract thinking—never before required . . . Until this century, at least 95 per cent of what an adult knew fell into two categories: practical or interpersonal. Both of these types of knowledge are concrete; they involve things one can see, touch and feel. Almost all of the remaining five per cent—the abstract knowledge—was comprised of myths, legends and religious beliefs passed down by the culture . . . Today from the moment they wake up to the morning news on the radio until the moment they turn off their TV at night, citizens must constantly process information about things they can't see, touch or really even imagine. Still, they are expected to decide whether the information is true or not and how to act on it. Those who are comfortable with all this abstraction thrive. Those who aren't flounder.[5]

In the industrial age, notions of value were closely associated with the production of material goods. Our cultural understanding of a market economy is founded on the concept of people making things which are then identified through market transactions as holding a particular quantity of material worth. Knowledge, of course, is not as easily quantified, nor can it be subjected to a mechanistic process of production. The intellectual paradigms of the industrial age lack a language of analysis for dealing with the political economy of a knowledge-reliant society. In particular, they struggle to adequately explain the means by which the values of society might be fashioned, not by material means, but through the citizenry's engagement in ideas and learning. It now appears certain that public issues of information access, especially in the cognitive skills required for the attainment of knowledge, have run an important new dividing line through society. The stratification of social opportunity and values is being determined as much by the divide between the information rich and the information poor as by conventional notions of material wealth and deprivation.

The march of permanent change has for many parts of society made this an era of permanent anxiety. For industries threatened by the mobility of capital, for workers challenged by the shift from industrial to knowledge-based employment, for citizens without the information skills required to overcome social and economic exclusion, for communities and locations left behind by the pace of change, our dynamic society looks nothing like a fair society. Inevitably, with the loss of most of the certainties of the industrial age, the spread of social and economic insecurity has broadened. Just as the advent of the Industrial Revolution turned society on its head—as labour moved from agricultural to manufacturing employment, as people moved from rural homes to urban communities, as the nation state emerged and then dominated our systems of government—the information age is just as thoroughly transforming the nature of work, society and national governance.

The old ideologies of the Left and Right, positioned around the industrial age struggle between capital and labour, do not appear capable of dealing with these issues, any more than the steam engine might now be regarded as an effective mode of transport. Internationally, parties are striving for new paradigms of governance suited to the demands of an information society and economic globalisation. The tricks of sophisticated electoralism—opinion polling, populist rhetoric and marginal seat campaigning—are without answers beyond the short term horizons of electoral manipulation. Likewise, the politics of nostalgia offers nothing more than a chimera of false comfort and expectations.

Politicians who engage in these particular methods bear a heavy responsibility for the substantial loss of public confidence and trust in our political system. There is something frightfully immoral about those in public life who know full well that the past is undeliverable yet because the electorate sometimes seeks shelter from insecurity by reviving impressions of how society used to be, they still proceed to throw back to the policies of the past and hold out false hope for the way in which nostalgia might somehow resolve the problems of the present. For political causes committed to the virtues of social progress, this technique is doubly dangerous. It not only fosters conservatism among the electorate by abandoning the desirability of social change, but also discounts the possibility of social progress through the skilful anticipation of change and adaptation of policy.

The cause of Labor is never weaker than when the Party has nothing more progressive to offer the electorate than a revival of ideas long past. The Party has never found electoral or policy salvation in such a path. As ever, Labor needs to take on the role of educator as well as reformer: explaining why a society in transition needs to find fresh solutions to issues of public prominence; exposing the deception and folly of the politics of nostalgia; and creating strong expectations for the need for policy reform. At a time when society and politics are so thoroughly in motion, this necessitates the reconsideration of the ideology and moral purpose of left-of-centre causes.

IDEOLOGY IN TRANSITION

Out of the Industrial Revolution, which harnessed machine power for commercial purposes, politics came to be defined around questions of ownership and control in the means of production. The owners of capital were said to be exploiting those who worked the machines. Questions of social equity and participation were understood and argued out within this framework of owners and non-owners. In the post-industrial era, however, it is clear that political issues are being driven by much more than the conventional dichotomy between capital and labour. The political spectrum no longer lies flat with an easy continuity from Left to Right. It has had additional layers of partisanship grafted on through the upward movement of capital, the rise of information skills and the changing nature of social connectedness. The political divide is now best conceptualised as a four-plane matrix, split by the struggle between capital and labour; economic nationalism and economic internationalism; the emergence of the information rich and information poor; and the realignment of social relations between individualism and community.

In many nations parts of this matrix have served as a catalyst for recasting the party political system. In New Zealand, for instance, the traditional parties of the Left and Right—Labour and the Nationals—have split in two in response to the issue of economic internationalisation. Left-of-centre, Labour has embraced an internationalist agenda while The Alliance continues to advocate the policies of a closed economy. Right-of-centre, Winston Peters' New Zealand First Party, was formed as a break away from the National Party to pursue a program of so-called economic nationalism.[6] This four-cornered party or candidate system is now reasonably common in Western European and North American elections. In Australia, albeit on a smaller scale with a different voting system, a similar process has taken place with the former Liberal candidate, Pauline Hanson, forming her One Nation Party and the maverick Labor MP, Graeme Campbell, establishing an Australia First Party.

Even within a more diffuse party structure, industrial age ideologies have been further fragmented by the advent of knowledge work and the values system of an information-based society. Cognitive skills are not only fashioning issues of social and economic participation, but also the way in which society is determining its spread of ethical and normative values. The information rich have a high level of engagement in abstract thinking, with the capacity to create new opportunities out of the change process. Within the context of globalisation, a clear set of social values has emerged: cosmopolitan, progressively tolerant and confident, generally embracing the rhetoric and horizons of a global village. A dynamic society is welcomed as an addition to life's interests, rather than a threat to life's security. The information poor, however, carry a vastly different set of social values: relying more on the practical certainties of life, the things one can see, touch and feel. The conceptual appeal of the internationalisation of economic and social relations is treated with greater caution, if not hostility. Notions of outward looking tolerance are perceived as better suited to the interests of those who have already attained a secure place in the new economy. Change is interpreted for its immediate consequences, more likely as a tangible threat than a chance for problem-solving abstraction.

These two ends of the cognitive spectrum have created an active political contest transcending the party system and the way in which, historically, the values and incentive structures of government have been framed. This has been a particularly challenging concept for left-of-centre thinking. A government which pursues and rewards the values of the information rich at the expense of the information poor would appear, at face value, to be working against some important equity principles. Yet the

Left has always looked to the power of learning and excellence as a means of building tolerance and social enlightenment. This paradox has produced a vigorous, still largely unformed debate over issues of so termed 'political correctness'; that is, the suggestion that a network of cognitive elites have captured the tools of opinion leadership—primarily through the public sector, academia and the media—and unreasonably imposed their values upon the remainder of society. While the partisan interests of many of those campaigning against political correctness might easily be dismissed (representing, as they do, a band of elite conservative opinion), the fundamentals of the argument require serious scrutiny.[7] Parties of the Left require a paradigm of analysis within which issues concerning the apparent divide between the information rich and poor can be reconciled in the political economy of the nation state.

Certainly the politics of the four-plane matrix is intensely challenging. The capital/labour binary concerns itself primarily with the distribution of society's material goods. The question of economic nationalism/internationalism represents an important reworking of the type of patriotism which first became prominent 200 years ago with the emergence of the nation state. The rise of social values to the centre of the political agenda is highly representative of the public partisanship of an information society. History tells us that 100 or even 50 years ago, the diffusion of social values was not as broad. After all, people are less likely to differ about the practicalities of life—the things they can see, touch and feel—than concepts that can only be dealt with in cognitive abstraction. The value systems of the industrial age had only to deal with the practical and interpersonal aspects of life. Now, with the wide spread of information and learning in society, the range of personal priorities, ethics and beliefs has multiplied exponentially. The conventional methods of party politics, however, are without a compass by which these value systems can be assessed.

Left-of-centre thinking has been slow to engage itself in the values debate. So too, it has taken insufficient interest in issues of community and place. Reformist techniques have tended to concentrate on a top–down relationship between governments and the citizenry, rather than on the quality of the relationship between citizens that might aid the formation of shared interests and community. That is, from its origins, the social democratic project has limited its role to the capacity of the state public sector to alter the distribution of physical capital and, more recently, human capital. It has not recognised the significance of a public sector beyond the strict functionings of government—the type of contact and association between people which gives rise to bonds of mutual trust and equality in the public arena. It has yet to actively engage itself in the debate concerning the formation and distribution of social capital. This has been a disappointing feature of social democracy: adopting a somewhat perfunctory view of social reform—much as a doctor might administer medicine to a patient—without pursuing a close interest in the relations between people which determine issues of equality and community in the non-state public sector. James Coleman has positioned the social capital question as follows:

> Just as physical capital is created by changes in materials to form tools that facilitate production, human capital is created by changes in persons that bring about skills and capabilities that make them able to act in new ways. Social capital, however, comes about through changes in the relations among persons that facilitate action. If physical capital is wholly tangible, being embodied in observable material form, and human capital is less tangible, being embodied in the skills and knowledge acquired by an individual, social capital is less tangible yet, for it exists in the relations between people.[8]

The changing relations between citizens in an open society have created a new generation of political issues. While the new sphere of international capital and cognitive excellence appears well suited to individualistic endeavour, opening up for many people fresh tiers of economic and social opportunity, there appears to be (particularly among those citizens excluded from these opportunities) a growing level of concern about the loss of community and interdependence in our society. The social policy agenda of most nations is now overflowing with issues of social fragmentation. The sense of public unease arising from the spread of lawlessness, street crime, drug dependency and the entrenched features of unemployment has broken the credibility and reputation of the welfare state as a solver of social problems. So many people now express a fear of what other citizens are doing or might do, thereby eroding the basis of social trust and respect. Everywhere people are declaring their support for wanting to do more things in common with others, but nowhere, they say, can they find the people to trust or the things to do.

Issues of community and place have formed a fourth plane of political differentiation. They reflect a broadening of life's responsibilities, further aggravated by the upward shift of capital and its attendant political issues to a global arena. In their daily activities, people, and those who represent them, are being confronted, more than ever, by matters spanning the local and regional spheres of public responsibility, through to the national and international.

While political leaders are now expected to master multinational forums, many of the issues that determine their election or defeat lie at a local level.[9] This is a striking challenge for all parties to the democratic system. Its resolution lies, at least in part, in a reaffirmation of the importance of community. As the pace of life has lifted, and workplace skills and social values have diversified, the need for expressions of commonality—the interests and ideals people can and should share with others—has risen in tandem. New forms of social connectedness and solidarity, however, are not possible unless people find new things to do and express in common. Although political leaders in all regions and nations have been keen to embrace the rhetoric of community values, the new work of community, and its relationship with the policies of the state public sector, still stand as an unformed issue. In particular, social democracy is yet to consider at length the type of activities and relationships in which people might usefully engage themselves in rebuilding social capital.

Australian Labor, like many of its fraternal parties internationally, has been struggling to reconcile its historic purpose with these additional layers of public partisanship. An odd thing about our term in government was the way in which Labor gained a reputation for doing things at opposite ends of the conventional spectrum. At one extreme the Party was seen as an agent of economic change, opening up new opportunities for global trade, investment and information skills. At the other end, it was regarded as pursuing income security measures for people outside the production system. For those in between—a newly insecure group of workers and their families—Labor's agenda had become blurred and, judging by the 1996 election result, unrepresentative.

One feature of a heavy defeat, however, is that it usually encourages one's opponents to reveal some of their research and thinking. Addressing the National Press Club in March 1996, the Liberal's Federal Director, Andrew Robb, declared 'there are now deep contradictions within the Labor Party in regard to what they stand for and who they represent'. The Liberal's exit polling revealed a nine-point lead over Labor among blue collar workers. In Robb's view 'it owes much to Labor's attempts over fifteen years or more to chase the votes of the socially progressive, often highly educated, affluent end of middle class Australia . . . along the way Paul Keating and his colleagues came to reflect far more closely the values and priorities of this narrow, affluent, middle class group'.

This summary of the last election result reflects, neatly enough, the shifting sands of Australian politics. It demonstrates how—with the emergence of a second, third and fourth plane on the political spectrum—political interests and constituencies have become more complex and fluid. Moreover, it exposes the limits inherent in what I would term 'binary politics'; that is, the idea that parties and politicians can target issues and constituencies on a single plane of the matrix without flow-on consequences elsewhere. In the old system of politics, based on the capital/labour divide, political decisions and outcomes were regarded as relatively predictable. They encouraged parties to take a distinctive position along the spectrum and build a coalition of support among the related interest groups. The ALP, for instance, argued for improved wages and conditions for workers knowing that, while this might upset the interests of the business sector, the Party was supporting the interests of its traditional constituency. Conventionally, the Liberal and National Parties advanced the interests of capital, explicitly defining this class during the 1950s and 1960s to include a new generation of professionals, artisans, passive shareholders and small business people. These examples provide a guide, albeit in fairly simplistic terms, to the characteristics of binary politics: the establishment of a party position on either side of the Right/Left spectrum by which a stable constituency of support could be commanded.

The four-plane matrix of politics in an open economy provides no such certainty. It is representative of the general trend towards major party dealignment, with a steadily increasing number of swinging voters and support for third and fourth party movements. It is not possible for parties to target issues plane by plane without significant inconsistencies arising elsewhere. The catch-all style of binary politics, governed by a comparatively simple set of win–lose scenarios, now flounders from the depth of interests and values guiding electoral behaviour down the matrix. Because none of the four planes sit in harmony, the ideologies of an industrial society have entered a period of transformation. From a Labor perspective, for instance, the interests of what had been known as working class citizens have been fragmented by the changing nature of work and new distinctions between the political values of the information rich and information poor. Likewise, Labor's opening of the Australian economy to internationalisation was clearly interpreted by many working people prior to the last Federal election as aiding the rate of dislocation in traditional forms of employment and social connectedness.

The mere passing of an election, of course, is not able to reconcile these tensions or competing constituencies. Already the record of the Howard Government has confirmed its determination to exploit Andrew Robb's thesis of 'deep contradictions' within ALP policy. On a range of social issues it has engaged in a strategy of wedge politics, aimed at forcing Labor to juggle its commitment to what Liberal strategists like to term 'the cafe latte set' and 'the blue singlets'. Bolstered by the benefits of incumbency this is, to be realistic, a menacing tactic. It uses issues like work-for-the-dole, migration cuts and native title as a way of splitting two Labor constituencies: the highly skilled, cosmopolitan internationalists and the less secure, more traditional working class.

The ALP—and for that matter, the nation—cannot afford to be overcome by the low-grade morality of wedge politics. This makes even more critical the task of ideological and policy transition. It confirms the need for social democracy to meet the core challenges of the new political economy—to develop a clearer public consensus on the policies and values of social inclusiveness and connectedness; to make welfare work so that the social safety net becomes synonymous with social mobility; and to ensure that international engagement and traded growth carry with them a stronger sense of economic security. In short, Labor needs to show that equity and electoral success can still go together.

Challenges such as these confront the electoral viability of parties like Labor and, no less critically, many of the principles upon which left-of-centre thinking has been based. For the ALP, however, they now take on a special significance. After thirteen years in government, pushing through a sea-change in Australia's circumstances, Labor needs to engage itself intellectually in the task of reconstruction. The scope of the economic and social changes, both here and abroad, is so broad that it cannot be dealt with—at least from first principles—by simply tracking, issue by issue, the flow of electoral opinion. One of the reliable laws of modern politics is that policy vacuums are filled by polling results. At this part of the political cycle, however, this is not a sound strategy for the ALP. Removed from the administrative and political pressures of office, the Party needs to vigorously debate, rethink and revise its core ideology: what we stand for and who we represent. This book aims to add value to this process of policy renewal. It hopes to find a way through the multi-layering of the political spectrum by which Labor and its historic purpose can find relevance in the politics of the post-industrial age.

THE NEW RADICAL CENTRE

A starting point is to examine the recent success of some of Labor's fraternal parties overseas. In particular, Tony Blair's New Labour in Britain and Bill Clinton's new Democrats in the United States have responded to the complexity of the new political economy with a fresh set of social democratic values. They have eschewed the coalition-building approach of binary politics in favour of the values of a 'new radical centre'. The policy prescriptions of the old Left and Right dichotomy have been abandoned as unsuitable during a time of globalisation and widespread insecurity. They have been replaced by the construction of a new social consensus around the values of responsibility, reward for effort, devolution and the interdependence of society. In his seminal book, *Behind The Oval Office* (1997), Clinton's long-time adviser, Dick Morris, has described this process as 'triangulation'. The new radical centre is formed by moving to the centre of the old Left/Right spectrum and, most critically, lifting above this plane of politics through the expression of new and radical social values (conceptualised as the apex of a triangle, with the Left/Right divide forming its base). In Blair's words, 'being radical is defined as having a central vision based around principle but liberated from particular policy pre-scriptions that became confused with principle'.[10]

The guiding principle of the new radical centre is to hold the cohesiveness and fairness of society together through new expres-sions of personal and collective responsibility. During this era of globalisation and insecurity, each of us as individuals plainly need to do more to advance our own interests—to study harder, to prepare and save more effectively for an uncertain future, to work smarter, to develop the competitive skills that deliver job security in an open economy. But just as much, we also need to do more together—to look out for each other, to aid those who are strug-gling to help themselves, to support each other in the values and interests we hold in common. The new radical centre is best understood as a political assertion of this heightened sense of responsibility, not just in the relationship between citizens and government, but also between citizens and society. It gives to the public sector two core functions: facilitating the opportunities and incentives needed among the citizenry to combat insecurity—eco-nomic and social—plus helping to develop the skills and effective freedom people require in the realisation of their life's potential. It rejects the core features of the ideologies of both the old Left and the New Right—that is, the notion of a nanny state, within which government is responsible for the provision of welfare without the reciprocation of personal responsibility; plus libertarian arguments favoring individual responsibility without the active role of government and the collective work of the public sector.

Morris refutes the idea of a narrowly self-interested electorate, maintaining that people are still willing to help others, as long as they can be guaranteed that these acts of collective responsibility are matched by the discharge of individual responsibility by others.

He describes this as the new politics of 'liberalism with standards. Give to the needy but exact performance and responsibility in return.'[11] Within this framework, the role of government is to act as a fulcrum between the two tiers of responsibility, ensuring an appropriate balance between public provision and individual effort. Policy needs to aim at marrying rights with responsibilities, at creating new social opportunities in tandem with the imposition of new personal obligations. Only by these methods can the citizenry, as individuals and as a society, guarantee a threshold of social and economic security all round.

The new radical centre declares the era of large-scale, centralised, paternalistic government to be at an end. It requires the devolution of many of the traditional functions of the state into the hands of self-governing communities of interest. Clearly, people are not likely to take suitable responsibility for their own actions if their personal control and dignity have been smothered by the decision-making power of others. Equally, however, not all individuals and communities, if left to rely on nothing more than their own resources and capabilities, will cope well with the challenges of economic and social change. Hence the new radical centre is incompatible with the *laissez faire* agenda of the libertarian Right. It rejects an ideological standpoint insisting, in the famous dictum of Margaret Thatcher, that there is no such thing as society. Indeed, it points to the growing significance of interdependence in an open society, with new forms of partnership between the state and its citizens—that is, the collective role of government as a raiser and distributor of public resources; and the role of individuals and communities in moulding these resources (in combination with their own efforts and responsibilities) to deal with the spread of uncertainty. All citizens are given a stake in society, with strong incentives and clear obligations to use their entitlements well.

In this way, the new radical centre develops a synthesis of public and private sector activity around the fulcrum of social responsibility. It fashions the work of government around rewarding the citizenry for the exercise of effort and responsibility. Whereas the tax debate, for instance, is usually conducted in terms of self-interest and social justice (with the Right favoring tax cuts across-the-board and the Left wanting to target them to the lowest paid), the new radical centre offers a fresh perspective. It casts tax concessions, not in terms of who receives them, but what citizens have done to deserve them.[12] Similarly, industrial relations and wages policies are framed to explicitly reward work (whereas the deregulatory policies of the Right often create poverty traps, encouraging people to move from work to welfare). The work of the welfare state is aimed at social mobility, framing the allocation of transfer payments as a second chance, not a way of life. The values of the new radical centre break the limits of binary politics by appealing to the interests and concerns of citizens in common.

The legitimacy of public sector action is interpreted as resting heavily on the capacity of government to positively influence the behaviour of its citizens. Perceptions of personal well-being now rely more on communal issues—the way in which the actions of others might impact adversely on one's life—than concerns about the generation and distribution of economic resources. Economic issues are likely to be judged in the public arena for their attendant social impact, rather than more abstract measures of social justice such as income equity. For example, public concerns about unemployment tend to be based on fears about the behaviour of those who are economically idle, with evidence pointing to a correlation between rates of unemployment and the spread of crime against persons and property. As Morris has written from the 1996 US Presidential campaign, 'Clinton tapped into a conclusion many people have reached in their personal lives: that the impediment to a better life is not primarily one's economic performance but communal problems—the quality of life for everyone'.[13]

While more than ever people are demanding a positive return on their taxes, this attitude is being cast in terms of a public desire for government to ameliorate the negative actions of other people. In this sense, the attainment of a fundamentally fair and decent society, displaying the virtues of economic inclusiveness and social connectedness, is by no means inconsistent with popular politics. If the taxation system was perceived as the price of making welfare work and achieving social mobility and social capital, then few people would resent its impositions. The problem for social democracy in recent decades, however, has been a substantial gap between this goal and the policy outcomes of government. In a democracy, the public inevitably pays on results. Until the social democratic project deals more effectively with issues of economic and social exclusion, it is likely to represent nothing more substantial than the nice rhetoric and political striving of a well-intentioned minority. Even worse, it might start to find comfort in a form of highbrow purity—resenting the values and aspirations of the popular culture because of its perceived failure to snugly fit the social democratic mould.

The values of the new radical centre aim to avoid these shortcomings. They reflect the virtue of politics in transition: responding to changed economic and social circumstances with the new tools of social cohesiveness. They recognise that in a post-industrial society, a party's relevance hinges on the quality and appeal of its values. In the old system, politicians were encouraged to define themselves with close reference to the binary divide: to draw a line in the sand and encourage a majority of interest groups to join them on one side of the debate. This led to issues being dealt with through the calculus of coalition-building. In its most corrupted form, the interest groups concerned would actually be invited to write the party policy. It seems likely, however, that this style of politics will continue to struggle with the complexity of a multi-plane system. Increasingly, electoral behaviour is being determined by views, ethics and morality expressed on more than one plane of the matrix. Just as questions of class (capital versus labour) no longer act as a primary determinant of political ideology, nor can matters concerning the nation state (economic nationalism versus internationalism), cognitive skills (the information rich versus information poor), or social relations (individualism versus community), be taken in their own right as definitive guides to electoral identity.[14] The days of simple issues and electoral analysis have ended.

It is for this reason the value-laden approach of the new radical centre is so significant. Values of this kind, framed as a cogent response to globalisation and insecurity, are able to find resonance across the citizenry. They cut across each plane of the matrix with a depth well beyond the scope of binary politics. In an open society with a wide spread of economic uncertainty, a good proportion of people are likely to appreciate the importance of social responsibility, rewards, interdependence and devolution. This represents a critical opportunity for social democracy. Themes such as these need to be used as the basis of a new framework of social inclusion and fairness. They have the potential to form the moral and political foundations of a rejuvenated social democratic project. A leading purpose of this book is to show how the values of the new radical centre can aid the cause of social inclusiveness in an open economy.

Quite often Tony Blair and Bill Clinton are dismissed as too slick and folksy in their language and purpose to have any lasting impact on the ideology of the Left. Some have argued that their politics actually represents the capitulation of social democracy to the anti-welfare, small government realities of globalisation.[15] This author comes to the debate not wanting, nor feeling compelled, to defend each of their actions and statements. This is not a matter for the argument at hand. Rather, I see significance in a broader issue: to recognise how the values of the new radical centre appear to have given social democracy renewed relevance in dealing with the equity issues of a post-industrial society. Its values provide a setting for the way in which new sources of social interdependence and inclusion might emerge. While this is, of course, an important observation for Australian Labor, it also, to be realistic, signifies nothing more advanced than a starting point. An active political cause, of course, needs more than an appropriate set of values: it requires a guiding sense of purpose and being. It needs to find the type of association between its values and policies that arises primarily from turning its mind to a philosophy of politics.

SOCIAL CAPABILITY

In its development as an ideology of Labor, social democracy came to stand for three things: a Keynesian strand of macroeconomics which relied on tax redistribution and full employment to deal with issues of economic exclusion; a planning strand which assumed that the state could successfully plan and provide for each of the needs of its citizens; and a welfare strand which identified minimum standards of material provision, health care and educational opportunity. In short, social democracy expected 'the state to continue its historic civilising function through public expenditure funded from a growing mixed economy'.[16] The clear evidence of market failure and social inequality arising from the 1930s and 1940s legitimised the role of government. In many respects this reflected the triumph of statism—an assumption that society's interests could be managed from above by parliamentary policy and bureaucratic action, with a focus on the relationship between citizens and the state (much more than citizens and society). Through the 1950s and 1960s—the long boom of economic growth and certainty— social democratic thinking acquired a disposition bordering on the complacent. The primacy of parliamentary power was thought to bring with it the certainties of governance: that the state would be capable of achieving all that it was asked to achieve; that policies turned into law would be policies implemented; and that the decisions of government would influence the citizenry as social democratic intent required them to be influenced.[17]

Each of the three strands of social democracy has been undermined by the features of a post-industrial society. The social and economic changes of the 1970s and 1980s effectively broke the social democratic mould. The international mobility of capital and production has reduced the relevance of macroeconomic strategies devised on the premise of a closed economy. New issues of economic exclusion and inequality have arisen from the changing nature of work and production. The effectiveness of the tax/transfer system has declined with the erosion of the tax base and an overloading of the functions and outlays of government. The easy era of social democratic expansion has been halted by the waning legitimacy of the welfare state and the widespread loss of socio-economic certainty. The entrenched problems of long term unemployment and underclass have conspicuously overwhelmed the capacity of service planning and passive welfare to deliver social mobility. Across society the ideals of welfare are struggling with new dilemmas of social diversity and fragmentation.

The need for a fresh assessment of the politics of the Left has rarely seemed more urgent. Just as Tony Crosland, in his canon of social democracy, *The Future of Socialism* (1956), argued that 'the intellectual framework of pre-war socialist discussion has been rendered obsolete . . . by the fact that we have a quite different configuration of economic power',[18] the wheel has now turned full circle. Large slabs of post-war social democratic thinking have been made moribund by the new political economy of globalisation. This has left a vacuum of policy and apparent purpose, resulting in a good deal of confusion about the philosophical underpinnings of parties like Labor. When social democrats now talk about their commitment to concepts like equality and social justice, it appears to be without clarity or a clear road map as to how these goals might be achieved. Throughout the Western democracies, the public memory of social democratic equality in practice is showing signs of strain.

The core of this dilemma lies in a basic flaw of reformist technique: the inability of state planning to cope with the dynamic and diverse features of a post-industrial society. From its origins, social democracy aimed to use the instruments of government intervention to even out excessive variations in the human condition. While it acknowledged the diversity of innate ability among people, it would not accept an economic or social system that converted these qualities into accumulated strata of privilege and inequality. It sought a 'democratic equality of condition' through the provision of a decent standard of material well-being for all and an equality of access to social goods of advancement, such as education.[19] The attainment of these fine goals, however, was founded on a problematic assumption about the role of the state. During an era of relative economic and social certainty—with standardised skills in the workplace, a standard (nuclear) family type and fairly stable social values and identity—it was assumed that the state, in the pursuit of equality, could successfully plan ahead and provide the necessary material and social goods. As long as variations in innate abilities and levels of income and wealth remained the root causes of inequality, the power of the planning strand was thought likely to prevail.

With the transformation from an industrial to an information society, however, the effectiveness of state planning has dissolved.

The growing diversity of values, economic outcomes, cognitive skills and social relations has made it difficult for government to anticipate and meet the needs of each of its citizens. This variety of circumstance has also made the conceptualisation and attainment of equality more complex. The passive provision of material and social goods, top–down from the state, is no longer likely to form the basis of equality in practice; just as variations in genetic outcomes and primary goods no longer represent the only causes of inequality. The diversity of a post-industrial society requires the construction of what the social theorist, Michael Walzer, has termed 'complex equality'. This reflects not only on the relationship between people and goods in society, but on the relations between people which form the basis of society itself. It also signifies an attempt to create a more sophisticated understanding of the interactions leading to a condition of equality. As Walzer explains:

> Simple equality is a simple distributive condition, so that if I have 14 hats and you have 14 hats, we are equal. And it is all to the good if hats are dominant, for then our equality is extended through all spheres of social life. On the view that I shall take here, however, we simply have the same number of hats, and it is unlikely that hats will be dominant for long. Equality is a complex relation of persons, mediated by the goods we make, share and divide among ourselves; it is not an identity of possessions.[20]

Social democracy has not responded adeptly to the question of social diversity. Its instinctive attachment to the planning strand and the inherent value of state intervention has not been conducive to a satisfactory redefinition of equality. As society has progressively emphasised new issues of diversity—such as gender, cultural values and ethnicity—social democracy has responded with new categories of equality and sources of state action. It has simply layered new definitions and expectations of equality onto its initial concern with material and social goods. This has inevitably produced a degree of confusion, as the purposes of social democracy have dispersed themselves across a wide range of goals. The simultaneous pursuit of an equality of opportunity, material conditions, social goods, gender, culture, sexuality, race and other rights is, in practical terms, a mission impossible. In the work of the public sector, several of these layers have become contradictory in their purpose, especially given the opportunity cost in allocating scarce public resources to one layer ahead of another. Moreover, in the popular culture, some of the new categories—perversely enough—have cultivated a feeling of exclusion. This is the problem with chopping questions of equality into a series of categories based on the personal characteristics of various citizens. It excludes those people who do not identify themselves with one or another category, yet still face in their lives more universal concerns about the impact of insecurity and disadvantage.

Social democracy requires a new paradigm of equality which deals comprehensively with the challenges of social diversity, much in the manner by which the values of the new radical centre have been able to reconcile the multiple planing of political issues. Social justice theories need to return to a sustainable conception of what is meant by notions of equality in an open society. An obvious starting point is to ask from first principles: equality of what? The American political economist, Amartya Sen, has provided an appropriate answer with his concept of 'social capability'. This recognises that personal well-being relies on more than the availability of material and social goods: citizens must have the capacity to effectively utilise these resources. For example, the effective use of income support is diminished for someone with a gambling problem. In this fashion, the capability paradigm forms a link between public rights and personal responsibilities. It also bridges the two conventional strands of social equality: equality in terms of primary goods (ownership and income) and equality of liberty and social freedom. Effective freedom—what Sen calls the 'freedom to achieve'—comes from taking advantage of one's innate ability and the enhancement of skills and assets in society to pursue one's personal desires and aspirations. As Sen writes, 'the capability set can be seen as the overall freedom a person enjoys to pursue her well-being'.[21] The interaction between personal liberty, primary goods and the skills of social and economic participation establishes a person's social capability.

This approach defines issues of advantage and disadvantage in terms of 'capability failure'—the loss of the freedom to achieve in society, not just simply a loss of resources. It is said, for instance, that Kerry Packer's favourite recreation is to watch sport on TV while eating pizzas. While this lifestyle option might also be available to welfare recipients, its implications in terms of social capability are vastly different. Packer still has an immense freedom to achieve in other aspects of his life; welfare recipients are not so fortunate. So, while in this recreational pursuit they technically have the same resources available to them (television and fast food), the exercise of control and choice in their lives—their capability set—could not be more varied. This confirms Dick Morris's point about the importance of lifestyle aspirations and options. Surveys of unemployed people, for instance, have shown that, for them, the worst thing about not having a job is not necessarily the loss of financial resources, but the loss of dignity and freedom to determine their own lifestyle.[22]

Sen answers the dilemmas of complex equality by urging social democrats to pursue a fairer distribution of social capability. This has the virtue of bringing social democracy closer to its initial purpose of a democratic equality of the human condition. It does so, however, in a manner consistent with the diversity of a post-industrial society. It recognises that the same set of resources can mean different things and produce different outcomes for people, depending on their personal aspirations and capacity to convert these resources into effective freedom.[23] The capability set also takes account of the relations between people, as well as between the state and its citizens. It recognises that capability relies, in good part, on sound social relations: the recognition, mutual trust and respect between people that fosters a stronger sense of social participation and connectedness. In this fashion, social democracy is chartered with an enhanced interest in the work of the public sector, state and non-state.

In the new political economy, social needs and wants are highly differentiated among the citizenry. People do not just have needs; they have a growing range of values, ideas and priorities impacting on the nature of their needs.[24] The likelihood of the state being able to specify these matters on behalf of each of its citizens, let alone plan for them, now appears remote. Whereas in the past, left-of-centre parties often aspired to eliminating the differences between people, a revised social democratic project now needs to accommodate social diversity—in work skills, family types, social values and interests. The planning strand, economic and social, has become moribund. A recurring theme in this book is the need for government to abandon its assumption that 'one size fits all' in the making of social provision. Whatever the state can do in securing the spread of social capability, it must do less by command and more by the customisation of service delivery and the devolution of public governance.

Importantly, the capability paradigm points to a resolution of the central tension in political thought this century—liberty against security, freedom against equality, the market against the state. Sen reconciles the apparent conflict between personal liberty and material equality by focusing on the interaction between both. Citizens need to make sound use of both their primary goods and personal opportunities to attain the freedom to achieve in society. Within the capability paradigm, collective institutions (helping to provide access to material and social goods), and individual liberty (providing the freedom citizens require in developing these goods for

personal and collective gain), are able to comfortably co-exist. This
further confirms the redundancy of the old binary form of politics.

Abstract rights and liberties are not in themselves sufficient to
guarantee social capability. All Australian families, for instance,
have the notional freedom to send their children to Scotch College;
only a small proportion have the effective freedom to do so.
Likewise, policies aimed at the achievement of absolute equality
are no longer appropriate. History shows that the compression of
income levels and assets, purely for the sake of material equality,
can take away some important incentives for the exercise of personal responsibility and endeavour. The elimination of poverty and
'capability failure' is a more important goal for social democracy
than the elimination of material inequality. Questions of the distribution of income and wealth, as with matters of personal liberty,
now need to be assessed through the prism of complex equality.
This casts our understanding of a fair society in terms of the
attainment of social capability across the citizenry. Society is made
fair, and our search for equality satisfied, in circumstances where
each citizen can access items of social merit—essential liberty,
primary goods, skills enhancement and social connectedness—from
which they, in the exercise of their personal attributes, efforts and
aspirations, can enjoy the freedom to achieve in society.

The role of the state, within this schema, is to ensure that
people have a platform of citizenship on which to stand: the tools
of economic and social participation by which they can pursue the
opportunities and effective freedoms of their choice. The capability
paradigm recognises that, in a post-industrial society, some
resources play a particularly important role in the spread of social
capability. This gives to the forums of public governance and
provision some special responsibilities. Access to education and
cognitive skill development is critical. Minimum standards of material living are still fundamentally important.

Perhaps, however, the greatest challenge to these ideals of
public provision lies outside the domain of the state—that is, in
rebuilding the foundations of mutual trust, recognition and support
across the work of the non-state public sector; and in re-estab-
lishing the feeling of community and place that offers, at least in
part, an answer to the threat of insecurity. If people do not see or
feel the need for mutuality in the public arena, then the top-down
programs of the state are not likely to win popular support. The
threat of insecurity may drive people closer to an individualistic
agenda and away from the logic of collective action. In addressing
the foundations of public mutuality, social democracy needs to give
closer consideration to the relations between citizens rather than
simply working from an assumption that all social issues can be

resolved in the state-to-citizen relationship. During an era of social diversity and uncertainty, the need for new forms of commonality, in the interests shared across society, has become particularly acute.

To be certain, during an era of economic globalisation and rapid social change, the citizens of the nation state have too few things left on which to rely. Interests held and expressed in common, especially in the attainment of social capability, have become all important. This requires a strong mutuality in the relations between people, as well as the successful reform of many of the formal institutions of government. This book maintains that if, as Australians, we are not willing to relearn the habits of collective governance and social connectedness then not only will the quality and equality of our society be much diminished, but so too will the capability of the nation itself.

OUTLINE OF THE BOOK

The remainder of this book deals with a range of policy ideas giving expression to the values of the new radical centre and egalitarian goals of the social capability paradigm. It proposes the means by which Australian Labor might seek to address each of the major issues now prominent in the new political economy. It commences with questions of economic internationalisation and distribution, then examines reforms to the welfare state, and finishes with an engagement in the social capital debate. The viability of a new program of social democracy is examined, spanning the economics of global capital to the politics of community and location. Readers with more specialised interests might find useful the following guide to the book's structure.

Part I deals with the growing bundle of issues arising from economic globalisation. It examines the decline of traditional expressions of national economic sovereignty, such as border controls, macroeconomic policy and heavy market regulation. It presents a critique of both the competitive advantage paradigm and orthodox economic theory. Part I also advocates the development of economic strategies and the expression of a new nationalism based on the skills and capabilities of the Australian people, especially in the nation's investment in education and research. It regards industry welfare approaches to economic policy as an inadequate response to the internationalisation of capital.

Part II describes the characteristics of the new economy, especially the impact of the changing nature of work and production. It addresses the failings of conventional economic policy and sets out a new framework by which social democracy might deal with the problems of economic exclusion and income inequality. The spatial features of the labour market are adopted as the key unit of analysis in this task. Part II also examines the means by which the ALP can repair the effectiveness of the tax/transfer system and guarantee, in the distribution of primary goods, a more equitable method of national gain sharing.

Part III considers the appropriateness of traditional theories of social justice during an era of widespread and growing insecurity. It examines the way in which the expansion of the welfare state has overloaded the resources of government and undermined the legitimacy of public sector action. Part III also questions the appropriateness of a policy approach based on 'segment-of-life' characteristics, such as race, culture and gender. It advocates a different set of priorities in the development of social justice strategies, with the customisation of public support and the primacy of economic insecurity and social capability issues.

Part IV considers the shortcomings of the post-war welfare state and proposes a far-reaching program of reform. It develops new systems of income support and educational opportunity aimed at the attainment of social capability all round. It advocates a new welfare relationship in Australia between the state, society and each of its citizens, advancing the virtues of self-providence and reciprocal responsibilities. Part IV also examines proposals for the place and case management of welfare communities.

Part V examines the means by which social democracy can play a role in the emerging debate about social capital and trust. It highlights the importance of strong relations of mutual trust, respect and recognition in society as one of the preconditions of social capability. It sets out a social democratic agenda for an engagement in issues of community and place, without having to follow the political Right down the path of a bidding war on law and order issues. Governments need to establish new forums and sources of social responsibility within which citizens can build their interdependence and create the virtues of equality in practice.

Finally, these themes and policy suggestions are pulled together in a conclusion, emphasising the viability of a new program of social democracy. Policies need to address the broadening of life's responsibilities, as people struggle to reconcile their involvement in local institutions with the spread of globalisation; as people everywhere deal with the new social pressures on family, community and citizenship. This can only be achieved by strengthening the basis of social and economic security, arising from the virtues of public mutuality and collective governance. Moreover, the conclusion dismisses the core ideologies of the political Right, with their emphasis on individualism and conservatism, as an inadequate response to the political economy of a post-industrial society. They serve only to add to the spread of social fragmentation and insecurity.

In most respects, however, it was ever thus. History tells us that parties like Labor have always been called on to aid the cause of a good and decent society; to keep responding to social change with the virtues of equity and inclusion. The reconstruction of the social democratic project—recasting the logic of collective action and public mutuality in a post-industrial society—is little different. It is much like the Yiddish story of the man sent to guard the city gates and wait for the new millennium: 'big task', he said, 'but at least the work is steady'.

Author's note

This book has been structured, within each of its six parts, around a series of short, relatively self-contained chapters. While in a few instances this may have produced some overlap, it also gives the reader the advantage of being able to selectively focus on his or her subjects of policy interest. I trust that this approach—especially in a lengthy and, at times, heavy piece of work—proves both convenient and informative.

PART I

THE CHASE FOR GLOBAL CAPITAL

There are elements of symmetry in the challenges the ALP faces in the 1990s, and those it confronted at the time of its formation in the 1890s. In its early decades Labor forged a political response to the emergence of national capital. The Party's origins lie in the dominance national capital secured over agrarian labour late in the ninteenth century. Concurrently, the push for Federation dissolved many of the barriers to free trade and investment between the colonies, thereby giving a national focus to questions of political economy. Political groupings coalesced around these new economic interests: the Free Traders and Protectionists represented competing interests within the sphere of national capital, with parliamentary Labor providing national representation for the working class.

A century on, the ALP has been grappling with the internationalisation of capital. During the 1980s, Labor in government increased the economy's exposure to international market forces by floating the exchange rate, loosening capital controls and dismantling tariff walls. Workplaces were restructured and enterprise bargaining placed at the centre of the industrial relations agenda. The public sector was exposed to corporatisation, privatisation and competition all round. The Keating Government pursued an internationalist agenda by advancing Australia's commitment to APEC and its objective for free trade and investment in the Asia-Pacific region. While in many other nations, political responses to the internationalisation of capital were framed by parties of the Right in government, in Australia this task was left to Labor.

The restructuring of capital to an international scale places pressure not just on nations, their industries and workforce, but also on political parties, and more so for parties interested in equity. Globalisation appears to be associated with new forms of

inequality and social exclusion. Nations with open economies tend
to develop patterns of income dispersion matching international
standards. Economic rewards are allocated according to levels of
skill. Low skill, low productivity workers and locations struggle to
share in the new sources of trade penetration and national income.
For some at the bottom of the skills pyramid this can mean an
entrenched cycle of unemployment. Economic flexibility also gives
rise to various forms of social insecurity and fragmentation. Internationally, the relevance of the post-war welfare state and
sustainability of social capital are under pressure.

Globalisation looms large over the future prospects of social
democracy. Economic and social restructuring, not surprisingly,
has produced elements of political restructuring. In many ways the
ALP, having moved in government from a relatively closed and
protected Australian economy to international trading arrangements, is still coming to terms with the consequences of these
changes. Federal Labor is still engaged in the development of
strategies that address the core issues of economic vulnerability in
an open society—that is, how to best offset the impact on people
and places of the dislocation costs and inequities of continuous
economic change and global competition. This is an enormous task
in updating the relevance of the Party's traditional role in Australian politics.

Labor's strategy for the new economy needs to respond to both
the internationalisation of capital and the changing nature of
production and work. This chapter deals with the former. It
examines Australia's transition from a national to a global sphere
of capital, and the options now available for developing new sources
of economic sovereignty. With the declining effectiveness of traditional forms of national economic control, planning and
regulation, new policies are required to cope with the mobile
geography of capital. Internationally, parties are struggling to close
the gap between globalised economic events and local electoral
demands. Policies pitched at crude isolationism and sloganeering
have shown themselves to be a poor response to this task. The
path to national economic sovereignty will not be found in repli-
cating the North Korean economic model, nor in reductionist
critiques of so-called economic rationalism. The challenge for
social democracy lies in reasserting the sovereignty of the nation
state without denying to national economies the competitive and
technological progress associated with the transfer of trade and
investment. This means developing policies aimed not just at the
attainment of a high growth/high wage economy, but also ensuring
that the process of economic adjustment does not leave behind
vulnerable people or places.

1

NATIONAL CAPITAL

FROM ITS ORIGINS the ALP's strategy for civilising national capital was laborism—that is, direct government intervention in the production process to guarantee the strength of trade unionism, decent wages and conditions, and a reasonable supply of blue collar jobs. Laborism reflected the working class culture of its time. Notions of equality were understood more by the symbols of a male-dominated, monocultural society than the state ownership of the means of production. This was how the Labor idealist, William Lane, was able to describe 'socialism as just being mates'. During the first decade of Federation, political Labor became the instrument by which laborist ideology was built into Australia's economic institutions. The ALP at this time was in a privileged position, holding the balance of power in the new House of Representatives. It developed a strategic agenda of 'support in return for concessions'.

This agenda was designed to protect Australian workers from the defeats of the 1890s: high unemployment, falling wages and broken strikes. So came the historic compromise of conceding tariff protection to manufacturing interests in return for centralised wage fixing. This was accompanied by support for White Australia, defending workers against an inflow of low wage Asian and Islander labour. Both business and labour urged the development of large public utilities to create transport and energy infrastructure and a steady supply of blue collar employment. At the turn of the century Australia had much to defend: the world's highest living standards, robust mining industries, strong agriculture and well-developed cities. On the back of the nation's primary industries, our production per man-hour was three times higher than most European nations, and more than 60 per cent higher than the United Kingdom and the United States.[1]

The policy settlement of the first decade of Federation made sense to both sides of politics. It enshrined the ethos of a lucky country: blocking economic threats from overseas while enjoying the national wealth harvested from successful pastoral and mining industries. In this fashion, laborism generated a gain sharing model for working Australians. Economic rents in agriculture and mining were distributed through a transmission mechanism of basic wage adjustments, tariff protected industries and a labour market buttressed by growing public sector employment. As long as Australia's resource endowments and world commodity prices remained strong, national standards of living and a claim to egalitarianism (albeit limited by gender and race) could be sustained.

Rather than adjusting to fluctuations in Australia's trading position, the post-Federation settlement adopted a defensive strategy. This involved tariff protection all round, centralised industrial relations, benevolent state monopolies, restricted migration and the emergence, particularly after the Second World War, of a residual system of income maintenance for those outside the workforce. Gradually, however, as other economies grew past Australia, domestic defence came to mean domestic decline. By locking out competition, protectionism denied firms the motivation to secure competitive niches in new markets and grow beyond the limits of the domestic market. By the 1970s it had led to the development of what Paul Keating described as 'Australia's industrial archaeology'. Moreover, the oil price shock of the period downgraded the importance of commodities on world markets, and knocked the top off Australia's comparative trade advantage. By the end of the 1970s most European and North American nations had overtaken Australia's productivity rate.[2] Through the 1980s Australia's terms of trade declined by almost 4 per cent per annum. The laborist gain sharing model had lost its milch cow.

SOCIAL DEMOCRATIC AGENDA

In other aspects of Labor policy, new agendas and constituencies were being created. In particular, Gough Whitlam's leadership of the Federal Party redefined the ALP's understanding of the role of government. Whereas laborism had essentially limited itself to the rights of workers (wages and conditions), Whitlam established a social democratic program concerned with the rights of citizens: land rights for Aborigines, equal pay for women, racially tolerant migration policies and the universal provision of basic community services. It was thought that strong, continuous economic growth could be distributed to new sources of social amenity and opportunity. Across the three budgets of the Whitlam Government (1972–75), for instance, social expenditure as a percentage of GDP increased from 12.9 per cent to 18.8 per cent.

This agenda helped to refashion Labor's understanding of equality. While laborism had concentrated on gains for one segment of society, essentially men in work, social democracy developed a wide range of equity programs. It did not attempt direct interventions in the production process, but rather looked to the countervailing role of the state as a means by which governments could correct the shortcomings of (in this instance) national capital. Social democracy set itself the task of sustaining those things the market was unable to provide citizens in a civilised society. Whitlam's agenda also had a strong spatial dimension, defining equality and social opportunity as much by where people live as how much they earn. Hence issues of distribution and redistribution were paramount: using the benefits of national economic growth to create new public resources and services; creating a new role for the national government in quality of life issues; taking an interest in the spatial form of cities so that public resources could be redistributed to areas of greatest need and growth.

In this fashion, Australian social democracy aligned itself with the Keynesian certainties of a closed economic model—that is, the use of tax policies, transfer payments and social expenditures which could, with precision, mould the distributional features of social opportunity. During the long boom of the 1950s and 1960s, an expectation developed that, once governments had successfully fine tuned the economy, public policy could turn to its central purpose of socioeconomic distribution and redistribution. Much like pulling the levers of a machine, as Crosland wrote, 'the government can exert any influence it likes on the income distribution and can also determine, within broad limits, the division of total output between consumption, investment, exports and social expenditure'.[3]

Labor's agenda declared new certainties in the manner by which the public sector, especially the Federal Government, could engineer new responsibilities and social outcomes. It could liberate the working class with the standards of learning, health care, housing and public provision suited to a civilised society. Thus Labor became a party interested, not just in the standard of living, but also the quality of life. It did so, however, assuming that the closed economic model could sustain the pressure placed on national income by the universal provision of social services. As Frank Castles has concluded in his study of Labor's transformation from laborism to social democracy:

The ALP began, for the first time, to pursue a more expansive, universalist and social wage oriented welfare strategy of the kind characteristic of western European social democracy. The irony, in hindsight, is that it sought a way out of its policy impasse of the mid-1960s by offering all citizens fair access to the good fortunes of the lucky country just at the point when the luck had begun to run out.[4]

ECONOMIC INTERNATIONALISATION

By the 1980s and the national election of a new Labor Government, it was clear that a closed system of national capital could no longer meet the preconditions of laborism—solid economic growth and gain sharing—let alone finance the expansive public outlays of social democracy. Ultimately both laborism and Whitlam's program of social democracy suffered for the weakness of national capital in changed economic circumstances. For this reason the Hawke and Keating Governments pursued the internationalisation of the economy as a new strategy for national income growth. For a decade or more, Labor's claim to electoral success rested on its capacity to deliver the twin virtues of economic competitiveness and social fairness. From this experience, however, it is not immediately clear that traditional social democratic ideals can be easily reconciled with the distributional features of global capital. While the opening of the Australian economy to global capital may have rendered the laborist model redundant, it has by no means guaranteed the sustainability of the social democratic project.

Prime Minister Keating was fond of reporting to the Federal Parliamentary Labor Party on his sophisticated social democratic model for Australia: an open and competitive trading economy supported by strong citizenship rights and an effective social safety net. He had much to be proud of, with a record, too rare in Australian public life, of turning good ideas into reality. Yet, perversely enough, the big picture was never quite big enough. Many of the distributional policy tools of the social democratic model are, in practice, made obsolete by the internationalisation of capital.

In particular, during Labor's time in government, the effectiveness of long-standing economic controls and Keynesian fine tuning declined, while the fiscal pressures of government weakened the viability of the tax/transfer system. Old certainties were replaced by new inequities. Australian Labor, like so many of its fraternal parties internationally, has more to learn about globalisation, particularly its impact on questions of earnings and employment dispersion, and the distributional capacity of the state public sector. This is a challenge by which the Party will determine whether its age old role in Australia's political economy remains relevant to the new politics of the 1990s.

Labor's recent experience poses a new set of issues and tensions. The Keating legacy has left the ALP with an imposing agenda for rethinking its strategies and policies. Social democracy confronts a wide range of policy dilemmas in an open economy. Is it possible to adequately fund the universal rights and services of citizens off an internationally competitive tax base? How can the declining legitimacy and effectiveness of the welfare state be reversed? Is it possible to offset the tendency of globalisation towards economic exclusion and inequality? Can Labor sustain its traditional role as a party of social protection in the face of economic insecurity and loss of national economic controls? Is it possible to reconstruct a model of income gain sharing which reconciles social justice with economic openness? Can the historic cause of Labor successfully adapt to the new political economy of global capital?

The restructuring of the world economic order is an event rare in history, especially given the scale of globalisation in recent decades. Economic restructuring inevitably gives rise to new social and political tensions. The issues now prominent on Australia's political agenda challenge not just Labor's capacity to deliver a fairer society, but also the Party's capacity to command a majority of electoral support. Labor needs to use its time in Opposition to think strategically about the attainment of social justice in an open economy. It needs to create from first principles a cogent response to the international mobility of capital. It requires strategies which deal with the decline of national economic controls and the new demands of international competitiveness. It needs to show how the distributional features of global capital can be superseded by the work of the nation state.

In government Labor was forced to deal incrementally with the process of securing economic change. The Party was more intent on debating the desirability of change, through questions such as privatisation and deregulation, than the strategic issues arising from globalisation. In many cases, policy responses lagged behind economic events. For instance, the 1994 Working Nation program, despite its innovations and successes, was essentially a delayed response to the 1990 recession and advent of structural, long term unemployment in Australia. Likewise, the structure of the prices and incomes Accord, which in its origins in the early

1980s was based on relatively closed economic settings, steadily became less effective in dealing with the wage equity issues of an internationalised economy. Free from making change, Labor now has an opportunity to respond more adeptly to the economic consequences of the spread of global capital.

2

GLOBAL CAPITAL

While it is somewhat premature to talk about a single, global capital market, it is indisputable that over the past three decades capital has become highly mobile and markets increasingly integrated. This may not be the first trend towards free trade and investment (Europe and North America experienced something similar in the late 1800s), but it certainly signifies the first move towards the integration of finance capital, production and commodity trade on an international scale. That is, global corporate strategies and the movement of finance and investment are everywhere breaking down the economic barriers between nations. The fall of ideological walls has complemented this process. The collapse of communism as a national ideology has added to the global reach of capital, and intensified the degree of competition between nations.

It is worth considering the raw statistics. The total stock of financial assets traded in the global capital market increased from $5000 billion in 1980 to $35 000 billion in 1992, equivalent to twice the output of the OECD economies. The McKinsey organisation has forecast that the market will swell to $83 000 billion by the year 2000, three times the GDP of the advanced economies. In 1973, a typical day of global foreign exchange trade amounted to $15 billion. In 1983 it was still a modest $60 billion. By 1995 it had reached $1300 billion, the relative scale of which can be judged by the $640 billion the central banks of the world's industrialised economies hold in foreign currency reserves.

The emergence of international financial markets has been complemented by the mobility of large holdings of multinational investment. Of the world's largest 100 economies, national and corporate, 47 are now multinational conglomerates. Through massive gains in transport, communications and knowledge-based

11

work, they have the capacity to make their products just about anywhere, and sell them everywhere. These businesses owe little loyalty to national boundaries; their core concern lies in the maximisation of profit. While these companies often maintain a distinct home base, the spread of their investment strategies has provided a new set of challenges for the governance of the nation state. Political jurisdictions, anchored in the electoral politics of nations and regions, have felt compelled to engage in the chase for capital across the globe.

By comparison with global finance, the rate of growth in the volume of world trade has seemed almost sluggish, rising by 500 per cent between 1960 and 1990. National governments have more thoroughly liberalised controls over financial capital than the trade of goods and services. For instance, even after the 1994 Uruguay round of GATT, which secured a 40 per cent reduction in tariffs, 56 per cent of world trade remained, to some extent, tariff protected. Trade liberalisation has been a politically sensitive issue for governments to master, especially in nations with a well-formed culture of economic isolation. While, for example, the openness of the Australian economy (measured by the ratio of exports/GDP) moved from 11 per cent in 1960 to 22 per cent in 1994, the OECD average also doubled through this period, but from 21 per cent to 42 per cent. Even though international trade has not replicated the mobility of finance and investment, and some nations remain less open to trade than others, it is still possible to talk of the progressive internationalisation of capital and the means of production. This clear tendency towards globalisation is unlikely to moderate and, most certainly, will not be reversed. It reflects the dominant trend in the new political economy of the nation state.

STRUCTURAL CHANGE

The structural causes of economic internationalisation have been two-fold. First, improvements in communications and transport technology after the Second World War made it easier for investors to circumvent national policy controls. During the 1970s, particularly with the breakdown of the Bretton Woods system,[1] national governments decided to liberalise their economic settings in response to the inexorable surge in capital mobility. With floating exchange rates and open financial systems, national policies focused more intensely on monetary policy and interest rate adjustments. It can be argued that these settings led to a more pronounced business cycle after the long boom of steady economic growth in the 1950s and 1960s.

These changes produced important flow-on effects in other aspects of economic policy. The intensification of competition between nations for investment capital promoted a worldwide trend towards product market and labour market deregulation. Political jurisdictions began to compete against each other through the quality of their business inputs: efficient markets, labour force skills and technological research and development. In this sense, economic change has driven policy change. Politicians worldwide are still grappling with what the global sphere of capital means for the relevance and effectiveness of the nation state.

Second, the oil price shock of 1973 fundamentally altered the way in which businesses and nations organised their economic inputs. Capital was increasingly substituted for energy, especially in nations where high rates of savings could easily fund new capital. In part, this explains the so-called Asian economic miracle—economic and political systems which effectively mobilised capital and labour inputs in an energy-deficient world economy. Conversely, many Western economies (among them Australia) found themselves constrained not just by a loss of competitive advantage in resource industries, but also by limited national savings and capital productivity.[2] An immediate response to these limitations was the abolition of capital controls and aggressive competition to attract footloose global capital. While these markets remain imperfect, and most nations still finance a majority of their investment from domestic savings, the policy intention has been clear: changes in production methods and capacity drove such policy changes.

The pace and scale of capital movements mean that economic activity no longer conforms to geographical or political boundaries. Increasingly, economic policies are conforming with the pressures of international capital. This has not been the stuff of blazing headlines but an incremental process over recent decades. Importantly, it does not infer the necessity of smaller government but rather, inexorable changes in the role of government, plus the advent of policy convergence between governments. The rise of global capital has had clear, albeit mixed, implications for national economic sovereignty and control. As Fred Argy has written:

> Financial globalisation has reduced the potential for domestic destabilisation arising from fluctuations in the terms of trade, export demand, inflation and liquidity; but on the negative side, it has powerfully increased the risk of international financial shocks, especially for economies with a relatively large dependence on portfolio capital. As a result, the pattern of international business cycles and the channels through which these cycles are transmitted to individual countries have fundamentally changed.[3]

Nations which choose short term consumption ahead of savings are not able to fund a high rate of investment and economic growth without a matching rate of company takeovers and foreign debt. The scale of international capital markets is such that no central bank has sufficient reserves to resist a run on its currency.[4] Moreover, there is a strong tendency, as capital exercises its mobility and discriminates between nations, for the conventional macroeconomic tools of nations—monetary and fiscal policy—to converge. While there is still some scope for autonomous national policies, the mobility of capital and the scale of international flows are now so immense that national settings are being pushed closer together. The sovereignty of national macroeconomic policy is in steady decline.

In the old model of closed economies, the power of government policy was based on its capacity to tax, to borrow, to print money and to spend. Centuries of economic theory and debate have involved nothing more than a series of configurations by which these four powers could be exercised. The growth of capital mobility has placed new disciplines on national economic policy. For instance, if a government sets its tax rates too high, capital may be driven to another political jurisdiction. Or if a government borrows excessively and allows inflation to get out of control, capital might seek out a more stable currency.[5]

MONETARY AND FISCAL POLICY

The history of macroeconomic policy in Australia over the past decades is a good example of the declining usefulness of conventional policy tools. The evidence shows how activist monetary and fiscal policies are likely to aggravate the domestic impact of the international business cycle. This is not surprising for a small, open economy with insufficient national savings and security against international capital movements. Given the footloose nature of capital, it is not possible to demand manage or fine tune away the structural weaknesses of a national economy.

The certainties associated with Keynesian pump priming, while attractive in a closed economy, are (at best) shaky in an open trading environment. The effectiveness of the Keynesian paradigm has been downgraded by the internationalisation of capital markets. It relies on the assumption of a closed economy, without dynamic trade and capital flows. Keynes' thinking was governed by the sovereignty of national capital: in 1941 he declared that 'nothing is more certain than the movement of capital funds must be regulated'. Now, given the global exposure of most economies, aggressive demand management is likely to magnify the national business cycle, a point confirmed in the recent Australian experience. The fiscal impact of the expansionary 1992 One Nation program, for instance, was not fully felt until 1994 (due to lags in capital construction projects), at which time it inflated aggregate demand. Interest rates were then increased to narrow the gap between national output and spending, and bring the current account deficit back under control. This demonstrates how a small open economy, with low savings, cannot grow faster than its trading partners without a high proportion of growth spilling onto the external account.

Internationally, passive fiscal settings have achieved better results than active policies. Passive settings rely on the capacity of tax and transfer regimes to automatically stabilise the economy across standard swings in the business cycle. The OECD, for instance, has estimated that fiscal stabilisers can reduce cyclical fluctuations by up to 50 per cent. Active policies, however, frequently suffer from spill-over effects. Unfunded spending lifts the demand for money and hence attracts a greater inflow of capital. An appreciating exchange rate, in turn, has a contracting impact on income. Under conditions of a floating exchange rate and constant money supply, active policies lose their impact as a fine tuning instrument. Fiscal intervention is now best applied to conditions of market failure outside the normal business cycle. This includes, for instance, relatively closed regional economies rutted into a cycle of low consumption and low employment. Otherwise, capital markets, more than ever, are demanding passive fiscal settings and stability.

Similarly, there are now sound technical and empirical reasons for governments to pursue passive settings in monetary policy. In principle, floating exchange rates allow governments to develop independent monetary policies as the supply of money is no longer impacted on by external circumstances. External pressures are absorbed through exchange rate variations. In practice, however, the volatility of capital movements is an impressive discipline on the convergence of monetary policies between nations. Markets are placing a premium on transparent, reliable forms of decision-making by central banks. These parameters have narrowed the scope of monetary policy to a one instrument/one target framework. It is increasingly difficult for central banks to juggle competing goals for price stability and employment growth. While the transmission mechanism for money impacts directly on price, its effect on economic activity and output is entirely indirect. It is generally accepted that monetary policy experiences a twelve to eighteen month lag between movements in interest rates and the

full impact on economic activity. With increasingly rapid movements in capital and economic information across the world
economy, long lag time instruments are comparatively crude and
risky in the management of domestic demand.

The Australian experience over the past decade highlights the
imprecise and problematic features of monetary policy. Under
conditions of financial deregulation, interest rate adjustments are
a blunt policy tool, impacting not just on consumers and savers
but also businesses and home buyers. Moreover, as a nationwide
instrument it lacks due sensitivity to the circumstances of regional
labour and consumption markets. The Reserve Bank's conventional
response to an imbalance between national expenditure (GNE) and
output (GDP), thereby defining a current account problem, has
been to lift interest rates to slow expenditure.[6] The counter-direc-
tional function of this policy, however, is that higher interest rates
and business uncertainty tend to knock down investment and
export competitiveness through the medium term. Perversely
enough, higher rates can increase expenditure in the short term
due to their favourable impact on household savings (for every
dollar of debt Australian households hold two dollars of credit).
Given that household consumption accounts for two-thirds of
GNE, the capacity of interest rate movements to repress short
term aggregate demand is spurious.

It makes clearer sense to tackle Australia's core economic
challenges—national savings, output growth and regional employment effects—at their source rather than through temporary and
tenuous macroeconomic methods. Figure 1.1 shows the relationship between the current account deficit and rate of unemployment
since 1970. Whenever the current account deficit (CAD) has
approached 6 per cent of GDP (in 1982, 1986, 1990 and 1995)
growth has had to be slowed from the top of the business cycle
(usually via blunt interest rate movements, producing lagged
increases in unemployment). The peak rates of unemployment in
Australia have coincided with the CAD coming under control at
3–4 per cent of GDP. This has led to the emergence of what can
be termed an externally constrained unemployment rate (ECUR)
of between 8 per cent and 10.5 per cent.

Makin has noted how the Reserve Bank's discretionary intervention in financial markets, operating on the basis of its
incomplete knowledge of economic behaviour, substantially
increases economic and investment uncertainty. He presents evidence of how activist policies have actually amplified Australia's
business cycle relative to the international cycle. A risk premium
related to uncertainty has been incorporated into Australian rates:

Figure 1.1 Current account deficit and unemployment

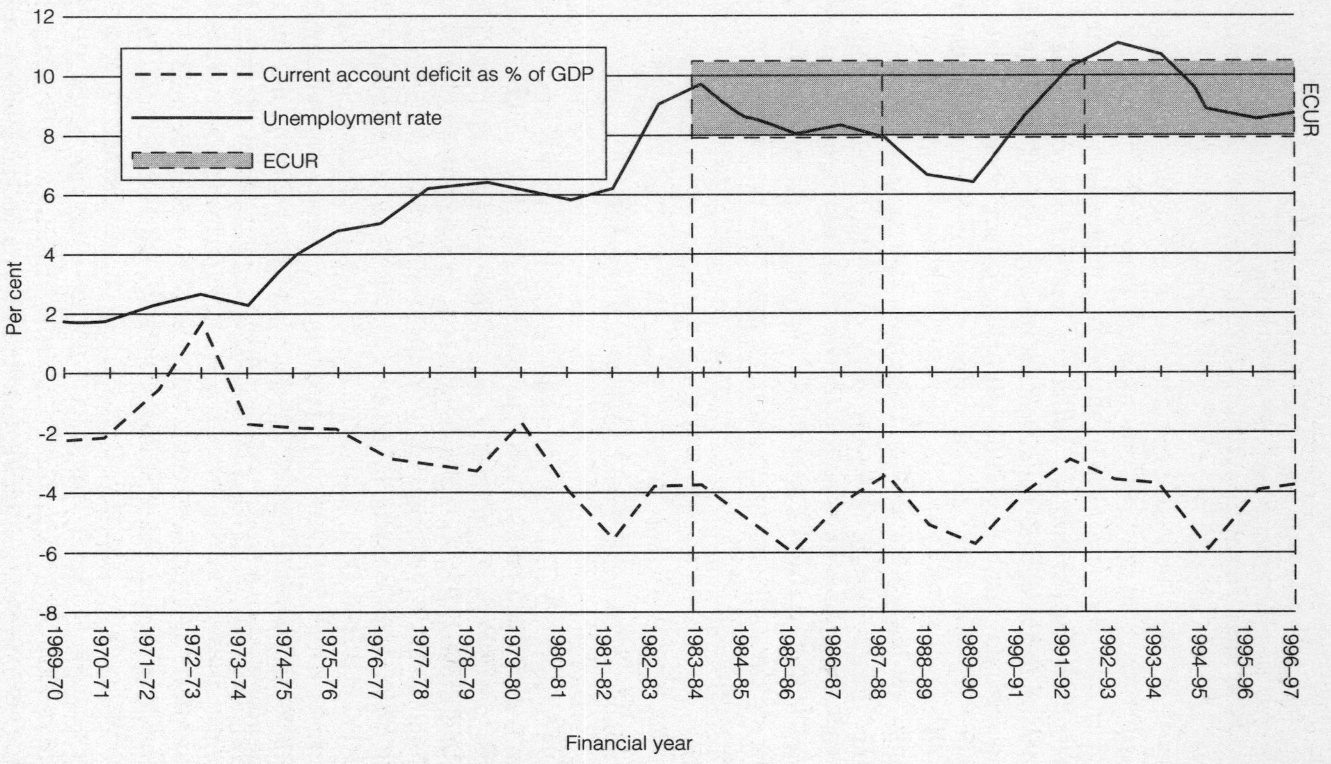

Per cent

Financial year

Source: Federal Parliamentary Library

Legend:
- - - - Current account deficit as % of GDP
——— Unemployment rate
▨ ECUR

Excessive Reserve Bank intervention in money markets also explains why short term rates are so often out of line with long-term rates. This has given Australia one of the most variable yield curves in the world. The related interest risk premium stymies investment expenditure, which impedes productive activity in the economy.[7]

Moreover, financial deregulation and innovation have made it harder for central banks to measure money and its economic impact. Interest rate movements in Australia now rely on strong announcement effects to influence market expectations. It is thought that the weak impact of incremental rate rises on market expectations in the late 1980s contributed to the misjudgment of policy and subsequent recession. Inevitably, however, markets alter their expectations in response to policy changes. This again highlights the nebulous relationship between monetary policy and output, especially in an environment in which daily media speculation about possible rate movements can only add to business uncertainty. As Keynes once put it, everyone in the market (including the central bank) tries to guess better than the crowd how the crowd will behave.

MACRO WAGES POLICY

Not surprisingly, the changing nature of monetary and fiscal policy has given greater importance to wages policy as a macro instrument. No Western economy has found a way to pursue high growth/low inflation policies without a macro wages strategy. Without this policy tool, high growth is constantly threatened by capacity constraints which, in turn, produce real wage adjustments well above rates of productivity. Wages policy is the only mechanism by which governments can directly influence wage outcomes. Otherwise they are forced to use monetary policy to indirectly influence wages growth. This mechanism suffers from the lags and transmission problems noted earlier. Monetary policy directly impacts on prices; it is a long way round to influence wages.

The internationalisation of economic activity has added to the usefulness of macro wage agreements. In an open, dynamic economy the upgrading of key labour force skills lags behind the development of new technologies and products. Skill blockages add to wage-push pressures. Moreover, in some industries the value of labour can now outstrip the value of capital. The bargaining power of these specialised skills can produce big wage and salary increases. In an internationalised economy, labour-based parties have a distinct advantage in economic policy making, given their capacity to lever macro wage agreements with the labour movement. This advantage remains a distinct feature of Australia's political economy.

ECONOMIC MULTILATERALISM

Other than by adopting passive monetary and fiscal settings and emphasising the significance of wages policy, how should governments respond to the macro policy implications of globalisation? A logical step is to foster policy cooperation between nation states. Just as capital has lifted its sphere of activity to a global level, so too should nations. It makes sense for national governments to cooperate within global forums to ensure, as much as possible, that the internationalisation of capital accords with economic interests within national jurisdictions. A commonsense response to the uncertainty associated with economic globalisation is to internationalise the regulatory and other macroeconomic functions of government.

Earlier this century, Keynes added to economic studies an understanding of how economic instability arises from a mismatch between the time horizons of capitalist finance and production.[8] The erosion of short term returns on financial markets can trigger a much larger adjustment in medium to long term production cycles. Hence nations have always used the prudential regulation and supervision of their financial markets as a public sector safeguard against these risks. It is now clearly desirable for national governments to apply the same principles to the volatility of global capital. This does not mean winding back trade liberalisation or the re-regulation of exchange rates and capital flows. Rather, it involves improving the supervision of national financial systems plus, more critically, establishing strengthened systems of cross-national intervention.

One option is to use pricing policies via turnover taxes on capital to deaden the impact of short term speculation across money markets. The so-termed Tobin tax,[9] for instance, would levy a modest rate (say 0.5 per cent) on all foreign exchange transactions. This additional cost would act as a disincentive to speculative activity while leaving long term investments relatively unaffected. Accordingly, such a tax would help increase the autonomy of nation states over monetary policy. Governments might also consider cooperative action, through global codes and regulation, to better manage the destabilising features of short term capital flows across national boundaries. In practice, however, these objectives sit at the long end of internationalist horizons. After all, their effectiveness relies on the participation of a large majority of governments worldwide.

Recent events point to more tangible outcomes being achieved on a regional scale, especially with the conversion of regional trade blocs into various forms of policy union. The Maastricht Treaty, for instance, is applying 'supra-national' controls on the financial policies of European Union nations. The treaty provides a time-table for a common currency, common central bank and monetary policy convergence. Nations need to satisfy four criteria—price stability, a stable currency, reasonable long term interest rates and sound budgeting[10]—to participate in the policy union. One of the key aspects of Australia's political economy in coming decades will be the extent to which regional trade initiatives like APEC, and bilateral agreements, such as the Closer Economic Relations with New Zealand, evolve in a manner matching the European experi-ence. The Reserve Bank of Australia has recently taken an important initiative with its move to establish an Asia-wide central banking institution, dealing with financial market developments, the management of foreign exchange reserves and banking super-vision. This is an agenda—the internationalisation of the nation state's command over global finance—which the ALP must be prepared to constantly advance.

3

COMPETITIVE
ADVANTAGE

The international mobility of capital has also restricted the usefulness of trade theories based on comparative advantage. This approach, first developed in the eighteenth century, was based on the relative value of industries to a nation, with an assumption that capital is mobile within nations but not between them. The internationalisation of the economy has called for a new approach in understanding the flow of trade, finance and investment between nations. This has led to the development of a new paradigm of competitive advantage, generally associated with Michael Porter's *The Competitive Advantage of Nations* (1990) and Robert Reich's *The Work of Nations* (1991). In most nations, including Australia, policies aimed at competitive advantage have superseded traditional systems of macro fine tuning and national economic controls. It is now argued that a nation's trading capacity, and hence its economic success, are determined by the international competitiveness of the companies and industries operating within its boundaries.

In this paradigm, nations matter only for the way in which they fashion inputs to the private sector. Governments are assigned the role and expectation of either upgrading the quality of these inputs or lowering their costs. The competitive contest between companies is taken to reflect, in aggregate, the competitiveness of nations. Politicians worldwide have responded by talking up the importance of this type of economic competition. In the words of President Clinton, each nation is 'like a big corporation competing in the global market place'. The policy tools of the competitive advantage model, however, are by no means homogenous. They reflect three distinct approaches to the question of international competitiveness.

The first, the 'business costs' approach aims at driving down the unit costs of doing business. It is not likely, however, that the

Western democracies, in most cases with their tax and wage systems geared around a civilised safety net, can compete success-fully for investment through low cost, labour intensive inputs. Social progress is not likely to be made by replacing the low income unemployed with a new generation of working poor. Where this approach has a more constructive role to play is in ensuring the competitiveness of non-labour costs, such as in transport, commu-nications, reticulated services and the costs of regulatory control. This reflects the goals of public sector competition policies and most forms of microeconomic reform.

The second, the 'human capital' approach, points to the impor-tance of a well-educated labour force, especially with the growing significance of knowledge-based industries. The path to economic success, it is argued, lies in a highly skilled workforce producing high value added goods and services. In the global economy most factors of production are footloose: investment, information, resources, even entire industries. Given the accelerated mobility of capital, Reich has defined the skills of a nation's people as its most important (and perhaps only) enduring resource in the struggle for competitive advantage:

> In the politics and economics of the coming century, there will be no national products or technologies, no national corpora-tions, no national industries. There will no longer be national economies, at least as we have come to understand that concept. All that will remain rooted within national borders are the people who comprise a nation. Each nation's primary assets will be its citizens' skills and insights. Each nation's primary political task will be to cope with the centrifugal forces of the global economy which tear at the ties binding citizens together—bestowing ever greater wealth on the most skilled and insightful, while consign-ing the less skilled to a declining standard of living.[1]

A third approach, often advocated by the corporate sector, is to use government as a crude subsidiser of business inputs. Com-panies are able to maximise their profits by seeking protection from government from the full impact of market competition. This strategy of 'industry welfare' aims to manipulate market forces through such measures as trade protection, tax concessions and direct financial transfers. While in the politics of nations it is often portrayed as a sign of national economic strength, this approach is not favoured among the theorists of competitive advan-tage. Porter, for instance, is critical of the crude subsidisation of capital. He points to the importance of industry upgrading, and the new investment, technology and skills which give companies a competitive edge on world markets. Corporations based in a particular nation succeed because their trading environment is dynamic and challenging, pressuring them to upgrade and widen their advantages over time. Competition in domestic markets gives rise to competitive success on markets abroad. Policies of industry welfare smother this competition and its impact on industry upgrading.

AUSTRALIA'S POSITION

Australia's place in the new paradigm is best understood from Porter's development of an historical model of competitive advantage. Within this framework, nations pass through the successive resource, investment, innovation and wealth-driven stages of economic development. This century only the United States, among those nations rich in natural resources, has progressed its economy through all four stages. The tendency among many resource-rich nations has been to rely predominantly on their natural endowments, too complacent to upgrade their economies with bold innovation and investment. For much of this century Australia could be classified among a small group of nations—including Canada, New Zealand and Norway—which bridged the resource-endowment and wealth-driven stages of development. National wealth was generated from rich agricultural and mining assets, avoiding the need to upgrade productive capacities in other parts of the economy. Company formation was based on takeovers and mergers rather than new enterprises and risk taking. This produced a fragile economy with an inadequate base of investment and innovation.

In the absence of substantial policy change, economies such as these struggle to progress beyond their natural advantages. The tell-tale signs are diminishing competition, adversarial labour relations and industry protection. The national focus is inward looking, with public policy geared to preserving the status quo. This analysis neatly fits the impact of the laborist model and closed national capital on Australia's economic development. It also describes the economic conditions the Federal Labor Government faced in 1983 and its rationale for the internationalisation of the economy. Australian industries, it was argued, needed to be exposed to external competitive pressures and market opportunities to upgrade their productive capacity. Significantly, both sides of Australian politics accepted this approach as a useful guide to national economic and trade policy. While differences remained about aspects of policy implementation, internationalisation emerged during the 1980s as an item of mainstream party consensus.

ROLE OF THE STATE

From a political perspective, however, competitive advantage theory is not without its tensions and contradictions. In the public arena a particular view of economic responsibility emerges: if companies are not competitive then, far from being any fault of the companies themselves, governments and their impact on the size, quality and cost of industry inputs are to blame. Herein lies the contradiction and imposing challenge of modern economic management. While globalisation has diminished the effectiveness of the conventional tools of national economic policy—trade protection, capital controls, fixed exchange rates and active fiscal and monetary policies—governments are now expected to deliver the tools of competitiveness to each industry sector. This dilemma, in turn, is aggravated by the immediacy of the electoral cycle. Non-government parties and the media, with their daily agendas driven by action and conflict, are forever keen to lift public expectations for the contemporaneous things governments can achieve in the competitive advantages of capital.

Under comparative advantage theory, the role of the state was to facilitate trade and exchange. Governments had a fairly limited role in dealing with national deficiencies in competitiveness and trade imbalances. The Bretton Woods system of fixed exchange rates and capital controls meant that current account deficits had to be financed out of official reserves. This restriction does not apply during an era of capital mobility. Nations with uncompetitive industries and low savings can sustain their current account deficits by drawing on the savings and investment of other nations. The loosening of policy controls has been associated with a massive shift in policy expectations. The competitive advantage paradigm has made the state responsible for most aspects of competitiveness and the consequences of competitive failure, such as high unemployment, sluggish growth and external deficits.[2] The public sector is now held responsible for the economic shortcomings of the private sector. In the popular culture, small business failures are more likely attributed to the supply side failures of government policy, rather than risk-laden investments or inadequate consumer demand. Business problems are not perceived to be the result of poor management skills or investment decisions, but the inability of public policy to improve the productivity of business inputs.

AUSTRALIA'S ECONOMIC CULTURE

These unrealistic expectations about the role of government are particularly relevant in Australia. Historically our economy has lacked a strong culture of business enterprise and entrepreneurialism. In its report on Australia's potential as an *Enterprising Nation*, the 1995 Karpin Committee concluded that our 'generally ambivalent to negative attitude toward business enterprise is culturally-based . . . [Australia lacks] a strong small business culture'. According to the Australian Manufacturing Council, only 10–15 per cent of the manufacturing businesses that could be exporting are actually doing so. Indeed, if companies reformed their own performance as substantially as they expect governments to change policy, Australia would be in a much stronger economic position. A series of World Competitive Reports have ranked the quality of Australia's workforce and governments well ahead of the quality of business management.[3]

Australia has a reasonable record of product invention, having been a world leader in medical research, biotechnology, agronomy, marine research, radio-astronomy and aspects of engineering. Our problems have come from failing to successfully invest risk capital and market new products. Even with the decline of protectionist policies and values, cultural issues are likely to continue to make Australia's success under the competitive advantage paradigm problematic: a nation's rate of economic growth is directly linked to, and perhaps, primarily determined by its entrepreneurial spirit. This is what Schumpeter described as the 'creative destruction' of market economies—the innovation, product development and growth phase which replaces old products and declining industries.[4] This approach to economic policy has downgraded the age-old debate about the relative share of savings, aggregated demand and capital accumulation on the national accounts. It emphasises the importance of culturally based aspects of economic behaviour, such as the work ethic, entrepreneurialism and personal thrift.

Other studies, such as Robert Putnam's work in Italy,[5] have shown how these cultural features rely substantially on the strength of social capital: the civil institutions and associations which develop a sense of social cooperation and creativity. While governments can influence economic outcomes, it is much harder to change social habits and attitudes. Australians, while gregarious and confident, are not great risk takers. There has always been an unusual defensiveness about the Australian character and culture. Perhaps this is the inevitable product of a nation long cautious about its place in the world. It also says something about our social capital.

Australia's civil institutions have lacked a strong tradition of social engagement. The pattern and timing of European settlement coincided with the rise of the nation state and central government. Our methods of governance have featured a unique combination of strong central authorities (used to settle Australia's vast and rugged terrain in the 1800s) and individualised subsidies, primarily through the state sponsorship of home ownership (used to settle Australia's cities in the 1900s). The dominance of these institutions has left only a limited role for the type of social cooperation which features in non-government, civil organisations. Equally, as a nation, Australia has not been known for a culture of long term planning and personal thrift. For many decades the 'lucky country' ethos promoted attitudes to wealth creation heavily reliant on commodity and property development (including a high premium on home ownership as the 'great Australian dream'). Elements of a hedonistic lifestyle promoted the virtues of spending now and worrying later (best reflected in the 'she'll be right' approach).

This is an appropriate framework for understanding Australia's risk-adverse business culture and relatively poor savings record. It again highlights the false expectations the competitive advantage paradigm places on the role of government. As long as cultural issues and the quality of business management are overlooked in the public debate there can be no meaningful assessment of Australia's competitive outlook. The public sector cannot be blamed for competitive failures if the tools of competitiveness sit primarily in the hands of private capital. The new paradigm forces a view that public resources should be directed solely at the enhancement of the international competitiveness and profitability of private capital. It undervalues the role of government in correcting market failures and developing solutions to economic problems outside the domain of the private sector. The economic benefits of public investment and employment, for instance, are downplayed.

In Australia's circumstances, a series of cultural issues—impacting on the nation's savings performance and the quality of business management—makes the attainment of competitive advantages problematic. While public policy can often influence and upgrade these cultural features, its impact lies more in the medium to longer term. Moreover, the opportunity for all citizens to participate in productive economic activity will not automatically be achieved from the application of competitive advantage. The internationalisation of capital, once its logic is applied to national jurisdictions, features clear elements of economic exclusion, especially in the dispersion of earnings and employment opportunities. This is an inevitable consequence of the competitive process between nations in the chase for global capital.

International competitiveness involves political jurisdictions pulling against each other to secure jobs and investment. Not all nations succeed in this contest and, even within highly competitive jurisdictions, not all citizens and locations are likely to share in the national growth gains of international competitiveness. It can be concluded, therefore, that even with the application of so-called best practice policies, the competitive advantage paradigm is not likely, in its own right, to deliver for all Australians the benefits of economic inclusiveness. The pursuit of competitive market advantages is not enough. Something else is needed. This means creating an active role for government in the policy tools of economic adjustment. Just as laborism sought to share the (ultimately limited) gains of national capital, this new model needs to lever national economic gains in a manner consistent with an equitable distribution of employment and earnings.

A precondition for this approach is a capacity to deal with new issues and contradictions in the relationship between capital, now in its global form, and domestic systems of representative government. That is, while private capital now moves on an international scale, political jurisdictions remain fixed in the geography of nations and regions. This dislocation between the spheres of capital and government, especially when expressed in the new paradigm of competitive advantage, has fundamentally altered the political economy of the Western democracies. It has helped to turn ideologies upside down. For more than a century the political Left argued a dialectical relationship between capital and labour. Business interests and their political representatives sought to highlight tensions between private capital and public systems of governance. In truth, the most prominent political tension of our time arises from neither private production nor public ownership structures but from the relationship between global capital and nation-based politics.

4

NEW POLITICAL ECONOMY

In the famous formulation of the US Democrat, Tip O'Neill, all politics is said to be local. By its nature, national democracy represents an aggregation of local electorates and local issues. With the geography of capital moving remorselessly to global arenas, an obvious dislocation has emerged between this level of economic activity and the structure of democratic politics. This tension has been reflected in the following ways: between international competitiveness and democratic institutions; in the changing nature of political conflict and partisanship; and the emergence of fiscal crisis in the public sector. These three trends, and the way in which they are driving the new political economy of the nation state, are examined in turn.

It is often argued within the competitive advantage paradigm that national economies need lower business costs and continuous micro reform to be competitive on world markets. Yet the local impact of these changes is invariably uneven and, in the eyes of many, unfair and unnecessary. In this fashion, governments are being squeezed by the competing geography of the new political economy: the formation of capital on a global scale; the formation of electoral majorities on a local scale. While the free movement of goods and investment might maximise economic welfare internationally, nations specialising in low skill, low value added industries will inevitably endure weak levels of income growth. Moreover, the spatial and structural impact of economic restructuring is far from uniform. The growth of new industries and jobs rarely matches the location and occupation of jobs lost in those industries previously excluded from the impact of micro reform.

POLITICAL TENSIONS

These trends have built new sources of tension into our systems of governance: the conflict between what is perceived as good politics and what are understood to be good policies. While, for instance, the international transfer of savings gives each nation greater scope for productive investment, nationalist sentiment in the electorate is sensitive to current account deficits and increased foreign debt and ownership. Under competitive advantage theory, the central goal of economic policy is long term productivity growth. Governments cannot control the competitive advantage of nations, they can only influence it over time. The political process, of course, demands results consistent with its immediate cycle of electoral conflict. Hence governments are often tempted to trade away protectionist policies and subsidies in return for electoral support. They might pursue short term demand management tools to artificially inflate the economy and improve their electoral prospects, despite the medium term consequences of a spill-over on the external account. Or they might even tolerate a structural gap between national investment and national savings, rather than risk an electoral back-lash from knocking down national consumption.

These tensions have placed new pressures on the hegemony of liberal democracy. Competitive advantage theory tells us that countries that lack a consensus around economic strategies, or where special interest groups wield partisan influence, are less likely to achieve solid long term rates of growth. This argument has been used in the so-called Asian values debate to issue a challenge to the sustainability of Western democracy. Asian leaders such as Singapore's Senior Minister, Lee Kuan Yew, and Malaysia's Prime Minister, Mahathir Mohamad, have argued that liberal values and freedoms tend to be incompatible with the demands of economic globalisation. Liberal democracy, it is said, does little more than register the self-serving interests of competing groups. It lacks the political authority and moral purpose required for strong compet-itive inputs to the private sector. Social cohesion, cultural discipline and purposeful government are interpreted as the core precondi-tions of national economic success. In the Asian values paradigm, a solution to the tension between global capital and local politics involves the downgrading of liberal democracy.

Globalisation has also fundamentally changed the nature of political campaigning and information. There is now a substantial gap in each of the Western democracies between the complexity of national issues and the superficial means by which the public receives its information about political events. In an open trading economy the linkages between economic phenomena are usually complex and indirect, while television (by far the most influential medium in modern politics) relies on uncomplicated stories conveying conflict and action. In Marshall McLuhan's terminology, the medium is the message. Thus while the world over the past decade has been able to watch the fall of the ideological barriers between nations (precisely because these events were suitable for television), there has been relatively little awareness of the extent to which economic walls have also fallen. The invisible hand of the global market is not easily televised. Consequently, massive changes in the nature of private capital have, in most respects, remained outside the scrutiny of the public arena.

POLITICAL PARTISANSHIP

While markets have become global in their reach, most citizens still work and consume locally. Their reference point for living standards and lifestyle issues remains locked into local communities, labour markets and economic systems. The average Australian, for instance, is perhaps less likely to alter his or her consumption habits and take personal responsibility for an imbalance on the external account as long as foreigners are willing to fund the excess of Australia's investment over national savings. In a democracy, individuals may only take direct responsibility for national circumstances if and when their nation moves towards crisis. Otherwise, electoral politics tends to follow a pattern of global action and local reaction.

In this fashion, the contradiction between international capital and nation-based politics has made the tasks of government more complex and challenging. While competition policies and other micro reforms may assist with international competitiveness and produce benefits for consumers, they are also intensely unsettling for producer interests. Interests on the production side—such as business groups, farmers and trade unions—tend to be better organised politically, more vocal and more visible than the dispersed interests of consumers. Globalisation has given a sharper edge to a process as old as organised politics itself. Five centuries ago Machiavelli wrote of how the protests of the disaffected can overwhelm the interests of a majority favouring reform. Without new sources of competitive advantage, the economic interests of a nation and with them, a government's electoral position, are likely to decline. However, policies to upgrade international competitiveness invariably unsettle producer and local interests. Given the pace of economic restructuring, governments are now required to reconcile acutely conflicting interests on the supply and demand sides of the economy.

The upward shift of economic space to the global arena has

also intensified the parochial features of democratic politics within the nation state. Not surprisingly, the political interests of opposition parties are usually framed through an ethos of sectionalism, avoiding responsibility for adding value to the national policy process. They are careful not to interfere with the difficult tasks of economic restructuring yet are keen to exploit the electoral consequences of economic change. This emphasises the disjunction in modern democracies between the qualities required for election and those needed to govern effectively. Opposition parties which take a superficial approach to policy making have set a familiar cycle in Australian public life: failure to think through a policy framework, absence of an effective mandate for change, broken promises once in government and hence, further aggravation of the public's distrust of the political process. It used to be said that good government relies on effective opposition. The quality of our democracy now relies on parties, whether in government or opposition, that are able to deal effectively with the electoral tensions between global capital and local politics.

FISCAL CRISIS OF THE STATE

Among the many contradictions between global capital and local politics, Labor's agenda is particularly disadvantaged by what has become known as the fiscal crisis of the state—that is, the gap between the revenue raising capacity of an internationally competitive taxation regime and the public outlays required to fund social democratic programs and the local costs of economic adjustment. This highlights a basic flaw in the methods of social democracy in an open economy. While they rely on government revenue catching a strong flow-on effect from national economic growth, the revenue net itself is limited by competitive tax policies. The movement of capital to a global scale has fostered strong competition between the spatial jurisdictions of government, manifest in both additional costs to the state and revenues forgone.

The term, the fiscal crisis of the state, was first used by James O'Connor in his 1973 book of the same title.[1] He and other neo-Marxists have written persuasively of the growing financial demands on Western governments. Social welfare legitimises the gap between the size of the labour force and the provision of employment opportunities. Industry welfare (subsidies and tax breaks) helps to prop up the rate of return to capital. Lowering business costs tends to drain revenue from public budgets. Similarly, public choice theory has explained how electoral pressures push tax rates down, while interest groups push outlays up. Both theories point to a structural gap between the revenue raising capacity of government and the expenditure required to fulfil a growing number of public functions.

The liberalisation of capital markets has allowed national governments to borrow more extensively, entrenching a pattern of semi-permanent public sector deficits across the Western democracies. In a closed economy, governments had to fund their deficits by paying higher interest rates to domestic investors. With access to global markets, however, smaller rate rises can attract the same volume of deficit finance. Hence, large increases in public sector debt have accompanied the integration of capital markets over the past two decades. In the 30 years to 1974 in the OECD economies, total net public debt fell progressively as a proportion of GDP. In the years since it has risen from 15 per cent to 40 per cent.

Deficit budgeting on recurrent commitments has been a feature of the Australian public sector since the early 1970s. The mobility of capital, and competition between political jurisdictions, have led to competitive fiscal federalism (whereby State Governments discount tax rates against each other) and the marking down of Commonwealth income and company tax rates. The limited scope of State revenue powers, with their focus on transaction and mobility taxes, has contracted even further.[2] The introduction of national competition policies is progressively eliminating the monopoly profits of both Federal and State public utilities. Moreover, the disaggregation of the scale of private sector production—manifest in the growth of the contract, consultant and franchise sectors—has weakened the Federal tax net on earnings and forced tax efficiency issues downstream to the point of expenditure and savings.

Attempts to widen the tax base in Australia, particularly with broad-based consumption taxes, have not been successful for equity and electoral reasons. The growth in new forms of services consumption has generally remained outside the scope of the existing wholesale sales tax and excise regime. In the decade to 1995, Commonwealth revenue declined by more than 3 per cent of GDP or $15 billion in current dollar terms. If revenue had maintained its share of national output, the 1995–96 Budget would have recorded a modest surplus. By no means could Federal Labor in office be regarded as a high taxing/high revenue administration. Indeed, Keating left Australia as the second lowest taxing nation in the OECD. Australia's average rate of personal income tax (including social security and health contributions) is around 18 per cent, compared to an OECD average of 22 per cent.

On the outlays side, the Whitlam, Hawke and Keating Governments each accepted new funding responsibilities. The changing nature of work—with the growth in female participation rates, multi-skilling and workplace flexibility—has led to new functions and outlays in child care and most forms of education and training. The Federal Government has carried most of the additional costs of human capital development. High rates of structural unemployment have broadened the scale of transfer payments and produced a new generation of labour market programs. Ageing demographics and improvements to medical technology have pushed out the demand for aged care and accommodation plus all forms of health care. General advances in consumer standards and recreational pursuits have also contributed to higher expectations about the functions of the public sector. Electoral influences have aided the entrenchment of new programs which, once established, tend to attract their own strong following.[3]

The overload of the modern state has left social democracy vulnerable to the small government agenda of the political Right. This is especially the case in Australia, where most programs are financed off the general budget instead of contributory schemes. Unlike many other national systems, Australians provide for most of their welfare in sickness, unemployment and retirement as taxpayers rather than self-funding citizens. In the economic orthodoxy, the public sector has been allocated additional responsibilities for its contribution to national savings through cost saving measures. This model has also been vulnerable to shifts in the legitimacy of the welfare state, particularly public expectations for the hypothecation of tax contributions to some form of personalised return. The overload of government has concentrated the role of the state on the rationing of scarce public resources. In Part III it is argued that this rationing role has undermined the legitimacy of government in its management of the public entitlements and services.

It is difficult to sustain Labor's social model and agenda without the resolution of the fiscal crisis of Australian government. The experience of Federal Labor in office confirms the tensions which inevitably arise from government's role as a rationer of scarce public resources. The Hawke and Keating Governments, remarkably enough, were able to manufacture a European-style social contract and safety net from revenues based on United States-style tax rates. This project could not be maintained, however, without the emergence of collateral equity and electoral concerns, many of which fashioned the 1996 election result. These included:

- selling a number of fixed capital assets to help fund the demand for recurrent outlay growth in other areas—a privatisation strategy which caused concern among some parts of the Labor constituency;

- cutting real grant monies to the States which, in turn, reduced the scale of community service provision and infrastructure development;
- engaging in public sector efficiency gains—such as corporatisation and contracting out—which, by their productivity-based objectives, reduced the public sector's role as an employer (particularly an employer of last resort in low employment regions);
- running down own-purpose capital and infrastructure outlays, which again restricted the Commonwealth's role in regional development;
- narrowing the scope of service universality through user pays pricing strategies and resource rationing, particularly in the health sector; and
- greater targeting of cash payments which led to some unacceptably high effective marginal tax rates for middle income earners (particularly two-income families) and consequent electoral resentment.

THE CAUSES OF FISCAL CRISIS

O'Connor has identified the cause of the fiscal crisis as:

> the contradiction of capitalist production itself—the fact that [the act of] production is social whereas the means of production are owned privately. In the long run, monopoly capital socialises more and more capital costs and social expenses of production. However profits are not socialised; the point of socialising costs and expenses is to raise profits.[4]

In fact, it is the footloose rather than monopoly characteristics of capital which have overloaded the fiscal capacity of the state public sector. The mobility of finance, and most commodities, has been able to extract an economic premium from nation states in pursuit of competitive advantages. The cost of business inputs and public subsidies has been progressively added to the expenses of government. Simultaneously on the revenue side, governments have been increasingly reluctant to appropriate public resources from private returns to capital for fear of footloose investment relocating to another political jurisdiction.

Globalisation forces upon the nation state additional public responsibilities and costs, while simultaneously driving down the public resource base. The chase for capital across the globe has induced political jurisdictions to subsidise the locational decisions of footloose capital. Moreover, the competitive advantage paradigm demands from government lower costs among a range of business-related services. It is also clear that globalisation adds to the costs of state action in dealing with the consequences of economic exclusion and uncertainty. These are expressed through additional measures of income support and labour market adjustment. The global integration of capital has given the state more work to do, yet fewer resources with which to discharge these responsibilities.

Both the spheres of global capital and local politics force additional public costs onto a restricted revenue base. Herein lies a critical contradiction in the role of the modern state: while it has been assigned (within the jurisdiction of national politics) the role of making capital competitive, it has also been identified (within national accounting systems) as the cause of current account deficits and foreign indebtedness. In the competitive advantage paradigm, the external account is taken as a balance sheet on each nation's degree of competitiveness. Deficits—in the trade and financial flows of capital between nations—are taken as a sign of national failure and are commonly reported as such. While footloose capital places additional demands on public sector outlays to secure competitive advantages at a national level, these same outlays are frequently taken as a sign of national disadvantage. This is the perspective of the twin deficits theory: that inadequate national savings are essentially a public sector problem; that a reduction in public budget deficits reduces the current account deficit.

In this fashion, the competitive advantage paradigm and consequent overload of government are antipathetic to the legitimacy of the state public sector. The globalisation of capital has left the state suffering from high expectations for its role in fostering national economic successes, yet with seemingly limited means by which it can fulfil its public functions. This double standard manifests itself in most parts of the public debate, with the economic orthodoxy condoning all things private—private sector initiative, spending, jobs and investment—while condemning most things public. The issue of national savings is commonly presented in terms of inadequate public sector savings, not deficiencies in the private sector. Private sector employment is portrayed as socially desirable (in the language of the Howard Government, constituting 'real jobs'), while public sector employment is interpreted solely for its potential for low cost business inputs. So too, the small business sector is said to embody the social virtues of industry and effort, while publicly provided services are portrayed in terms of their economic cost, rather than social utility.

These tensions, importantly enough, are aggravated by the demands placed on the fiscal capacity of the state by social democracy, especially with its emphasis on the universal rights and entitlements of citizens. It was noted earlier that laborism, operating within the sphere of national capital, secured most of its goals from regulatory interventions in the production process. This was part of a strategy of domestic defence: closing the economy to international competition and using the leverage of the state to share some of the gains of productive national capital among workers and their dependants. Social democracy, by contrast, represents a strategy of domestic compensation, relying on public resources to compensate citizens treated unfairly by the profit system of production.[5] The sustainability of compensation strategies of this kind is clearly restricted within the sphere of global capital, and the demands placed on government finances by the competitive advantage paradigm. It cannot be assumed in an open economy, even if competitive advantages are attained, that the revenue sources of government will be sufficient to support each of the objectives of social democracy. This is a fundamental lesson of Labor's thirteen years in government. A prominent argument through the remainder of this book concerns the resolution of the fiscal crisis of the state by reformulating the basic goals and purpose of social democracy.

5

ECONOMIC RATIONALISM

Acommon Left response to the emergence of global capital has been to denounce market forces by associating the recent period of reform with 'economic rationalism'. The use of this term commonly points to a vanguard of academics and financial interests who have secured a realignment of government policy towards free market forces.[1] It is suggested that strategies of so-called economic rationalism have released undesirable, globalised market trends. In practice, however, changes to markets have driven changes to public policy, not the reverse. As ever, events have had a much greater impact on policy than has political theory. As global capital began to seriously circumvent the effectiveness of national economic policies and controls in the 1970s, governments worldwide changed their policies. As an explanation of cause and effect in public policy, therefore, economic rationalism is no more helpful a concept than attempts by the political Right to demonise 'political correctness', or earlier Left efforts to identify a 'money power' conspiracy.[2]

These approaches are characterised by reductionist thinking: reducing complex issues to a single, all-purpose term of derision. This is a self-serving way of handling issues. It erects straw men solely for the purpose of knocking them down. These reductionist theorists rarely attempt to develop serious alternatives to their men of straw. Indeed, over time, theorists of the political Left have been just as guilty as those on the Right in making rationalist assumptions about the behaviour of participants in the market. For instance, Marx and Engels constructed a model for the rational accumulation of capital and income maximising behaviour. Even today, some parts of the industrial movement are struggling to accept that pure, rationalist models of labour exploitation have been overtaken, especially in post-industrial workplaces, by skill diversity and enterprise cooperation.

METHODOLOGICAL ERRORS

A more satisfactory critique of economic rationalism, properly understood, applies to economic theories (of either the old Left or Right) which rely on assumptions of rational market behaviour. This assumption goes to the heart of most of the methodological flaws in modern economic theory. The origins of economics lie in attempts 200 years ago to make sense of the Industrial Revolution. Classical economists, such as Adam Smith and David Ricardo, used the empirical tools of observation and description to assist their task. Throughout the remainder of last century, however, economics was transformed into a more rigid and precise discipline, using mathematical models and scientific methods to equate it to the laws of nature. As a profession, economics has never recovered from this methodological error.

The models and methods of conventional economics, as taught and practised throughout the Western world, are an inadequate way to describe and understand a market economy. They rely essentially on a flawed assumption about economic behaviour: that markets are dominated by rational participants displaying perfect knowledge and exercising perfect choice. Rationality is defined in terms of narrow self-interest and income maximising behaviour. In truth, nobody has perfect knowledge and no consumer has yet enjoyed perfect market choice. A more accurate understanding of market economies would incorporate elements of altruistic, as well as self-interested, behaviour. Similarly, cultural considerations—the set of values, beliefs and prejudices which hold society together—are important determinants of economic activity. Yet they are foreign to a rationalist framework. In practice, human behaviour can never be reduced to a set of formulas and assumptions abstracted from the social environment.[3]

None of this is to suggest, of course, that less than rational behaviour by market participants negates the usefulness of market forces. Indeed, no society has found a better way of facilitating growth and generating wealth than by holding out personal incentives and the profit motive. Ultimately markets, as imperfect as they may be, simply represent a mechanism for pricing and allocating resources and hence, stimulating economic activity. The dynamic nature of markets also makes stereotyping difficult. The robber baron images of the early 1900s, for instance, have been diluted by many thousands of smaller interests in the new economy, ranging from superannuants to shareholders and sole trader businesses. Equally, changes to the nature of production and work now mean that not all labour relations necessarily involve exploitation.

Simplistic ideas in economics have a habit of forming badges of identity for like-minded people and political views. The repetition of dogma becomes a substitute for the value of observation and empirical learning. In this fashion, economic libertarians have used the market behaviour of rational economic man to advance the merit of free market forces. At the other extreme, command economists have used the shortcomings of the market to promote supply side planning and regulation as their preferred solution to economic problems. In both cases, however, economic theories have been constructed primarily to justify a desired set of policy outcomes, rather than objectively deal with the complexities of a mixed economy.

AN INSTITUTIONALIST APPROACH

Economic paradigms which seek to simplify all issues and events into a self-contained and justified framework need to be treated with caution. Economic activity, national and international, is now far too complex for the reductionism of general theories or generalised critiques. There are no natural laws in economics, only dogmatists who try to invent them. Better results can be achieved through an institutionalist approach to economic analysis, with a reliance on the empirical methods of observation and adaptation. Economic behaviour is best understood by acknowledging its diversity: the likelihood of both rational and irrational behaviour; the coexistence of self-interest and altruism among market participants; and the strength of cultural influences and social circumstances. Market influences are supported for their positive contribution to economic growth, with a countervailing role for government in the correction of market failures and moderation of some market outcomes. Within the institutionalist approach, firms, regions and the political economy of the nation state are taken as the most useful units of empirical analysis.

This paradigm seeks to return the dismal science of economics to its origins in the social studies of political economy. It eschews a fundamentalist view of markets and their ownership features. It avoids the folly of both libertarian and socialist economics. While the first argues the logic of the market as a natural precondition of social good and political freedom, the other positions it as the antithesis of equality and liberty in practice. Both approaches tend to treat the market as an homogenous entity, more as an end in itself than a means by which, under certain conditions, a number of social goals might be realised. As the Australian polemicist, David Burchell, points out:

What is shared by all markets is little more than the fact that something is marketed in them. Otherwise they are highly differentiated, and there is little point in trying to analyse the functioning of the market without further specification. Markets always operate under institutional conditions . . . [For example] the market conditions created by privatisation, corporatisation and so on, for the most part, bear little or no resemblance to the ideological picture of 'free markets' and are never likely to. Rather, they are for the most part highly administered, necessarily highly regulated, artificial 'quasi-markets'. Hence the picture of economic rationalism as creating free markets in place of government regulation conceals the important extent to which these quasi-markets are themselves the product of a careful and highly differentiated regime of governance.[4]

Too frequently, social democratic thinking has been guided by an assumption that the replacement of private markets with various forms of state intervention is intrinsically good. Functionalism of this kind sells short the diversity and potential of market forces. It does not logically follow that because a commodity or service is important to society, the private market should be automatically discounted as the most effective method of social delivery. For instance, two of the essentials of life, food and clothes, are regularly exchanged through private sector transactions, without socially unacceptable results or the public demanding the creation of state-run alternatives. Likewise, a belief in the primacy of market-based economies does not imply that private markets are always likely to produce optimal outcomes. Rather, free markets are in some circumstances inconsistent with the fair distribution of material and social goods, thereby necessitating the active role of government as a regulator, redistributor of resources and provider of services outside the profit system. The differentiated nature of markets makes it difficult to construct a general theory for the countervailing role of government. This again underlines the usefulness of an institutionalist approach: fashioning a mix of market influences, public interest regulation and public sector delivery as circumstances might demand.

THE FOLLY OF ISOLATIONISM

Significantly, the critique of economic rationalism has also been associated with populist calls for a return to a relatively closed economy. The rejection of market methods has inspired a feeling that Australia might productively disengage itself from the global market.[5] Clearly, however, isolationist strategies of nationally defined capital are no longer viable. National economic barriers acceded decades ago to the volume and velocity of international capital. The technological and economic changes driving this agenda for policy liberalisation are not likely to be reversed. Isolationism, therefore, is best understood as an electoral slogan appealing to the politics of nostalgia. Modern economic history points to the way in which the central planning and capital controls of the nation state have fundamentally failed due to their inability to make better judgments about the system of production and distribution than those directly involved in the market. The international evidence points to nations, on the basis of some exceptionally unproductive experiences, moving to abolish trade protection, financial controls and long term industry intervention, not restore them.

There are three formidable barriers to Australia returning to a relatively closed economy. First, the costs of closure would be enormous given the openness of our markets and the prospective withdrawal of financial capital from Australian markets. Second, a closed economy loses a large slice of its transmission mechanism for sharing the benefits of global advances in technology. In dynamic industries like information technology, for instance, nations do not have permanent competitive advantages; rather, they have an omnipresent chance to capture the economic benefits of the next wave of technological change. Third, Australia would detach itself from each of the potential economic gains of world trade liberalisation, both at a bilateral and multilateral level. Most of our industries are unlikely to prosper if restricted to Australia's domestic markets for consumption. A nation with just 0.3 per cent of the world's population needs to expand its markets through the virtues of aggressive multilateralism and economic openness. It is difficult to understand what a small trading nation like ours can achieve from jeopardising its access to international markets through the restoration of a policy paradigm which, by the time of the 1970s, offered little more than a national inventory of over-protected and inefficient industries.

From an ALP perspective, there is simply no way back to a laborist model of income gain sharing. The diminution of Australia's farming and mining trade advantages has eliminated the possibility of income transfers to the industrial sector from commodity-based economic rents. Just as much, in an era of open and liberalised capital markets, there is no such thing as a convenient half-way house between an open and closed economic model. The market's tolerance of capital controls, heavy regulation and macro policy adventurism has well-defined limits. Policies running counter to internationalisation will most likely be ineffective. One of Labor's ongoing strengths, in this regard, is its commitment to free trade and investment in the Asia-Pacific region by the year 2010 as part of the APEC process.

6

ECONOMIC
NATIONALISM

While orthodox economic studies have failed to deal adequately with national economic systems, their shortcomings with regard to the significance of economic globalisation are even more pronounced. Economics, by and large, has failed to develop a satisfactory framework within which the tensions between global capital and nation-based political jurisdictions can be examined. Hence the political economy of most nations is now framed around a narrow trade-off between national benefits (drawn from the competitive advantage paradigm) and national autonomy (drawn from electoral resistance to the upward shift of capital to a global arena). While politicians have held out the potential benefits of international competitiveness, public concerns have more likely centred on the dislocation costs of capital's growing mobility. The Australian political economist, Dick Bryan, has expressed this dilemma well:

> The gulf between the extremes of nation as a discrete economic space, and nation as an arbitrary part of an international space, lacks a language of investigation. It has proved very difficult to develop a language or analysis in which global accumulation is part of the domestic economy, and the local is understood as a specific representation of global processes. Similarly, it has been difficult for economics to develop a conception of the role of the state which is not predicated upon a nationalist conception of accumulation, and the belief that the state's role is to secure 'national' benefit. So international economics and political economy continue to baulk at the ambiguous constitution of boundaries, reverting to the apparent conceptual clarity that is nationalism. Notions of national autonomy being secured or subverted, and gains and losses to the national economy from

international interaction, are the terms which continue to dominate debate.[1]

Bryan, writing from a neo-Marxist perspective, maintains that
the chase for capital has transferred the class conflicts of the
industrial age into the national conflicts of a globalised economy.
The key to this process, he argues, is the way in which the working
class of each nation has been convinced, through the ideology of
patriotism, that competitive advantages represent 'an agenda of
labour as well as capital'. It is thought that nationalism, 'dignifies
competition [between labour] as an expression and experience of
social commitment to a collective good'.[2] As long as workers regard
their interests as matching those of footloose capital, distributional
conflicts are externalised into national contests for competitive
advantage. Economic leverage passes to the global sphere of capital,
creating new issues of economic sovereignty and equity. Within
the terms of this analysis, the durability of nationalism is explained
away in terms of capitalist hegemony. It is not available to social
democracy, however, restricted to national systems of parliamentary democracy, to simply ignore the strength and political
importance of nationalism. It needs to develop, consistent with its
equity goals, a satisfactory response to the pressing nationalistic
tensions between the globalised sphere of capital and the localised
features of governance.

BIDDING WARS

Bryan's analysis highlights the kind of strategic advantages capital,
in its multinational form, now exercises over national jurisdictions.
The governments and workers of the nation state have been willing
to compete against each other in pursuit of competitive advantages
and footloose investment. Governments everywhere are struggling
to capture and keep a share of global capital, both in securing its
locational decisions and finding ways through the taxation system
by which it might make a financial return to the public sector.
With the disaggregation of the scale of production in many industries, politicians can no longer rely on the sunk costs of investment
to hold productive capital within the boundaries of the nation state.
Even in traditional areas of heavy industry, such as steel and
automotive manufacturing, investments appear to be in a constant
state of rationalisation on a multinational scale. Governments have
fallen into the habit of bidding against each other to attract
footloose investment, often with open-ended subsidies, tax concessions, border controls and the promise of wage restraint. The

political economy of the nation state faces a dilemma best explained in the language of supply and demand: capital investment enjoys worldwide demand and the advantages of substantial mobility; nations have decided to aggressively compete against each other to secure scarce capital resources; and accordingly, multinational capital, in the exercise of its locational decisions, has been able to extract substantial economic premiums from within the boundaries of the nation state.

Capital has been able to use its international mobility to lever financial benefits through the political pressures of the competitive advantage paradigm. The bidding war between political jurisdictions has aided the interests of profit maximisation on an international scale. This has inevitably been at the expense of national interests, as these premiums have to be paid for by the government and citizens of the nation state. In some industries this has forced real wage reductions. In the public sector, it has forced a general increase in business-related outlays (adding significantly to the fiscal crisis of the state) plus the application of competition policy to various public utilities. In return, there is little evidence to suggest that the owners and managers of multinational capital have been willing to engage in the exercise of social responsibility or the advancement of national interests.

Internationally, left-of-centre parties are still grappling to frame an adequate response to the economic leverage of footloose capital. The development of a policy bridge between globalised economic events and localised electoral issues remains unformed. Yet without the resolution of these tensions it is difficult to perceive how social democracy can ensure the basis of a socially just system of economic distribution. The capture of large economic premiums from the citizens of the nation state by global capital is not conducive to a fair allocation of primary goods. The realisation of a number of important equity goals now relies on the development of new strategies of national economic leverage. Nations need to be able to maximise their influence over economic events, as well as the economic returns available to their citizens.

SPATIAL STRATEGIES

This requires, in Bryan's words, a new language of investigation in the political economy of the nation state. It is not sufficient for governments to indiscriminately throw ever more resources at the chase for global capital. Incrementalism of this kind simply results in a crude bidding war and the attendant problems of the fiscal crisis of government. Rather, policy makers need to think strategically about the most effective means by which the nation state can re-assert its leverage and sovereignty in its relationship with international finance and production. They need to devise an approach which ensures that the economic assets of the nation state, anchored and secure within its boundaries, are developed to their full potential. Old ways of thinking about the economic process need to be replaced by new strategies of economic nationalism. Just as capital has established a new sphere of space and mobility, the economic strategies of nations now need to be cast in explicitly spatial terms.

In conventional economic analysis, inputs to the production process—capital, information, labour skills, raw materials, infrastructure and government support—are not considered for their spatial features. The factors of production are each assumed to be mobile and flexible. In practice, of course, this is never likely to be the case. What distinguished the old economy, however, was the way in which the relative immobility of capital brought it under the clear jurisdiction of nations. Just as the geography of capital has fundamentally altered, the work of the nation state now needs to devise a complementary response. This necessitates a reconsideration of the role of government, based on the geography of each of the nation state's inputs to the production process. The framing of policies impacting on immobile factors of production needs to be distinguished from business inputs which are easily manipulated by the portable geography of capital. In this regard, the potential policy tools of competitive advantage—business costs, human capital investment and industry welfare—need to be differentiated on the basis of their spatial features and impact.

Governments need to invest heavily in the new economy on those factors of production that remain relatively immobile, knowing that the benefits of these public outlays will continue to be realised within the boundaries of the nation state. This points to the significance of the public's investment in human capital, plus the fixed assets of regional infrastructure, such as transport and communication links. The geography of each of these inputs to the production process remains predominantly anchored within nations and regions. By contrast, outlays directed at a crude bidding war between political jurisdictions—such as the financial subsidisation and protection of footloose capital—represent a less effective strategy. The benefits of industry welfare, with its purpose centred on the enhancement of profit, tend to be captured by international capital and thereby remain subject to its mobile geography. Subsidies and concessions paid directly to multinational companies are lost to the nation state once the companies, as is most likely, embark on the further rationalisation and relocation of their operations. To be certain, scarce public resources engaged in the competitive advantage paradigm need to be devoted to inputs and factors of production which maximise the economic leverage of the nation state.

This spatial dimension in the framing of economic strategies helps to alter the nature of the national economic debate. First, it recognises that the interests of internationalised capital do not necessarily reflect the interests of the citizens and workers of the nation state. Second, it acknowledges the importance of the distributional conflict between nations and the global sphere of capital in pursuit of economic benefits. And third, it positions the role of government in this distributional competition as attempting to maximise the income and economic growth available to its citizens. An appreciation of the diverse geography of the various inputs to production also helps to demonstrate that national benefits can actually be consistent with enhanced national autonomy. Competitive advantages can be attained by investing heavily in the primary assets of the nation state—the skills and insights of its people, plus the development of its fixed economic infrastructure. Economic sovereignty can be expressed through the economic growth and premiums achieved in the success of this strategy. In this fashion, social democracy can reposition the question of economic nationalism in the political arena. It needs to argue that, faced by the spread and influence of global capital, the strength of the nation state fundamentally relies on its capacity to invest in and develop its remaining economic assets: its human capital and fixed economic infrastructure.

CORPORATE INTERESTS

This approach can also help to resolve social democracy's somewhat incongruous relationship with the business sector. During the long boom of the 1950s and 1960s, left-of-centre parties moved into the habit of regarding corporate interests as matching the national interest. This not only suited the public mood of the time, riding on the back of strong and continuous economic growth, it also suited the ideals of national economic planning. The distributional functions of social democratic government relied on the solid growth of the national sphere of capital. In Australia, for instance, the ALP went out of its way, especially after the term of the Whitlam Government, to rebuild its reputation for economically 'responsible' policies. In an era of globalisation, however, this relationship is not without its flaws and tensions. Most of Labor's traditional constituencies have been unsettled by the rationalisation and inequities of multinational capital. They have not necessarily shared the perception, still propagated by some sections of the ALP, that corporate interests are synonymous with Australia's interests. After the corporate excesses of the 1980s, the public mood remains disenchanted with the ongoing evidence of tax evasion, consumer exploitation and other forms of socially irresponsible behaviour by large holdings of capital.[3]

It is no longer sufficient for parties like Labor to allow themselves to be positioned as a facilitator, seemingly at any cost, of interests at the big end of town. On the plane of issues being argued out along the economic nationalist and internationalist divide, social democracy needs to define a more appropriate purpose than this. It has to recognise that issues of nationalism now need to be judged not just as a contest between nations for competitive advantage, but also, no less pointedly, as a contest between the nation state and global capital for economic premiums. The upward shift of the geography of capital has added to the complexity of the public expression of economic nationalism. Citizens adversely affected or concerned by the impact of globalisation are just as likely to feel antagonistic to the interests of international finance and investment as the interests of other nations. This represents a basic point of departure for social democracy in the framing of economic policy.

DUAL NATIONALISM

Labor needs to give expression to both strands of the nationalistic contest and feeling. It needs to develop policies that allow Australia not only to compete effectively in the short term chase for investment and growth, but also to enhance the enduring economic strength and sovereignty of the Australian people. Without these twin goals it is not possible for social democracy to overcome the nature of Bryan's critique—that it is without a language of analysis and political purpose by which the economic interests of the nation state can be differentiated from the interests of multinational capital. Nationalism, expressed solely in the chase for investment can convince people—as workers, producers and taxpayers—that their sacrifices in the distributional share of income is an acceptable way of furthering the national interest. Social democracy needs to become more than just another political expression of the three strands of competitive advantage, more than just another voice calling for economic efficiency as well as more subsidies for capital. It needs to engage in strategies dealing with the distributional conflicts between large holdings of multinational investment and the citizens of the nation state. As footloose capital owes no loyalty or responsibility to any political jurisdiction, it should be the legitimate target of patriotic feeling and policy making.

The repositioning of economic nationalism as a contest between nations and footloose capital has the potential to reconcile several of the political dilemmas facing social democracy. First and foremost, it helps to demonstrate that the interests of capital and labour do not always coincide and that in such instances, the public sector has a role to play in pursuit of greater distributional equity. From this position, many of the false expectations of the competitive advantage model can be overcome. Social democracy needs to show that national account deficits are more likely to represent a failing of business culture and methods than inadequate public policy. It needs to focus public concerns about competitive weaknesses in the national economy on the quality of business management, rather than solely on the public sector's control of business inputs. It needs to allocate to government an active role in developing strategies of national economic leverage, plus dealing with the failings of the private sector. It needs to develop the legitimacy of public sector employment and investment as an answer to the problems of economic exclusion in an open economy. These policies, outlined at length in Part II, represent the most effective means by which the shortcomings of the competitive advantage model, expressed in the durability of unemployment and economic inequality, can be resolved.

The approach outlined above, of course, is essentially untested in the new political economy of nations. One of social democracy's problems is that it has become, in the electoral politics of most nations, largely indistinguishable from its opponents in the framing of economic policy. The upward shift of capital has forced parties across the political divide to engage in the chase for footloose investment. Economic policies have seemingly moved into an era of convergence. There are sound reasons, however, why this does not need to be the case. Social democracy, with its powerful interest in distributional issues, needs to engage itself more comprehensively in the raft of policy matters arising from the relationship between the nation state and global capital. This does not require a policy retreat from internationalisation; rather, it necessitates the development of a policy framework embracing the dual features of economic nationalism. National benefits and national autonomy need to be made compatible. Labor's economic policies need to pursue competitive advantages, not just at any cost, but in a manner that invests heavily in the nation's fixed economic assets. This means embracing, as a policy structure, new growth theories of national economic success.

7

NEW GROWTH
POLICIES

It has become common in the political debates of the nation state to focus on the economic problems of over-consumption. This is a characteristic of the national accounting systems implicit in the work of the competitive advantage paradigm. That is, to define national economic issues in terms of the twin deficits: the excess of recurrent consumption over revenue on public budgets, and the excess of consumption over production on the national accounts. It assigns to the public sector responsibility for the paucity of national savings and the consequent problems of a current account deficit. This has become an awkward issue for social democracy. While ever the debate focuses primarily on the public sector's contribution to national savings, governments have to juggle a commitment to fiscal consolidation with their support for the broader work of the public sector. Coupled with the general evidence of fiscal crisis, the horizons of collective governance in an open economy are inherently restricted.

It is, therefore, critical to develop a new framework by which issues of over-consumption and the twin deficits can be more suitably addressed in the public arena. As mentioned earlier, this involves consideration of a range of cultural issues, especially in the failings of business management and corporate risk taking in Australia. It also relies on an appreciation of how the shortfall in national savings can be attributed more to the paucity of private savings than public savings. Moreover, there are now sound reasons why the political focus on these matters should shift from the twin deficits to consideration of a third, and more important, deficit issue: Australia's under-investment in the skills and inventiveness of its people and institutions.[1] This represents something of a new radical centre in political economy. While the old Left has always argued for more recurrent spending as a way of boosting economic growth, and the Right has focused narrowly on the scale of public saving and dissaving, better results can be achieved by stimulating the processes which create, from first principles, new sources of economic growth. As Paul Romer, a founder of this new growth paradigm, has argued:

> A recent branch of work in economics that goes under the label of endogenous growth theory validates some of the concerns about competitiveness, innovation and discovery expressed by people who are not economists. It suggests that both the save-more and the spend-more macroeconomic policy prescriptions miss the crux of the matter. Neither adjustments to monetary and fiscal policy, nor increases in the rates of savings and capital accumulation can by themselves generate persistent increases in standards of living. The most important job for economic policy is to create an institutional environment that supports technological change.[2]

In the conventional theory of economic growth, inputs of capital and labour were taken as the only valid determinants of variations in output. Quite remarkably, new pools of knowledge and inventiveness were regarded as outside the parameters by which growth outcomes and forecasts could be modelled. In the neoclassical approach, for instance, it was assumed that a constant, exogenous rate of technological change generated a steady rate of per capita growth. The new growth theorists have been able to overcome this deficiency and demonstrate how, in the new economy, the long run rate of growth in real per capita output depends entirely on the rate at which technological knowledge grows. Moreover, it is argued that the development of knowledge does not occur outside the economic process. The decisions of the public and private sectors in the rate of research and development, investment in the education system, upgrading of equipment and allocation of other economic resources, have a profound impact on the scale of technological change and attendant rate of long term growth.[3]

KNOWLEDGE AS AN ECONOMIC RESOURCE

With the advent of knowledge-based industries and employment, these new theories of growth have the potential to fundamentally redefine economic theory and the sovereignty of the nation state. Even though knowledge has become an important economic resource, within most forms of economic study it still lacks clear parameters of analysis. It sits outside the measurement techniques of conventional economics, in the quantification of its value, cost and productivity. In the words of Peter Drucker, 'so far there are no signs of an Adam Smith or a David Ricardo of knowledge'.[4] The new growth theorists, however, have provided the basis of a fresh understanding of the current wave of economic change. Just as the Industrial Revolution produced new and extraordinary rates of economic growth through the mobilisation of industrial capital, the information age is based on the application of new forms of technological knowledge to the marketplace. The economic advantages of nations now rest with their capacity to mobilise the know-how and investment required to establish and expand these new industries.

The new growth theories also provide important support for the value of economic openness. Nations which lose the transmission of technological advances in the international exchange of trade and investment quickly fall off the leading edge of technology in the development of knowledge-based industries. Economic nationalism expressed through crude border controls is now more likely to represent an assertion of national folly. Notions of economic sovereignty are better expressed through the skills and capacity of a nation's people to add value to the new growth process. This helps maximise the prospects of employment growth in a post-industrial economy.

It needs to be appreciated, contrary to some of the nonsense circulating in Australian politics, that knowledge-based production realises higher employment returns than older forms of manufacturing output. It is estimated, for instance, that information technology companies generate ten to twenty times more employment per million dollars of investment than heavy industry concerns, such as steel production.[5] While both forms of output rely on elements of automation (and neither could be judged, especially by the standards of the agriculture or industrial ages, as labour intensive), newer industries at least have the advantage of a strong catalytic effect in the creation of new jobs. Through the twin virtues of openness and knowledge enhancement, nations are able to capture the new growth impact of knowledge-based output. For instance, it is estimated that Australia, in the development of this approach, has the potential to lift its exports in information technology from $4 billion per annum to $25 billion by the year 2005.[6] Accordingly, correction of Australia's third deficit has the potential to overcome the twin deficits.

Like any other economic resource, knowledge needs to be paid for in a way that necessitates opportunity costs for other forms of consumption and investment. In the new growth paradigm, governments have a critical role to play in ensuring that nations invest adequately in education and technological research. They need to ensure that other forms of national spending do not divert resources from endogenous growth strategies. Private markets are not likely to meet the large commencement costs implicit in the development of technological advances, thereby necessitating public outlays in the development of human capital. While it is expensive to develop new economic know-how, in the invention and design of new products and services, these unit costs decline as the new knowledge spreads to other parts of the economy. As no single producer can capture the full economic benefits of the new technology, the private sector is unlikely to invest to its full potential and social benefit. Hence technological progress carries some of the features of a public good, requiring a strong level of public investment. This is in sharp contrast to the neoclassical model within which government has no direct role to play in fostering economic growth. It is also at odds with macroeconomic advice urging governments to think about the business cycle and little else.

EDUCATION AND RESEARCH POLICY

In the information age, the public sector needs to invest in the enhancement of knowledge no less fulsomely than the industrial age invested in machines. A nation's commitment to research and development is all-important. So too is the effectiveness of a nation's education system as a means by which new ideas can be produced and used. The new growth theorists maintain that the engine of economic expansion lies in the development of these various forms of human capital. Evidence across a large number of nations shows that human capital formation—the spread and success of education and research—is a key contributor to growth.[7] In the spatial context of national economic strategies, this opens up a critical opportunity. Not only can a nation grow its economy through the skills of its people, but the enhancement of these assets and advantages—education, research and development—can produce economic benefits that remain strongly fixed within the boundaries of the nation state.

The theory of global capital requires a perfectly mobile labour force and set of workplace skills. In practice, however, the relative immobility of people, anchored in the geography of localism and nationalism, has given to the nation state a potential source of economic leverage. Its significance lies in the implications of the new growth paradigm and the changing nature of work and production in a post-industrial economy. Increasingly, economic value is being created by the skilful adaptation of information and symbols to new sources of economic demand. Skilled citizens are able to attract an economic premium commensurate with their value adding capacity. Clever countries have worked out that footloose investment is increasingly drawn to the skills of highly trained knowledge workers. Education and research thereby stand as the best investments to be made in a nation's future. They serve as a self-replenishing pool of resources for a country's success in the global economy. Otherwise governments are left with nothing more sovereign or satisfactory than a bidding war, conducted through an ever worsening spiral of wage reductions and industry welfare, by which economic leverage is conceded to multinational capital.

Within the competitive advantage paradigm, the development of the education system and human capital is seen as one portion of a menu of business inputs aimed at the competitive struggle between nations. With the repositioning of economic nationalism, however, it is an essential part of the leverage of the nation state. The new growth paradigm not only secures national benefits, it has the capacity to develop a heightened sense of national economic autonomy. It defines the economic sovereignty of a nation primarily in terms of the knowledge skills of its people. It uses the spatial features of the factors of production to target public outlays at the economic capability of citizens (instead of multinational companies). In meeting this goal, it is important to preserve the integrity and independence of a nation's education and research system. Education resources need to be devoted to the competence, skills and personal development of citizens, rather than simply substituting for the short term training costs of industry. Equally, research institutions need to be able to maintain control of their intellectual property, rather than having it treated as if they were just another market commodity.

AUSTRALIA'S NATIONAL INTEREST

In Australia a great deal of the public debate about globalisation has focused on what is said to be an unlevel playing field with our Asian competitors, especially with regard to tariff walls and wage rates. If this is so, it is all the more reason to regard the Keating Government's initiatives in APEC trade liberalisation as a policy of genuine nation building significance. Nonetheless, it is likely that the greatest tilt in the playing field, working against our national interests, has actually been self-inflicted. In terms of the status, universality and success of its education system, Australia is allowing itself to fall behind the standards of many Asian nations. Singapore is a clear example of how economic nationalism, properly defined and understood, needs to be expressed through a nation's commitment to high quality education, research and life-long learning. Highly skilled knowledge workers and technological progress have formed the basis of a highly prosperous economy. The high earning and spending power of Singapore's skilled workforce has, in turn, created the basis of a large, non-traded sector (within which goods and services are not transportable to other nations), leading not just to full employment but over-employment.

In Australia, by way of contrast and folly, education and research spending has been made the chief target of the Howard Government's budget cuts. At a time when other areas of spending have been quarantined, our Education Ministers seem to delight in wearing the size of their portfolio cuts as a badge of honour. Attempts to close the Federal deficit have simply increased the size of the third deficit. In particular, the resourcing of Australia's university sector and research centres has been substantially weakened. New school funding policies are draining resources from government schools, aggravating the problems of educational marginalisation in disadvantaged neighbourhoods. Moreover, as a product of budget cuts, Australia's investment in research and development is being pushed below 1.5 per cent of GDP. This is well short of the OECD average of 2 per cent and alarmingly below the level of national investment in competitor economies such as Japan (3 per cent), Germany (2.8 per cent) and the United States (2.7 per cent). Among the many inadequate policies of the Howard Government, nothing is more likely to damage Australia's future prospects than its abandonment of the new growth virtues of education and research support.

Australia's leading economic priority should be to reduce its deficit in new growth investment. An obvious source of funding lies in progressively shifting the nation's outlays on industry assistance, particularly the open-ended protection and subsidisation of capital, to public investments in education and research. This is an essential part of a sound strategic response to globalisation. Indeed, it is a measure of the misguided priorities in Australia's political economy that the subsidisation of the corporate sector has formed such a prominent part of public sector outlays. For instance, through the 1990s Federal outlays on industry assistance (at an estimated $10.2 billion per annum) have only been marginally lower than expenditures on education ($10.6 billion). Spending by the three tiers of government on industry support ($17.7 billion per annum) has not been substantially different to the sum of resources allocated by the States and Territories to education ($18.8 billion). For every public dollar Australia has been spending on industry assistance, the nation has devoted just $1.60 to secondary and tertiary education.[8] Seen through the prism of the competitive advantage model, priorities such as these pass with little public comment. With a repositioning of nationalism and economic leverage, however, they can be seen as an unconscionable act of national folly. To be certain, the enduring sovereignty of the Australian people now lies in the investment we are willing to make in ourselves as a highly skilled, learning society.

8

INDUSTRY POLICY

It is no longer sufficient for social democracy to assume that all forms of government intervention in the market system are desirable. The upward shift and mobility of capital require the public sector to be highly selective in the framing of industry-related policies. In particular, the fiscal crisis of the state means that public resources now need to be used with a clear sense of national economic strategy. Just as the tools of national economic management are in transition, social democracy needs to engage itself in this strategic debate. One of the problems for Australian Labor has been the way in which, for a decade or more, the internal party debate has focused primarily on whether the traditional economic methods of government—financial regulation, state ownership, macro management and industry sector planning—should be maintained. Little attention has been given to what might logically replace them in an open economy. The Party has fallen into the habit of believing that all forms of public intervention in the economy have the same impact and merit. A more important issue lies in determining the types of intervention that make most sense in the construction of an effective response to globalisation.

The reductionist critique of economic rationalism has sought to create a view that government economic interventions, no matter their form or purpose, are inherently effective. The demonisation of the market has been used to turn policy instruments into ends in their own right. It is argued that if government were prepared to do more in the economic arena—more subsidies, more regulation, more restrictions on trade and investment—the state would be able to exercise more leverage over private capital. While in the sphere of nationally defined capital this argument may have been defensible, it represents an inadequate response to the internationalisation of capital. The scope and mobility of global

investment has subverted the effectiveness of crude intervention-
ism, especially when expressed in the form of industry welfare.

This approach seeks to chase capital by offering to corporations
a range of tariffs, bounties, subsidies and tax concessions, each
funded at a public cost to taxpayers and consumers. It is argued
that if a government is willing to underwrite a strong return to
capital through the provision of public resources, corporations will
exercise their locational decisions in favour of that jurisdiction. In
this fashion, the decisions of government are driven by a corporatist accommodation with the owners of multinational capital
aimed at the maximisation of profit. Crude subsidies paid out of
the pockets of the Australian people, however, are not an effective
strategy for dealing with the footloose features of capital. The
inadequacies of the industry welfare approach were demonstrated
during the course of two major economic events in Australia in
1997.

FOOTLOOSE INVESTMENT

Nothing has more thoroughly exposed the Australian people to the
characteristics of economic globalisation than the controversies
concerning BHP's relocation out of Newcastle and the manner in
which the Federal Government decided to freeze car tariffs till the
year 2005. After decades of public subsidisation and support, BHP
was able to use its global investment strategy to pursue even more
generous subsidies at locations offshore. Australia became an
under-bidder in the chase for global capital. The earlier payment
of industry assistance, having been absorbed by the company and
built into its profits, became a casualty to the mobile geography
of capital. Unless an input to production is relatively fixed in its
geography it is not likely to represent, among the outlays of
government, a satisfactory investment. The rate of technological
progress and capital rationalisation in the new economy, even
among older forms of industrial production, has undermined the
effectiveness of crude bidding contests for capital.

In June 1997, following strong recommendations from the
Productivity Commission, it was expected that the Federal Government would continue the phase down of tariff protection levels
for the car industry. Until faced with threats from the car companies to take their foreign-owned investments out of Australia, John
Howard had wanted to cut car tariffs to 5 per cent. The Prime
Minister was told, however, that overseas shareholders would
accept nothing less than a freeze on tariffs at 15 per cent, or the
payment of a $1.8 billion public subsidy.[1] For commentators and

voters who might have thought that Australia's elected government still ran the Australian economy, the decision on car tariffs, acceding to the threats of the car multinationals, stands as a useful piece of shock therapy. It shows that, in the application of corporatist industry policies, overseas shareholders effectively have the power to determine Australia's economic policies (in this instance, the rate of tax Australians pay on the purchase of imported vehicles or the public revenue needed to secure the locational decisions of Ford, Toyota and Mitsubishi). It is indeed a peculiar expression of economic nationalism to allow the decisions of a national government to be determined by the threats and urgings of multinational boardrooms.

Subsidising the locational decisions of capital simply adds to the economic leverage exercised by the mobile geography of capital. The more intensely jurisdictions compete against each other, the greater the scale of national economic premiums paid to capital. When political jurisdictions within a nation compete against each other, the results are likely to be even more counter-productive. This has been an unsatisfactory feature of competitive federalism in Australia, where the States and Territories have engaged in a bidding contest for the locational decisions of economic investments and events. Major companies have been able to bargain up the payment of subsidies and tax concessions—heavily at the expense of the Australian taxpayer but without any net gain in national employment. The South Australian Government, for instance, has been willing to provide subsidies of up to $32 000 per job. In total, the States and Territories each year outlay $2.5 billion in direct subsidies to the private sector and $4.8 billion in payroll tax concessions.[2] Clearly the Australian Government needs to curtail this process, either by way of agreement between the States and Territories, or by the use of financial sanctions in the allocation of Commonwealth general revenue grants.

To be sure, crude bidding wars between political jurisdictions do not favour nations and their workers. Rather, in circumstances where investment is locationally mobile and governments compete by way of industry welfare policies, the prospective location of jobs will remain uncertain. The loyalties of multinational capital lie in profit maximisation rather than within the boundaries of the nation state. This is why, in the case of footloose industries, the corporatist accommodation of capital is unlikely to provide the basis of employment security. Protection and subsidies in one political jurisdiction are frequently overtaken by other jurisdictions also bidding for capital investment. Beyond the short term, industry welfare cannot guarantee the locational tenure of investment or the security of work. Its lasting purpose is to subsidise profits through the transfer of competitive premiums from nations to the owners of capital. Far from serving as an expression of economic nationalism, it incrementally adds to the sovereignty and economic leverage of global capital.

INDUSTRY WELFARE

Corporatist industry policies are not likely to add to the rate of national employment growth. By its nature, industry welfare allocates economic resources to less efficient activities which, in turn, limits the effectiveness of national strategies for economic growth and the creation of new jobs. It establishes a relationship of dependency between the public sector and private capital which further erodes national economic performance. It is difficult to understand how shielding capital from its own rationale—the competition inherent in a market economy—can foster new forms of employment and strengthen the economic leverage of the nation state. Indeed, the Australian experience has consistently shown a close link between levels of business welfare and rates of job shedding.

The industries that have lost employment and discarded workers most rapidly in Australia have always been those with the highest level of protection and public subsidisation. The automotive industry, for instance, shed twice as many jobs in the decade prior to 1985 as it did in the decade that followed, even though tariffs had been placed on a schedule of steady reduction.[3] It is not employment that industry welfare defends, but the rate of profit among its recipients.[4] Corporatist industry policies allow capital holdings to maximise their returns to investment, at a substantial public cost to national jurisdictions, while still pursuing global strategies for technological upgrading and automation. On the night of the car tariff decision, for instance, the Ford motor company aired advertisements on Australian television boasting of its advanced robotic technology. National strategies for employment creation now need to focus on the changing nature of work in the new economy. As a response to the newly formed issues of economic exclusion, policies aimed at industry welfare are not likely to be successful.

As a distributional strategy for social democracy, industry welfare is doubly damaging. It subsidises global returns to capital at a public cost frequently met by regressive forms of taxation. Low income earners bear a disproportionate share of the costs of industry protection. It is estimated, for instance, that between 1968 and 1992, the total value of subsidies paid to the car and clothing industries in Australia was $150 billion, the equivalent of one-third of Australia's GDP. Currently, the average Australian family is still forced to pay an additional $22 per week to meet the public costs of tariff effects in these industries.[5] As a strategy for employment security and social justice, industry welfare represents an unattractive option. The Labor movement is never weaker than when pursuing the open-ended subsidisation of footloose investment: conceding public money to the sovereignty of multinational capital; aggravating inequality in the distribution of living standards; yet offering nothing more substantial in employment policy than temporary relief from the portable geography of capital (for the most part, in industries where jobs are being lost through corporate strategies aimed at automation).

As a political strategy, industry welfare is sullied by the worst features of corporatism. It requires no more strategic thought and focus than menu selection with the captains of industry (much like the 1960s ethos of protection on demand). Contrary to Labor's equity goals, it promotes the subsidisation of profits at the wrong end of town. This approach also adds to false expectations about the role of government. It deflects attention from the inadequacies of business management and risk taking. It creates an impression in the public arena that failures of national competitiveness are simply a product of the inadequate public subsidisation of capital. The fiscal crisis of the state becomes more acute as the costs of production are socialised, while returns to capital remain privatised on a global scale. As noted earlier, this process erodes the public legitimacy of the state public sector and discounts the desirability of economic strategies outside the domain of the profit system. Public expectations are framed around a mounting cycle of industry assistance: creating further cash transfers to capital and shelters from market competition, each at an opportunity cost to other, socially useful outlays.

SECTOR PLANNING

Industry policies of this kind reflect a throwback to the planning ethos of the post-war decades. There is always a temptation for some politicians to believe that they can remake the market and plan adeptly for its contingencies. In the new economy, however, the type of market assumptions used in sector planning across the medium term are likely to be eroded by the rapid flow of capital, technology and competitiveness. As Hirst and Thompson have concluded from their study of economic globalisation:

If macroeconomic management is problematic, so too is that supply side alternative, a centralised state-directed industry policy. Technologies are currently changing too rapidly for the state, however competent and well informed its officials, to pick winners on a national basis. Moreover, the population of firms that the state would have to bring into such a policy is less stable and easy to interact with than it was in the 1960s. Many major products are now the result of complex inter-firm partnerships. These are factors that traditional state institutions and uniform systems of industrial administration find it hard to cope with.[6]

The pretensions of sector planning seek to deny the inexorable diversity of corporate performance in the new economy. Industry sector classifications are no longer a reliable guide by which the needs and competitiveness of particular firms can be assessed. In 1995–96, for instance, the Australian Government awarded 135 Export Market Development Grants worth $7.9 million to companies in the textile, clothing and footwear sector, plus 63 grants totalling $3.2 million to automobile manufacturers in Australia.[7] Thus, while in one aspect of public policy, a number of firms in Australia's two most protected industries were competitive enough to secure export penetration grants, in other decisions of government they were deemed to require tariff barriers to import penetration. From the perspective of the companies themselves, this represents nice work and good returns in the allocation of business welfare on both sides of the customs desk. The changing nature of corporate form and production is making a farce of broad-brush measures of industry support and planning. Internationalisation, especially with the advent of floating exchange rates, has eroded the logic and effectiveness of blanket industry measures such as border controls and tariffs.

In any case, the experience in Australia and elsewhere has shown that the lasting impact of long term patterns of sector assistance lies in the creation of a dependency relationship between government and industry. Companies inevitably lose the incentive for innovation and upgrading if they are allowed to rely on semipermanent props of government support. This reflects the folly of tariff walls and ongoing subsidies: creating a complacent corporate environment within which the allocation of industry welfare becomes a substitute for competitiveness. Corporate upgrading is unlikely to occur without the disciplines of competitive pressure and the transmission effects (such as new technology and research) arising from an open economy.[8] A satisfactory framework for industry policy now relies on the development of new growth policies by the public sector and the application of competition policy to the traded sector.

GROWTH AND INNOVATION

Australia's economic circumstances have magnified the significance of this set of policies. The major obstacle to the nation's competitive success is its risk-adverse and generally inadequate culture of corporate management. National economic strategies need to be directed at overcoming this problem. As was argued earlier (and is advocated in detail in Part V), this requires the strengthening of our social capital through the devolution of public responsibilities and resources to civil institutions. It also requires a strengthening of Australia's potential for endogenous growth and innovation. This potential is not likely to be realised solely on the back of a greater public investment in education and research. It also necessitates a fundamental shift in the culture and methods of Australia's private sector. In this regard, the reforms of the Hawke and Keating Governments in opening the economy to international competition not only need to be maintained, but also extended.

Progress in building a culture of corporate risk taking and innovation in Australia will be halted if companies are granted a breather from the disciplines of market competition. Australia's national interests do not lie in its politicians acceding to the requests of the corporate sector for special treatment, subsidies and protection. Economic rivalry pressures firms to innovate and improve. It forces them to create new processes and products, to improve quality and productivity. It exposes them to the new growth horizons of active competition which, in a market system, remains the only reliable guide to success and failure. Firms operating in Australia, attracted by the skills and capabilities of our workforce, are not likely to upgrade if they believe that government assistance will shelter their interests and profit margins from domestic or external competition.

There are just two means by which a small nation such as Australia can maintain a strong level of corporate competition and productive capacity. First, it keeps its markets open to international competition and second, it aims at an acceptable scale of product demand by growing its export markets in areas of specialised advantage. In a knowledge-based economy, these advantages depend on a nation's enhancement of endogenous sources of growth and employment. Other aspects of industry policy need to be directed at anti-competitive market practices, especially obstacles to the formation of new enterprises. The market system often fails because of the way in which competition is stifled by barriers to market entry. The public sector has a role to play in overcoming blockages to the free flow of competition, skills development and new sources of market information and access. This highlights the importance of short term, targeted interventions—such as the Keating Government's establishment of AusIndustry as a source of information and advise for prospective businesses. The outlay of public funds in industry policy needs to facilitate new market entrants and competition, rather than prop up existing enterprises. Generally, the costs of industry policy should remain privatised unless, of course, their benefits can be socialised.

9

CONCLUSION: RESPONDING TO GLOBALISATION

Often in politics, particularly during a time of widespread economic and social uncertainty, there is a temptation to resurrect strategies framed and applied from an era past. Self-evidently, however, back-to-the-future scenarios are a poor way of dealing with changed circumstances, especially given the ongoing implications of globalisation. Old assumptions and ideals are not likely to answer the challenges posed to social democracy by the internationalisation of finance and production. Laborist strategies of domestic defence, while admirable in their gain sharing goals, do not represent an appropriate response to the new economy. Just as much, globalisation has reduced the effectiveness of the national tools of macroeconomic management. It has forced governments to pursue competitive advantages by influencing the quality of inputs to the production process. This approach, while capable of generating new sources of economic growth, rarely produces an equitable distribution of the benefits of growth. In the new economy, national growth does not necessarily trickle down and universally create the virtues of economic inclusion. Moreover, the competitive advantage paradigm tends to present a one-dimensional view of economic nationalism and the functions of government. It positions the economic contest as solely between nations, and places expectations about the role of the state entirely in pursuit of these cross-national competitive advantages.

Labor's term in government highlighted the dilemma of false expectations in economic policy. The idea that politicians can pull the levers of short term economic management to achieve full employment and income equity is seriously flawed. Expectations about the functions of government need to be broadened so that they include pursuing the economic leverage of the nation state over footloose capital, plus expanding the role of the public sector in creating new sources of economic inclusiveness. In this sense, social democracy requires a new paradigm of economic strategy. It needs to look beyond old Left formulas for regulation, intervention and capital subsidisation at any cost. It needs to counter new Right paradigms relying exclusively on the freedom of the market as an answer to economic issues. It needs to respond to the dual features of economic nationalism in an open economy. It needs to bridge the gap between the localised sphere of governance and the globalised sphere of capital. It needs to demonstrate that national benefits can be made compatible with national autonomy. The primary argument of Part I has been that social democracy's capacity to satisfy these objectives relies heavily on the policies from which the economic assets of the nation state, relatively fixed and secure within its boundaries, are developed to their full potential.

ECONOMIC INSECURITY

Concerns about economic globalisation and job security now fill the public arena in Australia and many other Western nations. For those who know that the process of economic change is irreversible, the challenge is to find something more substantial in the framing of public policy than the siren song of nostalgia. This is why the development of new growth strategies is so important. This approach accommodates both aspects of the new economic nationalism—the competitive contest between nations, plus the struggle for economic premiums between national citizens and multinational capital. It adds to Australia's economic growth and development by pushing its industries up the value adding chain of knowledge-based output. It also responds effectively to the mobile geography of capital by casting Australia's economic strength and sovereignty in terms of the knowledge, skills and inventiveness of its people. It expresses patriotism in the investment Australians are willing to make in themselves—as a community and a nation—through the development of education, research and a learning society. It uses the spread of social capability among the nation's citizens as a way of reconciling localised politics (and its collective provision of services) with the demands of globalisation. That is, the capacity of the citizenry to cope with an era of permanent change rests on the universal attainment of economic and social skills.

In the new economy, knowledge skills and the value they add to the production process are the most effective means by which nations can secure economic benefits against the mobility of capital. These benefits, in turn, need to be harnessed by the public sector for distributional purposes. The premiums available to a highly skilled workforce are comparatively fixed in the geography of nations and regions. The international experience shows that patterns of investment, particularly in new industries, tend to follow the location of well-educated and highly skilled workers, producing new sources of traded sector wealth. Moreover, these gains in national income and their associated boost to domestic consumption have the capacity to produce employment gains in the non-traded services sector. This is an important transmission effect between the traded and non-traded sectors which, if strong enough, can substantially reduce the rate of unemployment. In Part II it is argued that this linkage holds the key to an equitable distribution of national income growth in the new economy.

The new growth paradigm defines Labor's understanding of issues of economic security and social responsibility in terms of the values of the new radical centre. Society's sense of security and obligation is expressed through the primacy of education and lifelong learning. In the new economy, workers are not likely to enjoy jobs for life, at least in the sense of holding down the same, standard skill job throughout a working career. Job security as our parents or grandparents might have known it, has been dismantled by the changing nature of work. The best today's labour market entrant can hope for is 'employability security'; the certainty of knowing that if he or she falls out of employment, they have the quality skills required to be offered new work.[1] The quality of a nation's education system is fundamental to this type of security. It equips people, no matter their background or vocation, with the skills required to adjust successfully to economic change. So, too, a learning society carries a strong sense of reciprocal obligations in the relationship between the state and citizens.

The attainment of new economic and social skills requires an active partnership and reciprocated flow of responsibility between the skill recipient and skill provider. As Part IV makes plain, it also reflects each of the other core values of the new radical centre: the importance of social interdependence and commonality of interest; the creation of opportunity and social mobility; plus social incentives for the encouragement of effort and reward of endeavour. This is an important point of departure from the methods of the business costs and industry welfare strands of competitive advantage. Their construction of social responsibility flows just one way: government's responsibility for either driving down the costs of doing business or directly subsidising returns to investment. In this fashion, global capital has become important to the nation's success, yet without the discharge of responsibility to the nation's people. Corporate leaders in Australia have become proficient in urging for the exercise of responsibility in the discharge of social welfare policies, while ignoring this responsibility themselves in their receipt of industry welfare.

As a nation, Australia needs to find the capability to adapt successfully to the challenges of globalisation. This will not be achieved by denying the inevitability of economic change, nor by allowing our national institutions the luxury of pausing for a break from change. A nation relying excessively on strong natural endowments, no matter its past luck, is not likely to prosper in the global economy. The lucky countries will be those that have developed the new growth horizons of a highly skilled and innovative society. Economic policies will need to look well beyond the management of old industrial forms of capital in the national arena. They will need to accommodate the demands and spread of internationalisation through the development of new economic skills and social inclusiveness. This does not mean an end to national economic policies or sovereignty, but their redefinition and expression in a substantially different form. Such are the economics and politics of transition.

NATIONAL STRATEGIES

This part of the book has advocated new national strategies in response to economic globalisation, primarily in the enhancement of new growth policies. It has been argued that social democracy also needs to strengthen the economic leverage of the nation state through three related measures. The first concerns the advancement of economic multilateralism. This means supporting the development of multinational forums for the macroeconomic and regulatory functions of government. Just as capital has lifted its sphere of activity to a global scale, so must nations reposition their trade, financial and investment controls through the virtues of aggressive multilateralism. Within each nation, appropriate macroeconomic settings now rely on the development of passive monetary and fiscal policies and macro wage agreements. Second, footloose capital must be made to compete. Nations weaken their economic leverage whenever scarce public resources are directed to the subsidisation of capital's mobility. It should not be the way of social democracy to shield capital from its own rationale for market competition. This simply adds to the economic premiums demanded by capital from political jurisdictions. The regulatory and industry policies of government need to maximise the virtues of economic competition. Policies designed only to please the owners and managers of multinational capital are generally counter-productive. Protection and subsidies merely delay innovation and the new horizons of growth.

A third strategy concerns the capacity of the public sector to play a countervailing role in the permanent process of economic restructuring. The accelerated mobility of investment, upward shift of workforce skills, and substantial loss of industrial age employment have created enormous problems of economic adjustment. The labour market has seemingly entered a perpetual state of imbalance, with the supply of skills at each location rarely matching the availability of skill-suited work. The competitive advantage paradigm has not been able to fully resolve the problems of entrenched unemployment and growing income inequality. Increasingly, the viability of economic change relies on providing each of society's participants with a stake in the economy and a share in its growth.

The public sector has an important role to play in easing the strain of economic adjustment, not just through the creation of new skills but also the creation of new forms of employment. This strategy relies on the enhancement of the fixed economic assets of nations and regions, especially in the public investment in infrastructure and direct employment creation. Social democracy needs to be able to supersede the distributional features of the market in answer to the crisis of unemployment and the growing extremes of affluence and poverty in the new economy. It is to these issues of economic exclusion and inequality that the book turns.

PART II

POLICIES FOR THE NEW ECONOMY

Globalisation and the changing nature of work have transformed the key features of economic activity. As a discipline, economics is yet to develop a comprehensive response to either the growing mobility of capital or the emerging dominance of knowledge as an economic resource. In particular, theories of the labour market have struggled to deal with the diversification of work and workplace relations. These changes have lifted a new generation of equity issues to the centre of the political agenda. The new economy features two fundamental sources of imbalance and inequality. First, there is an imbalance between the demand for labour and skill levels in certain segments of the labour market. This has produced, in all Western economies, a large residual group of the unemployed, a problem of economic exclusion that is, seemingly, beyond the scope of theories of competitive advantage. Second, there is an imbalance between the financial rewards accruing to internationally competitive workforce skills and those accruing to skills in the non-traded economy. This has produced a growing dispersion of income and economic opportunity.

A central task for social democracy is to develop a framework within which these imbalances and inequities can be ameliorated. The new economy requires not only the recasting of labour market theory, but also the development of new strategies of economic inclusion. The distributional tasks of social democracy have been placed under immense pressure. Issues concerning the income share of capital and labour within nations have been compounded by the distributional struggle between the nation state and footloose investment. The changing nature of work has also led to the development of a range of income equity issues within the sphere of labour. Highly skilled workers have been able to draw an economic premium exponentially greater than the returns available to unskilled labour. Moreover, substantial changes in the nature of production have eroded the revenue base available to government, thereby jeopardising the effectiveness of the tax/transfer system of distribution.

The ALP needs to be able to ensure that the benefits of national economic growth are distributed fairly throughout society. Policies for the new economy need to be directed towards a model of national gain sharing, so that the distributional features of an open economy are superseded by new policies of economic leverage and equity. Growth and competitiveness are not in themselves sufficient to deliver equity: the state has a role to play in ensuring that their benefits, at least in part, are able to overcome the entrenched problems of income inequality and structural unemployment. This is a daunting task given the way in which globalisation has dismantled many of the conventional measures of national economic control and macroeconomic policy. Notions of economic planning, state ownership and open-ended welfare are not likely to form the basis of social justice in the new economy.

10

THE NEW ECONOMY

Changes in the nature of economic activity are having a lasting impact on the role of government. Internationalisation has transformed the geography of capital and labour, producing a new generation of economic interests. The disaggregation of production has facilitated new forms of flexibility in the market place. The liberalisation of capital markets has aided the corporate sector in taking over and discharging some of the traditional functions of the public sector. The emergence of new labour market structures has fragmented the economic interests of labour and challenged the effectiveness of the trade union movement. In response, old ideologies and parties are struggling to reconcile their goals and programs with the characteristics of the new economy. Social democracy needs to adjust its thinking and stragegies to cope with the rapidly changing nature of production, work and economic interests. It needs a new framework of analysis for the construction of its economic policies.

THE CHANGING NATURE OF PRODUCTION

In a post-industrial economy, capital and labour have been joined by knowledge skills as major inputs to the production process. This has been facilitated by a revolution in the technological basis of economic activity. In every advanced economy, advanced communication networks have emerged which foster the seamless transfer of information between nations. Digitalisation allows texts, sound and pictures to be transmitted at the speed of light. This has not only introduced new, knowledge-based skills to the workplace, but also altered the locational features of work. Increasingly, production processes based on information skills are adopting a global,

24-hour format. For instance, engineers based in Asia, Europe and America can each take an eight-hour shift working continuously on the same production process, spun around the globe by advanced information technology. Likewise, the potential for telecommuting has changed the collective features and location of the workplace in many industries.

These technological changes have helped to transform the scale of production. In many parts of the economy, the value of information has become greater than the value of equipment and products. Wealth is being generated through the exchange of data, information and knowledge, downgrading the traditional significance of industrial machinery and raw materials. The technology has become so flexible it is now possible to produce products and services in much smaller quantities and still be cost effective. Customisation has become comparatively cheap, inventories small and capital requirements low. Whereas the old economy relied on large-scale enterprises to take advantage of high volume/standardised methods of production, post-industrial enterprises tend to reflect smaller, virtual units of output and value. In Australia, for instance, more than 95 per cent of the nation's non-agricultural businesses employ fewer than 20 people.[1]

With the disaggregation of the scale of production, the small business sector has emerged as a major market force. These issues of scale are demonstrated from the way in which more than one-half of Australia's 781 000 small businesses are not actually engaged in employment.[2] As an economic unit, their optimum size lies on a scale of one. These are information workers, consultants, designers, tradesmen and service providers who previously worked for large corporations, but have now established their own enterprises as sole trading contractors, outsourcers and franchisees. At the same time, large sized firms have become reliant on a network of small sized suppliers and contractors. Many information workers, operating as small businesses in their own right, design and create services which are then delivered to the market by larger scale enterprises.

In this fashion, corporations have the capacity to operate on a more substantial scale by virtue of their budget and results, not necessarily the size of their payroll or direct ownership of plant and equipment. This has not necessarily meant the end of the large corporation but rather, the emergence of organisational principles based on networking. Network organisations have the dual advantage of achieving economies of scale while also avoiding the high overhead costs of large, centralised entities. Strategies for corporate competitiveness have moved from a reliance on high volumes, driving down unit costs, to innovative forms of product differentiation and customisation. Mass production and mass consumption have given way to customised products and niche markets. The proliferation of product types—in industries as diverse as household goods, personal effects, finance and entertainment—has been one of the defining features of the post-industrial economy. These characteristics have also made economic activity more dynamic and time intensive.

The age-old belief that 'time is money' has found new relevance. The key benefit of smaller economic units is their adaptability to changes in technology, production types and market preferences. That is, they have a shorter time horizon and production cycle by which they can turn new ideas and markets into corporate revenue. Under conditions of global capital and fluid technological change, time becomes critical, with knowledge turning over at an ever faster rate. In the metals industry, production technology is said to turn over every five years; in information technology it is now less than two years. Inevitably, these trends have had a profound impact on macroeconomic patterns of production and consumption. Appendix I presents an outline of the new macroeconomics of a post-industrial economy.

FRANCHISING

The spread of networking has also opened up new distributional tensions within the production system, especially through the proliferation of franchised corporate relationships. Franchising has become a leading characteristic of the new economy. It has allowed multinational capital to enjoy an economy of central scale in the design and marketing of products, while also realising economies of decentralised scale and consumption. Parent companies can combine the standardisation of product design and marketing with the dispersal of business risk and customer delivery. McDonalds and other fast food restaurants are the most prominent example of the adaptability of capital in its franchised form. Global returns can be accumulated from a vast network of service outlets, each functioning on the strength of geographically restricted consumption markets. Capital has been able to build a bridge from its globalised format to the localised features of product and services consumption. This applies to markets as diverse as food, clothes, petrol and the outsourcing of household functions.

In the franchise sector, capital has established a production format based on the principles of global localisation. It is important to recognise, however, that the interests of the global and local spheres of capital are far from homogenous. Distributional conflict

is a recurring feature of relations between central franchisors and
local franchisees. Both are contesting the appropriation of profits
from the same, geographically defined consumer market. In most
cases, the market strength and globalised features of the franchisor
allow it to dominate the business relationship and rate of return
to capital. This is an issue of equity within the domain of capital
ownership that requires the attention of public policy. It opens up
a new regulatory role for government in guaranteeing fair trading
in the franchise sector, with a fair distribution of economic
resources between franchisors and franchisees.

Franchising has emerged as one of the fastest growing sectors
of the Australian economy, with more than 30 000 outlets and
300 000 employees. Its share of GDP, already over 15 per cent,
seems certain to continue to expand.[3] With the restructuring of
the economy, a large number of citizens displaced from older and
automating industries have converted their personal assets into
franchisee holdings. The public sector needs to develop a policy
framework within which these economic interests can be protected
against the market advantages of franchisors and multinational
capital. Traditional systems of competition and trade practices law
are not sufficient. The regulatory potential of franchise law lies in
its expression of economic nationalism, firmly defending the
localised interests of franchised holdings.

The differentiation of interests within the sphere of capital
points to the way in which—with the changing nature of production—the pattern of economic transactions and relations has
become more complex. The traditional binary of capital and labour
no longer holds. For instance, as capital has disaggregated and
opened itself to public subscription, it has come within reach of a
large number of workers. More than 20 per cent of adults in
Australia, some 2.6 million investors, own shares. With the growth
of mandated superannuation, around 90 per cent of Australians
now indirectly hold an interest in shares, bonds and other fund
investments.[4] The spread of franchises and economic outsourcing
has turned a generation of workers into entrepreneurs. Notions of
competition between capital and labour in the distribution of
national income are no longer clear cut. In terms of the expression
of economic interests, many Australians now barrack for both sides.

Moreover, the differentiation of economic interests has made
conventional interpretations of corporate and workplace law less
satisfactory. It is often difficult in the new economy to characterise
market participants within a dichotomy of employers and employees. The discrete paradigms of business regulation and labour law,
neatly framed to suit the old economy, have started to blur. For
example, should sub-contractors in the building industry retain

their labour rights for collective bargaining or be subject to business codes outlawing collusive practices? Should franchisees be classified as labour because they carry out functions downstream from the main body of corporate capital, or should they be regarded as businesses because they carry a share of market risk? Should highly skilled, well-remunerated people, acting as sole traders in the production process, be regarded as entrepreneurs because of their earnings capacity, or as workers because they own nothing more than their labour?

In most nations, these issues are forcing the establishment of a new framework of economic regulation, aimed at adapting the role of the state to the core features of post-industrial production and work. Social democracy has a role to play in enacting economic regulations that guard against the dominant market power of multinational capital. This is an essential part of its response to economic globalisation—guaranteeing fair trading conditions for the nationally defined sphere of capital. In an era of internationalised markets and aggressive capital movements, social democracy needs to counter inequities within the split geography of the corporate sector, as well as maintain its traditional role in protecting the interests of national labour.

THE CHANGING NATURE OF WORK

Economic restructuring has not only involved new forms of production, it has also meant fundamental changes in the labour force skills required for employment. The spread of information-based skills, accelerated by the internationalisation of the economy, has intensified the rate of labour market change in Australia and overhauled the nature of work. In the 1950s and 1960s, young Australians looked forward to employment once they had acquired, through the education system, relatively simple and repetitious skills. This was because our economy was organised around systems of high-volume, standardised production. Whether in agriculture, manufacturing or office work, each employee took a simple but related part in the production process, through which productivity was guaranteed by high volumes and low unit costs. This type of work was labelled 'Fordist', given its association with the production line methods pioneered by the Ford motor company in the United States at the beginning of this century.

Through the 1970s and 1980s, however, this mechanistic production process was transformed by the advent of knowledge-based technology. New information systems and skills flattened the production hierarchy and fundamentally changed the nature of workplace organisation. Whereas under the Fordist system, the use of specific knowledge and information skills had been restricted to management personnel, tasks requiring diverse skills were progressively dispersed across the workforce. The nature of work moved from a standardised format to a post-Fordist model of skill diversity. For a significant proportion of the labour force, a successful working life now requires a range of adaptable skills with a lifetime commitment to learning and re-skilling. The threshold of skills required for employability security has moved to a new plane of cognitive capacity.

Not all forms of work, however, reflect these arrangements. This is an important feature of the economic transition from industrial to information age employment. Generations of workers have grown familiar with a different type of work and skills base than that being produced from the restructuring process. While a significant number of jobs are being created in knowledge-based industries, they rarely feature the same skills and location as the type of work being discarded in older industries. This has placed immense pressure on the capacity of the political process to manage the transition of work skills and employment. In the tension between globalised economic change and localised political institutions, governments are often tempted to deal with these transitional issues by opposing the process of change itself. These strategies, which mostly take an industry welfare approach, do not, however, represent an adequate response to workplace change. They can achieve little more than marginally slowing the pace of change. Most likely, the public subsidisation of profits diverts resources from the development of more effective adjustment strategies.

Sound labour market policies now lie in the development of an analytical framework within which the diversification of workplace skills and employment opportunities can be addressed. The changing nature of work requires a new theory of the labour market and the role of government in the process of economic adjustment. It is proposed, for the purposes of this chapter, to follow Reich's method of labour market categorisation.[5] This identifies three modes of work, reflecting the growing complexity of the labour market during a time of economic transition. The first category concerns 'symbolic-analytic' or knowledge workers, who have the creative skills to identify and solve problems and thereby add large slices of value to the production process. These skills can be traded on global markets and hence command vast financial returns, in many cases outstripping the value of industrial capital. Symbolic analysts often work alone or in small teams. They are indicative of the way in which advanced technology has broken down the production process into a series of skill-based units, often producing a highly customised output in response to specialised consumer demand.

These workers typically include engineers, consultants, information technology specialists, artists, entertainers and creative designers. They:

> solve, identify and broker problems by manipulating symbols. They simplify reality into abstract images that can be rearranged, juggled, experimented with, communicated to other specialists and then, eventually transformed back into reality. The manipulations are done with analytic tools sharpened by experience.[6]

Knowledge and skills of this kind substantially add value to the economic system. Their discrete features have allowed symbolic analysts to draw a significant earnings premium from the means of production. With the rise of knowledge work, the number of symbolic analysts has increased considerably in all Western economies since the 1970s. It is estimated, for instance, that one-quarter of the Australian workforce now falls within this category of employment.[7]

Second, 'in-person service providers' represent the outsourcing of personal or household functions to commercial enterprises. Services and work previously provided for on an unpaid basis in the home are purchased (for convenience or entertainment reasons) from other sources, thereby creating new markets for paid services and work. Examples include restaurants, cleaning services, child care, security guards and even tourism. Generally these services are not able to be traded between nations (while tourism notionally earns export income, its services are of a domestic nature). The volume of production and earnings capacity of in-person service workers relies heavily on domestic demand conditions. It does not necessarily require the exercise of knowledge skills. The scale and personalised nature of this form of work is conducive to small teams or even sole traders, again breaking down the standardised features of production.

In-person service providers represent Australia's largest and fastest growing employment sector. This reflects a general shift in economic activity from commodity production to service provision; from the features of an industrial economy to the emergence of personal service and knowledge-based industries. Over the past three decades, the proportion of the Australian workforce employed in production-type industries—on the land, down mines, in factories or on construction sites—has fallen from 46 per cent to 28 per cent. During the same period, employment growth was concentrated in the services sector, with an increase from 2.6

million to 6.0 million workers—or 54 per cent of the workforce in 1966, to 72 per cent in 1996. Consistent with this trend, the tourism, hospitality and business services industries in Australia now account for 18 per cent of national output, compared to manufacturing's 16 per cent. In the new economy, more Australians are employed by McDonalds than in the steel industry.

This transformation in economic activity and employment is likely to continue through the accelerated outsourcing of household activities. Already, tourism (outsourcing facilitated by travel) and prepared meals (restaurants, takeaway food and home delivery) have emerged as substantial employment sectors. Other forms of household outsourcing—such as home maintenance, home-order information services and educational tutoring—have been gathering momentum and are likely to emerge over the next twenty years as major growth industries. In the decade to 1995–96, the fastest growing occupational group in Australia, with 91.3 per cent additional employment, was personal service work (classified by the ABS to include child care workers, enrolled nurses, home aides and tourist guides). During the same period, the accommodation, cafes and restaurants industry grew by 67 per cent, while cultural and recreational services increased their employment by 48 per cent.[8]

Third, 'routine production workers' reflect the remnants of the Fordist system of production. This involves making items of economic value through high output, standardised methods of production. These routine systems, however, are not restricted to older primary and secondary industries; they also feature in some parts of the business services sector, such as data processing tasks. In all industry sectors, given the way in which the Fordist system has been copied and transferred between nations, routine production workers are exposed to international competition. As a consequence, especially with the standardised nature of this work and enhanced mobility of capital, routine production workers have few sources of international competitiveness, other than by reducing their wages and tightening their work conditions. In recent decades, the scale of economic restructuring has substantially reduced the number of routine production workers in Australia, especially in blue collar manufacturing work.

Changes in the characteristics of work have been driven not just by technology, but also by a transformation in patterns of consumer demand. The cost of manufactured goods has fallen appreciably due to gains in labour productivity and improvements in transport and communications. This has helped to free up consumption in a new generation of information and leisure related services. Whereas at the turn of the century, on average, Australians spent approximately 70 per cent of their daily disposable income on goods, they now spend this proportion on services. This makes an important point about the framing of public policy in response to the restructuring of the labour market. In a market economy, the power to decide which industries prosper and expand and which industries contract or even disappear, rests with consumers, not governments.

Public figures who maintain that goods-based production is inherently more valuable than the consumption of services, are not likely to be any more effective than their counterparts last century, who railed against manufacturing because of its displacement of agriculture as the main employer of labour. Policies for the new labour market need to reflect something more substantial than the dogma of the old economy.

NEW ECONOMIC INTERESTS

The growth of post-Fordist production and work has posed a fresh set of issues for the Labor movement. The binary divide between capital and labour, based on the ownership of industrial investment, is no longer sufficient to deal with the key questions of economic distribution and equity. Internationalisation has opened up new distributional conflicts within the sphere of capital and added exponentially to the dispersion of earnings among workers. The spread of knowledge work has created a new economic divide based on the cognitive skills of labour market participants. The changing nature of work has also posed a different set of challenges to the organisation of labour. The political divide can no longer be adequately conceptualised along the lines of profits versus workers, businesses versus unions, capital versus labour. Freshly formed layers and causes of inequity have emerged that require a different approach, with a different way of making policy. The equity goals of social democracy need to be cast around these new sources of economic stratification.

In particular, the rise of knowledge work is causing the industrial wing of the Labor movement to have to fundamentally rethink its purpose. In a market economy, with an endless series of economic transactions, the exercise of market power relies on two preconditions: items of differentiated value in the market place and an imbalance between market demand and supply. In the old economy, a worker acting in isolation was not able to exercise sufficient industrial power to alter the terms and conditions of production. Most forms of labour held a standardised value in common, available in the labour market to a point of excess supply. Workers had no other way of influencing economic activity than by organising themselves collectively. The undifferentiated skills of one worker were easy to replace; the bargaining strength of all workers carried a value which could influence the terms and conditions of transactions in the labour market.

By contrast, knowledge work carries a value which stands alone in the production process. The nature of these skills, held uniquely in the personal capacity of each worker, carries a strong demand in many parts of the new labour market. The owners of knowledge skills are thereby able to exercise substantial market power in their own right. The bargaining power of highly skilled, internationally competitive labour can often outstrip the value of capital. In a post-industrial economy, not all workers are vulnerable, in the sense of having their labour exploited. Some workers receive an economic premium on the contribution their skills make to the production process. If this contribution is expressed through the international production system, then the value of the premium is usually multiplied several times over. In this fashion, the advent of symbolic-analytic work has recast the theory and practice of the labour market. Distributional issues have now arisen within the sphere of labour, with a growing dispersion in the income available to various types of workers.

These changes in the expression of economic interests have also impacted on the relationship between workers and trade unions. Under Fordist production techniques, with workers sharing standard skills and economic interests, the logic underpinning collective representation in the workplace was strong. In the conflict between capital and labour, workers looked to unions for a collective expression of their rights and interests. A standardised scale of mass production provided a natural format for mass unionism. Under post-Fordism, however, the skills and interests of workers, along with the logic of their representation, have been dispersed. Workers with individualised skills and diverse bargaining positions clearly find it difficult to set their interests within a framework of mass unionism. The smaller scale and flexible format of enterprises is not consistent, in organisational terms, with the mobilisation of the collective interests of labour. Moreover, the emergence of symbolic-analytic workers has helped to overturn conventional notions of exploitation and representation in the workplace. The labour market bargaining power of these workers is exceptionally strong. Their education and skill level is such that they are likely to believe that they can adequately represent their own interests without the involvement of a trade union official.

These factors have played a catalytic role in the decline of trade unionism throughout the Western world. In Australia union membership has fallen from 51 per cent of employees in 1976 to 31 per cent in 1996. Most disturbing of all, fewer than 10 per cent of small businesses in Australia now have a union member among their employees.[9] In summary, each of the trends and organisational principles of a post-Fordist economy sit uneasily with the basics of trade unionism. Whereas in its origins unionism was a force for economic change and progress, it has now fallen into the habit of opposing change in its contribution to most issues. In Australia there is little evidence to suggest that the leadership of the union movement has adapted successfully to the demands of the new economy. For instance, at a time when the mode of production and commonality in worker interests is down scaling, it is difficult to appreciate the logic behind the ACTU's strategy for union amalgamations. Unless unions can demonstrate their effectiveness in the small-scale, virtual workplace of the new economy, then their membership coverage will continue to retreat to the public sector and the routine production workplaces of the old economy. The danger for the relevance of political Labor lies in the way in which this narrow base of unionism might foster a concentration of employment strategies on capital intensive manufacturing industries at the expense of the growth potential of the services sector.

A 30/40/30 SOCIETY

On each of the contemporary issues of Australian political economy—the changing nature of production and work, new distributional tensions throughout the economy and the challenge to mass unionism—the Labor movement, at both its political and industrial wings, requires a new paradigm to guide its policies and purpose. It requires a new manner of conceptualising questions of economic restructuring and inequality. It requires, in the framing of economic policy, a way of dealing with the matrix of issues in a post-industrial economy: the divide between the national and international spheres of economic activity; the rise of knowledge as an economic resource, with its dichotomy between the information rich and the information poor; and the lingering significance of issues based on the ownership of capital and labour.

A useful guide to this task lies in the conceptualisation of a 30/40/30 society.[10] This reflects an analysis and set of economic interests consistent with society's transformation from an industrial base to the information age. It sets out a relevant framework of social stratification and the type of equity concerns upon which Labor might base its distributional strategies. This analysis identifies:

- an affluent 30 per cent of citizens with competitive skills, high productivity and growing incomes—best understood as those with a major ownership stake in the system of global capital, plus the new group of symbolic analysts. By virtue of their knowledge-based skills, these citizens carry with them a high earnings premium and a predominantly internationalist out-look. They frequently work, trade, travel and communicate at an international level.
- a middle 40 per cent who, while gainfully occupied, lack economic certainty in both their employment tenure and earn-ings capacity; that is, they have incomes but not income security. This group might typically include downstream fran-chise holders, in-person service workers, routine production workers and the new generation of casual, part-time and tem-porary employees; generally those citizens who do not carry a market premium from internationally competitive skills. Many have had to cope with the challenges of economic restructuring (and still fear its consequences). This newly insecure, middle group predominantly draws its income from the non-traded portion of the economy. Its social values still hold an affinity with traditional notions of place, community and the practical-ities of life.
- a further 30 per cent of citizens excluded from the production process: the unemployed, chronically ill, the aged and other economically inactive people. With the changing nature of work and the impact of ageing demographics, this group com-prises a growing proportion of society in most Western nations. It includes those who, as a product of long term economic exclusion, have often grown alienated from society, plus those who, in their active retirement, are often disappointed with society's direction. A large proportion of this group draws its standard of living from state income support.

This framework sets aside the conventionally defined interests of capital and labour. It responds effectively to the changing nature of production work and economic interests. It extrapolates issues of earnings capacity and employment from the relationship be-tween the nation state and the global integration of capital. It defines economic interests from the value that might be added and the premiums that might be drawn from the internationalised production system. It takes issues concerning the access and devel-opment of information skills as a setting within which inequities in the distribution of income can also be understood. It recognises the diversity of skills and earning capacity inherent to the post-Fordist system of production.

Accordingly, the 30/40/30 framework is able to accommodate the two distinguishing features of a post-industrial economy: the internationalisation of capital and the advent of knowledge as a significant economic resource. It brings together the distributional impact of the new geography of capital, and the new growth potential of information-based production, in tandem with conventional notions of capital and labour. It is, therefore, a useful means by which questions of equity, interests and representation might be judged in the new economy, both in the workplace and the framing of economic policy. Most of all, as the following chapters set out, it assists Labor with the development of a satisfactory response to the critical issues of income inequality and entrenched unemployment in an open economy.

11

INCOME INEQUALITY

In the Fordist system of production, high incomes were generally a product of access to capital and managerial positions. Below this income tier, the comparative uniformity in labour force skills was an equalising force in the distribution of income. The lowest incomes were generally restricted to those excluded from the work-force. The dispersion of labour force skills in knowledge-based industries, however, has led to a wider dispersion of income levels. Combined with the opening of the Australian economy and exposure of parts of the labour force to international competition, it has been possible to chart the hollowing out of the Australian labour market. A new layer of income inequality has emerged, directly linked to the value labour adds to the internationalised production system. As a nation's economy becomes more open, income relativities tend to move closer to those of its trading partners.

A range of studies has confirmed the widening spread of earnings in Australia since the 1970s. This trend ended a long period of stability in the pattern of earnings dispersion. In the mid-1970s, for instance, Norris was able to conclude that 'the dispersion of earnings in Australia is probably very little different to that 60 years ago'.[1] Between 1975 and 1994, however, the proportion of full-time workers earning between 90 per cent and 110 per cent of median earnings fell from 29.4 per cent to 23.8 per cent. Through the same period, the proportion of workers earning less than 75 per cent of median earnings rose from 10.9 to 15.7 per cent. Among male workers it increased from 9.8 per cent to 17.7 per cent. One would reasonably expect even greater dispersion if casual and part-time workers were included in these calculations. The ABS data, however, are restricted to full-time employees. Table 11.1 highlights the clear trend of these workers to greater inequality.

Table 11.1 Proportion of employees by earnings band (per cent of all full-time adult non-managerial employees)

Percentage of median earnings	Males			Females			Total		
	1975	1985	1994	1975	1985	1994	1975	1985	1994
Less than 75%	9.8	13.4	17.7	6.7	7.4	10.7	10.9	11.6	15.7
75–90%	23.6	22.3	19.9	21.9	23.2	24.2	23.1	23.8	21.9
90–110%	30.0	26.0	22.8	39.9	33.4	27.2	29.4	26.2	23.8
110–150%	27.2	26.9	27.9	25.6	27.1	27.9	26.6	26.6	27.6
More than 150%	9.4	11.5	11.9	5.9	8.9	9.9	10.1	11.8	11.0

Source: ABS data presented in Federal Parliamentary Library Research Note, No. 9, 28 August 1995.

The dispersion of income in the new economy can be explained in terms of the three broad categories of work and earnings capacity. Knowledge workers accrue high incomes from the high value their skills bring to the global economy. Routine production workers rely on volume rather than skill-based productivity. As they are exposed to cross-national competition, their wage rates tend to be driven down as a function of globalisation. Routine production enterprises are more likely to seek out low wage settings in developing nations than persevere with high wage workers in advanced economies. Given their standardised skills, these workers are not able to compete effectively on the basis of productivity. Their job prospects have usually rested on historic patterns of investment, public sector subsidies and wage rate reductions. In developed economies with highly deregulated labour markets, such as the United States, this has produced a new generation of the working poor. It is estimated that more than one-third of working Americans earn wages no higher than the poverty line.[2]

In-person service providers tend to fall between these two patterns of income relativity. As their skills, services and products are restricted to local markets, their income earning capacity is usually a function of domestic spending power and demand. If, for instance, an economy has a strong proportion of high income knowledge workers outsourcing a large share of their personal consumption, this leads to a strong in-person services sector with relatively high income and employment levels. As the nature of in-person service expenditure is restricted to the domestic economy, these effects can vary substantially between geographically defined markets of service consumption.

This is a defining feature of the new economy. While some workers, symbolic analysts and routine production labour, are engaged by the chase for capital across the globe, the prospects of many other workers are anchored by the spatial features of in-person service provision. The mobility of capital in knowledge-based and routine production industries has fostered a new sphere of labour market competition linked to the skills and capabilities of each worker. In the in-person services sector, how-ever, labour is the central component of the production process. With the relative immobility of labour, service markets of this kind are limited in their scope for active competition. Local service providers do not compete on a global or even national scale. Hairdressers in Sydney, for instance, are not threatened by the skills or wage levels of hairdressers in other parts of the nation or overseas. Their earnings capacity is a function of localised con-sumption and skill/wage competition in the regional labour market.

This sector of employment have also been responsible for the extraordinary growth of part-time and casual work. The labour intensive nature of in-person services, plus the demand for around-the-clock service provision, have encouraged enterprises to develop flexible working hours and conditions. Inevitably this has weakened the role of full-time, standardised jobs. In Australia between 1984 and 1994, part-time employment, as a proportion of the workforce, rose from 17.8 per cent to 24.3 per cent, while casual employment increased from 15.8 per cent to 23.7 per cent. This trend has created the problem of a dual labour market segmented on the basis of working time—that is, the creation of a layer of earnings dispersion between competitive 'core' workers, and a growing periphery of casual and part-time workers. This raises important equity issues for labour market and wages policies. It also signifies the need for welfare state reforms aimed at a new generation of income support mechanisms dealing with earnings insecurity. (These themes are further developed in Part IV.)

COUNTERING EARNINGS DISPERSION

The changing nature of production and work has broadened the range of factors determining the earnings capacity of labour. This diversity, in turn, has driven the tendency towards greater earnings dispersion. The income return to labour is no longer set by broad banded skills in secure, standardised jobs. A matrix of factors—including internationalisation, capital mobility, knowledge-based skills, local service consumption and time-at-work—now impact on the earnings of each worker. For the first time, strategies aimed at income equity need to counter the growing dispersion of incomes and assets among workers. This is a freshly formed policy task for the political Left. Never before has it focused on social justice issues within the band of labour earnings.

In the old economy, workers held standardised skills suited to Fordist systems of production which, in turn, yielded standardised, basic wage entitlements. An open economy, however, places a high income premium on internationally competitive skills. It also tends to anchor returns to lower productivity workers at minimum rates. Routine production workers face intense wages competition as a consequence of the mobility of capital. In-person service workers face problems in the strength of spatial consumption markets, and the tendency towards the casualisation of work. Social democratic ideals and thinking have now been confronted by income equity concerns within the wages share of national income.

Three related strategies are available to the Labor movement to ameliorate the trend towards earnings dispersion. Their purpose is to reduce the proportion of wage earnings falling unacceptably below the median band of income earnings. Strategies aimed at the leverage of the nation state over footloose capital are obviously important. As outlined earlier, these assist in maximising the income premiums available to national economic systems and labour. Nothing matters more in this regard than universal access and social mobility in the education and training system. In the post-industrial era, economic opportunity is being defined not so much by access to financial capital, but human capital. This is a critical opportunity for political causes interested in the foundations of a fair society. It can be argued that the capacity of collective institutions and interests, led by the state public sector, to influence the formation of information-based skills exceeds their capacity to influence the ownership and formation of capital. The equity functions of government have been re-ignited by the role of the public sector as a provider of public education.

In the new economy education is the fulcrum on which the issue of income security rests. It is the most effective means by which disadvantaged citizens can lift their skills and come within reach of a decent economic premium. An example of this process can be found in the correlation between education and earnings levels in the United States. In 1979, college-educated men earned 50 per cent more than males with a high school qualification; by 1994 this gap had nearly doubled to 100 per cent. For women, the gap moved from 44 per cent to 85 per cent. While in Australia the impact of education on earning relativities has not been as pronounced, mainly due to the strength of our union and award safety net system, skill levels are emerging as a key determinant of earnings dispersion. Borland has identified an increase in the relative earnings of workers holding a degree, trade qualification or diploma over the past decade. Prior to the mid-1980s, there had been a decline in the relative earnings of these educational categories. An important cause of this turnaround has been 'a substantial increase in the relative demand for workers with higher levels of educational attainment'.[3] The diversity of the new economy and its skill requirements also appear 'to have had a large effect on earnings dispersion' within broad bands of education and work experience categories.[4]

A second strategy concerns the extent of workplace solidarity. The decline of trade union membership in Australia has been linked to the growth of income inequality. Research at the University of Melbourne shows that trade union coverage is an important force for earnings equality. It particularly assists low skill, low productivity workers with their labour market bargaining and wage movements. Between 1986 and 1994, the fall in union density in Australia accounted for approximately 30 per cent of the increase in earnings variance for full-time male employees and 15 per cent of the increased dispersion for full-time female earnings.[5] In the new economy, trade unions are important for the fairness of our society as much as the direct provision of workplace services.

Workplace solidarity relies on the cohesiveness of collective representation, bargaining rights and laws guaranteeing a strong industrial safety net. The need for these initiatives has been made more significant by the Howard Government's industrial relations agenda, which defines every worker as an individual instead of every workplace as a cooperative enterprise. The introduction of individual employment contracts and diminution of collective bargaining strength in the workplace can only lead to greater insecurity and inequality for the bottom tier of wage earners. By contrast, policies which recognise the significance of the membership and bargaining strength of trade unions aid the cause of income equity.

A third strategy, perhaps most critical of all, is to establish a formal system of income gain sharing for the benefit of low skill, low productivity workers. This requires a legislated model of income redistribution which counters the tendency of an open economy towards earnings dispersion. It acts as a precondition for income security: to provide lower productivity workers—the newly insecure, middle group—with gains in disposable income commensurate with gains in national economic growth. As the national economy grows, the lowest band of wage earnings needs to be guaranteed a reasonable share of this income growth. The Australian claim to egalitarianism has always relied on a clear, structured approach to earnings justice. Historically, from the Federation settlement to the opening of the Australian economy in the 1980s, basic wage adjustments and tariff protected manufacturing put together a loose model for national gain sharing. Economic rents in agriculture and mining were transferred to manufacturing and other urban-based workers.

Labor is still struggling to successfully adapt the concept of gain sharing to the new economy. The major shortcoming of the Prices and Income Accord 1983–96, especially with its ultimate emphasis on retirement income ahead of disposable income, was its failure to establish an active gain sharing mechanism to the satisfaction of lower productivity workers. While the Labor Party boasted of a record period of national economic growth, the distributional features of GDP did not necessarily lift the living standards of the economically insecure. It should be remembered, of course, that in its origins the Accord was not designed to cope with the competitive pressures of an open economy or a produc-tivity-based wages system. It was a prices and incomes strategy aimed at breaking the back of inflation by trading money wages increases for social wage gains.

DEVELOPING A GAIN SHARING MODEL

Social democratic thinking now needs to turn to the development of a gain sharing model for an open economy. This is an important guarantee against economic insecurity: a guaranteed share of national economic growth for workers without internationally com-petitive skills. Productivity-based wage bargaining and small safety net adjustments are not enough. In several parts of the non-traded economy—most notably, the housing construction and road trans-port sectors—it is difficult to extract labour productivity gains from work practices which have already reached international best prac-tices. The only way truck drivers transporting goods from Melbourne to Sydney, for instance, can increase their productivity is to bend the law even further. It is not satisfactory for workers in industries such as these to be denied decent prospects for steady wage increases. Moreover, the productivity-based system is made problematic by the difficulty most service-type workplaces face in actually measuring labour productivity. This is particularly the case in the growing in-person services sector.

A system of industrial relations based solely on decentralised bargaining steadily aggravates the extent of earnings dispersion and income insecurity. It widens the gap between high skill, core workers and the poorly paid periphery of part-time and casual workers. It aggravates the relative economic premiums available to internationally competitive labour and workers in the non-traded, in-person services sector struggling with weak markets of spatially defined consumption. It makes it difficult for routine production and in-person service workers to secure wage increases based on identified productivity gains. It tends to anchor these workers on or near minimum rates, and reduces their earnings in real terms. In its interaction with the social security system, it can also take away the reward for work.

A particular problem with labour market deregulation strategies is the creation of poverty traps. Reduced real wages for the working poor can lead to incentive problems in the interaction between the transfer payment and wages systems. Low minimum wage rates can act as a disincentive for people seeking work and moving off unemployment support. It is estimated that the gap between minimum wages and unemployment payments (which are indexed to average earnings) in Australia has fallen from 36 per cent to 11 per cent since the mid-1970s.[6] Further deregulation of the labour market, and lower wage levels, mean that poverty traps cannot be avoided other than by also lowering the social safety net and level of income support. The Howard Government's support for individual employment contracts and decentralised bargaining can only aggravate the poverty trap problem.

The challenge for the Labor movement is to develop a gain sharing model consistent with sound macroeconomic objectives such as low inflation and passive monetary policy. The ACTU's 1996 living wage submission should be seen as an important catalyst for this approach. It recognises the equity features of a minimum wage based on the living costs of active citizenship and participation in our society. In the new economy, sustained economic growth and the resounding evidence of affluence have not guaranteed the benefits of a living wage and a fair distributional share of national income growth for all. The industrial relations system needs a strong floor of adjustable minimum rates to achieve these goals.

This requires the establishment of a two-tier wages system. The first stream relies on a productivity-based bargaining approach for internationally competitive workers in the traded sector. The second entrenches a living wage system of gain sharing for the in-person services sector. High levels of personal consumption by symbolic analysts serve as a transmission mechanism for income transfers between the two streams. As national income grows on the back of international competitiveness, it is possible to ensure, through adjustments to the living or minimum wage, that the incomes of low paid workers also grow. A dual wages system is essential if governments are to cope with the equity consequences of labour market segmentation in the new economy. It combines the features of an adjustable safety net with a separate stream of productivity-based gains and workplace incentives.

The establishment of a living wage is reflected in the second plank of the ACTU claim: a more substantial floor under the award system by increasing minimum wages for entry level job classifications. These adjustments are critical to the attainment of earnings equity. Importantly, beyond these movements in minimum rates, there is also a need for safety net adjustments for low productivity workers without the capacity to negotiate pay increases under the bargaining system. However, unlike the first plank of the ACTU claim (which pursued a flat $20 per week increase), these adjustments need to be weighted carefully on the basis of wage equity—that is, it is important to link the size of the safety net adjustments with the proximity of wage earners to the living wage minimum. This system ensures that gains in national income are distributed across all bands of earnings and productivity. The greatest gains will still be enjoyed by high skill, high productivity workers. The purpose of the gain sharing model is to ensure that the living standards of low income earners, especially in-person service workers, are also reasonably enhanced.

In orthodox economic theory it has been argued that wage movements beyond gains in productivity effectively price workers out of a job. This real wage overhang argument, however, is not well suited to the labour market diversity of the new economy. Highly skilled knowledge workers, for instance, tend to be price setters in a labour market for which the price-driven substitution of capital for labour is not relevant. Capital and other factors of production are also limited as substitutes for labour in most in-person service industries. In the new economy, only routine production workers are likely to act as price takers as predicated by the conventional labour market theory based on factor mobility and the seamless interaction of supply and demand.[7] In short, it is not appropriate to simply assess the price of labour, as one would assess the price of fish and chips, as an exercise in free market supply, demand and equilibrium price outcomes. The post-Fordist labour market is highly segmented, with a considerable range of pricing and employment possibilities.

EMPIRICAL EVIDENCE

This analysis is supported by recent research in the United States showing that higher minimum wages in many parts of the labour market do not lead to the overpricing of labour and unemployment.

Empirical studies by David Card and Alan Krueger at Princeton University have led to the conclusion that:

> minimum wage increases have not had the negative employment effects predicted by the textbook model. Some of the new evidence points toward a positive effect of the minimum wage on employment; most shows no effect at all. Moreover, a re-analysis of previous minimum wage studies finds little support for the prediction that minimum wages reduce employment. If accepted, our findings call into question the standard model of the labour market that has dominated economists' thinking for the past half century.[8]

In industries featuring in-person service work—such as fast food outlets, restaurants and bars—it was found that a rise in the minimum wage can actually increase employment. At an enterprise level this type of employment tends to be relatively price inelastic, while higher wages produce a positive impact on macro consumption patterns. In the in-person services sector, wages impact more as a determinant of spending power than a supply side cost item. This is especially the case in lower skill, low employment regions suffering a demand side crisis in spending power. Moreover, studies have consistently shown that patterns of employment by small businesses in the non-traded sector are more aligned to demand conditions, than to supply side issues like unfair dismissal laws. If demand declines, then no level of wage reduction will generate new employment. Furthermore, most small businesses are comfortable with the simplicity of the award safety net system and do not regard it as a barrier to enterprise flexibility.[9]

At least with regard to labour market analysis in the new economy, Labor can lead the charge against economic correctness. An economy with a strong traded sector, enjoying the growth potential of high productivity and export penetration, can sustain a strong floor under award wage levels in the in-person services sector. A formal, indexed link between the living wage and general movements in earnings can create the basis of income gain sharing in the new economy. Card and Krueger's research shows how minimum wage movements are a key distributional tool in the new economy. They have a significant impact on the living standards of less skilled workers, and help to offset the tendency of an open economy towards wages dispersion. They act as an important income transfer mechanism with relatively small efficiency losses. Minimum wage increases also help to create a 'ripple effect', whereby low productivity earnings above the minimum band are likely to be enhanced.[10] This is an important consideration in the framing of safety net adjustments above the living wage minimum.

In determining a formal method of indexation for movements in the minimum wage, Card and Krueger correctly caution against a direct correlation with either the CPI or average weekly earnings. The former runs the risk of an entrenched inflationary impact, while the latter is likely to produce an undesirable spiral effect, given the way in which minimum wages are included in the calculation of average wage levels. An effective gain sharing index for the Australian labour market, therefore, most likely relies on partial earnings indexation, framed with reference either to mean incomes (such as AWE minus X) or less-than-average earning bands (such as full indexation to the 30th or 40th percentile).[11]

MACRO WAGE AGREEMENTS

In each aspect of wages policy, Labor's relationship with the trade union movement should be seen as an asset of strategic potential. This is why measures aimed at improving the relevance and coverage of unions in the small, virtual workplaces of the new economy are so important. With the globalisation of capital, the usefulness of active fiscal and monetary policies has declined. Wages policy remains the one autonomous macro policy tool still available to national governments. Only unions, as a collective agent in the labour market, can lever wage outcomes in the national interest. Only by agreement with the trade union movement can governments directly influence wage and inflation outcomes. Otherwise they need to use monetary policy, with earlier and bigger interest rate movements, to pre-emptively strike against a tightening of the labour market. The Governor of the Reserve Bank confirmed these fundamentals in July 1996, pointing out that if the Bank 'could be more confident that these influences [wage movements in line with low inflation expectations] would win the day, it would be easier for the Bank itself to adjust to low inflation'—that is, ease official interest rates.[12] With the abolition of the Accord process, Australia's central bank has lost its security blanket for assessing future wage outcomes.

In the absence of macro wage agreements, enterprises and unions are left with the equivalent of a prisoner's dilemma in the labour market: why should one group of workers exercise wage restraint (in the name of collective benefits via lower interest rates) if they cannot be certain of bargaining outcomes in other workplaces. Workers surrendering their labour market bargaining power on wages have no guarantee of other workplaces doing the same.

Yet as much as any other part of the economy, they will face an increase in interest rates as a result of wage claims elsewhere. In this environment of uncertainty, public calls for wage restraint by central bankers or politicians have no practical standing. The abolition of the Accord encourages each workplace and union to press its wage claims to the full extent of its labour market power.

Macro wage agreements are also able to assist with issues of equity in the dispersion of earnings. As noted earlier, the Labor movement needs to address income equity issues within the band of wage and salary movements. Macro wage agreements should aim at containing high income movements in recognition of the importance of living wage adjustments. This trade-off at either end of the wages spectrum assists with the maintenance of low inflation and passive monetary policies. Cooperation of this kind between the political and industrial wings of the Labor movement can produce a fairer dispersion of earnings and gain sharing, consistent with sound macroeconomic policy.

The basis of this strategy was recognised by the Australian Industrial Relations Commission in its decision on the living wage claim in April 1997. It granted a safety net wage increase of $10 per week, plus established a federal minimum wage for full-time adult employees of $359.40 per week (substantially short of the ACTU's goal of a minimum wage of $380 at stage one, gradually lifting to $456 per standard 38-hour week). Significantly, however, the Commission pointed out that a sensible macro wages agreement would have facilitated a more equitable outcome on minimum rates:

> It was always implicit in the enterprise bargaining system that a gap would arise in the wages of bargainers and non-bargainers. If that gap is seen as being, or becoming too wide, it is our view that the best prospect of correcting the situation is a moderation in the levels of claims and settlements in enterprise bargaining . . . We regret that we cannot now go further [with low to middle level wage increases]. Progressive recognition of the new, non-inflationary environment [would] lower the level of settlements so as to leave 'space' for a more generous treatment of workers fully or substantially dependent on award wages.[13]

An unacceptable aspect of the wages debate in Australia, especially under the Howard Government, has been the way in which expectations for restraint are directed at lower to middle income earners. The earnings data, however, show that the bulk of the real income gains, often ahead of productivity, are enjoyed by the highest band of earners. Between May 1994 and May 1996, for instance, average weekly total earnings rose by 6.9 per cent, to which gains by managers, administrators and professionals contributed one-half. This highlights the importance of earnings dispersion strategies which tackle the issue of executive and professional salary increases. Restraint and the exercise of social responsibility at the top end of the income scale would leave much greater 'space' for better living standards for the poorest paid band of Australian workers. An effective Federal agenda in this area is an important means by which the macro viability of the living wage model can be enhanced. One proposal, examined in Chapter 13, is that the allocation of any public sector assistance to the private sector be made conditional on the proper exercise of executive and managerial earnings restraint.

In summary, the Labor movement should never sell short the value of a cooperative agreement between its political and industrial wings. While a replay of the Accord will not be possible—nor, in all its detail, desirable—it is in the interests of both the ALP and trade union movement to declare a mutual commitment to new systems of gain sharing for the new economy. This should involve the establishment of a dual wages system, the virtues of the living wage approach and the effective use of macro wages policy. In each of these strategies the Labor movement can aid the cause of a more equal society by superseding the distributional features of an open economy. This also requires, of course, the development of new strategies aimed at countering economic exclusion.

12

ECONOMIC EXCLUSION

A leading paradox of modern capitalism is that it has seemingly solved the problems of production and wealth generation, yet a significant number of citizens remain excluded from the production process. The semi-permanent high rates of unemployment in most Western nations are a result of market failure: a mismatch between the mobility of capital on a global scale, and the relative immobility of labour market skills and participants. As capital restructures and relocates itself, the growth of new industries and jobs rarely matches the location and skills of the employment lost. These problems of market failure in skill formation and employment location lie outside the scope of orthodox economic theory. Enhanced national productivity, while always desirable throughout the history of private capital formation, is no longer sufficient to clear the labour market.

Thus, the unemployment crisis in Australia and other Western nations also reflects a crisis in economic theory. As a discipline, economics is yet to adapt successfully to two sea changes in economic activity. First, globalisation has made capital, in the form of finance, investment and commodities, exceptionally mobile. The chase for capital across the globe has made traditional macroeconomic remedies and national controls largely redundant. Second, the widespread disaggregation of the scale of production, and the advent of new information-based technologies, have dramatically lifted the skills base for most forms of employment. This is reflected in the spatial concentration of unemployment. A substantial gap has emerged between the changing labour force needs of industry and the relatively fixed location of labour force skills.

Australia's major cities were structured, during the period of substantial suburbanisation after the Second World War, on a broad correlation between industry types and the location of

labour. Outer suburbs, through cheaper land and new public housing stock, housed a workforce predominantly engaged in routine
production work. The more attractive housing sites were taken up
by the owners of capital and managerial and professional types.
Now, in the 1990s, labour skills and rewards are being determined
by the exposure of companies and industries to trading competition. White lab coats are replacing blue overalls on the factory
floor as manufacturing enterprises seek higher levels of technology
and skills with which to succeed on world markets. The rapid pace
of restructuring has broken the correlation between the location
of job opportunities and the geography of the Fordist labour force.

Not surprisingly, the rationalisation of capital—domestic and
international—has outpaced the restructuring of urban areas, both
in terms of residential location and the upgrading of labour force
skills. While the changing nature of work has opened up new and
improved career opportunities for knowledge workers and many
in-person service providers, it has disadvantaged a certain type of
regional labour market. Regions which traditionally relied on routine production employment have, over the past 10–15 years, had
to deal with two sources of economic adjustment: exposure to
trading competition, as well as higher standards of competitive
labour skills. The combined structural impact has concentrated
rates of unemployment on a regional scale. As Bob Gregory and
Boyd Hunter conclude from their study of the spatial structure of
the labour market:

> the structural change of Australian employment into less manual
> work in the service sector has favoured those workers in the good
> regions with more education. The workers in the low status areas
> have largely failed to secure employment in the growth industries
> and appear to move into the unemployment pool once they lose
> their jobs in manufacturing.[1]

For workers and locations affected by the decline in routine
production industries, the in-person services sector is critically
important. It represents the most prominent sector of employment
growth in the Australian economy not requiring internationally
competitive labour skills. This confirms the way in which
knowledge-based industries have produced a new form of segmentation in the Australian labour market. That is, economic rewards
no longer rest simply on the dichotomy between capital and labour,
but on the competitiveness of labour skills in the global market.
Knowledge workers—whether in primary industries, manufacturing
or services—are highly skilled and highly paid. By contrast,
employment in the non-traded services sector (including household

and business outsourcing and a range of public sector services) features a weaker base of skills and wages.

THE DUAL LABOUR MARKET

This phenomenon signifies the emergence of an 'upstairs/downstairs' segmentation of the Australian labour market. Knowledge workers tend to live in the same, more expensive, housing locations. Their high incomes and high propensity for household outsourcing produces a strong demand for in-person services and employment. These locations, with their strong base of upstairs employment, enjoy a strong flow-on effect in downstairs enterprises and the employment of less skilled workers. Conversely, weaker regions have struggled to replace jobs lost in routine production work with new sources of employment from the services sector; nor have they been able to achieve an internationally competitive set of labour market skills for the creation of high income, high value added work.

These regions have a low proportion of upstairs employment, leading to relatively weak consumption of downstairs services. The National Institute for Economic and Industry Research, for instance, has estimated that the propensity for services consumption on Sydney's North Shore is up to 100 per cent higher than in Western Sydney, with regional employment multipliers at least 200 per cent higher. That is, for every one downstairs job generated by household consumption in Sydney's west, three or more are created on the North Shore. In this fashion, low growth regions face a stagnating cycle of low upstairs employment, low household consumption, low downstairs employment, still lower aggregate demand and poor rates of business investment. The employment figures for these areas point to a spiralling pattern of disadvantage. Once jobs are lost in the weak regions they are infrequently regained, leading to the growth of long term and intergenerational unemployment. Since the mid-1980s in Australia, sustained periods of national economic growth have had little positive impact on the spatial concentration of long term unemployment.

Among the many changes produced by economic restructuring in recent decades, the most pronounced has been in the geography of employment. This is demonstrated in Figure 12.1, from which Gregory has concluded:

In 1976, if you walked across Australia crossing from high socio-economic status areas to low socio-economic status areas you would notice that access to employment did not change very

Figure 12.1 Employment–population ratio and socioeconomic status

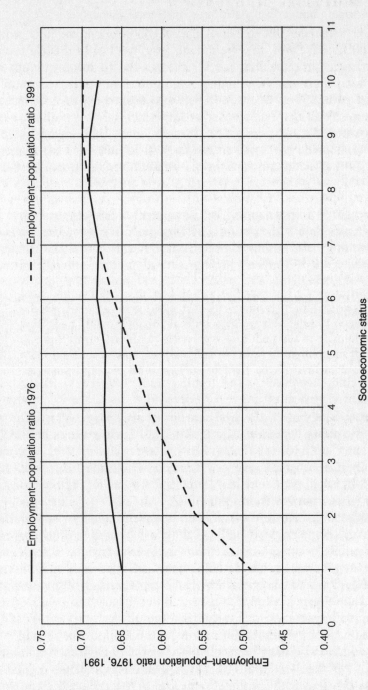

Source: Bob Gregory, 'Unemployment: What To Do?', *The Sydney Papers*, Sydney Institute, Spring 1994, using census data 1976–91.

much. The income differences produced across areas were derived from different wages not from different levels of employment. If you walked across Australia along the same path in 1991 you would notice that the income differences among some areas have become exaggerated. The principal reason is the change in employment opportunities. The income of the poor areas is falling because of lack of jobs.[2]

The emergence of this spatial differential in rates of employment has been driven largely by demand influences. Supply side factors, such as population shifts and variable participation rates, tend to moderate the differential. This points to a particular interaction between the skill-based features of the new economy and the personal characteristics of labour market participants in weak regions. Unskilled workers are more likely to be unemployed because there is less demand for their services, especially in areas with low levels of downstairs consumption.[3] The changing nature of work and relationship between upstairs and downstairs modes of employment has given a strong, even dominant, spatial dimension to the labour market.

In the old product-based economy (with a high proportion of employment in agriculture and manufacturing), goods were produced across a range of locations (dispersing the spatial share of employment opportunities) and then transported to consumer markets. The mobility of services employment from household outsourcing, however, is constrained by the intensely local and personalised nature of the services provided. Variations in household spending power on a spatial scale are rarely factored into economic policy decisions in Australia. Yet the structure of regional labour markets and composition of consumer demand are now key determinants of employment outcomes. The suburbanisation of employment opportunities has spatially fragmented the functioning of the labour market (see Table 12.1).

Regions move towards low unemployment as they reach skills and spatial labour market balance. This reflects one of the ironies in the public debate about unemployment in Australia. The quest for full employment has actually been achieved, but only in a particular type of labour market in certain parts of the country. These are regions with a strong set of upstairs skills and the consequent generation of a large number of downstairs jobs. To be certain, high unemployment is not a problem across the macro-economy. It is spatially concentrated among those locations most affected by the loss of routine production work. These regions include Western Sydney, the Hunter and Illawarra (NSW); Northern and Western Melbourne, Dandenong–Springvale, Gippsland

Table 12.1 Regional differences in rates of unemployment

State	Highest rate of unemployment (%)		Lowest rate of unemployment (%)		Ratio High: Low
NSW	Auburn (Sydney)	19.4	Northern Beaches (Sydney)	2.9	6.7
Victoria	Sunshine	14.1	Cheltenham (Melbourne)	4.9	2.3
Queensland	Caboolture	17.2	Central West	3.0	5.7
South Aust	North West (Adelaide)	11.9	South East	5.4	2.2
Western Aust	Rockingham	11.1	Country North	5.6	2.0
Tasmania	Brighton	23.9	Kingborough	5.9	4.1
Average		**16.3**		**4.6**	**3.8**

Source: Department of Employment, Education, Training and Youth Affairs, local labour market data, June Quarter 1996. Figures for Tasmania represent statistical local area estimates.

Table 12.2 Dual labour market in the Campbelltown LGA

Indicator	Public housing estates*	Remainder of Campbelltown LGA %
Unemployment rate	41.7	10.7
Proportion of LGA unemployment	25.7	74.3
Proportion of LGA labour force	8.1	91.9
Proportion of adult population (15 years or more) in employment	21.3	63.5

*   Claymore, Ambarvale, Macquarie Fields and Airds are broadacre public housing estates with a combined population of 17 976 (part of Campbelltown LGA's population of 135 898). The estates feature intergenerational unemployment and high rates of welfare dependency (around 70 per cent of all families).
Source: 1991 census data

and the Central Crescent (Vic.) Northern Adelaide (SA); Kwinana–Rockingham (WA) Bundaberg–Maryborough (Qld); and Tasmania. They typically feature unemployment rates twice those of surrounding regional labour markets, and high levels of long term unemployment. Table 12.1 highlights the spatial imbalance of the Australian labour market.

Further, within statistical regions, neighbourhood effects can produce even wider variations. In the Australian labour market, suburbs have become the most appropriate unit of spatial analysis. Gregory and Hunter take this approach through the reconstruction of Census Collector Districts. Even within local government areas, dual labour market effects can be identified. Take, for instance, the extraordinary difference in unemployment rates between privately owned and public housing estates in Campbelltown, on Sydney's south-west fringe. Table 12.2 points to severe labour market segmentation on a suburban basis.

LABOUR MARKET POLICY

These trends represent a paradigm shift in our understanding of the labour market and employment activity. In particular, the spatial concentration of unemployment weakens the effectiveness of conventional macroeconomic policy. Spatial imbalances in economic activity make it more difficult to pursue high growth fiscal and monetary policies without the emergence of inflationary wage pressures. Strong regions are likely to develop skill-based bottlenecks which threaten the maintenance of price stability and thereby, the durability of macro growth strategies. The benefits of the growth cycle are not likely to reach depressed neighbourhoods once inflationary wage pressures are exerted by those in the strong neighbourhoods tapping the benefits of economic expansion and skills demand.[4] Thus, spatial labour market policies are needed to maximise the effectiveness of macro policies for growth and inflation. The significance of macro wages policy is also reinforced. The moderation of wage movements in high skill neighbourhoods helps to prolong the growth cycle and its potential for employment creation among the weaker neighbourhoods.[5]

The dual features of the labour market have formed a link between two-core distributional issues: the growing dispersion of earnings in the new economy and the spatially uneven distribution of work. In recent decades the Australian economy has maintained its demand for high skilled occupations while the demand for low and middle skilled jobs has fallen appreciably. This is the reason why, since 1970, one in four full-time male jobs has disappeared. It reflects how speculation about the disappearing middle of the Australian labour market actually involves the deterioration of the bottom tier of routine production work. As Gregory has noted, 'the individuals who would normally be employed in the middle of the earnings distribution have remained in or moved into lower paid jobs. When there are insufficient jobs in aggregate [reflecting the loss of standard skill commodity production], this serves to bump the least skilled off the earnings ladder.'[6] The spatial features of a dual labour market have moved to the centre of the employment policy task.

The new pattern of jobs distribution has supplanted the significance of other labour market issues, such as functional flexibility and deregulatory policies. Even though, for instance, labour market laws in the United States and Australia are fundamentally different, Gregory's work shows that the pattern of job growth in the two countries in recent decades has been remarkably similar. Both labour markets have hollowed out, with a loss of semi-skilled work, an anchoring of worker earnings at the bottom end of the income ladder, and the residualisation of poorly skilled people into long periods of unemployment. The net result of labour market deregulation in the United States has been to increase wages inequality without necessarily creating any greater proportion of semi-skilled jobs than those reflected in the Australian experience. In a spatially and skill-fragmented labour market, the restoration of full employment lies 'in a direction other than reducing the wages of the low paid'.[7]

It also lies in a direction other than simply assuming a trickle down of national economic growth to low skill neighbourhoods. National productivity gains, desirable as they may be, are not sufficient to clear the problems of skill and spatial imbalance in the new labour market. The segmentation of skills, earning capacity and employability has created a new bundle of labour market effects. Increasingly, material benefits and lifestyles are being determined by people's access to information skills and their involvement in the internationalised production processes. High incomes bring with them access to high cost housing areas and a high propensity for outsourcing household consumption, thereby creating a strong upstairs/downstairs labour market. By contrast, low skill areas are locked into a cycle of low downstairs consumption and high unemployment. Successful individuals often move out of these areas while new, poorly skilled residents move in, producing an urban churning effect. The framing of policies aimed at the distribution of incomes and employment among individuals now needs to be founded, first and foremost, on the spatial features of the dual labour market.

As a discipline, economics clearly needs to reformulate its approach to employment issues. Labour market deregulation is not an effective course to follow; it simply drives down wages and creates a new generation of the working poor. Competitive advantages alone are not enough in the chase for footloose capital—some locations will still be excluded from the growth cycle. Business welfare is not desirable: subsidising the locational decision of investment simply socialises the costs of production while returns to investment remain privatised and increasingly globalised. National economic controls and macro fine tuning can no longer be regarded as a sufficient starting point for employment policy.

Spatial labour market and skill blockages need to be resolved before high growth/low inflation macro strategies become feasible.

Economic theory needs a new unit of labour market analysis addressing the global integration of capital and skill-based features of production. Orthodox micro and macro theories need to give way to the type of neighbourhood effects identified above. A spatial analysis takes account of the mobility of capital, plus the particular skill requirements of each location. Old left-of-centre responses to unemployment relied on Keynesian notions of nationally aggre-gated demand as the correct unit of labour market analysis. Neoclassical economics has analysed labour like any other market, with a focus on micro reform. In the new economy, however, national labour markets are heavily segmented, with capital and labour no longer acting as close substitutes, thereby discounting the usefulness of both the conventional macro and micro approaches. The correct unit of labour market analysis lies at a neighbourhood level. This reflects a new countervailing role for government in the creation of full employment: customising its programs in vocational education, wage subsidies, infrastructure and public sector services to suit the employment needs of each location.

SUPPLY SIDE MEASURES

Governments need to develop spatially framed strategies on both the demand and supply side of the labour market to ensure that labour force skills correspond with the creation of suitable work. Supply side measures need to be targeted at the quality of skills development in weak neighbourhoods. In the new economy, edu-cational qualifications and income bands tend to be closely correlated at a neighbourhood level.[8] With the changing nature of work and upward shift in skill requirements, the allocation of employment opportunities is essentially determined by educational achievement. Weak neighbourhoods are now doubly disadvantaged by poor levels of education and training: first by less access to well-paid jobs and second, by less access to any form of employment at all. Gregory and Hunter's research has found that the education–employment relationship has shifted since the mid-1970s 'so at each neighbourhood education level there is 15 percentage points less employment'.[9]

As employment skills have become more specialised, especially with the advent of knowledge work, the labour market has become more segmented on the basis of education and training. Segmen-tation of this kind has been felt most acutely on a locational scale.

Low skill neighbourhoods face a cycle of entrenched exclusion. Poor skills lead to long term unemployment, low expectations and a running down of self-esteem. These problems, in turn, further diminish social and economic capability. When they pass from generation to generation, the neighbourhood itself and its history of educational under-achievement become an identifiable source of disadvantage. The problems of a suburb or region become much greater than the sum of its component parts (the characteristics of each resident) might otherwise indicate. As McDonald's 1994 study of economic disadvantage in Australia concluded:

> the unemployment of fathers has a significant negative effect on the self-concept of teenagers . . . there is a danger that the so-called vicious cycle of poverty will be revisited in the next generation. The tragedy is that, where unemployment is region-ally concentrated, whole neighbourhoods of young people will have low self-concept and low expectations. In this setting, schools have an impossible task in attempting to reverse the outlooks of their students. It is no accident that rates of teenage unemployment are highly correlated with the rates of unemploy-ment for all ages and that participation rates in higher education of younger people from regions of high unemployment are so low.[10]

Other research has confirmed the close link between low socioeconomic status, educational disadvantage and unemploy-ment.[11] It highlights the critical role of education and skills development in breaking entrenched cycles of disadvantage. During the post-war period of full employment, Australia's education system gained a reputation as an important instrument of social meritocracy. School leaving qualifications provided access to a broad band of standard skill jobs. The new economy, however, requires a higher level and more diverse band of educational attainment across the citizenry. This has forced a new generation of policy reform issues, particularly with regard to the creation of opportunity and social mobility in disadvantaged neighbourhoods. The spatial concentration of unemployment requires policy makers to address not only issues of institutional design for schools, and lifelong vocational education, but the relationship between educa-tional opportunity and the home learning environment. These matters are explored at length in Chapter 27. In short, it is argued that the most effective labour market program on the supply side is a successful disadvantaged schools program.

The problem of spatially concentrated unemployment, particu-larly in its intergenerational spread, challenges the capacity of an essentially passive welfare state to deal with issues extending beyond the minimum safety net of income support. Generally the work of government has not been designed to deal with the entrenched social problems of low expectations, low self-esteem and poor skill development; nor does it cope effectively with a range of other labour market difficulties facing disadvantaged communities. These issues include poor transport access and the potential dislocation and financial costs of attempting to move to high employment areas.[12] Employment opportunities are further diminished by elements of labour market discrimination, on the basis of race (high unemployment regions invariably feature a high proportion of migrants) and/or location (the stigma commonly attached by employers to people living in low socioeconomic status areas).

The experience of the Keating Government offers an important guide to the means by which shortcomings on the supply side of the labour market can be addressed. The 1994 Working Nation program was an impressive catalyst for rethinking the fundamentals of the welfare state and questions of socioeconomic disadvantage. It pursued the customisation of training support for the long term unemployed, developing case management techniques and an active agenda for skills capability. The dysfunctional nature of the new labour market, with its semi-permanent imbalance between skill levels and job types, demands interventions from the public sector aimed at skills enhancement. Wage subsidy or workfare programs can also be a useful tool in improving the employability of the long term unemployed. It needs to be noted, however, that these measures invariably suffer from substitution effects, whereby enterprises have an incentive to replace full-cost employees with subsidised labour. Workfare should not be seen as a creator of additional employment but rather, a means by which employment opportunities can be improved for target groups, according to both the duration and location of their unemployment. Solutions to unemployment in the aggregate lie elsewhere.

On the demand side of the labour market the conventional approach to employment policy has been to rely on a trickle down effect from improved efficiency and competitiveness. In the new economy, however, even the most aggressive programs of micro reform and competitive advantage are likely to still leave a significant proportion of citizens and locations excluded from productive activity. The chase for capital across the globe does not treat weak neighbourhoods well. The insatiable demand of the private sector for lower costs and higher subsidies is not able to overcome the structural flaws of the new labour market. Deregulatory policies aimed at notional efficiency in the supply of labour are not able to solve the slow burning crisis of unemployment in Australia. Even desirable supply side measures, such as re-skilling and workfare programs, are unable to directly compensate for the structural decline in the demand for employment in weak neighbourhoods. They are simply one-half, albeit an important part, of spatially defined labour market solutions. Governments must also pursue demand side interventions targeted at the creation of new forms of employment, in balance with the supply of labour force skills at a neighbourhood level. This represents a relatively fresh agenda for the ALP in employment policy.[13]

13

EMPLOYMENT CREATION

The capacity of Western economies to achieve full employment has been progressively undermined by the internationalisation of capital, the changing nature of work and large increases in the labour force participation rate. Strategies aimed at national competitiveness have not been able to counter the remorseless loss of full-time jobs or accommodate the number of citizens wanting to join the workforce. Even our understanding of what is meant by the term 'full employment' has been challenged by the rise of part-time, temporary and casual work. The new economy features a growing number of people working either longer hours, reduced hours or not working at all. While the number of two and three job household units has grown, so too has the number of households in which no one can find work. The growth of long term and intergenerational unemployment has meant more than a loss of earnings capacity: it has also diminished the status and social recognition available to a significant proportion of the citizenry. The provision of work has taken on a welfare function in society that sits well outside the scope of market theory. The spatial features of the new labour market have forced onto government a charter for pursuing non-market solutions to unemployment.

In most Western nations the agenda for economic competitiveness is now reasonably settled. It is recognised that efficient product markets are superior to the wasteful allocation of economic resources. It is accepted by most economists that international capital should be made to compete, free from the folly of corporatist industry policy. Items of contention now centre on the appropriate regulation of the labour market and the role of government in employment policy. While the attainment of competitive advantage certainly remains desirable it is not, in itself, sufficient to move the labour market to a point of full employment.

These issues represent items of lively political distinction for social democracy. Its support for substantial regulation of the labour market aimed at fair patterns of income distribution, plus an active role for the public sector in labour market adjustment programs, contrasts sharply with the deregulatory agenda of the libertarian Right. In the new economy, however, the problem of entrenched exclusion is more challenging still. It requires a radical rethink of the responsibilities of government on the demand side of the labour market.

SPATIAL STRATEGIES

The starting point for successful employment strategies lies in the recognition of the distinctly spatial features of macroeconomic growth. The benefits of strong national economic growth are likely to be concentrated in the neighbourhoods and regions with the strongest skills base. Employment trends in all parts of the economy are running against the interests of the unskilled and poorly educated. Public policy now needs to ensure a heavy bias in the creation and location of additional jobs towards those who live in depressed areas. Gregory has shown that, in returning the Australian economy to full employment:

> For each additional job taken up in the top five per cent of socioeconomic status areas, about 12 jobs are needed for those from the lowest five per cent of SES areas. It seems unlikely that macro policy alone will be able to achieve this outcome . . . Since 1976 the unemployment curve has moved in ways which suggest that job offer slip-overs [the trickle down effect in employment growth] have become weaker and, as a result, it has become more difficult for macroeconomic policy alone to achieve full employment without generating inflationary pressures.[1]

Accordingly, the economic strategies of government require a strong spatial focus. The Australian economy should not be regarded as an homogenous entity; it needs to be treated as a series of highly differentiated regional economies and neighbourhood labour markets. Internationalisation and the changing nature of work have eroded the usefulness of the nation state as a unit of analysis for employment policy. This signifies an important challenge, not only to the macro settings and language of orthodox economics, but also to assumptions of national uniformity and centralised decision making. Australia, for instance, has not had a strong tradition of setting regional policy at the centre of its national interests. This is somewhat surprising for a geographically large and isolated nation, with dispersed centres of population and economic activity. An awkward federal system of government has failed to sustain an appreciation of regionalism and the need to address spatial inequities. The national ethos, perhaps drawn from the uncertainty of Australia's origins as an outpost of British colonialism, has emphasised the importance of strong, centralised governance. This has produced a system of political power highly concentrated in Canberra and the State capitals, with the weakest tier of local government in the Western world. Australia's policy structure for regional economic development has been remarkably frail.

The post-war experience points to the failure of public policy to swim against the tide of the rationalisation of capital. The locational subsidies and tax breaks favoured by State governments in the 1960s (and revived in the 1990s under the banner of competitive federalism) were not able to secure lasting regional advantages. Ultimately, they negated the need for firms to upgrade their competitiveness and form strong regional clusters of industry advantage. In the 1970s, the Whitlam Government pursued a program of decentralised growth centres with only moderate success. In the 1980s the drive for fiscal restraint, plus the corporatisation of a wide range of public services, impacted harshly on levels of regional employment. The Hawke Government tended to rely on notions of national competitive advantage to provide a trickle down effect to the regions. Not until the Keating Government's One Nation and Working Nation programs were attempts made to establish a policy framework for regional development. The first, in 1992, represented a counter-cyclical boost to infrastructure spending while the second, in 1994, following the recommendations of a report by the McKinsey organisation sought to emphasise the significance of regional leadership strategies and self-help.[2]

Neither of these measures, however, was able to sustain an effective spatial strategy. The infrastructure boost, while an important initiative for many regions, was limited by its one-off nature. The McKinsey material, dealing with the quality of local personnel and initiative, was based on a premise that regional economic problems are a product of failed regional leadership. This is obviously not the case. The primary cause of uneven regional development in Australia has been the uneven spatial impact of the rationalisation of capital. With the enhanced mobility of investment, the locational decisions of the private sector, drawn by the maximisation of profit, are not bound to any particular jurisdiction. Investment decisions are exercised to satisfy corporate interests,

often by parent companies well removed from regional circumstances. Policy makers should be sceptical of how much any amount
of 'self-help' and 'bottom-upwards' leadership can achieve in relatively weak regions. It is not difficult to use the natural strengths
of a region like North Queensland (chosen by McKinsey as a
development model) to generate strong tourism markets and
regional growth. Yet even the most successful 'leadership' strategy
is not likely to be able to reverse the downscaling of domestic and
international capital in regions with poor and declining inputs to
production. This places the contribution of local issues, such as
planning and marketing, in their proper perspective. That is, while
they might add marginally to the success of high growth regions,
their likely impact on inherently weak regions is more problematic
and certainly insufficient to deal with the problems of entrenched
neighbourhood unemployment.

One of Labor's leading tasks in opposition is to develop an
effective response to the spatial characteristics of the labour
market. Market forces alone will not suffice. Distance often makes
markets dysfunctional. Vast nations like Australia do not easily fit
the economic textbook model of seamless factor mobility and
trickle down effects. If the public sector does not fund the extra
costs of distance in service delivery, basic infrastructure and
employment opportunities, it is unlikely that the free market will.
Shrinking the role of government is not an answer for regional
Australia. If regions are not able to establish new sources of
economic activity to substitute for the loss of public sector services,
then Treasury-talk of a crowding-in effect from budget cuts
(whereby they supposedly increase private investment) simply
becomes a mirage. Australia needs to declare its preparedness as a
nation to fund the extra costs of distance and regional development.
If, in our type of country, regional centres are not guaranteed a
basic threshold of public sector employment and essential private
sector services (such as banking and fuel) then they will continue
to fall below the critical mass of economic activity needed to
survive. Regional development has become a critical function of
the collective responsibilities of governance in an open economy.

INFRASTRUCTURE DEVELOPMENT

The work of the public sector—as a funder of infrastructure, as a
provider of services and employment in its own right and as a
regulator of private sector activity—needs to pursue a distinctly
spatial role. That is, it needs to ensure that the demand for labour
at a neighbourhood and regional level closely corresponds with the

supply of labour force skills. This objective requires the development of five related strategies. First, transport, communications
and other infrastructure investment needs to be increased and
targeted on a regional scale. In recent decades in Australia, capital
spending has been used as a swing instrument in the Federal
budget, reaching significant levels only during times of economic
downturn. Better outcomes can be achieved through consistent,
long term strategies aimed at regional development. The economic
benefits of infrastructure investment tend to be realised within the
boundaries of regions and nations, thereby facilitating an effective
means by which government can boost private sector productivity
and employment growth.

A number of economists have identified a positive relationship
between the stock of public capital, labour productivity and rates
of economic growth. When targeted at low growth regions the
gains in employment growth can be substantial. At a national level,
the possibility of public capital crowding out private investment is
easily offset, beyond the short term, by positive spill-overs in
private sector productivity. These studies suggest that over a 3 to
5-year period, public infrastructure outlays crowd private investment in, not out.[3] Otto and Voss, from the University of NSW,
have estimated that, for the period 1966–90, every 1 per cent
increase in the public capital stock in Australia lifted private sector
productivity by between 0.38 per cent and 0.45 per cent. These
results are similar to Aschauer's work in the United States, which
has identified a public investment/productivity correlation of 0.4
and the likelihood that, 'public infrastructure capital [is] four times
as potent in affecting the macroeconomy as private investment'.[4]

Australia can no longer afford to ignore the substantial regional
growth potential of infrastructure investment. Current levels of the
stock of public capital are low by historical standards, following a
sharp decline in public investment in both the late 1970s and late
1980s.[5] Australia has been living off the benefits of past infrastructure spending and failing to invest adequately in the prospective
growth of its regions. Compared to other Western nations, our
economy suffers from low rates of investment and productivity,
more so on a regional scale. It is estimated, for instance, that our
capital productivity is 10 per cent below the OECD average.
Australia and its regions require a major boost in employment
growth off the back of enhanced infrastructure investment.

Fiscal expansion on the capital account should not be regarded
as inflationary or inequitable (between generations), given the way
in which it finances productive investment. Just as private companies borrow to finance part of their investment load, it makes good
sense for the public sector to debt finance long term investments

in Australia's regional infrastructure. Another means of financing infrastructure is through land value capture. That is, where the development of infrastructure leads to unearned gains in corporate capital and land values, these windfall benefits should be returned to the public sector through the taxation system. Infrastructure needs to be funded and constructed as one of the core functions of the public sector in employment policy. As the Labor MP, Lindsay Tanner, has proposed:

> The Federal Government should restore some balance to the infrastructure funding process. The debate about private sector involvement in infrastructure should be one about allocative efficiency rather than the evils of public debt or a belief that the private sector inherently does things better than the public sector. Where risks depend largely on future government decisions and the cost and benefits of the use of infrastructure are enjoyed by people other than direct users, public ownership is not only socially desirable, it is economically optimal. The government should establish a specific fund to provide loans for infrastructure projects in regional Australia to be developed through local and regional bodies. Public sector accounts should be separated into capital and recurrent accounts to enable more rigorous and transparent analysis of infrastructure decisions.[6]

PUBLIC SECTOR EMPLOYMENT

A second strategy aimed at regional employment growth concerns the spatial distribution of public sector services. The service functions of government are rarely assessed for their employment impact on a locational scale. These outlays, however, should be used to compensate for the shortfall in spending power and service sector employment in low growth regions. Government needs to use its role as a service provider and employer to break the cycle, now common in the upstairs/downstairs labour market, of inadequate demand and low employment. While the stimulation of aggregate demand is now limited on a national scale due to the likelihood of spill-over effects on the external account, redistributive strategies between regions can have a positive employment impact. This is due to their capacity to target, on a spatial scale, the provision of skill-suited services work at the needs of low employment neighbourhoods. The number of in-person service jobs is increased through the role of the public sector as a community services provider and employer.

In many respects these services represent a form of household outsourcing, with the collective role of the state substituting for the necessity of private provision. Community services such as municipal maintenance, environmental programs, urban renewal initiatives and ancillary services in education, health and transport are not only socially useful, but provide a critical source of employment for semi-skilled labour. In the public arena, however, they do not appear to have acquired the type of credibility accorded to the private sector in its provision of in-person services. While the growth of private sector industries in the hospitality sector and leisure-based services has been embraced as an important new source of employment in Australia, the supply of equivalent, yet publicly funded, services—such as child care, sporting facilities and accommodation for the aged—is more often interpreted for its additional cost to public budgets, than its critical role in the generation of new employment opportunities.

Several European nations have shown how the public sector's commitment to service provision not only provides jobs, but also has the potential for new sources of national growth and income. Denmark, for instance, has become a significant exporter of expertise in aged care and leisure services. Community services are also funded to aid the interface between work and family responsibilities: most notably in the way in which child care and pre-school services directly provide a substantial number of jobs, plus help to facilitate the re-entry of parents to the workforce. Even in the emergence of the East Asian economic miracle, public sector employment strategies have played a role. The city state of Singapore, for example, is best known for the virtues of traded competitiveness: high value adding and productivity, personal thrift and global economic integration. Yet the Singaporean economy also has a small army of public employees undertaking valuable work in the non-traded sector, particularly in civic maintenance, gardening and public health. To be certain, the dual features of the new labour market require the provision of a substantial pool of semi-skilled services work to bring the national economy closer to full employment.

It should be noted that this proposal does not signify a return to the short term, make-work schemes of the Regional Employment Development (RED) (1974–77) or Community Employment Program (CEP) (1983–89) initiatives in Australia. Rather, it represents a permanent reallocation of resources, and an increase in the role of the public sector as a services provider and employer. Government funding formulas need to ensure that the location of these additional employment opportunities is closely targeted at weaker neighbourhoods and regions. With its strong focus on national economic management, the Hawke–Keating Government did not give a great deal of attention to this issue. In many cases, socioeconomically disadvantaged regions did not receive adequate priority in the distribution of Federal funding.

The child care system, for instance, was managed more as an instrument of gender equity than locational equity. In the distribution of financial assistance grants to local government, one-fifth of the funding was preserved for most affluent municipalities (comprising 22 per cent). Similarly, issues of locational advantage and disadvantage did not bulk large in the construction of the government's funding formulas for health and other community services.[7] The next Federal Labor Government will need to explicitly entrench the employment needs of disadvantaged locations in the criteria by which each of its direct grants is allocated. The charter of the Commonwealth Grants Commission will also need to be modified to ensure that State and Territory community service programs are carefully targeted at regional employment needs.

CIVIL SECTOR EMPLOYMENT

A third strategy concerns the pursuit of employment growth outside the conventional domain of private capital and public enterprises. This recognises the impact of technological change in the new economy in eliminating a large number of semi-skilled tasks. The upward shift in employment skills is now being felt in several parts of the services sector, while at the same time, automation has wiped out most forms of unskilled farm, mining and manufacturing work. Routine production jobs are being lost in service functions such as the processing of data and financial transactions. While economists have always argued, in the long cycle of economic growth, that job numbers lost in old industries are ultimately replaced by new industries and new forms of employment, the current changes are distinctive in two key ways. First, post-Fordist work reflects a much higher plane of skill level in the production process. It draws on well-developed cognitive skills and capacities. The replacement of standardised, physical labour with knowledge work has obvious features of exclusivity in the labour market. Second, foreseeable employment replacement effects, arising primarily from the outsourcing of household functions, display clear elements of locational imbalance.

These problems of exclusivity in skill formation and the spatial distribution of employment have rarely entered the political debate in most Western nations. In recent decades the political Right has argued the case for labour market deregulation even though, in the new economy, this only adds to the problems of earnings inequality and insufficient spending power in weak neighbourhoods. Conversely, for the past 60 years, the political Left has seen macroeconomic stimulation, in national fiscal policy and pump priming, as the only way—in the words of the US economist Paul Samuelson—'to cheat the devil of ineffective demand'.[8] This again confirms the prudence of a new, radical centre in employment policy, not only using regions and neighbourhoods as the primary unit of labour market analysis, but also seeking the creation of new forms of socially useful employment beyond the conventional binary of the public and private sectors. Whereas in the old economy, the political debate centred on the appropriate balance between government and private markets, fresh issues are now forming around the relationship between the private, public and civil sectors.

In the creation of civil sector employment, policy makers have an opportunity to bring together the interests of the over-worked and the under-employed. A growing number of citizens seem to be finding that, through the pressure of having to work longer hours or because of their role in two-income families, they have less time available for civic participation. They have not been able to find the time required for the level of commitment to local community organisations, sporting groups and charity work that they might otherwise choose. As a result, many of these organisations are now struggling to carry out their socially useful role in the development of non-state public services and social connectedness. Conversely, a substantial number of people, as a product of either part-time work or full-time unemployment, are finding their time and capacities under-utilised in the paid economy. Unfortunately, many of these citizens, with a loss of social recognition and worth corresponding to their loss of employment, have grown alienated from society and its community purposes. The strength of our society and its civil functions do not appear to be coping well with the uneven distribution of work and leisure time in the new economy. As Jeremy Rifkin has written:

> Even with the technological strides of the information revolution, most people in the foreseeable future will still have to work in the formal market economy to make a living . . . As for the increasing number for whom there will be no jobs at all in the market economy, governments will be faced with two choices: finance additional police protection and build more gaols to incarcerate a growing criminal class or finance alternative forms of work in the third [civil] sector.[9]

The resolution of these issues lies in the capacity of the public sector to support and resource a range of civil responsibilities as a new source of semi-skilled employment. Projects such as these can help to strengthen social capital and connectedness (as is argued at length in Part V). The targeting of civil sector employment on a locational scale also serves as an appropriate response to the spatial features of the labour market. Governments need to revive their role as a facilitator of employment of last resort, even if this responsibility is ultimately discharged by other (community-based) organisations. The public sector can create new, socially useful forms of work by ensuring that people excluded from the market system contribute directly to civic projects. This type of work actively compensates for the loss of comparable jobs in other parts of the economy. It matches skill levels across the labour force against the availability of skill-suited work. It places a social premium on non-market solutions to the crisis of unemployment. Society should no longer restrict its view of legitimate work to an engagement in private and public sector activities. In a post-industrial economy, conditions of full employment increasingly rely on society's willingness to fund and provide civil sector jobs.

Rifkin has proposed the establishment of a community allowance as an alternative to welfare benefits. This would facilitate the retraining and placement of long term unemployed people in jobs in the third sector. It would also complement the granting of resources to non-profit organisations to help them train and recruit new employees. In this fashion, civic associations should be able to sponsor work activities which strengthen their role in society. With the widespread depletion of social capital, a range of projects are available: transport services for the frail aged; meals on wheels; assisting local sports clubs; improving municipal infrastructure and maintenance; environmental programs; assisting local schools; and adding to the work of service clubs, parishes and charities. The public sector needs to devolve the scale and authority of some of its own functions and place more resources and responsibilities in the hands of civil society. This requires, in part, a redefinition of the way society views employment. It requires governments to resource the civil sector in a fashion no less legitimate than its conventional services. It requires the creation of a civil sector economy from which the attainment of full employment is a social priority.

Significantly, some of these measures are already being pursued in other nations. In the United States, especially with President Clinton's emphasis on welfare-to-work programs, several States are using federal funding to create new sources of civil sector employment. The Massachusetts plan, for instance, requires all able-bodied persons on welfare for more than twelve months to enrol in a community service program. In return, government provides an income subsidy and family support services such as child care.[10] The Blair Labour Government in Britain is pursuing a similar approach, with a menu of workfare, civic employment and training options for unemployed people under 25 years of age, funded from a special tax on the windfall profits of privatised utilities. Obviously these programs, in terms of their affordability, save for society the deadweight costs of economic exclusion, such as property-related crime, drug abuse and other social problems. The local application of civil sector work is further explored in Chapter 25 under the banner of place management.

ECONOMIC COOPERATIVES

A fourth strategy is to pursue new structures of economic ownership as an alternative to the rationalisation of capital. While in Australia the cooperatives movement has remained relatively small, in most parts of Europe it is an integral part of the economic adjustment process. Cooperative banks and credit unions have been able to mobilise local capital for the establishment and expansion of producer and consumer cooperatives. A substantial number of manufacturing, retail and service enterprises are owned jointly by their workers and consumers.[11] This has provided the basis of solid productivity gains and a virtuous cycle of local and regional economic activity. Surplus funds are distributed to members who have an incentive to purchase their goods and services locally. Cooperatives provide the basis by which labour can hire capital (rather than the reverse) and engage in participatory decision making in the management of enterprises. Moreover, the ownership features of cooperatives disallow the possibility of equity investment, thereby ensuring that the economic benefits, control and ownership of these ventures remain anchored in the nation state.

With the disaggregation of the scale of production and relative ease of market entry in the new economy, the establishment of cooperative enterprises is becoming a more feasible form of economic adjustment. Opportunities should be made available for retrenched workers to use their accumulated savings and benefits to form cooperative ventures, either in their existing industry or new markets. Presently a large number of displaced routine production workers are entering the in-person services sector, either as prospective employees or franchisees. The cooperatives movement, displaying the virtues of nationally defined ownership and worker control, offers a more satisfactory process by which this transition can be made. The public sector can assist the growth and potential of this new source of economic activity and employment in Australia through carefully targeted measures, such as the provision of advisory services and seed capital to ease the costs of market entry. Cooperatives of this kind also represent a means by which the resources and leadership of the trade union movement might find renewed relevance.

CORPORATE RESPONSIBILITIES

A fifth strategy concerns the social obligations of the private sector. In orthodox economic theory, the responsibility of corporations extends no further than the maximisation of profits. Participants to the market are judged to be amoral, that is, without a sense of the moral norms—the rights and wrongs—that commit people to a sense of common purpose in a social environment. This is, however, an inadequate framework within which to assess the functions of the corporate sector in an open economy. The private sector, self-evidently, does not operate in isolation from the rest of society; its decisions have a profound impact on all manner of social relations. While within the national sphere of capital, governments often assumed that corporate interests would readily coincide with the national interest, globalisation has changed forever the relationship between the state and capital. Corporations are now less likely to feel any obligation or attachment to a particular political jurisdiction. There is, therefore, a need for government policy to develop stronger safeguards against the immorality of corporate behaviour.

The enhanced freedoms and scope of globalised markets carry with them additional social responsibilities. This is a core moral proposition of the new radical centre: that the furthering of rights in an open economy and society also requires a furthering of responsibilities. In the corporate sector, raw economic competition is not enough; corporate decision making must also have regard for the importance of social cooperation and cohesiveness. The regulatory and funding powers of the state, given the link they provide between corporations and citizens, have a significant role to play in pursuit of this goal. As noted earlier, social democracy should not assume that corporate interests are synonymous with national interests. Especially in the exercise of economic nationalism, policies often need to include a range of incentives and sanctions that force from corporations a proper sense of moral obligation.

The feasibility of these measures, of course, depends heavily on a nation's success in applying the new growth strategies of economic leverage. Once capital is attracted to the growth potential of a certain jurisdiction, it is much easier for public policy to calibrate an appropriate set of social obligations. In an open economy, government carries a strong responsibility for overcoming the chronic problems of economic exclusion. It is not unreasonable, therefore, to require the private sector, particularly in its provision of essential economic services, to have regard for the spatial features of the new labour market. For many years public policy in Australia has demanded a reasonable spread of telecommunications facilities through the community service obligations imposed on Telstra.

This standard might also be applied to the provision of financial and energy services by the private sector. Two examples stand out in the exercise of this responsibility. First, it is possible for the Federal Government to set, in the issuing of bank licenses in Australia, strong standards for the locational availability of a basic threshold of face-to-face banking services. Second, in guaranteeing a geographic spread of fuel outlets and businesses, Federal competition laws need to declare petroleum terminals as an essential economic facility. This would help to break the monopoly market power of the petrol multinationals and provide country petrol retailers with fair and competitive access to wholesale petrol supplies.[12] Both measures represent an important means by which the viability of economic services and employment levels in regional Australia can be maintained.

There is also a sound moral argument for the reciprocation of responsibility in the assistance governments might provide to the corporate sector. One of the problems with the business welfare approach to industry policy is that it promotes a one-way flow of social responsibility. Governments are said to be obliged to make ever more concessions and subsidies for the benefit of private profit, without businesses being bound to socially responsible commitments in return. This has been a common practice under the Howard Government. With the abolition of unfair dismissal laws, for instance, business managers in Australia are no longer required to take responsibility for the mistakes they might make in the selection of staff. In their interaction with the taxation, regulatory and funding policies of government, firms should have to provide a guarantee that any publicly provided benefits will be used to actually create employment. In some parts of the United States and Western Europe this principle has led to the introduction of 'clawback' provisions, whereby firms are required to 'pay back all or part of subsidies if they fail to deliver, under-perform or over-promise'.[13]

Similarly, firms receiving public assistance should have to

comply with a public code of corporate governance. This would specify clear social obligations for employment practices, executive salary restraint and the rights of shareholders in corporate decision making. At a time when the nation state is redefining its relationship with capital, these responsibilities are an important means by which the moral standing of corporate governance can be brought into line with public expectations and interests. In Australia and elsewhere, the public's concern about outrageous executive salaries, corporate tax avoidance, and shoddy business practices is no less acute than public hostility to social welfare abuse. If public policy, for whatever reason, allocates assistance to the private sector, it must be on the basis of reciprocated obligations to the public and national interest.

These five strategies, applied in tandem, form an effective response to the spatial characteristics of economic exclusion in the new labour market. They recognise that while the pursuit of competitive advantage can produce new sources of growth in the national economy, growth alone is not likely to clear the labour market. Active supply and demand side interventions are needed to cope with the spatial features of the new economy. The concurrent movement of capital to international arenas and refashioning of the labour market into neighbourhood effects has led to a new charter for the work of government. This agenda—the public sector's role in the development of new growth strategies, education and re-skilling programs, employment creation and regional programs—in turn creates a fresh set of issues in the resolution of the fiscal crisis of the state.

14

FINANCING GOVERNMENT

A leading task for social democracy is to resolve the overload of modern government and repair the viability of the transfer system. In an open economy, government tends to be allocated additional responsibilities off a steadily contracting resource base. This inevitably leads to unsatisfactory outcomes in the work of the public sector, with responsibilities either discharged inadequately or not at all. Public confidence in the role of government will not be enhanced by the continuation of this piecemeal approach, or its associated rationing of scarce public resources. The legitimacy of public sector action and the adequacy of its revenue base need to be restored. In part, this requires the rationalisation of public sector functions, such as the argument in Part I for phasing down the level of industry welfare. In other areas, it requires the hypothecation of particular types of revenue to an appropriate set of public functions. For example, public sector debt should be dedicated to the funding of productive infrastructure on a regional scale.

More generally, the public sector needs to overcome the false expectations imposed on it by the competitive advantage paradigm. It needs to argue that substantial gains in Australia's international competitiveness lie more in the remaking of corporate cultures and management than the endless subsidisation of profit or an excessively narrow focus on driving down the costs of business inputs. Nothing serves the interests of the corporate sector and its management more fulsomely than to have both sides of politics constantly engaged in a bidding war for the highest level of industry welfare and public sector micro reform. It allows the performance of corporations and the captains of industry to escape public scrutiny, while also allowing corporations to establish a dependency relationship with government in answer to the challenges of market competition and profitability. Social democracy needs to clearly distinguish between these interests and the national interest and, in this process, ensure that capital is made to compete on its merits.

Scarce public resources need to be directed primarily at overcoming the inadequacies of the profit system—its failure to invest adequately in the skills of a nation's people; its failure to deal with the entrenched problems of economic exclusion on a spatial scale. In this way, social democracy is able to eliminate any tension or inconsistency between its general support for market forces and its moral commitment to the active role of government in the redistribution of income, public resources and economic capability. The work of the public sector needs to concentrate on providing those things the market either cannot provide or actually takes away. This means sustaining a solid base of public revenue and arguing the legitimacy of spatially framed measures of employment creation and skills development. It also means countering false expectations in the framing of national savings policies.

As noted earlier, one of the contradictions of the competitive advantage paradigm is the way in which it loads extra responsibilities onto the budgets of government while also seeking, in the accounting systems of nations, to blame public sector dissaving for the problems of a current account deficit. Social democracy needs to confront this contradiction and end the narrow obsession in much of the economic debate with public sector budgeting. This requires, at least in Australia's circumstances, an emphasis on the way in which the nation's savings shortfall is attributable more to the performance of the private sector than the public sector. The debate about the correct balance of national savings and national investment (a surplus of investment over savings produces a current account deficit) needs to consider, first and foremost, Australia's cultural adversity to long term planning and savings. There are sound arguments for Labor to consider and advance its response to the national savings question primarily in terms of the responsibilities of the private sector.

PRIVATE SAVINGS

In recent decades, movements in Australia's current account deficit have corresponded closely with changes in the level of private savings, much more than changes on the bottom line of the Federal budget.[1] Any decline in the level of public savings in Australia since the 1970s has been accompanied by a fall in public investment and infrastructure spending, ensuring that the net public sector borrowing requirement (and hence its direct impact on the current account deficit) has remained reasonably stable. This is partly reflected in the way in which, by 1996–97, public debt interest, as a proportion of Commonwealth budget outlays, remained steady at its 1972–73 level of 7.2 per cent.[2] Indeed, the greatest impact on Australia's savings performance this decade has come from the secular decline in private savings, with the household ratio (net savings as a proportion of disposable income) falling from 7.5 per cent in 1990 to just 2 per cent in 1996. Notably, on the back of financial deregulation and easier personal finance, housing and consumer debt relative to household income spiralled from 176 per cent, in March 1992, to 229 per cent in 1995.

Close examination of the Federal budget papers confirms this pattern across the longer term. Since the early 1970s, household savings have fallen by 8 per cent of GDP, while public sector net lending has declined by just 3 per cent.[3] On an international comparison of private and public net lending performance over the past decade, the Department of the Treasury has noted that

> private sector net lending in Australia has been consistently negative, indicating that private sector saving has fallen short of private sector investment. In contrast, private sector lending in the United States has been positive, or at worst marginally negative and, for industrial countries on average, it has been positive.[4]

By contrast, Australia's level of public sector net lending has been more modest than the United States and far superior to the industrial countries' average. One might reasonably conclude from this evidence that official concerns about Australia's savings performance most productively might be focused on the private sector. Yet, in this regard, the Commonwealth Treasury has managed to conclude that, 'since Australia has a saving shortfall from the private sector, the public sector cannot draw on national savings'.[5] That is, private savings may be the problem but Treasury only ever recommends the twin deficits theory and its advocacy of public sector cuts as a means by which this issue might be addressed. In this fashion, orthodox economic opinion and advice acts against the viability of public sector action. The flaws in this approach, both theoretical and practical, are set out in greater detail in Appendix II.

TAXATION REFORM

Labor's economic strategy needs to be founded on the legitimacy of government intervention on both sides of the labour market.

These measures should not be diminished or sacrificed in the name of national savings. Rather, policies aimed at improvements in national savings need to be cast in a way that explicitly addresses the cultural foundations of this issue in Australia—primarily our culture of consumption and ephemeral economic activity. This, in turn, highlights the necessity of a prescriptive approach to private savings, such as compulsory and other self-provident measures. The Keating Government made a series of important advances in the development of these policy methods through its reforms in super-annuation. The means by which this strategy can now be broadened, particularly through the enhancement of pre-retirement savings and the associated reform of Australia's transfer payments system, is examined at length in Part IV. To be certain, the greatest gains in Australia's savings performance lie in the restructuring of our welfare and taxation regimes. As Fred Argy has concluded:

[Compared to the Federal deficit] a more credible basis for policy concern about saving and the current account deficit is that the policy environment does not offer the community a 'neutral' choice between present and future consumption. We have a tightly targeted social security system which discourages saving and a tax system which favours consumption and produces one of the highest rates of tax on saving in the developed world.[6]

Moreover, taxation reform is needed to address a range of other economic and social concerns. Primarily, the changing nature of work and production has undermined the effectiveness of the tax system as an instrument of economic equity. This has compounded the long standing problems of tax minimisation and avoidance in Australia, and substantially narrowed the revenue raising capacity of the public sector. In its original form in most nations, the taxation system was not designed or intended to support the outlays required by the scale of the modern welfare state. Even without the spread of globalisation, the tax system would be in need of constant repair and reform. Not withstanding the pitfalls of tax reform in the electoral arena, this process now seems unavoidable in Australia. The effectiveness of the taxation regime, both in its adequacy and equity, has become a first order issue for social democracy. The aspirations and endeavours of parties like the ALP have, for most of this century, relied heavily on the success of the tax/transfer system. Without an adequate revenue base, the public tasks of social opportunity and equity are made increasingly improbable.

As the economy makes its transition from national systems of industrial capital to the internationalised features of post-industrial production, the foundations of tax policy also require an overhaul. Most notably, several irreversible economic trends are placing pressure on traditional forms of tax that levy their rates at the point of earnings. These pressures are pushing the incidence of taxation from the income of individuals and corporations to 'down-stream' points of consumption and savings (once acquired, all earnings must either be spent or saved). For instance, the changing base of economic activity has prompted more than a decade of debate about the reform of the Australian tax system. The shift to services consumption, with the growth of household outsourcing and recreation-type spending, has led to calls for a broadening of the indirect tax base.

More generally for all nations, the footloose features of capital have forced policy makers to drive down their corporate tax rates in search of international competitiveness. If a nation taxes earnings too severely, corporations and even some citizens have the capacity to move to a more generous jurisdiction. Like so many other aspects of public policy, the taxation system needs to respond to the mobile geography of capital. This means ensuring that the incidence of taxation falls, as far as possible, on items of economic activity which remain relatively fixed within the boundaries of the nation state. Conceivably, these items might include the personal consumption decisions of national residents; the transfer and real-isation of the value of personal assets; plus land and other property-related holdings.

The competitive advantage paradigm has opened up a broad range of tax deductions and concessions for the corporate sector, ostensibly to create investment and private sector growth. The Australian taxation system is riddled with benefits of this kind, such as negative gearing on rental properties, the proliferation of trusts and other income-splitting devices, plus a myriad of specific indus-try measures.[7] Each of these concessions substantially weakens the tax base. For instance, there are now some 500 000 trusts in Australia (which if taxed at the full company rate would produce an additional $3 billion in revenue per annum), while at least $8 billion of revenue is lost each year in interest and other deductions on rental properties.[8]

The changing nature of production has also served to narrow the tax base on earnings. With the disaggregation of business form, taxpayers are moving in substantial numbers from the PAYE stream to corporate arrangements. The growth of sole trading contractors, consultants, franchisees and outsourced work in the new economy has facilitated the widespread use of company structures, with the benefit of a 14 per cent gap between the top personal tax rate and

Table 14.1 Income taxes and multiples of average earnings, Australia

	Average income tax rate Proportion of average earnings (%)[a]					
Year	33	66	100	200	400	800
1977–78	0.0	14.8	21.1	31.4	44.4	53.6
1981–82	6.6	19.3	23.5	33.8	46.0	53.0
1982–83	7.4	19.0	22.9	33.9	46.8	53.4
1984–85	8.7	18.9	23.7	37.5	49.1	54.6
1987–88	9.1	18.9	25.0	35.7	43.0	46.6
1990–91	9.7	16.8	24.1	35.3	41.8	45.0
1992–93	9.7	15.2	22.8	34.0	40.5	43.8
1994–95	10.4	16.3	22.2	33.0	40.0	43.5
1996–97[b]	10.9	17.3	22.8	33.8	40.4	43.7

Note: These figures equal the average tax rate applicable in certain years to income levels, expressed as a proportion of AWE.
a   Average total earnings for all male employees.
b   Estimates
Source: *Average Weekly Earnings, States and Australia*, various (ABS Cat. no. 6302.0), Australian Taxation Office.

the company rate in Australia. The use of family income splitting by these tax units produces a further loss of public revenue. In aggregate, these trends have placed considerable stress on the PAYE stream and undermined public confidence in the fairness of the Australian tax system.

It now appears to a large number of Australians that the system is weighted in favour of those interests most likely and able to exploit the complexity of the tax laws and thereby minimise their obligations to the rest of society.[9] The taxpayers with the wealth and capacity to engage the best tax lawyers seem to be able to find holes in the tax net faster than the capacity of policy makers to eliminate existing anomalies. When the Tax Office reports, as it did at the beginning of 1996, that the wealthiest 100 Australians are avoiding $800 million in tax, while every day the burden on lower to middle income earners grows more acute, our tax system has reached a point of sclerosis. For the past 20 years, Australia's income tax rates have become less progressive (as Table 14.1 shows). This has been the inevitable consequence of fixed, tax-free thresholds, compressed rates and the incidence of bracket creep (where through income growth and non-indexed tax rates, taxpayers progressively move into higher marginal brackets). Whereas the top marginal tax rate in Australia in the 1950s cut in at 19 times the level of average weekly earnings, this ratio has now fallen below 1.5.

The Liberal and National Parties have responded to these trends by advocating a goods and services tax. The economic impact of this measure, however, is highly questionable. Any immediate benefit in the competitiveness of exports would soon be wiped out by an appreciation in the floating exchange rate. The employment and growth consequences of moving the incidence of taxation downstream from the declaration of earnings to the expenditure of earnings are also problematic. As even John Howard has admitted, 'all taxes, with the exception of those on economic rent and inherited wealth, have some [negative] employment and economic growth effects'.[10] The only discernible benefit of a GST appears to lie indirectly in the enhancement of allocative efficiency from a more consistent treatment of the taxation of goods and services consumption.

Clearly the regressive features of a GST, plus the acute problem of framing a permanent package of compensation for low income earners, make it unacceptable as a system of income redistribution. Its inflationary impact also raises a number of economic concerns. The GST's relevance in the tax debate in Australia seems to rest heavily on its ability to broaden the tax base and shift the revenue burden from the earnings stream. Yet even in this regard, however, several aspects of the new economy seem to be moving against the efficacy of taxing transactions. The rise of knowledge-based industries has created a new bundle of tax avoidance issues. In particular, the international spread of electronic commerce, such as the purchase of goods and services off the Internet, has raised doubts about the capacity of the nation state to effectively police and tax the flow of economic transactions. Even if a Coalition Government were able to introduce a GST, its foundations would most likely be eroded over time by the growing spread of cross-national electronic commerce.

From Labor's perspective, the public interest and controversy associated with prospective tax reform need to be taken as an opportunity to reassess the Party's own policy principles. The viability of the tax/transfer system—and with it, most of the aspirations of the social democratic project—now relies on the development of a tax system capable of satisfying the following eight objectives:

- an adequate base, such that the tax regime aids the resolution of the fiscal crisis of the state;
- capacity to fund the work of government in addressing the wide spread of economic insecurity, especially in resourcing the education system and new sources of employment creation and regional development;

- the achievement of progressive and redistributive outcomes, consistent with the goals of a national gain sharing model;
- potential to counter the footloose features of capital by focusing the incidence of tax on nationally defined forms of economic activity;
- capacity to adequately address downstream issues in the taxation treatment of consumption and savings;
- suitability in overcoming, in tandem with other policy initiatives, the paucity of private sector savings in Australia;
- consistency with allocative efficiency goals and the development of a high growth/high wage economy; and
- potential to restore public confidence in the integrity of the tax regime, by guaranteeing that those citizens most able to contribute taxes actually make such a contribution.

PROGRESSIVE EXPENDITURE TAX

Within the terms and possibilities of the decade-long tax debate in Australia, with its narrow focus on a flat consumption tax, the satisfaction of each of these principles appears remote. This is why Labor needs to broaden the debate and pursue a substantially different approach to the issue of tax reform. The viability of large slabs of the tax/transfer system in Australia now rests on the success of this policy task. With the advent of economic internationalisation and the changing nature of production and work, social democracy needs to think boldly about the purpose and structure of taxation. The habits of incrementalism and caution, which plague so much of the tax debate, are clearly inappropriate. A useful starting point for social democracy's overhaul of tax policy involves the examination of the so-called Kaldor tax.

This system, first raised by the British economist, Nicholas Kaldor, in *An Expenditure Tax* (1955), holds out the possibility of a progressive tax regime levied on the value of personal and corporate expenditure. It aims to shift the incidence of direct taxation from earnings to spending, and then apply a highly progressive set of tax rates to the total value of these consumption decisions. It does this by calculating a level of 'taxable consumption' for each tax paying unit (whether corporate or personal), whereby allowable items of savings and investment are subtracted from the total value of all sources of income. This recognises, of course, that a taxpayer's net outlays for consumption purposes equals their income minus savings. By registering the deductibility of savings and investment items according to their value to the economy, governments are able to ensure that the tax system only

Table 14.2 Assessment of liability for a progressive expenditure tax

ADD		
1. *Personal income receipts*		
Wages	XX	
Salaries	XX	
Dividends	XX	
Interest	XX	
Rent	XX	
Profits	XX	
Royalties	<u>XX</u>	
		XXX
2. *Capital receipts*		
Realisation of capital assets	XX	
Amount borrowed	XX	
Receipt of repayment of past loans	XX	
Reduction in money balances	<u>XX</u>	
		XXX
3. *Windfall incomings*		
Inheritances	XX	
Gifts received	<u>XX</u>	
		<u>XXX</u>
Total chargeable items		XXX
DEDUCT		
4. *Non-consumption outgoings*		
Acquisition of assets (investments)	XX	
Amount lent	XX	
Repayment of past borrowings	XX	
Increase in money balances	XX	
Gifts made	XX	
Direct taxes paid	<u>XX</u>	
		(XXX)
Total allowable deductions		<u>(XXX)</u>
5. *Chargeable balance*		
(Representing 'taxable consumption')		XXX

Source: Report of a Committee (Chaired by Professor Meade), *The Structure and Reform of Direct Taxation*, The Institute for Fiscal Studies, London, 1978.

promotes and rewards productive forms of economic activity. For instance, it would most likely be decided to treat personal luxuries, such as art collections and vintage cars, as a form of consumption rather than items of appreciable investment. Conversely, all forms of capital market savings and investments in new technology and equipment would be treated as tax deductions. The 1978 Meade Committee,[11] which reported on the possible implementation of the Kaldor tax in Britain, identified the items shown in Table 14.2 as indicative of the way in which the calculation of tax liabilities might be made.

The residual amount of taxable consumption would then be subject to a progressive scale of tax rates, so that those taxpayers with the highest level of consumption would pay the highest proportion of tax. Compared to the current system of earnings taxation, the Kaldor tax offers enhanced scope for progressivity. Because the incidence of tax is shifted from earnings to consumption, high marginal rates are not able to act as a disincentive for earnings and economic effort. In this fashion, a progressive expenditure tax (PET) removes from the armoury of the political Right its chief argument—expressed with some success for most of this century—for narrowing the fairness and scope of the tax system. In the absence of earnings disincentives, it is possible to extend both the adequacy and progressivity of the tax system.

High progressive rates of expenditure tax, levied on people with the income and wealth required for lavish consumption, serve only as a disincentive for the act of conspicuous consumption itself. If high income earners choose to save or productively invest a solid proportion of their revenue, and thereby add to the growth of the economy, then the PET's impact is entirely reasonable. Its purpose lies in ensuring that the realisation of affluence, expressed in the form of excessive consumption, is accompanied by a progressive contribution to the tax system. At the other end of the income scale, a tax-free threshold could be established to effectively exempt for each taxpayer a basic amount of expenditure on life's essentials, such as food and clothing. The impact of a PET, in terms of both its equity and allocative efficiency, is also enhanced by the way in which it facilitates the abolition of a raft of regressive, indirect taxes. In Australia's circumstances, the equity inherent in the Kaldor tax stands in contrast to the Liberal Party's obsession with a GST and its negative impact on the interests of low to middle income earners.

It is important to note that the PET is levied on the net sum of each tax unit's consumption, rather than on each spending transaction. Accordingly, it avoids the huge volume of paperwork associated with the indirect taxation of consumption, plus the emerging issue of tax minimisation through the use of electronic transactions. It also ensures that the focus of the tax system rests heavily on those items of economic activity anchored within the boundaries of the nation state. Citizens would not be able to avoid the PET's impact on their personal consumption decisions unless they decided to change their nation of residence; so too, companies would need to pay the new tax while ever they continued their operations within the levying nation. The PET deals with other relatively fixed economic items—such as the holding of property-related assets and personal transfer of wealth—by ensuring that the realisation of these assets into income and then consumption triggers the progressive and comprehensive payment of tax. Quite simply and equitably, the PET is able to reduce the real value of unproductive wealth by requiring tax to be paid whenever this form of wealth is spent.[12]

BENEFITS OF PET

The introduction of a progressive expenditure tax in Australia would most likely benefit the average working family by producing a fairer spread of the tax revenue burden. Its potential rests in forcing those Australians who enjoy a high standard of consumption and affluence to actually pay, after decades of avoidance, a decent share of the nation's taxes. This is a critical step in restoring the public's confidence in the integrity of our tax system. It also allows the public sector to harvest a return on the extraordinary amount of wealth and affluence being generated in the new economy. The advent of internationalisation and the high earnings premium paid on information-based skills have delivered for many Australians—the top 30 per cent group of knowledge workers and large capital holders—a growing proportion of national income. This has converted itself, driven by the consumer ethos of our society, into a new generation of lavish personal consumption: the luxury cars, boats, homes, holidays and other forms of extravagant recreation which characterise the lifestyle of this 'new money' group. By any assessment of a reasonable threshold of personal capability in our society (the primary goods required in the attainment of each individual's freedom to achieve), material benefits of this kind are superfluous.

The redistributive functions of the public sector now rely on its capacity to harvest a return on these resources, from which it can then fund the new policies of economic inclusion. The PET establishes a transfer mechanism by which the Federal Government, through the additional revenue raised from taxing the new money affluence, can effectively discharge its responsibilities in regional development and neighbourhood employment. Even if the PET system were limited to a special levy (supplementary to the current tax system) on the expenditure decisions of the wealthiest Australians, it would still be able to achieve some important redistributive functions. In terms of Rifkin's argument for the creation of third sector employment:

The newly emerging symbolic analyst class, who are the immediate beneficiaries of the high-tech global economy, are asked to

redistribute a portion of their purchasing power to help those
who have been cast aside by the market forces of the [informa-
tion] revolution. Providing a community allowance to excluded
citizens, in return for performing meaningful work in the civil
sector economy, will in turn benefit both the market and public
sectors by increasing purchasing power and taxable income as
well as reducing the crime rate and the cost of maintaining law
and order.[13]

Kaldor's proposal reflects a relatively fresh and I believe,
increasingly relevant, way of expressing the principle of tax equity.
It is argued that those who absorb the highest level of resources
in the economy should pay the highest level of tax. In terms of
the capability paradigm, the PET's impact can be expressed as
follows: those citizens who consume the largest amount from the
overall supply of primary goods should be required to make the
largest contribution to the common pool of public resources. These
resources then allow the public sector to advance the capability of
disadvantaged people and places through skills development and
the creation of socially useful forms of employment. Governments
are able to transfer the surplus use of primary goods among
society's most affluent group towards the benefits of economic
participation among the bottom 30 per cent cohort. This perspective—the role of excessive consumption in depleting a nation's
supply of primary goods (and hence part of the capability set)—
further strengthens the view in a post-industrial economy that the
most appropriate unit of taxation lies in acts of expenditure, rather
than earnings.

Productive effort and initiative are required to build a satisfactory base of primary goods and capability, both for individual and
collective purposes. The earnings derived from this process of
economic growth are not in themselves an issue within the capability paradigm; it is the downstream use of earnings that
determines their overall utility. Earnings directed towards the
enhancement of national savings and productive investment need
to be encouraged, while earnings directed at the over-consumption
of primary goods need to be discouraged. These economic and
social goals are embodied in the Kaldor system—earnings and
effort are rewarded among the citizenry; only the excessive consumption (and consequent dissaving) of these material benefits is
penalised financially.

A progressive consumption tax offers an active incentive for
productive investment and the virtues of saving.[14] This is particularly important in the circumstances of an open economy, where
society—through both the effort of individuals and the collective

system of governance—needs to thoroughly plan and provide against the contingencies of economic change. Moreover, this savings effort, once expressed on a national scale, needs to be seen as a powerful source of national sovereignty. Only by funding more of the investment made in Australia through our own sources of savings is it possible to resolve the nation's chronic problems on the current account and its attendant levels of foreign ownership and debt. In an era of global capital, economic sovereignty now lies in the advancement of a nation's skills, infrastructure and savings.

IMPLEMENTATION OF PET

Curiously, particularly given its potential benefits, the progressive expenditure tax model has not been adopted in any part of the world (although in several nations, pension savings are treated with an expenditure tax methodology—whereby inflows are tax deductible and outflows are taxable). The Meade Committee's report was not proceeded with in Britain in the late 1970s due to the absence of computerised tax records and resistance to its requirement for an annual cycle of tax returns. Neither of these issues, of course, arise in Australia. Taxpayers here have grown accustomed to a system based on regular returns and computerised information. Indeed, recent advances in information technology by the Tax Office have made the data collection task for the administration of a PET comparatively simple.

The Australian tax system is also well placed to handle the other major transitional issue in moving to the Kaldor system; that is, the possibility of intergenerational inequities. It can be argued that because people and corporations have already paid taxes in the accumulation of their assets, to now register these assets for the purposes of a PET would amount to a form of double taxation.[15] In Australia, however, with one of the weakest bases of asset and wealth taxes in the Western world, this is not an irreconcilable problem. Moreover, the introduction of a capital gains tax (which has many similarities to the PET) in the 1980s demonstrated the means by which wealth accumulated out of taxed income, and wealth from non-taxed sources, can be differentiated. A range of other administrative issues in the possible introduction of a PET in Australia is dealt with in Appendix III.

In any aspect of public policy, especially the transitional costs of major tax reform, it is always important to consider the cost of doing nothing. In terms of the adequacy of the tax/transfer system in an open economy, social democracy is rapidly losing the comfort of the do-nothing option. If it does not restore the base and fairness of the revenue system, then inevitably the political Right will be able to further develop and implement its agenda for regressive and indirect forms of tax. This difficulty has become particularly acute in Australia. At least through the PET proposal, Labor would be able to advance a clear alternative to the introduction of a GST, consistent with its commitment to tax equity and the seven other key principles of tax reform outlined earlier. The boldness of the PET approach should not be used as an alibi for inaction. As one of Australia's leading economists, Vince Fitzgerald, has lamented:

> Looking back over the tortuous path that the debate about taxation reform in Australia has taken over the past decade and a half, how much better off would Australia be now, if we had been the [first] OECD country to move towards taxing persons primarily on a [progressive] expenditure basis—with, of course, parallel changes to the corporate income tax; that is, moving it from a tax on profits towards a tax on cash flow, thereby removing immense complexities over the treatment of depreciation and encouraging business investment.[16]

15

CONCLUSION: SUPERSEDING THE MARKET

The first two sections of this book have highlighted the dual features of policy development in the new economy. The split geography of the market system—the advent of global capital and neighbourhood labour markets—has pushed spatial issues to the centre of the economic debate. The internationalisation of capital requires policy makers to concentrate their outlays and investments on nationally defined items of economic advantage, such as education, skills development and fixed infrastructure. Likewise, the emergence of an upstairs/downstairs labour market requires a new approach to policies for employment creation and labour force re-skilling.

As a discipline, economics has to some extent been 'topped and tailed'. In the creation of wealth and prosperity, economic theory is struggling to adjust to the rise of knowledge as a leading input to the production process. In the distribution of growth and economic opportunities, most Western nations have struggled to cope with the newly formed spatial features of the labour market. National economic policies are now required to deal with these two diverse aspects of economic activity: the search for new sources of endogenous growth to attract capital and investment on a global scale; and the development of new labour market interventions to guarantee a decent share of economic activity and employment on a neighbourhood scale. At each level, governments need to successfully manage the politics of economic adjustment.

In the public arena, there is a considerable amount of concern about the way in which industrial-type manual work is being replaced with the cognitive skills of knowledge work.[1] For many people, the most valuable form of employment is still expressed through the work of the hands, rather than the head. This represents an important distinction between the political economy of the information rich and the information poor in our society. It points to the difficulties in successfully managing the politics of economic transition. Public perceptions often lag behind the pace of technological and workplace change. However, the development of job replacement strategies to compensate for the inexorable loss of routine production work is not without its dilemmas in the public arena. The creation of community and civil sector work at a neighbourhood level is often criticised for not producing 'real' jobs. This is a consequence of popular perceptions of economic legitimacy and the role of government arising from the paradigm of competitive advantage.

There is always a temptation for both sides of politics, especially when driven by short term opinion polling, to exploit these views. Parties of the old Left sometimes try to use corporatist industry policies to raise public expectations about the means by which the loss of routine production jobs might be halted. Parties of the Right tend to engage in the rhetoric of small business growth, arguing that the labour market can be cleared only through the growth of private sector employment. They can also be susceptible to the special pleading of the corporate sector for ever more welfare and subsidisation. Both approaches, of course, represent an inadequate response to the issue of unemployment in the new economy. One diverts scarce public resources from the generation of endogenous growth, while also smothering the dynamic process of industry upgrading; the other sells short the direct and essential role of the public sector in resolving the spatial inequities of the labour market.

One of the problems with the economic debate in Australia, especially when placed in the hands of the old ideological divide, is that arguments and issues tend to be reduced to the level of dogma. The debate seems to pivot on whether more or less government intervention is appropriate for all parts of the economy, rather than analysing, issue by issue, the type of policy methods that make most sense. The need to match alternative forms of economic policy, whether relying on market or command methods, against the new geography of capital and the labour market, tends to be overlooked. This is where the flexibility of an institutionalist approach to economic policy can be most beneficial. It has the capacity to apply, from the methods of both the market and the state, a policy mix suited to the split geography of the new economy—that is, the application of new growth and competition policies to the traded sector; plus the use of targeted public sector interventions to overcome the deficiencies of the downstairs labour market. In this fashion, national economic policy can bring together the twin themes of economic reform and adjustment.

First, in response to the upward shift of capital, this approach recognises the high growth/high wage potential of the international transfer of trade and investment, complemented by the shift in economic activity to knowledge-based production. Moreover, it seeks to extend Australia's share of these global benefits and premiums through the nation's commitment to new sources of endogenous growth. This requires a substantial investment in Australia's core economic assets: the quality of our education and research systems; the scope and efficiency of our economic infrastructure; and the extent of our national commitment to savings. It also requires a permanent commitment to upgrading Australia's corporate culture and management through the competitive pressures of an open economy. As Romer has argued:

> Nations that can sustain a policy stance that tolerates or perhaps even fosters the process of creative destruction can count on sustained economic growth that will carry them into the next century. Those that are most successful in creating institutions that foster discovery and innovation will be the worldwide technological leaders. Through mechanisms like free trade and transfers of technology, nations that are less successful in the cultivation and commercial exploitation of science and technology can still follow comfortably along in the wake of the leaders. But nations that try to resist change by protecting inefficient firms, impeding flows of goods and ideas, and making a high level of income an entitlement instead of a reward will slowly be left farther and farther behind.[2]

Second, in the local and regional characteristics of the new labour market, public policy needs to respond to the insecurity generated by an era of permanent economic adjustment. The restructuring of the production system is intensely unsettling for a range of interests in the old economy, inevitably leading to demands for government to protect people from the impact of economic change. This does not require an end to change but rather, the development of new sources of economic security. Governments need to intervene on both sides of the labour market to assist the capacity of the labour force to successfully manage change. This is a basic requirement of the capability paradigm, the interdependence of government and its citizens in ensuring that all parts of society have the capacity to adapt to the demands and opportunities of perpetual change. In Part I, employability security was identified as a critical intervention in the skills and capability of labour. This part of the book has identified two other prerequisites for security in the new labour market: 'earnings security' in the establishment of a living wage and income gain sharing model;

and 'job replacement security' in the creation of new forms of employment on a locational scale.

As enterprises and workers are displaced from the routine production sector, they invariably move into the labour market for in-person services. This, in turn, especially in the weak neighbourhoods, creates downward pressure on wage levels through the over-supply of labour, plus the associated problem of structural unemployment. Two direct forms of government inter-vention are needed to ease the strain of this adjustment process. The first is to guarantee for semi-skilled, low productivity workers a decent and continuous share of the benefits of national income growth. This security in real earnings capacity is made feasible by the heavy segmentation of the labour market and the development of macro wage strategies aimed at a fairer dispersion of income. The second intervention involves the creation of new forms of work and regional development to supplement the demand for labour in poor neighbourhoods. Displaced workers need to have the security of knowing that not only can their skills and employ-ability be upgraded but, within their regional labour market, replacement forms of work are also available.

NATIONAL GAIN SHARING

This policy approach gives rise to a new model of national gain sharing. It deals with the split geography of the market system by focusing on the transmission of income and economic opportunities between the traded and non-traded sectors. In the post-Federation settlement, economic rents and wealth from Australia's primary industries were used to support the income share of secondary industries. In the new economy, the appropriate transmission effect is from internationally competitive enterprises and workers (the top 30 per cent group) to enterprises and workers anchored in the domestic economy (the middle 40 per cent), plus those citizens excluded from economic participation (the bottom 30 per cent). Income premiums earned in the traded sector are distributed to other parts of the economy through the following transmission mechanisms:

- the progressive taxation of consumption (which primarily raises public resources from the expenditure decisions of the top 30 per cent group) allows government to fund programs on both sides of the labour market;
- strong earnings capacity in the upstairs labour market leads to solid employment in downstairs industries, plus facilitates

income gain sharing through the establishment of a living wage system;
- spatially targeted public sector employment programs are able to supplement the demand for labour (primarily in the non-traded sector) in weak neighbourhoods; and
- new forms of economic regulation protect the interests and income share of the local (non-traded) sphere of capital against the market dominance of multinational capital.

Unlike the post-Federation settlement, this model relies heavily on the free movement of trade and investment. Self-evidently, the beneficiaries of national gain sharing—non-traded economic activities—do not require border controls. Indeed, in the new economy, the absolute level of economic rents and prosperity available to the non-traded sector is inexorably linked to the success of the traded sector. Without the foundations of new sources of endogenous growth and investment, there can be no effective gain sharing or transmission effect. This further confirms the folly of the industry welfare approach, especially from a social democratic perspective. It also demonstrates the need for a suitable balance between policies aimed at economic change and growth, and policies framed for the purpose of economic adjustment.

The Australian economy needs to increase its competitive output of tradable commodities to help clear its problems on the external account. Equally, however, it needs to increase its outlays on non-tradable products and services to help clear the labour market. If the former happens at the expense of the latter (that is, a stable level of GDP switches from non-traded to traded output) then the problem of unemployment in the weaker regions will be aggravated. This is why, for instance, the Howard Government's use of contractionary fiscal policy to deal with the current account deficit has been so damaging. If the latter occurs at the expense of the former (expenditure switches to the non-traded sector) then the external account will become an even tougher restriction on the sustainability of national economic growth.[3] This was why the over-heating of the economy in late 1994, coming off the lagged impact of the One Nation program and a series of interest rate reductions, was so undesirable.

These issues confirm the desirability of passive macroeconomic policies and the need to address Australia's structural economic problems by dealing with 'third deficit' issues. New sources of economic growth are needed to concurrently lift the threshold of non-traded consumption and add to the pool of national savings. This creates a virtuous cycle of growth, employment and savings. The role of government is to ensure that the growth process is accompanied by policies of economic adjustment and inclusiveness. The process of 'creative destruction' in a market economy requires public policy to guarantee, on a locational scale, the provision of employability and job replacement security. In particular, government policies aimed at structural reform and enhanced competitiveness, which often alter the skills and location of work, need to be matched by appropriate adjustment strategies.

These policies enable social democracy to bridge the gap between global economic change and its local impact. They apply strategies of national economic leverage to maximise Australia's long term rate of economic growth, while also ensuring that the distributional features of national growth are based on the economics of gain sharing and inclusiveness. They build the legitimacy of public sector action by focusing policy concerns on the adequacy of private sector savings and management methods; plus the development of strategies aimed at resolving the fiscal crisis of the state. They reflect the values of the new radical centre—rewarding work and savings; building the social responsibilities of the corporate sector; expressing society's interdependence in overcoming the problems of economic exclusion and inequality; and devolving many of the labour market programs of government to take account of neighbourhood effects. They demonstrate how the processes of economic change and inclusiveness need to be seen as symbiotic.

Most of all, they give social democracy its best chance to supersede the distributional features of an open economy; and, at least in the distribution of primary goods, set a platform for the attainment of social capability all round. To take Castles' words:

> the only way in which a small country can square the circle of obtaining the economic benefits of competitive trade and protecting the vulnerable is by superseding the market as the source of the distribution of economic rewards to the extent necessary to guarantee all citizens, irrespective of their labour market status, an equitable share in the national product.[4]

Despite the spread of global capital and the shifting sovereignty of the nation state, I would maintain that this goal remains— through the development of appropriate policies for the new economy—within reach of the social democratic project.

PART III

MANAGING THE COMMONS

The core purpose of this book is to examine the policies and structures by which social democracy, responding to the challenges of the post-industrial era, can foster the universal attainment of social capability. This requires all citizens to have available to them certain items of social merit. As Parts I and II have argued, the distribution of income and employment is important for the establishment of minimum standards of material living. Access to a high standard of education is also critical to the capability of individuals and, in aggregate, the nations in which they reside. The satisfaction of this complex form of equality requires the identification of needs in a social context. Social democracy, however, with its attachment to the planning strand of state provision, has clearly struggled to cope with the diversity of individual and community needs in a post-industrial society. It will be argued in this section of the book that its most basic assumptions about the foundations of social provision are also under challenge.

The collective functions of public governance rely not only on the identification of needs, they also rest on the identification of membership. While items of social merit must be made available to the members of society to assist the satisfaction of their needs, they also must be made available in a manner that sustains the very basis of membership. Without mutual membership there can be no mutual provision. The goals of public resource pooling are, therefore, relatively plain. The pool must be managed in a way that not only sustains the resource and maximises the effectiveness of its use, but also ensures that those with access to the resource pool are willing to maintain their contributions to it. The evidence in most Western nations, however, points to a fundamental problem for social democracy in meeting these goals. With the signs of social diversity and fragmentation all round—competing values, competing aspirations, competing lifestyles—a growing number of citizens are declaring their dissatisfaction with the management of the common pool. Their commitment to membership and the maintenance of their contributions appear to be in retreat.

This represents more than just a loss of public trust in the institutions of the state public sector. It also signifies a series of problems with the theory and practice of social justice. The collective wants and needs of a post-industrial society are substantially different to those of the post-war decades. The reasons for belonging and contributing to the common pool are in fundamental transition. The roles and responsibilities of government have become overloaded, giving rise to the fiscal crisis of the state, and the severe rationing of public resources and entitlements. In these circumstances, the effectiveness and sustainability of the pool are showing signs of decline. Social democracy needs to reconstruct, from first principles, a new approach to the management of the public commons. The capability of the citizenry, especially during a time of widespread change and insecurity, relies on rebuilding its common membership and commitment to the goals of public governance.

16

THE THEORY AND PRACTICE OF SOCIAL JUSTICE

The social democratic project has interpreted the work of the state public sector as a social contract. In this fashion, social democracy has moved in the tradition of Locke, Rousseau and Kant, with antecedents as old as the sophists of Greece. Social contract theories represent society as based on an original settlement between the people and government. An agreement is reached among the citizenry about the items required in the conduct and interactions of society, and then the means by which these goods might be provided in common. In this process, it is expected that individuals are prepared to forgo certain personal freedoms to facilitate the advancement of common needs and interests.

To give just three instances: law and order restrains the freedom (in an absolute sense) some individuals might wish to exercise in violating the property rights of others; the coercive practice of taxation converts the freedom of individuals to enjoy all parts of their personal income into a pool of public resources; forestry plans limit the freedom corporations might use to maximise private economic gain at the expense of a scarce public resource. It should not be thought, however, that the social contract negates freedoms without also creating them in other socially useful ways. In the three instances above, these are: the freedom to enjoy property rights without violation; freedoms associated with the well-being many citizens derive from the tax/transfer system; the freedom each generation holds to enjoy carefully preserved natural resources. These examples draw the distinction between negative and positive freedoms under the governance of a social contract.

RAWLSIAN SOCIAL JUSTICE

The social contract features of the Western democratic system, at least in their original purpose and theory, represent an expression of common will. Whereas totalitarianism, for instance, relies on tyranny and social oppression to force a contract of governance onto society, the legitimacy of democratic government relies on the consent of the governed to convert personal freedoms into shared gains. Social democracy has attempted to legitimise a social contract founded on notions of fairness and social justice. The terms and conditions of this ideology are best understood from the work of John Rawls, who has profoundly influenced social democratic thinking through the development of his theory of justice.[1]

Rawls argues that the principles of justice are those that would be agreed to by rational citizens calculating their own interests from a position of relative ignorance. That is, they do not know enough about themselves, their background, personal capability or position in society to know how the principles decided on would affect them in practice. This is the Rawlsian 'veil of ignorance' from which an abstract theory of social justice can be constructed. In the development of the principles of justice, no citizen is necessarily advantaged or disadvantaged by the outcome of natural chance or social circumstances. Rawls assesses this initial situation as 'fair between individuals as moral persons, that is, as rational beings with their own ends and capable of a sense of justice'.[2] The fairness of the original position gives rise to an interpretation of justice as fairness.

In this fashion, Rawls sets aside the utilitarianism of the classical liberals—Hume, Smith, Bentham and Mill. Once the principles of justice are understood from an original agreement in a situation of equality, citizens become much more than functional maximisers of personal utility. They are no longer isolated from an appreciation of the common good. As Rawls argues:

> it hardly seems likely that persons who view themselves as equals, entitled to press their claims upon one another, would agree to a principle which may require lesser life prospects for some simply for the sake of a greater sum of advantages enjoyed by others. Since each desires to protect his interests, his capacity to advance his conception of the good, no one has a reason to acquiesce in an enduring loss for himself in order to bring about a greater net balance of satisfaction . . . Thus it seems that the principle of utility is incompatible with the conception of social cooperation among equals for mutual advantage. It appears to be

inconsistent with the idea of reciprocity implicit in the notion of a well-ordered society.[3]

Rather than pursuing utility, narrowly defined, Rawls maintains that rational persons, taking choices from behind the veil of ignorance, would arrive at two core principles of social justice. First, equality in the assignment of basic rights and duties, which is essential as a safeguard against the accidents of natural endowment and social contingency. Second, social and economic inequalities are deemed to be just only if they result in compensating benefits for all citizens, particularly the disadvantaged, and only if the positions of advantage are attained by way of competition under systems of equal opportunity.

It is not difficult to understand, given the Rawlsian framework, how citizens might arrive at these choices as the basis of a socially just contract with the state public sector. Uncertainty about the future can only be rationally countered by guaranteeing for each citizen a threshold of material well-being, personal liberty and social opportunity, provided for from the common pooling of each citizen's resources. In circumstances when, such as in Rawls' original position, all citizens are made to deal with uncertainty, these guarantees take the form of universal rights, delivered in common through the universal obligations of the state. Hence the principles of Rawlsian social justice, justifying the need for public universality, rely on the universal spread of uncertainty among the citizenry.

This theory of social justice has emerged as a common expression of the social democratic ideal. Unlike other forms of socialism—such as Marxism, with a focus on equality through ownership of the means of production—social democracy has pursued a moral code relying on equal rights and obligations, especially an obligation on citizens to cater for the interests of others. This form of social contracting seeks to express interests held in common, using the assumption—under conditions of uncertainty in an individual's natural endowments, economic outcomes and social behaviour—that interests held apart between citizens today can just as easily be interests shared among citizens tomorrow. The uncertainty of social change is used to legitimise the collective functions of the state.

THE SOCIAL CONTRACT IN PRACTICE

As an abstract expression of the principles on which a just society might rely, it is difficult—morally and intellectually—to find fault in the Rawlsian framework and its construction of the social democratic project. Less favourably, however, social contracts are not framed and nor do they function by theory alone. The work of political movements and politicians committed to a just society involves narrowing the gap between social democracy as an ideal and the terms and conditions of the social contract in practice. Unhappily, the evidence in Australia and most other Western nations points to the gap widening, not closing, with signs of crisis in the effectiveness of the broad welfare state. Social democracy needs to be able to adapt to these trends and reformulate the relationship between social justice theory and the practical application of a just social contract.

An appropriate starting point is to qualify several aspects of the Rawlsian framework. First, it must be understood that the consequences of social justice theory are inherently dynamic. As societies change, as they alter their norms for social wants and needs, so too must a socially just contract change. It is not possible to assume that social justice principles automatically adjust to the change process and simply strike a new equilibrium for the practical consequences of a just society. The relationship between theory and practice is never this plain. In Rawls' conception of social justice, primary goods—liberty and opportunity, income and wealth, and the bases of self-respect (itself determined by society's declaration of equal rights and opportunities)—are to be distributed equally unless an unequal distribution of any, or all, of these goods is to everyone's advantage. Injustice, then, is understood as inequality not held to the benefit of all.[4] Primary goods are understood to be those things that every rational person is presumed to want. As wants change, no matter how rationally defined, so too must a just social contract be reformed.

An obvious catalyst for the changing nature of social wants is technological progress. For instance, improvements in health technology have had profound ramifications for the public provision of health care. Similarly, advances in information technology are likely to revolutionise the provision of public education. The emergence of modes of high speed travel have clearly altered social expectations and wants for the provision of public transport and infrastructure. In each of these areas, indeed throughout the work of the state public sector, the threshold of public wants has risen this century.

It is, after all, only rational for each citizen to want the highest standard of health care, education, transport, housing, community services and recreation that technology can facilitate. Not so easy in our modern democracies, of course, has been the task of funding a higher plane of social wants through the public resources of the state. Rawls, quite rightly, points out that, at least theoretically,

'by giving up some of their fundamental liberties men are sufficiently compensated by the resulting social and economic gains'.[5]
Firm evidence of a fiscal crisis of the state, however, indicates that
citizens are not as prepared as they might be, at least by the
standards of social democracy, to trade away their loss of financial
liberty for gains in public provision. This is a sign that changes to
the task of social contracting, driven by new technology and new
public wants, have widened the gap between the theory and practice of social justice.

Further, it cannot be assumed that progress towards a just
society will be without flow-on consequences for other parts of the
social contract. This point has been relevant to the overload of the
modern state. For instance, it is reasonable to suggest that the
wider application of rights in education has created a higher level
of wants for other learning amenities, such as public libraries.
Equally, progress towards the equal rights of women in the labour
force has led to public consideration of a new set of rights in child
care and family support. Invariably the application of social justice
principles to the social contract can take on the features of chaos
theory: action and reaction do not have a simple, linear relationship. Reactions are often skewed by consequences in other parts
of the social contract. To use the example of women's rights, some
of the progress towards universality in recent decades now appears
to be threatened by morally conservative opinion, critical of the
public costs of child care and changes to the family unit. A key
challenge for the social democratic project is to adapt effectively
to the dynamic features of social wants, arrived at by citizens (either
by rational or irrational means).

This leads to a second qualification of the Rawlsian theory of
social justice—the difficulty in imagining a social contract devised
by an unsituated set of contractors (not knowing their place in
society). By any practical purpose, no citizen's view of society and
their future interests can be fully obscured by a veil of ignorance.
As Rawls himself writes, 'no society can, of course, be a scheme
of cooperation which men enter voluntarily in a literal sense; each
person finds himself placed at birth in some particular position in
some particular society, and the nature of this position materially
affects his life prospects'.[6] The extent to which citizens might freely
and voluntarily adopt the social contract of a just society are
essentially left to circumstance and the practical work of social
democracy.

Clearly, however, the veil of ignorance is an important consideration in the application of this task. To the extent to which no
citizen can have full certainty about his or her future prospects,
the theory of justice has value. To the extent to which uncertainty

is a feature of society, the logic of collective action, based on a common appreciation of shared interests, is irresistible. This proposition immediately raises a question of great importance. If, as was argued earlier and seems widely accepted, the modern era of globalisation is associated with new tiers of economic and social uncertainty, why does the practice of collective action everywhere appear to be shrinking—not just from public universities, public schools, public health and public welfare—but from the very foundations of shared interests and common responsibility? Why is it in so much of our public morality, the idea of helping disadvantaged people has come to be seen by so many as adverse to the public interest? What has happened for the theory of social justice to appear to be falling so far short in practice?

These are matters best understood from the third and final qualification arising from Rawls' work. It may be that the rational choices of citizens under conditions of overloaded government are inconsistent with the logic of social justice expressed through collective action. Rawls' theory assumes that the unsituated citizenry has no knowledge or experience of the methods and performance of government. It is chartered with constructing a theory of social justice, not just from first principles but also from year zero. Rawls implicitly assumes an equilibrium between social wants dealing with the contingencies of uncertainty and the capacity of the state to raise resources for public purposes. His social contract precludes the possibility of citizens, acting on their accumulated knowledge of how government works, engaging in a contest for the allocation of scarce public resources.

This framework assumes that citizens will view the state apparatus through the prism of win–win game theory; that is, no action of the state harms the interests of any of its citizens. In practice, of course, the work of the modern state—especially with the overloaded features of government in an open economy—is understood by most citizens as representing a zero-sum game. The state has become a rationer of scarce public resources, struggling to cope with the growing needs of its citizens and public demands for new and improved measures combating socioeconomic uncertainty. In the public arena, government has become a contest for entitlements among competing interests and social segments.

In these circumstances, the rational choices of citizens are very different to those postulated behind the Rawlsian veil of ignorance. Whenever the work of the state is viewed through the parameters of a zero-sum game, the logic of collective action is significantly weakened. Citizens are less likely to support the practice of collective provision if they perceive, in the distribution of entitlements, a likelihood that their particular needs will be overlooked or even damaged, especially when assessed against the opportunity cost of putting their public revenue contribution to personal use. The rationing of public resources by the state diminishes large slabs of the rationale for collective action. This process, contrary to the Rawlsian theory, is especially acute during an era of widespread social and economic insecurity. Without significant doses of altruism, citizens are not likely to engage in the logic of collective action unless the common pool of resources addresses their own sources of lifetime uncertainty. The common inevitably retreats to the protection of self-interest. Individualism replaces collectivism as a common method for combating insecurity.

From its original position, Rawls attempts to advance his work by accommodating the importance of social values and behaviour. This framework, however, does not address the dilemma of a social contract framed around zero-sum choices. Rather, it relies on the 'natural sociability' of humankind to construct an 'overlapping consensus' around the virtues of social justice.[7] Under conditions of socioeconomic insecurity and overloaded government, this is little more than an exercise in wishful thinking. Sociability is moulded as much by the circumstances and choices available to the citizenry as by any of the innate characteristics of people. Acute public sector rationing effectively shatters Rawls' overlapping consensus and replaces it with a divisive contest for scarce public entitlements. This also seems to explain, from recent evidence and measures of public opinion, the erosion of the social democratic consensus in Australia, an issue to which the next chapter turns.

17

QUESTIONS OF
LEGITIMACY

After a decade of economic and social restructuring we have now entered a period of political restructuring. As noted in chapter 10, we have become a 30/40/30 society: 30 per cent of citizens with competitive skills, high productivity and growing incomes; another 40 per cent who have jobs but not job security—a newly insecure, middle group who face the uncertainty of economic restructuring and reskilling; plus a bottom 30 per cent of citizens outside the production process—the unemployed, chronically ill and elderly. This new structure is challenging many of the values and assumptions on which the inclusiveness of our society has been based. Conventional views about power and elitism (that the greatest threat to the working class comes from unbridled privilege and wealth) have been replaced by the advent of downwards envy.

A growing proportion of newly insecure workers see their interests being threatened, not from people and groups above them on the social ladder, but from below: welfare recipients, the unemployed, single mums and so on—generally people outside the system of production. This involves a perception of double standards in the entitlements system of the welfare state by a middle group, who are themselves exposed to continuous change and uncertainty in the workplace, while they perceive that other citizens are the recipients of guaranteed government income. In so much of the public arena—talkback radio, tabloid TV, the exchange of political views—Australians have turned from cutting down tall poppies to a punishing mood of small poppy resentment. This mood has aggravated a latent source of social tension: those who add value to the economy and pay their taxes increasingly resent the transfer of these resources to recipients not involved in the production process. This represents a basic redefinition of society's categorisation of deserving and undeserving citizens.

Notions of exploitation and exclusion have been superseded by the distributive features and morality of 'entitlement politics'. Within this paradigm, citizens' entitlements are defined more by their contribution to the production system than by personal circumstances of need and deprivation.

WINNERS AND LOSERS

Economic restructuring seems to have sharpened the divide between economic winners and losers in our society. As the winners, a minor yet powerful section of the economy, have grown more self-assured about their competitive success, they have been less willing to personally contribute to the common pool of public resources. This is akin to lifting the Rawlsian veil of ignorance on the work of the state public sector. These trends are doubly dangerous for the egalitarianism of society. Not only does the unveiled constituency question the merits of inclusiveness and the work of the welfare state, it also gives little credit to the role of the public sector. As a group, symbolic analysts are more likely to credit their own hard work, industry and skills for their economic success, rather than acknowledge any contribution by government.

In the old economy, with standardised skills and employment all round, economic interests were shared across a wider band of the citizenry. In the new economy, skills and interests are more sharply segmented. It is harder for the state to identify interests and values held in common. As Reich has asked, 'what do we owe one another as members of the same society when we no longer inhabit the same economy?'[1] This dilemma appears to have prompted the growth of downwards envy among the newly insecure, middle group in society, plus the creation of what Galbraith has termed a 'culture of contentment' among the band of economic winners.[2]

Significant changes in the nature of mass communications appear to have aggravated each of these trends. The cohesiveness of our public morality has been weakened in tandem with the rise of the electronic media. In many respects we have become an electronic democracy, with the public forum shifting from parliament to the air-waves. Television and, to some extent, radio, rely on conflict and confrontation as the basis of popular entertainment: portraying winners and losers, majority and minority interests in every story. The mass media needs to be understood as another type of commerce, pitching its appeal at popular forms of entertainment. Within this framework, politics is presented as info-tainment, while public issues are portrayed solely through a prism of conflict. This is why the electronic media spend so much time stereotyping unemployed people, welfare recipients and other subjects of downwards envy. Just as the Romans had the Colosseum, and Tudor England the village square stocks, we have ACA with Ray.[3]

John Howard is the first Australian political leader to set about the active exploitation of these trends. Never before has an Australian government made a virtue of the politics of downwards envy. Each of the deliberate Cabinet leaks and setpiece media announcements of the Howard Government has been designed to punish so-called (unproductive and undeserving) minorities: restrictions on migrant benefits, cuts to universities and their students, reductions in Aboriginal funding, diarising the dole plus working for it. This is what the Coalition parties mean by mainstream values. Their policies are not aimed at positively assisting insecure workers. (Indeed, the promotion of individual employment contracts and social wage cuts can only add to economic and social insecurity.) Rather, the government's electoral strategy is to target the groups and interests perceived by the middle segment of society as adding to socioeconomic insecurity. As much as members of the middle group feel threatened by people and interests below them on the social ladder, Howard will seek to position himself as their champion, echoing their views and dealing with perceived threats. In terms of the overload on government, the Coalition strategy declares the contest for entitlements in favour of 'mainstream battlers' at the expense of so-termed minorities.

LEGITIMACY OF THE WELFARE STATE

Political restructuring of this kind challenges not only the legitimacy of the post-war welfare state but also the effectiveness of the ALP. Ultimately, Labor's hopes for a more just society rely on a certain judgment about human values: the belief that while people will always defend their own interests, they also care enough about the society in which they live to advance the interests of others, particularly the needy and disadvantaged. Labor has always sought vindication of this judgment in the Australian claim to egalitarianism and a fair go for all. The rise of downwards envy, however, threatens the core assumptions on which the social democratic project has been based.

In this respect, three challenges have entered the frontline of Labor politics. First, how to strengthen the legitimacy of the welfare state by strengthening the effectiveness of its programs and outcomes. Ultimately, the critics of the social safety net can only be answered by ensuring that welfare works. Second, how to convince the middle group that the greatest threat to its interests comes from the top of the social ladder, not the bottom. Some of the policy implications of this approach have been addressed in previous chapters, especially in the discussion of the social responsibilities of the corporate sector. Combating insecurity often involves countering the interests of global capital. Third, how to resolve the overload of government and restore the sound management of the public commons. This is the key to reconstructing a public consensus around the virtues of social justice.

It also represents a silver bullet guiding Labor's electoral prospects. It highlights the irony by which Federal Labor, having been elected in 1983 on a platform of national reconciliation and consensus, was voted out amid claims of social fragmentation and partisanship towards sectional interests. Labor now needs to return the state public sector, in perception and substance, to a genuinely public purpose. Government needs to represent something more than a scramble for entitlements from which conservative politicians can engage in an ethos of divide and rule. On each of the issues in Australian politics conveying downwards envy, the Coalition tactic is to split Labor's constituency; that is, to force a choice between the competing interests of the top 30 per cent of society (outward looking symbolic analysts), and the middle 40 per cent (more socially conservative workers). These tensions, whether to Labor's liking or not, are real enough and need to be resolved. It is plainly not practical to run a political movement by trading away support, issue by issue, among constituent groups and interests. As ever, social democracy requires a public interest framework within which the competing values and needs of a pluralist society can be dealt with justly.

By the end of its thirteen years in opposition, the Coalition was able to craft a political strategy but not a strategy for governance. In government, Howard's tactics have been brutally simple: to use the public contest for scarce public resources during an era of economic uncertainty as a way of dividing the nation politically. This is the politics of the wedge: to set so-termed mainstream battlers against a host of minor streams. It echoes the type of advice Pat Buchanan forwarded for Richard Nixon's consideration in the late 1960s. 'We should tear the country in two', Buchanan wrote in a memo to the President, 'and then pick up the biggest half'.[4] Labor requires new principles to guide the work of social justice and help rebuild a common sense of public morality. It needs to strengthen the citizenry's commitment to membership and support of the public commons.

A starting point is to deal with the overload of government and problems of public resource rationing. This reflects the central paradox of the state in an open society: it has so many more functions and responsibilities to discharge, yet there are clear restrictions on the size of the public resource pool. This tension, in part, has forced the rationalisation of public sector finances through policies of privatisation, corporatisation, user pays and higher debt. It has also led to a perception that governments are now primarily concerned with the arbitration of competing public interest and rationing of scarce resources. Common ground has collapsed into a contest of targeted entitlements. Everywhere in the public arena, citizens seem to be seeking more assistance to combat the spread of social and economic insecurity.

18

OVERLOADED GOVERNMENT

Even though in an open economy more citizens rely on government to offset the impact of economic competition, government itself faces new restrictions on its capacity to finance additional commitments. The public sector is now expected to fund the cost of the competitive advantage paradigm. Workers facing economic insecurity, understandably enough, also place a higher call on the resources of government for income support. Similarly, the public sector faces mounting fiscal pressures in meeting the needs of citizens excluded from the production process, most notably from an ageing society and from the public costs of high structural unemployment. Concurrently on the revenue side, the taxation coverage of government is in need of repair. A significant structural gap has arisen between the revenue raising capacities of the state and the public outlays required to fund social democratic programs, universal service access, and the social costs of economic restructuring.

The fiscal crisis of the state is undermining the tax/transfer systems of social democracy. As the focus of taxation internationally has shifted from earnings to downstream questions of expenditure and savings, most governments are finding it harder to rely on tax progressivity as the basis of their redistributive functions. On the outlays side, the original purpose and relevance of universality is now being challenged. During the long economic boom of the 1950s and 1960s it was assumed that universal services and entitlements could effectively supplement the standardised, basic wage of a broad band of workers. In an open economy, however, internationally competitive capital and labour (perhaps one-third of society) are able to access these services through private income rather than public provision. Across the public sector this trend has strengthened the case for targeted entitlements and service provision.

New social justice strategies need to resolve these tensions and effectively tackle the overload of government. A starting point is an inventory or stocktake of the type of service provision most likely to deliver equity in an open economy. Clearly, emphasis needs to be given to the state functions most likely to assist in the satisfaction of social capability. By these priorities, an assessment can be made of the responsibilities best left with the individual, set apart from responsibilities best discharged by the collective provision of the public sector either through state or non-state institutions. Within the work of government a judgment then has to be made about the appropriate mix of means testing, targeting and free universal provision. In Australia this task has been made more urgent by the Howard Government's fiscal consolidation program, and its concerted attack on the principles of universal access, most notably in health, higher education and child care services. These policies are likely to create tiers of social opportunity based on personal income and wealth, rather than on social merit and need.

POLICY INCREMENTALISM

One of the problems with the social democratic project has been its incremental approach to the work of government. Since the Second World War, in most Western nations, new responsibilities have been loaded onto the role of government without due consideration of their impact, taken in totality. New concepts of equality, largely in response to changing social wants, have given the state additional tiers of fiscal responsibility. The welfare state commenced with an emphasis on the quantities of life: primary goods—such as food, clothes and shelter—provided for through an adequate level of disposable income and financial assets. This involved the establishment of income support programs and the state's interest in employment creation. The second tier of programs concerned the qualities of life that go beyond a basic threshold of material well-being; that is, skills and learning, health care quality, recreational interests and a range of creative arts. In many ways these reflect wants arising from the emergence of cognitive skills and abstract knowledge as items of social worth. The third and final tier, arising primarily since the 1970s, has sought the involvement of the state public sector in the behavioural characteristics of life—the relatively fixed characteristics of people which help to fashion the context of social interaction. These features include gender, sexuality, culture, race, nationalism, language plus personal values. This new tier of state activism has involved programs such as affirmative action, multicultural funding, cultural development and national identity.

The social democratic project is now groaning under the accumulated weight of these layers of equality and public sector commitments. This highlights the political folly of incrementalism: drawing on the common pool of resources without adequately tending to the sustainability of the commons. The contemporary work of the state has been reduced to a public contest for the allocation of scarce resources and entitlements. The logic of collective action, as a statement of moral value and social inclusiveness, has been much diminished in our public culture. Downwards envy has inverted a large slab of the public's appreciation of social justice and progressively undermined the legitimacy of the welfare state.

ZERO-SUM CHOICES

Unguarded incrementalism, over time, can also produce contradictions in the construction of equity programs. New concepts and tiers of equality can unwittingly conflict with earlier layers of state activism. This is especially the case under conditions of overloaded government. New programs have a clear opportunity cost, expressed in the priority which could otherwise be given to existing programs. For instance, public funds allocated to measures dealing with the behavioural characteristics of life have been criticised by a large number of people who, in dealing with insecurity in their own personal circumstances, have set a far higher priority on the quantities and qualities of life. Sound social democratic practice needs to avoid zero-sum choices in the construction of the social contract. Programs of positive discrimination—a prominent part of the recent tier of state activism—make this point clearly. By definition, these measures establish a new set of rights for certain categories of citizens at the expense of others. It is not possible to set quotas or reserve places for one group of citizens, however, without concurrently diminishing the opportunities available to the remainder of society.

Positive discrimination is indicative of the substantial recasting of the rights agenda of liberal democracy. In their original form, the rights of citizens were framed in a defensive fashion; that is, they were defined in terms of the legal protection by which citizens could preserve their freedoms and interests against the oppression of others. These rights included freedom of speech and assembly, freedom under the rule of law from arbitrary arrest and intimidation, refinement of the rights to hold property, the rights of a free democracy and basic protection against various forms of discrimination. Defensive rights are highly valued within both the social democratic and liberal traditions. Without the protection of the state, the exercise of basic liberties would constitute a primary source of uncertainty for all citizens. None of us could guarantee our right to core elements of participation in a free society without fear of oppression and exploitation. Hence, one of the defining features of the Rawlsian theory of social justice is the establishment of the equal liberties of citizenship. In classical liberalism these rights were identified as an article of faith. For instance, in John Stuart Mill's famous formulation:

> The sole end for which mankind are warranted individually or collectively in interfering with the liberty of any of their number is self-protection. That the only purpose for which power can be rightfully exercised over any member of a civilised community is to prevent harm to others.[1]

In recent decades, however, social democratic policy has featured a fresh generation of rights, based on the establishment of positive discrimination for people displaying various segment-of-life characteristics. Supporters of this approach argue that it is no longer sufficient to assert an equality of rights under the rule of law. In circumstances where negative discrimination and inequality remain entrenched, affirmative action and other special programs have been introduced. A defining feature of this approach is the way it absents issues of socioeconomic background from the construction of equity programs.[2]

No one portion of a person's nature or circumstances, in isolation, can offer an adequate explanation of life's deprivations. Poverty is a process, not an isolated event or personal characteristic. It reflects a complex range of factors leading to capability failure. From first principles, questions of advantage and disadvantage are formed from socioeconomic circumstance: the interaction of an individual's material well-being, skills and motivations with prevailing conditions of social opportunity. The sterile isolation and segmentation of personal characteristics are poor ways to understand this process. Likewise, the construction of categories and public programs around these segments-of-life is a poor way to deal with the processes of socioeconomic disadvantage and capability failure.

These measures also suffer from the dilemma of a zero-sum game. In the execution of positive discrimination policies there are clearly defined winners and losers. Behind a veil of ignorance there is no rational reason why an unsituated citizen would regard these policies as socially just; citizens could just as easily benefit from them in the future as they might suffer. With the veil fully or partially lifted under conditions of overloaded government, these policies, understandably enough, can cause considerable resentment about the terms and conditions of the social contract. In dealing with the contingencies of life, zero-sum parameters are an ineffective means for the development of social justice strategies.

Each of these tensions points to the need for rethinking the social democratic project from first principles—that is, to work back through the accumulated layers of equality and state activism and, from a greenfields stance, reconstruct an appropriate role for government in an open society. This means dealing with questions of globalisation and dynamic social change without the burdens of incremental policy making. Social democracy needs to judge new policy proposals, not only for their good intentions, but also their sustainability within systems of public provision. For Australian Labor, rebuilding after its heavy election defeat in 1996, greenfields thinking is an essential discipline. It is simply not possible to resolve the dilemmas of downwards envy and overloaded government without returning the practice of social justice to first principles. The Howard Government's wedge issue politics can not be countered without the development of clear public interest considerations to guide the work of the public sector.

19

FIRST PRINCIPLES

The theory of social justice points to the importance of uncertainty. Citizens are most likely to want to pool their resources and deal with each other fairly if such action addresses their common interest in dealing with the uncertainties of life. The logic of collective action is directed at the contingencies of change. For unsituated citizens this framework makes sense because all aspects of their life, self-evidently, are uncertain. The lifting of the veil of ignorance, however, forces new disciplines onto the methods by which collective action might be implemented. The construction of social justice, for citizens who know their situation in society, narrows to a set of principles dealing with the primary sources of life's insecurity.

Questions of security and certainty are fundamental to the human condition. Without a sense of certainty about our place in society and what the future might hold, none of us can fulfil life's quest for recognition and self-esteem. Anxiety is the natural antithesis of personal dignity and self-respect. Without a sense of control over the things happening within life's circle, the human condition is much diminished. Esteem, dignity and confidence are replaced by insecurity and, inevitably enough, the search for expressions of self-interest, narrowly defined. As the Australian social commentator Hugh Mackay has written:

> Insecurity breeds our disproportionate fear of crime and violence.
> It erodes our sense of trust in institutions and each other. It fuels
> our stress and our cynicism and makes us vulnerable to the siren
> song of nostalgia. It makes us tougher, less compassionate, less
> tolerant . . . [it turns our morality inwards], from social justice to
> 'real justice'; that is, each citizen starts to treat their attitudes and
> values as if they are the only ones that should be taken seriously.[1]

This is not to suggest, of course, that people are not capable of handling change. Change and insecurity are very different entities. Insecurity arises when the change process sits outside the control and interests of the individual. It challenges one's worth and threatens anxiety. By contrast, self-esteem and recognition are enhanced by individuals moulding the change process to their personal satisfaction and needs. Social justice programs should aim to deal with insecurity, not change *per se*. It is the way of the conservative to instinctively resist change and all its potential for social progress. In any case, as Churchill once suggested, the only social institution ever likely to successfully resist change is to be found at the graveyard.

ADDRESSING INSECURITY

From these parameters, the purpose of social justice in practice must be to address the primary sources of insecurity in society. This process, of course, is inherently dynamic, moulded by circumstance and socioeconomic structures. The first principles of social fairness are plainly unsuited to the static equilibrium analysis advanced by Rawls and many other social democratic thinkers. Social justice strategies need to be able to adapt, in their interaction with the citizenry, to changing sources of insecurity. Under conditions of economic globalisation, insecurity presents itself, first and foremost, in the economic domain. The capacity of each citizen to engage themselves in the production system is an endemic source of uncertainty in an open economy. This positions issues of gainful employment, income support and skills development at the heart of an alert social democratic agenda.

The widespread nature of economic insecurity in a globalised economy provides a compelling source of logic and legitimacy for the benefits of state action. If only a minority of citizens—the owners of global capital and skilled knowledge workers—is likely to find opportunities (as opposed to threats) in the internationalisation of capital, then for a good proportion of society, an enduring answer to economic insecurity most likely lies in the collective. Sufficient incentives exist, therefore, for society to protect itself against the exigencies of economic change and provide each of its citizens with an acceptable threshold of material well-being. This is the basis of a socially just contract, made possible by the way in which a large proportion of citizens are unsituated with regard to their prospects in a globalised economic environment. It makes sense of the three forms of economic security advanced earlier in the book: employability security in the enhancement of skills;

earnings security in a formalised system of income gain sharing; and job replacement security in state-led solutions to the spatial features of unemployment.

The other basic source of insecurity in our society concerns the physical well-being or health of each citizen. The public sector has had a long standing role as an insurer and provider against temporary ill-health, accidents, disability and chronic illnesses. It has also enacted measures aimed at protecting the standard of environmental health. These are, obviously enough, core state responsibilities as citizens deal with the uncertainties associated with their quality of life. Moreover, with the ageing demographics of society, the public sector will need to expand its role as an insurer and provider of the various forms of aged care. In both health and aged care services, the private sector has generally struggled to cope with the risk management features of universal pooling. It also tends to produce unacceptable externalities (indirect consequences) in the impact of economic activities on the physical environment.

It follows from this analysis that social justice strategies will be much less effective when aimed at the relative certainties of life. This highlights the problem with state activism concerning segment-of-life characteristics. Situated citizens obviously know their own race, nationality, gender, culture and personal identity. Indeed, these features represent the few remaining certainties of life left to us in an open society. The development of programs dealing with life's behavioural characteristics by the principles of positive discrimination serves primarily to create zero-sum options in the social contract.

As noted earlier, there is no rational basis on which unsituated citizens would regard these policies as socially just. They might just as readily be disadvantaged as advantaged by them. Moreover, for most citizens in practice—knowing their situation in society and expecting the state, first and foremost, to deal with the pressing issues of socioeconomic insecurity—these programs provoke considerable resentment. They are, unfortunately enough, given their initial purpose in the programs of social democracy, a leading cause of downwards envy. Initiatives intended to deal with a perceived tier of disadvantage in society have, in practice, passed down the path of folly. This is because their consequences, under conditions of overloaded government, are inconsistent with the logic of collective action. Social justice is reduced to a zero-sum contest between winners and losers designated, not by the uncertainties of life, but by personal characteristics which are, of course, relatively certain and secure in life. Better results can be achieved by building the socioeconomic capabilities of the citizenry and maintaining a strong set of state sanctions against negative discrimination.

ONE SIZE NO LONGER FITS ALL

Definitions of social justice should not seek to break society into a set of categories disconnected from the primary conditions of socioeconomic circumstance and uncertainty. In the popular culture this does not build confidence in the inclusiveness of the commons. Labor's starting point must be socioeconomic status and capacity, not a loose assumption that people sharing a certain segment-of-life characteristic also share the same access to economic and social resources. The public sector must approach the problems of disadvantage in a customised way, without the inadequacies of standardised categories. In a fundamentally diverse society, one size or category no longer fits all.

It is increasingly difficult for governments to generalise about the causes of skill deficiency. For instance, equity programs for higher education in Australia assume an inadequate level of access for non-English-speaking background (NESB) people, particularly newly arrived migrants. In practice, however, given the diversity of parenting and work ethics among different cultural groups, young NESB people have higher participation rates than English-speaking background people. In many cases, such as found with Chinese, Korean and Vietnamese speakers, the level of participation is strikingly high.[2] With the diversification of skills and socioeconomic background in the new economy, the broad banding of government programs has become less effective. Diversity of this kind requires customisation in the relationship between citizens and the state. In a dynamic society, with changing wants and needs, the planning strand of social democracy now sits outside the domain of sound social justice principles.

Segment-of-life categories are a poor guide to socioeconomic outcomes. To use another example from the multiculturalism debate, there is, in practice, enormous diversity among NESB people, depending on their age, generation of residency, country of origin, cultural traits and economic status. A non-English-speaking background itself does not indicate a single, homogenous level of disadvantage in English language skills. Among first generation migrants to Australia, for example, the use of English in the home varies between the Dutch (57.8 per cent of families) and Taiwanese (2.9 per cent), and at the second generation, between the Dutch (95 per cent) and Greeks (21.8 per cent).[3] Skill diversity of this kind is not suited to a one-size-fits-all approach to public administration. Indeed, governments no longer give their best support to multiculturalism (itself based on the virtues of diversity) through monolithic programs and categories which, in their delivery, end up defying diversity.

These issues also point to the importance of the social capability paradigm. Accumulated tiers of equity programs have left social democracy without a satisfactory definition of what it means by equality in practice. The habit of incrementally layering new programs on top of the old has led to conflicting equity goals and the creation of zero-sum choices. The conceptualisation of social capability helps to return social democracy to a sustainable theory of equality. It cuts through the multi-layering of state programs and rationalises social democratic goals into a single notion of equality in practice. It also makes plain the link between issues of security and the attainment of social capability. In a post-industrial society, where economic and social change abounds, the extent of personal capability is virtually synonymous with an individual's capacity to cope with change. Social wants, properly understood, bind social capability and security together.

From this approach to social justice, the work of government is readily apparent. The pooling of public resources aims at resolving each of the core issues of insecurity. Matters of economic security and health-related services have been highlighted above. Obviously the functions of the state in national security (defence and related services), and personal and property security (through law and order services), are also critical. Outside these purposes, however, the work of government is likely to represent a second order priority. Some public outlays, especially with regard to segment-of-life programs, are likely to add to the overload of government without necessarily achieving any of the goals of social justice. The design of state institutions, in the management of the commons, needs to be arranged in a manner that fosters and sustains the logic of collective action according to these priorities. This understanding of social justice and its attendant public administration establishes a framework by which the ALP can apply public or national interest tests to the formulation of policy. It points the way forward to a sustainable format for social democracy.

20

THE PUBLIC
COMMONS

Principles of fairness are not well served by government's role as a heavy rationer of public resources. In many respects, this is a challenge of institutional design. It is possible to understand the work and shortcomings of the modern welfare state by comparing it to the task of managing a mass commons—that is, the circumstances in which a finite pool of common resources are managed to maximise returns to each of those with rights of usage on the commons. In pure form, the welfare state involves a large-scale pooling of resources and risks by citizens, not just now but across several generations. Each of us pays to the state part of our surplus income, with an expectation that it will assist with each of the needs and contingencies of life that we, as individuals, cannot deal with effectively. It is assumed that our act of good faith in contributing to the common pool will be reciprocated, with some degree of consistency, even when our contributions have ceased.

The classic commons is a piece of land,[1] the use of which is controlled by the principles of collective interest rather than private property. The successful management of the commons poses certain dilemmas of institutional design and regulation. These relate to questions of how to ration use among those with access rights, and how to balance the benefits of immediate use against the opportunity cost of future resource depletion. Garrett Hardin has described the dilemma of uncontrolled over-use as the tragedy of the commons. Take the circumstance of open grazing rights for all herders. No one can limit grazing rights by anyone else's flock. If one herder alone limits his use of the commons, he alone loses. It is, therefore, in the interests, narrowly defined, of all herders to maximise their grazing. Hardin concludes:

therein is the tragedy. Each man is locked into a system that compels him to increase his herd without limit—in a world that is limited. Ruin is the destination toward which all men rush, each pursuing his own best interest in a society that believes in the freedom of the commons.[2]

Critically, this is not an argument against the commons, but rather the absolute freedom of each individual to draw on its resources. It is in the interests of those who access and control the commons to regulate its use. The collective interest, a healthy commons available to all generations, can only be advanced by restricting the freedoms attached to individual interests. The character of these restrictions will determine the fairness and sustainability of the use of the commons.

Both the welfare state and the commons are finite yet renewable resource pools to which the tragedy of overloaded use can apply. Hence the study of the management principles of the commons can assist with the positive reform of the welfare state. Two issues are particularly relevant: the question of intergenerational equity and the question of how best to design the institutional features of a common resource pool. If not properly handled, both matters can contribute to the institutional failure and decline of the commons.

INTERGENERATIONAL EQUITY

The question of intergenerational fairness in welfare is closely linked to the problem of the fiscal crisis of the state. If one or several consecutive generations draws more from the common pool than they contribute then this obviously increases the burden for future generations. The burden is plainly expressed through mounting levels of public indebtedness and/or diminishing returns and entitlements. If one generation draws too heavily on the commons it can reduce the resource management of future generations to a point of unsustainability. The New Zealand historian, David Thomson, has made this point well in his analysis of the trans-Tasman welfare state:

Resources are not proving to be 'on loan', but are taken and absorbed by some generations without return. New Zealand's winners are those born between about 1920 and 1945, with the children of the 1930s at their core: in Australia and elsewhere the boundaries vary slightly, but not greatly. The losers are those

born later, and the further one's birth from 1930 the greater the
lifetime loss is looking to be.[3]

Further, Thomson has calculated that a typical New Zealand
couple born in 1930 will pay lifetime income taxes equivalent to
perhaps six years of their earnings, taking inflation and economic
growth into account. Their returns from the pool, however, from
the cash benefits and services provided by the state, will equal at
least 37 years of their gross earnings. By contrast, if the sample
couple had been born around 1955, they are due to pay at least
15 years of earnings for perhaps 25 years of benefits.[4] The inequity
in such a trend is not difficult to identify. An unsituated citizen
behind a Rawlsian veil of ignorance, in this instance not knowing
the generation into which he or she will be born, would rationally
choose consistency in the costs and benefits of the welfare state.
By risk alone, and with no measure of justice, why would any
citizen design the management of the commons so that it meets
the needs of one generation more fully than another?

Hitherto, the theory of justice has not been closely associated
with issues of intergenerational equity and inequity. It is apparent,
however, that the design features of the welfare state cannot be
blind to the needs of future generations. It is manifestly unfair for
one generation to overload the commons knowing that, in all
likelihood, future generations will not have the same opportunity
to satisfy their collective interests. Consistency should be seen as
a virtue in the intergenerational characteristics of the welfare state.
A basic understanding of this principle requires intergenerational
systems of government financial accounting. Without quality information on the future impact of today's use of the commons, quality
decisions will not be possible.[5] Governments should also place a
premium on measures which spread their benefits across several
generations, such as infrastructure spending. As noted in Part II,
one of the unfortunate trends in recent public policy has been the
secular decline in Australia's infrastructure stock. The fiscal pressures of the state are such that politicians frequently trade away
intergenerational outlays in their determination to preserve measures with an immediate time horizon.

An interesting paradox of contemporary politics is that questions of intergenerational fairness have been broadly associated
more with agendas of the Right than the Left. This can be taken
as an unhappy sign of the moral decline of the social democratic
project. Perhaps the inequities of the present have been so pressing
that social democrats have not been able to adequately consider
the intergenerational design features of the welfare state. Conversely, economic liberals, in their determination to wind back the

scope of the welfare state, have latched onto intergenerational issues as an appropriate alibi for their reductionist agenda.

Social democracy needs to recapture a moral sense of inter-generational purpose and responsibility. If those committed to the ideals of collectivism do not care for, and effectively manage the commons, then others will act to dismantle it in the name of individualism. Under conditions of overloaded government and intergenerational inequity, as Thomson writes:

> a system of pooling, intended to relieve personal anxiety and to turn thoughts towards the community good, instead works over time to the opposite end. As it becomes clear that the common is being depleted, and that future benefits drawn from it must shrink, a switch towards an individualistic ideology becomes attractive.[6]

If those who claim publicly to care most for the commons and its value to society do not guarantee its sustainability, who will? The practice of social justice has no clearer moral purpose than to act diligently as custodians of the commons.   ,

THE LOGIC OF COLLECTIVE ACTION

The institutional design of common pool resourcing is, by this basic criterion, all important. This, in turn, reinforces the argument against incrementalism. In the nature of politics it is often convenient to initiate additional measures of equity without considering their impact on other parts of the common pool. Yet the commons, by definition, does not represent the aggregation of disconnected uses and functions. By virtue of its foundation on a shared pool of resources and access rights for all, it must be managed as a whole. In the propagation of collective interests there can be no more important management principle than this. The overload of government is, in part, a function of incrementalism: the ease with which well-meaning reformers can load new functions onto the commons without understanding the proper limits of its carrying capacity. After generations of extra loading, one of the central tasks of social justice, inevitably enough, is to return the commons and its management to a point of sustainability.

A rich body of management studies, primarily dealing with the use of natural resources held in common, offers a guide to how this might be achieved. The telling aspect of this literature is that it points to a very different set of issues to those which conventionally drive political debates on the future of the welfare state.

The type of functions performed by common pooled resources do not matter as much as the scale by which their institutional features are determined. Politicians arguing solely about the scope of government have overlooked a key determinant of institutional success: the organisational scale and limits by which the commons is managed. Most likely, the organisational scale of the modern welfare state has far exceeded the sound management of the commons.

In the conventional wisdom of rational group behaviour, it is assumed that individuals with interests and objectives held in common will generate action collectively to maximise the satisfaction of their goals. This is a principle entirely consistent with the theory of justice. The problem may be, however, that it is only valid among small-scale groups for which, in practice, the commonality of interests and action is highly transparent. In dissecting *The Logic of Collective Action* (1965), Mancur Olson concluded that, 'unless the number of individuals is quite small, or unless there is coercion or some other special device to make individuals act in their common interest, rational, self-interested individuals will not act to achieve their common or group interests'.[7]

Olson, with due logic, argues that when the number of group participants is large, the typical participant will know that his/her own efforts and assessment of interests (personal and collective) will not make much difference to the course of collective action. The contribution that each participant will make towards attaining the item of collective benefit will become smaller as the group becomes larger. Hence the incentives system for group behaviour breaks down: a participant who cannot be excluded from obtaining the benefits of group action has little incentive to contribute properly to the group. Importantly, this is not a denunciation of the commons but, rather, an important insight into the means by which it might function, or fail. Olson arrives at a conclusion for the logic of collective action connected, not directly to the number of participants in a group, but to the visibility of each participant's actions. If participants can find a reason for their contribution then collective action will proceed. If the group can exercise effective sanctions against the free rider problem, then the benefits of collective action will be sustained.

In many respects, the design features of the modern welfare state have become dysfunctional. Large, centralised bureaucracies have not been able to create behavioural visibility for stakeholders to the commons. Participants have lost a sense of control and input from the patron/client relationships of the state public sector. They are now most likely to assess behavioural norms on the commons from information presented in the mass media. This, in turn, has led to a perception, rightly or wrongly, that free riders are everywhere, and everywhere they remain unsanctioned. Public alienation and the punishing moods of downwards envy have diminished the legitimacy of the welfare state commons.

The creation of the nation state last century coincided with the emergence of mass welfare and centralised public provision. The functions of local communities, parishes and districts were aggregated under the administration of the nation state. This had the benefit of spreading more thoroughly the risks associated with common pooling, plus aligning the functions of government with the rise of nationalism. An unwelcome consequence of this process, however, has been the loss of behavioural transparency. The mass welfare state has lost the visibility and behavioural sanctions inherent in welfare communities. It has functioned more like an open access regime than a common with clearly defined and understood boundaries. This has made the public control and policing of the commons problematic. In Thomson's phrase, mass welfare 'provides anonymity and dims the sense that an individual's actions necessarily have consequences for others'.[8]

Unless the connection between individual action and collective consequences remains visible and direct, popular confidence in the management of the commons is bound to decline. Perceptions of widespread free riding become endemic. In the current political context, this helps explain the rise of public resentment about the payment of taxation and the clarion call for hypothecated returns on contributions to the common pool. It also says something about the significant erosion of public trust in the institutions of democratic government.

Public choice theory maintains that the state public sector has reached a scale from which its representative functions are limited to contact with peak sectional interests and organisations.[9] Liberal democracy was founded on the idea that everyone should have a say in the decisions of government impacting on their lives. The sheer size of the post-war state, however, has forced governments to replace direct democracy with representations from sectional interest groups. As decision makers have become isolated from small groups and interests, they have found it convenient to form policy around the views of articulate, well-organised peak bodies. In a complex democracy where power is centralised, only the privileged few can resemble Rousseau's ideal citizen, 'ever ready to fly to the public assembly'. This process works against some of our important values. Liberal democracy breaks down when elected representatives are exposed only to those organisations capable of lobbying. Participation becomes impossible for all but the opinion leaders of the major groups. Equality breaks down as political influence is concentrated among sectional organisations. Freedoms are eroded as citizens are expected to conform with decisions made primarily to satisfy vested interests.

INSTITUTIONAL DESIGN

These are critical public concerns to which social democratic thinking has been slow to devise a satisfactory response. Common welfare pooling should not be left to survive by coercion alone. Social justice strategies now need to redesign the welfare state to strengthen its sustainability. Lessons can be drawn from the management principles which sustain the use of common pool natural resources, such as grazing grounds and fisheries. Elinor Ostrom's study of these systems has shown that cooperative strategies can succeed. They require, however, design principles which fortify the logic of collective action.[10] These are summarised as follows:

1 The core task of design is to deal with circumstances of an uncertain and complex environment. If the rationale for common resource pooling is lost (in the case of natural resources, to deal with the contingencies of nature) then institutional failure will inevitably follow.

2 Consistency in design is a virtue, in terms of providing intergenerational stability and fairness over time.

3 Institutions need to create extensive norms among participants which help to define proper behaviour, fostering interdependence and trust. As Ostrom records, 'a reputation for keeping promises, honest dealings and reliability in one arena is a valuable asset. Prudent, long term self-interest reinforces the acceptance of norms. None of these situations involves participants who vary greatly in [a way which] could strongly divide a group of individuals'.[11]

4 The boundaries of the common must be clearly defined, both in terms of access rights and the characteristics of the pooled resources. A small number of participants makes the spread of information about behaviour, rules and sanctions highly transparent.

5 The rules of appropriation should be relevant to both the system of provision and the particular circumstances of the common resource pool. That is, institutional design should not be framed in a manner abstracted from practical, local conditions.

6 Individuals affected by the operational rules should be able to participate in modifying the rules.

7 Those who monitor pooled resource conditions and behaviour

should be fully accountable to the participants to the common, if they are not, in practice, participants themselves.

8 Those who are assessed as violating the operational rules should be subjected to a graduated scale of sanctions, depending on the seriousness and context of the offence.

9 Low cost mechanisms should be available for resolving conflicts. High cost methods subvert the logic of the commons.

10 The capacity of participants to the commons to design their own institutions should not be overruled by external government authorities. Autonomy is all important.

These principles highlight the need to reformulate questions concerning the raw size of government. Conventionally this debate has proceeded with regard to the share of national resources devoted to the public sector. Both sides of politics have tended to present size, understood in gross terms, as an end in itself. More likely, however, matters of public sector size are best understood through the prism of organisational scale—that is, the creation of boundaries, behavioural norms and accountability visible to each of those drawing from the common resource pool. It is the scale and norms of public sector systems, not their aggregated size, which should form the focus of social democratic reform.

In an age of widespread economic uncertainty, the need for common welfare pooling is indisputable. It is just as clear, however, that the mass welfare state no longer offers the most appropriate scale of organisation by which a system of common pooling can be sustained. The diversification of skills and interests in the new economy has fragmented the basis of a truly mass commons. The policy challenge for social democracy involves a fresh bundle of welfare and organisational issues. Can smaller scale units of welfare pooling be made compatible with comprehensive standards of safety net provision? Can the virtues of transparent welfare communities be combined with nationwide systems of minimum entitlements and actuarial risk sharing?

The success of the commons relies on a scale of organisation within which stakeholders are not only exposed to the behaviour of others but also have an appreciation of how their actions impact on the interests of others. At the same time, however, there are clear benefits in the sharing of pooling risks across a wider proportion of the citizenry. The reform of the mass welfare state by these principles stands as a first order task for social democracy. Otherwise the weakening legitimacy and effectiveness of the welfare state will continue to undermine the prospects of a just society. These issues are dealt with more substantially in the remainder of the book. Suffice, at this stage, to concur with Thomson's conclusion:

> Successful commons require openness, highly visible decisions and widespread awareness and acceptance of the rules of participation. This is not the case with the welfare state . . . A welfare common of sorts [is] necessary, but it has to be managed much more carefully than we have achieved of late. A first step is to recognise that the welfare state is a form of common. The unit of pooling may need to be much smaller than the nation. The boundaries between private, true commons and open-access property will need to be firmed, made explicit and patrolled. Rights and responsibilities towards the pool will have to be clarified and insisted upon, something we have been very reluctant to do as yet. More difficult still will be the need to give close consideration to what should be in the pool and why, and what can best be left out.[12]

21

A ROLE FOR GOVERNMENT

It is plain from the reconstruction of social justice theory that social democracy needs to focus its public purpose on the basic economic and social uncertainties of life. It should aim at ensuring for each citizen an acceptable threshold of social capability. These two themes—dealing with uncertainty and enhancing social capability—are a fine expression of what it means to talk about equality in an open society. They define a role for government which updates, under conditions of social and economic globalisation, Australian Labor's commitment to the public expression of social interests held in common. Society's transition to the post-industrial age forces new questions of relevance and purpose onto the social democratic project. Social change forces reform in the policies and organisational methods of the state.

In terms of organisational form, the approach outlined in the previous chapter advances the virtues of small-scale systems, transparent group behaviour and aspects of self-governance. Among the debates of the political Left, the organisational methods of the state have always held a special status. They have often been taken as a purpose in their own right, more so than the attainment of social goals. Means have frequently superseded ends. Concerns about the immutability of social democracy's methods—strategic state ownership, supply side planning and universality principles—have tended to overshadow the importance of ends and objectives. This highlights a curious feature of parties like the ALP: forever talking the language of social change, yet within party structures and policy making forums, instinctively resisting changed means and methods.

Labor politics has always featured a seemingly irreconcilable tension between the practicalities of social change and the need for continuity in its own traditions. As a party of reform and social protection, it has had to be responsive to the changing nature of economic and social circumstance. Yet as a party conditioned by the need for internal solidarity and collectivism, it has taken strength from its history and traditional methods. As Graham Freudenberg has explained, Labor's unity and purpose has relied on 'its sense of continuity. The ALP is a collective memory in action. That is why our history is so important to us; and why so much of the internal debate in the Party is about the interpretation of that history.'[1]

These tensions are frequently expressed between the forums of parliamentary decision making and the beliefs of Labor's rank and file members. This has produced a clear cycle of reform, reaction and then the redefinition of Party traditions. During the 1960s, for instance, Gough Whitlam's program of social democracy was frequently denounced as selling out Labor's commitment to state ownership and economic planning. Today it is taken by many Party activists as a 'real' source of Labor ideology, almost to the point of deification. During the period of the Hawke and Keating Governments, the tension between policy pragmatism and Party tradition expressed itself mainly through issues of privatisation and market liberalisation.

ENDS AND MEANS

The successful management of this process has been made more acute by the magnitude of economic and social change in recent decades. The global integration of capital and attendant reformulation of social structures is an event unique in history. To be certain, Labor needs to skilfully adapt to these changes and refashion the tools of social equity; yet it also needs to maintain a sense of continuity in its public purposes. If it does not do the former, its effectiveness and electoral relevance will inevitably decline. If it does not do the latter, then Labor's traditional core of support might fracture beyond repair. This is why the separation of political ends and means is so important.

If the Party's methods are taken as an end in itself then plainly the inexorable tensions between social change and party traditions cannot be resolved. Labor's methods would become immutable and, over time, by the standards of an alert political cause, irrelevant. Means should only be pursued for what they can achieve. In practice, there is nothing intrinsic in state ownership that eliminates economic uncertainty, or in supply side planning that produces a threshold of social capability. Nor is it possible to guarantee the sustainability of universal entitlements under conditions of overloaded government. By extension, it cannot be held that the use of market forces by policy makers is intrinsically inconsistent with any of these goals.[2] In each case, the means towards Labor's declared purpose rests heavily on the logic of circumstance: the changing nature of social wants and conditions to which the Party applies its objectives.

By this analysis, it makes best sense for the ALP to draw strength from the continuity of its political goals. These include an enduring commitment to the basis of a good and decent society—protecting vulnerable people, places and interests against the worst vicissitudes of the profit system; and equipping citizens with the skills and security needed to cope with the inevitability of socioeconomic change. Its methods should be devised solely to achieve these goals. This approach gives Labor its best chance to manage the tension between its history and contemporary political circumstances. It can take strength, not just from its historic purpose in Australian politics, but also from the relevance of its policy reforms and adaptability. In its origins and through its history, the ALP has been a political force for civilising capitalism. Increasingly in the modern era, its methods have had to turn to the task of civilising global capital.

These methods, as noted in Part I, rely on the capacity of the state public sector to exert leverage over the global integration of capital. In economic policy this is best achieved by making capital compete, and focusing the resources of the state on the skills and capacities of its citizens. It is a strange proposition indeed, yet frequently advanced by some, that governments can exercise leverage over footloose capital by shielding it from market competition and directing scarce public resources to the subsidisation of profits. Policies pursuing a subsidised halfway house between open and closed markets are a misguided strategy for the Labor movement. Social democrats should not argue that the public interest is best served by doling out protection to private capital, and sheltering the profit system from its own rationale for market-based competition. Morally, intellectually and in the practice of market policy, private capital should be made to compete.

CORRECTING MARKET FAILURES

In social policy it is obvious that private markets, whether sheltered or competitive, cannot satisfy each of the social wants and needs of the citizenry. An acceptable threshold of social capability will not be provided by private means alone. This is why the state has a countervailing role to play against the inadequacies of private production. This means government activism is required to compensate for the shortcomings of the private market system—what economists have termed market failure. These failings can be summarised as follows:

- natural monopolies and oligopolies—industries in which the costs of market entry are prohibitively high—require government intervention to protect consumers against imbalanced market power;
- the existence of externalities—by-products of production for which consumers cannot be charged—often requires government regulation and coercive pricing (especially with regard to environmental protection);
- free markets tend to undersupply public goods; that is, goods and services which all consumers can draw on without the rationing characteristics of the pricing mechanism (such as defence forces and law and order services);
- open markets for many social or merit goods, such as education, often malfunction due to shortcomings in the pricing mechanism, factor mobility and consumer knowledge, thereby leading to an unsatisfactory allocation of resources and social opportunity;
- markets often fail to successfully administer risky projects, such as social insurance schemes, due to their inability to spread risks universally (and hence discount future cash flows at risk-free rates of interest), plus their inability to overcome the problem of adverse selection (when those most likely to suffer loss are covered in greater proportion than others);
- in the development of most forms of long-life infrastructure, private markets have difficulty in accommodating financial risk and establishing a pricing mechanism for positive externalities; hence, the most efficient allocation of economic resources often rests with public sector ownership and financing;[3]
- open markets lack a mechanism by which the collective costs of economic adjustment can be adequately assessed, especially in terms of dislocation, and social and environmental costs;
- market-based incentives can produce a distribution of income and wealth which distorts social harmony and cohesiveness through the creation of intolerable levels of inequality;
- finally, markets are without a mechanism for assessing the cultural, social and national imperatives by which public sector intervention is frequently deemed desirable.[4]

These parameters help to guide the ownership features of the public sector. Markets are recognised for their valuable (but not perfect) contribution to the efficient allocation of economic resources. Market failures can be addressed by regulatory policy or, if this falls short of the public interest, the replacement of private capital with public capital. These are the countervailing or safety net principles by which the purposes of public sector ownership can be established.

Logically, it cannot be argued that the private sector is universally more efficient than the public sector. Market failures—such as ownership concentration, factor immobility and opaque pricing—usually involve high economic and social costs. The state has a well-defined role to play in the management of social risks (such as lawlessness), and economic risks (such as long-life infrastructure), which private markets are unable to cover. Public ownership can also act against the appropriation of merit goods in private hands, usually in markets with rapidly changing technology and social wants. The educative potential of the information superhighway, for instance, is a sound reason for the public sector maintaining its ownership stake in Telstra's cabling system.

OWNERSHIP NEUTRALITY

Importantly, however, the ownership of public assets cannot be used as an end in itself. In a dynamic economy the methods of government are not suited to (and rarely find) a form of static equilibrium. In recent decades the liberalisation of capital markets has allowed governments to shift their fixed capital investments from markets featuring competitive private capital, to the enhancement of human capital. The experience of the Hawke and Keating Governments shows that it is possible for the public sector to vacate its ownership role in industries like banking and airlines without a loss of economic efficiency or social equity. It is difficult to perceive a lasting role for the state public sector in the ownership of large slabs of industrial capital, especially when its agenda for the development of social capability and the associated skills of its citizens is so extensive.

The problem with Labor's privatisation policies in government was that they were driven, not by the principles outlined above, but by the exigencies of the budget bottom line. Sound principles for the role of public capital were undermined by fiscal pressures on the state. Under conditions of overloaded government, the public sector suffers from investment and risk adverse shareholders. Public capital has not enjoyed the same depth of equity finance as its private sector equivalents. In many instances, public utilities and services have been allowed to wither on the vine, a situation from which privatisation has then been presented as unavoidable.

Generally, under conditions of dynamic economic and social change, governments need to embrace the virtues of ownership neutrality. Questions of ownership should not be determined through fixed ideological preferences for either private or public sector activity. Rather, optimal outcomes will arise from an assessment of market structures, social wants and public interest imperatives. Within this paradigm, governments do not have fixed assets and methods, but an entirely adaptable function in correcting market failures and establishing the capability set of a just society. In the United States, Osborne and Gaebler have published the virtues of *Reinventing Government* (1992) as a clearing house for the innovative provision of basic services. The focus is on outcomes instead of ownership. The roles of the public sector as a funder, purchaser and provider of services are separated, opening up contestability for government contracts between publicly and privately owned providers. This breaks the assumption that public use can only be facilitated through public ownership and operational control. In Deng Xiaoping's famous dictum, 'it does not matter if the cat is black or white, as long as it is a good mouser'.

QUASI-MARKETS

The efficiency features of the market can also be applied to the social goods sector; that is, when outcomes other than material welfare are being pursued. However, a note of caution is required. Governments need to recognise the limits of demand side market forces as a distributor of social goods and opportunities. While the construction of quasi-markets on the supply side, forcing competition between service providers, can often boost efficiency without the diminution of equity principles, the construction of demand side mechanisms is sometimes problematic. The introduction of one-off voucher payments for access to large-scale capital facilities might maximise individual choice but, by definition, the most disadvantaged consumers often have the poorest access to market information and transport mobility, thereby restricting their capacity for effective choice and equal access.

Take, for example, the Liberal Party's proposal at the 1993 election to treat universities as open demand side markets. In practice, a market system such as this would suffer from the immobility of its capital and labour inputs, imperfect consumer knowledge, and a highly restricted pricing mechanism. Universities facing unexpectedly high demand at the start of each year would struggle to accommodate extra students due to the inflexibility of their factor conditions. It would not be possible to rapidly move buildings and courses from low demand universities to high demand facilities. Equally, institutions would each year encounter the risk of inappropriate fee settings, from which they would be unable to successfully adjust to market demand. Market pricing mechanisms are fundamentally flawed if consumer decisions can only be exercised once every twelve months. An open university market would also fail to address any mismatch between student preferences and the suitability of skills in the labour market. In Australia more than 50 per cent of students leaving high school hope to pursue careers which relate to less than 20 per cent of jobs in the workforce. A demand side market in tertiary education would produce a large number of unemployed lawyers, doctors and accountants.

Few private markets operate without imperfections, a situation which requires government to stay involved in the creation and distribution of public resources. In the provision of social goods, the use of supply side market forces can secure benefits in the competitive efficiency of service providers. The possible application of market systems on the demand side, however, relies on adequate levels of factor mobility, consumer knowledge and active use of the pricing mechanism. These preconditions are not likely to be met for services with high sunk capital costs. In other service areas, such as child care and most parts of the health system, demand side benefits are possible. These reforms, consistent with a full range of public interest considerations, can boost consumer sovereignty and flexibility and thereby assist with the propagation of social capability. Generally in the social goods sector, reform strategies need to aim at the mix of public provision and private contributions which establishes a decent threshold in the capability set.

REDEFINING UNIVERSALITY

All sides of politics have accepted the virtue of the public sector providing pure public goods such as defence and law and order. Less clear is the way in which the principles of universality should be framed for the role of merit or capability goods in the delivery of new skills and social opportunities. Recent experience in Australia has shown that the promise of publicly provided universality has been cut short by the fiscal pressures on government. A range of services—most notably public hospitals, child care, housing subsidies, aged care, community arts and recreation facilities—have suffered from rationing and/or inequitable access. Under these circumstances the basis of social democratic service provision needs to be recast.

Traditionally, universality has been interpreted as a right associated with one's open-ended participation in a civilised society. Public entitlements have emerged irrespective of the capacity for private provision. Over time, these rights have expanded from the core insecurities of life—income support, education and health—to take in a range of leisure-related services. These additional commitments have not only compromised the public sector's capacity to fund universality, but also produced some inequitable outcomes. These arise whenever low income taxpayers, without access needs (according to their own priorities and interests), are made to assist the immediate access rights of high income earners. The extensive public subsidisation of the high arts in Australia is an example of this process.

The principles of universal service provision, as noted above, are equivalent to the task of managing a mass commons. It is difficult to sustain a system whereby some citizens might contribute to the commons, yet not have any reasonable expectation themselves for drawing on its resources, either directly or indirectly. Contributions to the commons only make sense if each of its supporters can benefit from its use. Rights of access are not enough. Outcomes are all important, either through direct use and the satisfaction of personal needs, or through someone else's use and the creation of indirect benefits. This latter process involves the creation of positive externalities, whereby the shared provision of a service results in shared benefits, even though not all of the beneficiaries are direct users of the service. The strong economic growth benefits of public education are an example of a positive externality.

Accordingly, social justice strategies need to shift from systems of funding support based on universal access rights, to criteria premised on universal use and/or externalities. Services should be universal in their provision, not because citizens have abstract rights and entitlements, but because the collective provision of services by government brings to the citizenry a shared benefit. For instance, as a community and a nation, we are all made stronger—especially in terms of economic growth and shared prosperity—through the universal provision of quality education and skills training. People do not necessarily need to attend a university to realise its new growth benefits. Other examples of the logic of universality can be found in the public provision of health services, and investment in infrastructure.

In areas where universal benefits cannot be demonstrated, governments need to contain their activities to safety net services designed to enhance the equality and inclusiveness of our society. This means targeting (through income support and locational programs) public resources to those circumstances in which the availability of private resources is not sufficient to aid the tasks of social capability. This raises a critical point with regard to the legitimacy of safety net services. They should be judged not just in terms of equality and inequality, but also by the principles of externalities enjoyed in common. Especially under conditions of economic openness, each citizen derives some benefit from the effectiveness of the social safety net. Individual inventiveness and creativity are not likely to be maximised if the consequences of failure in such endeavours are too severe. As Thomson has noted:

> Nothing in my historical study indicates that substantial public welfare action can or should now be avoided. Students of the rise of capitalism and subsequent urban industrial society all stress that the population, family and other productive structures under-lying that success were all predicated upon large elements of public welfare action: the welfare state is in important senses not new. Individuals could be encouraged to take the necessary risks involved only if clear and substantial fall-back support was in place.[5]

Fall-back support becomes even more important in a post-industrial society. A nation's economic success relies heavily on risk-positive business and workplace practices, especially with the disaggregation of business size and structure. Obviously people are more inclined to take risks if society has in place an effective safety net. The legitimacy of the public sector, in the eyes of its taxpayers, is strengthened by the casting of universality in terms of positive use and externalities, rather than notional access rights. During a time of economic insecurity, citizens are understandably reluctant to fund the rights and entitlements of others when they themselves have few guarantees for the future. More than ever, social democracy—in advocating and advancing the active, equalising role of government—needs to frame its case in terms of the provision of services and externalities enjoyed in common.

22

CONCLUSION: SUSTAINABLE SOCIAL DEMOCRACY

One of the paradoxes of contemporary government is that everywhere it is being challenged for failing to deal with the growth of insecurity; yet the post-war welfare state was established expressly for the purpose of giving the citizenry peace of mind about the future. This indicates a level of dealignment between dynamic social wants and the relatively fixed methods of government. In the transition towards a post-industrial society, social democracy has fallen into the habit of loading extra responsibilities and functions onto the state public sector. In this process, it has struggled with the identification of social needs and served to loosen the collective commitment to membership of the public commons. The overload of modern government is strangling the legitimacy of the welfare state. If social democracy is not able to make the ideals of public governance work, then it remains permanently vulnerable to the small government agenda of the political Right.

For Australian Labor, a focus on segment-of-life programs has been accompanied by the segmentation of policy making. As core concerns about the uncertainties of life have been matched on the Party's agenda by the prominence of positive discrimination programs, policy making itself has drifted towards interest group capture. In this way, policies for gender equity come from the women's committee; policies for multiculturalism and immigration come from the NESB committee; and so it goes for each interest group activity. The result has been a loose coalition of policy segments, often with conflicting goals and purpose. For those citizens who do not closely identify with one segment or another— perhaps even a majority of people, with a more general concern about the impact of socioeconomic insecurity in their lives—perceptions of neglect and misplaced priorities inevitably arise. In the

191

reconstruction of social justice around the prime issues of insecurity and social capability, the ALP needs to abandon its segmentation of policy based on the behavioural characteristics of life. The sustainability of social justice in an open economy does not lie in programs of positive discrimination, such as the zero-sum application of quotas, special categories and interest group funding.

Social democracy needs to realign the priorities and methods of government with the social wants of the post-industrial era. Reform of the social contract becomes a logical consequence of this task. The principles presented in this part of the book point to an overhaul of the way in which the social democratic project deals with questions of social justice. Five related strategies have been advanced:

- a core focus on the socioeconomic uncertainties of life and downgrading of positive discrimination programs aimed at segment-of-life characteristics;
- an understanding of social equality aimed at providing for each citizen a threshold of social capability dealing with social wants and insecurities;
- the application of sound management principles for the public sector commons, with an emphasis on intergenerational equity and small-scale, transparent units of administration;
- the clear separation of political ends and means, with the pragmatic use of the countervailing tools of the state in response to market failure; and
- the casting of universality principles in terms of service use and positive externalities held in common, rather than the open-ended access rights of citizenship.

This approach holds potential for addressing the dilemmas of overloaded government and downwards envy. It aims at the sustainability of social democracy in an open economy. It seeks to rebuild from first principles the common values and interests which make for the logic of collective action. It takes the role of the public sector, in the expression of collective interests and responsibility, as the solution to issues of insecurity arising from globalisation. It maintains that just as few citizens live without various forms of private insurance, none of us should live without the role of the state as an insurer of last resort against the exigencies of socioeconomic change.

The past twenty years have told many Australians that there are too few guarantees left in our society; yet the search for guarantees, the things we might fall back on when individual effort and industry still leave us short, remains an essential part of the human condition. Without them there can be little security or peace of mind. And an answer? It might just be that amid the flurry of change, in Australia and beyond, the only true stabilisers the citizenry will find, the only enduring buffer it has against insecurity, lie in the things it holds in common and is willing to express through public action. Ultimately, society's interdependence is its only lasting guarantee against the contingencies of change in the post-industrial era. If it is not possible, through the work of the profit system, to rely on employment and income security for all, or on stable units of work, family and community, then what remains other than the countervailing role of the public sector? By this test of logic alone, Labor should not shy away from the principles on which the stabilising role of government is based. The moral purpose of social justice has not declined, only the effectiveness of its methods and conception of social justice.

By these reforms Labor can establish a role for government above and beyond the shortcomings of the old Left/Right dichotomy. The standard Left call of more money for more programs, and the focus on segment-of-life characteristics have overloaded government and eroded its credibility. Right wing agendas for winding back the welfare state and practising wedge politics crudely divide the public interest and, in their impact, add to insecurity. Labor needs to pursue a different role for government: one which matches rights with responsibility; one which advances the capability of each citizen in a customised way; one which concentrates the work of government on offsetting insecurity; one which manages the commons with a sense of shared interests and intergenerational equity; one which breaks the mould of centralised, supply side planning and creates a transparent, more virtual scale of public organisation; one which gives social democracy new relevance by radically updating its methods. This is not the time or place for more of the same.

PART IV

A POST-FORDIST WELFARE STATE

The overload of modern government has placed immense pressure on the legitimacy and effectiveness of the welfare state. All sides of politics seem to acknowledge the need for significant reform. Unfortunately, however, most proposals have focused on concerns about the raw size of government, rather than its functions, transparency and organisational structure. The policy debate seems bogged down in a struggle between those arguing for small government as an end in itself and those, at the other end of the binary, who simply want more money for more programs. On no other issue has the politics of the libertarian Right and old Left failed as badly as the reform of the post-war welfare state. These shortcomings, however, do not indicate a crisis of purpose in the work of the welfare state, but rather, one of relevance. The moral purpose of public governance, the civilised ideal that society should pool its resources to deal with needs and interests held in common, is as valid now as it was half a century ago. It is just that the systems of service delivery devised in the 1950s and 1960s are no longer directly relevant to the changing structure of society and its economy. Welfare needs and interests have changed and, if its purpose is to survive, so too must the welfare state.

A new generation of policy issues now dominates the welfare agenda: how to provide for the diverse and dynamic needs of the citizenry during an era of widespread insecurity; how to adapt the organisational methods of government to deal with the crisis of entrenched exclusion in the new economy; how to create adaptable systems of income support as a buffer against economic uncertainty; how to reform the education system so that citizens can draw on the skills needed for active economic and social participation. Social democracy needs to rethink each of the principles upon which it has organised the work of government. In particular, it needs to restore a proper sense of transparency, behavioural norms and public participation to the management of the commons. It needs to place in the hands of its citizens the opportunities and responsibilities which, in tandem with an effective safety net of public provision, give rise to social capability.

Social democrats can no longer assume that systems of passive welfare, the immediate replacement of earnings through various categories of transfer payments, are sufficient to create the basis of active citizenship. Much more is required to overcome insecurity in an open economy and deal with the entrenched problems of disadvantage in an information-based society. The planning strand of welfare needs to be replaced with customised service delivery. The advancement of the rights of the individual needs to be matched by the reciprocation of responsibility. The single, extemporaneous purpose of transfer payments needs to be supplanted by new methods of lifelong income support and provision. The functions and structure of the education system need to be broadened into adaptable systems of lifelong learning. New opportunities need to be created for the devolution of public governance and welfare provision. Most of all, social democracy needs to be able to answer the Right's depiction of the social safety net as a hammock by making welfare work; by showing how welfare reform in practice can lead to springboards of social mobility.

23

SHIFTING SANDS

The welfare state was primarily a product of social democratic thinking after the Second World War. It was assumed that full employment required little more than Keynesian fine tuning of the economy. Governments turned their policy aspirations to issues of distribution; primarily, how to supplement a growth economy with the universal services and rights of citizenship. During an era of Fordist production, governments themselves became mass producers of standardised services: comprehensive education, universal health coverage, large state utilities and public works. It was assumed, with some comfort, that the public sector could plan for the social needs of citizens and communities. Like all supply side solutions, these assumptions relied on static social wants and conditions. Welfare state planning was premised on circumstances by which the nuclear family would remain the dominant social unit, the workforce would continue to be predominantly male, and work itself would remain standardised.

With full employment it was assumed that all citizens had the skills to access and make best use of universally provided services. Transfer payments were designed to assist those who had either reached the end of their working life or were simply moving between jobs. Fixed capital assets were planned and located around predictable patterns of private investment; in the case of public housing stock, for instance, to accommodate a blue collar workforce near tariff protected manufacturing sites. Since the 1970s, with the internationalisation of capital and transformation of work, each of these assumptions has been made redundant. Dynamic capital movements and technological advances have disaggregated the scale of production and nature of work. The new economy has produced new welfare needs.

The welfare safety net was initially intended as a residual system of short term earnings replacement. It was designed to complement a core system of basic male earnings and family income support during an era of full employment. The growth of structural unemployment, earnings dispersion and part-time and casual work, however, has eroded the availability of a living wage across the labour force. The nuclear family has also declined as a social norm and traditional income unit, with a large rise in zero- and two-income family types. This trend has been associated with the surge in female labour force participation and emergence of long term and intergenerational unemployment. With the decline of standardised labour, a working life is now likely to include a range of skills, jobs and earnings capacity. The amount of time spent by the labour force away from work has increased substantially, whether for reasons of unemployment, under-employment or the time taken for re-skilling.

These factors, combined with society's ageing demographics, have reshaped the ideals and affordability of universal entitlements and service provision. In its earliest form, welfare state universality had a relatively small impact on the fiscal carrying capacity of the state. For instance, at the time of the establishment of the first universal age pension, by Bismarck in Germany last century, only 1 per cent of each age cohort was expected to live long enough to access it. Benefits for the aged were made affordable by the small proportion of aged citizens. Similarly, after the Second World War, the long economic boom ameliorated the cost of transfer payments for the unemployed. Now, of course, throughout the Western World these demographic and economic circumstances have changed fundamentally. In Australia, the age dependency ratio, which measures the proportion of the population aged less than 15 years and more than 65 years, increased from 33.1 per cent in 1947 to 50.2 per cent in 1995. The income dependency ratio, which measures the proportion of the adult population relying on transfer payments as its primary source of income, has also increased substantially: from 12 per cent in 1973 to 27 per cent in 1994.[1]

The sheer fiscal weight of this task, combined with the politics of downwards envy, have placed enormous pressure on the sustainability of the tax/transfer system. Across the board, the appropriateness of the post-war welfare state has been in remorseless decline. Table 23.1 offers a guide to the shifting sands of socioeconomic circumstance. It charts the diversification of work, skill and family types. It reveals an end of certainty in the type of assumptions on which welfare planning might take place. The challenge for social democracy is to adeptly redesign the institu-

Table 23.1 Changing socioeconomic conditions

Indicator	Pre-1980s	1995
Labour force		
Full-time work (% total)	90.2 (1966)	75.1
Part-time work (% total)	9.8 (1966)	24.9
Female participation rate	36.3 (1966)	54.0
Unemployment rate	1.7 (1970)	8.6
Long term unemployment (% total)	4.5 (1970)	32.0
Service employment (% total)	58.0 (1970)	73.0
Education		
Year 12 retention rate	29.0 (1970)	72.2
Tertiary participation	16.0 (1970)	52.4
Family Unit		
Births outside marriage (% total)	5.1 (1961)	26.6
Couples co-habitating prior to marriage (%)	16.0 (1975)	56.0
Two-earner families (% total)	34.3 (1980)	42.0
One-earner families (% total)	42.2 (1980)	30.3
No earner families (% total)	23.4 (1980)	27.8
Single parent (% total)	7.0 (1980)	13.9
Demographics		
Aged 65 years and over (%)	8.5 (1966)	11.9
Dependency ratio[a]	37.9 (1966)	50.2
Social security		
Recipients (% population)[b]	8.7 (1966)	32.4
Expenditure (% GDP)	4.3 (1966)	9.6

Notes:
a   population aged less than 15 and more than 65 years as a proportion of total population
b   includes all Department of Social Security (DSS) and Department of Veterans' Affairs (DVA) income support payments, excluding (basic) family payment and its predecessors
Source: Various ABS; Department of the Parliamentary Library; EPAC Paper No. 12, 'Future Labour Market Issues for Australia', July 1996

tional features and methods of the welfare state, and restore its relevance. A starting point is to acknowledge that orthodox, supply side methods of service delivery are no longer sufficient to cope with the dynamic features of economic opportunity, family types and lifestyle aspirations. The planning strand is no longer likely to cope successfully with the identification of social needs. The complex equality implicit in the social capability paradigm requires a fresh approach. Social democracy needs to rethink the relationship between citizen and state; and in so doing, establish new ways of dealing with diverse social needs and wants.

SOCIAL CAPABILITY

Under information-based systems of production, economic opportunity is defined more by access to human capital than physical
capital. The distinction between capital and labour has been
blurred by the advent of knowledge as an economic input. With
changes in the nature of production, variable skill levels have
become a leading determinant of lifetime opportunities in society.
The capability set defines the rights of citizens in terms of competence: their capacity to participate in society to a point of
personal satisfaction—that is, their freedom to achieve. The ownership of assets, public and private, matters only to the extent that
it might influence this process. The skills of participation, economic and social, are all important. Welfare policies need to
respond by shifting from income-based definitions of poverty to a
more comprehensive understanding of capability failure.

The welfare state was founded on the basis of universal freedoms (defined as rights) and universal entitlements to a basic
standard of material living. This led to a relatively simple conceptualisation of equality and the role of the state: it was not
pitched at the type of interaction between citizens and state that
leads to notions of social capability and complex equality. Indeed,
the welfare state assumed a threshold of capability from which
citizens might take advantage of the universal provision of services.
In a post-industrial economy, however, large segments of the
labour market lack an effective skills base. Individuals affected by
long term and intergenerational unemployment often lack the
lifestyle skills to make best use of services. Their capacity for active
citizenship has been depleted by joblessness and other social problems. This has become a sad feature of our society: the distortion
of social norms through extended poverty; the displacement of the
habits and memory of regular work by a cycle of personal crises
and despair.

Public policy in Australia has been slow to respond to the
entrenched problems of capability failure. Governments still deal
with poverty more through transfer payments than an appreciation
of complex equality. Standards of well-being tend to be assessed
through updates of the Henderson poverty line which, in its
methodology, still reflects a set of statistics and analytical tools
from the 1960s.[2] This has perpetuated a view that the alleviation
of poverty simply relies on more generous transfer payments. The
answer to capability failure, however, does not lie in rolling out
more benefits and more programs of the old kind. As the British
social analyst, Geoff Mulgan, has written:

Nationally standardised approaches mirror both the conventional liberal view of welfare as based on a set of rights, and the distributional ideas of John Rawls that have continued to have a surprising influence on the labour movement. The combined effect has been disastrous, diverting so much thinking about welfare away from ends and onto means. We have (albeit ill-defined) rights to health care, income support, schooling, but not to health well-being or understanding; and a relentless focus on distributing money rather than cultivating competence.[3]

In some respects, the distribution of money has even become counter-productive. In the popular culture, social security often carries a stigma which reduces the aspirations of those receiving transfer payments. This gives an important insight into the alleviation of poverty in a post-industrial society. Minimum standards of material living need to be complemented by the personal skills needed for active social and economic participation. The provision of transfer payments often represents a symptom of economic exclusion and participation failure, rather than a sign of social equality. In the case of long term unemployment, citizens can be rutted into a vicious cycle of welfare dependency. Labour market studies have shown that the duration of unemployment is inversely correlated with the likelihood of job offers and the aspirations of job seekers. Paid work now represents something more than the attainment of earnings: it has a welfare function in its own right, closely linked to the value of participation and self-esteem in society. Policies of welfare reform need to aim, first and foremost, at the creation of full employment. In the new economy, as Part II pointed out, this means shaping government's role to include its potential as a local employer of last resort.

The resolution of poverty requires changes in circumstance and capability beyond a safety net of material well-being. Policy requires a broader focus, recasting the role and measurement of the welfare functions of government. Social democrats can no longer assume that each citizen is able to utilise the universal supply of services and rights with the same threshold of self-esteem, confidence and skills. In a skills-based society, minimum standards of income support are not in themselves sufficient to overcome poverty and foster social mobility. Capability failure can only be dealt with by addressing the interaction between primary and social goods. The most effective standard of material well-being is one that individuals have been able to earn from their own skills and capability. To be certain, welfare works best when it lifts the recipients of government assistance to a new plane of personal capability. This, in turn, requires a number of fundamental changes in the relationship between citizens and the state.

RECIPROCAL RESPONSIBILITIES

A starting point is to recognise that skill formation is an interactive process. Its success relies on a partnership between the skill provider and recipient. This is a substantial break from the ethos of transfer payments and their passive relationship between providers and recipients. Under conventional forms of welfare, governments have provided a minimum level of income support as one of the rights of citizenship, without regard for the responsibilities citizens might exercise in the use of this support. Policies aimed at social capability, however, need to replace this passive relationship with active forms of welfare. This means entrenching a sense of reciprocal responsibility throughout the work of the welfare state. It means funding social responsibilities as well as rights: the rights of needy citizens to receive government assistance but, just as much, their personal responsibility to make best use of this assistance. Skill formation relies on the efforts of both providers and recipients. It makes the welfare state a two way rather than one way street.

These principles of reciprocal responsibility have arisen in two comparatively recent developments in Australian public policy. First, the Keating Government, in a little publicised aspect of the 1994 Working Nation program, sought to establish reciprocal responsibilities in its programs for the long term unemployed. Assistance under the Job Compact was made conditional on the discharge of certain responsibilities. The recipients of unemployment income support were obliged to accept a training position or subsidised job placement, otherwise, their benefits were withdrawn. These reforms offered the long term unemployed an active incentive for helping themselves: for making their best effort at training and skill development; for using the opportunities provided by government to re-engage themselves in the workforce. Second, the Howard Government in 1997 sought to cast its work-for-the-dole scheme under the banner of mutual obligations. This program, however, lacks a training component and proper sense of social partnership. Participants are no more likely to find work or have their skills enhanced by the end of the program than at its commencement. In this respect, the program develops a passive relationship between its participants and the role of government: the state uses its coercive powers to make unemployed people work part-time, for which they receive income support but no enhancement of their personal capability.

These two initiatives point to important differences in the way in which the ALP and Coalition have approached the issue of social responsibility. The Coalition has developed a commitment to what can be termed 'functional obligations'—that anyone receiving government assistance has an obligation to reciprocate, not by virtue of what they can do for themselves (or even society for that matter), but as a narrow function of the act of assistance itself. This view of human nature discounts the possibility of altruism, the idea that people might help others on the basis of need and compassion, rather than a functional expectation of reciprocity. Obligations such as these narrow the role of government. Instead of acting as a point of partnership between the individual and society, the public sector is reduced to an entirely coercive role. It uses its public authority to impose reciprocation for no other moral purpose than reciprocation itself. In its political context, work-for-the-dole was devised as a wedge issue, relying on downwards envy to set the interests of those in employment against the social entitlements of the unemployed.

By contrast, the ALP has sought to develop the virtues of 'positive responsibilities'—the role of the public sector in creating reciprocal social responsibility in a manner mutually satisfying to both society and the recipients of welfare. Reciprocation is seen as more than an end in itself. It is aimed at the enhancement of labour force skills and personal capability which, in turn, aids the strength of society. Unlike the Coalition's functional obligations, these positive responsibilities do not attempt to set the interests of one part of society against another. They aid the unemployed by developing their skills and reconnecting them with the benefits of work and active citizenship. Society benefits from this boost to its collective skills base and the full utilisation of the economic capacity of its citizens. Positive responsibilities give each Australian a threshold of social capability and, if they seek it for themselves, social mobility.

These principles demonstrate how questions of social responsibility should not be regarded as the political property of the Right. Indeed, the moral purpose and social gains inherent in the expression of positive responsibilities make this an essential part of the cause of Labor. Social democracy has long held that citizens hold responsibilities in common; it just seems that in the political arena these have never been well expressed. The welfare state has been allowed to drift too far down its one way street. Yet in its original form, society's interdependence relies fundamentally on the preparedness of its citizens to trust in and care for each other, and to express this relationship through a series of reciprocal responsibilities. People can best advance their interests, not only by maintaining their membership and contribution to the public commons, but by drawing from the commons themselves in a manner that takes proper responsibility for the interests of every other citizen.

A welfare commons based on passive and open access rights is too easily corrupted into a scramble for short term, narrowly cast, self interest. The discharge of positive responsibilities, however, reflects a different moral code. It says that the best governance arises, not only from helping people, but by defining the social contract in a way that also makes people responsible for their willingness to help themselves. In this fashion, with the discharge of responsibility by both citizens and state, the altruism and compassion of society are actually strengthened. Social democracy's approach needs to rely on this powerful mix of social assistance and social responsibility to engineer the benefits of social mobility.

SERVICE CUSTOMISATION

Programs aimed at social capability also recognise the diverse nature of welfare needs. The skill requirements and capability threshold of each individual are unique. The interaction between primary goods, skill development and personal circumstance and effort represent the expression of a form of complex equality. In a post-industrial society, governments can no longer assume, particularly with their supply side solutions, that one size fits all. Public sector programs need to be customised to suit the needs of clients, rather than an expectation that individuals need to mould their circumstances around the rigid categories and supply side systems of government. Segment-of-life categories and broadbrush planning are no longer sufficient to meet the diverse capability set of each citizen.

The post-war welfare state explicitly relied on both full employment and traditional family structures. It was assumed that men in work would earn a wage sufficient to cover the living standards of the nuclear family. This framework has been broken by the diversification of family types and working hours, plus the rise in female labour force participation. The family unit now faces the pressure of managing the demands of work (dual income families, casual and part-time work, split shifts etc.) against the responsibilities of parenting and a wider range of leisure options. These aspirations do not necessarily fit the rigid supply side methods of government. Child care services in Australia are a clear example of the inability of central planning to meet the customised needs of families. Demand side solutions, such as capitation payments, where parents can buy in services according to their own needs and priorities, are an important means by which government initiatives can flexibly match family circumstances. (A proposal for the flexible delivery of family services and income support is developed in chapter 26.)

The key change in family life has been the growth in two-income and no income families. For the latter, representing the increase in long term and intergenerational unemployed, the welfare state has been particularly inadequate. When unemployment passes from generation to generation it not only diminishes material well-being but also social skills and personal capability. The passive provision of universal services can have little positive impact if needy citizens lack the skills and responsibility to make effective use of these services. This is where the case management approach to service provision, also pioneered in the Working Nation program, becomes critical. Each long term welfare recipient is expected to work in partnership with a case manager, who acts on that person's behalf to help secure the most appropriate package of training and employment programs. In this fashion, the services and role of the public sector are built around the needs of recipients.

These principles follow an 'agency' approach to meeting the needs of disadvantaged people. That is, case managers act as an agent for welfare recipients by matching public sector resources to the needs of each disadvantaged person. They play an intermediary role in ensuring that resources are customised and reciprocal responsibilities discharged. This role compensates for the diminished skills and capability of many long term welfare recipients. The case management approach brings together two of the core principles of welfare state reform: recipients should no longer be required to fit their needs and circumstances into the universal programs of the welfare state; and welfare itself should no longer rely on an unreciprocated flow of responsibility. In the attainment of social capability, one size no longer fits all, just as social responsibility needs to be more than a one way street. A third and related principle, in redefining the relationship between citizen and state, concerns the establishment of greater flexibility in the delivery of public services—a set of reforms detailed in the next chapter.

24

FUNCTIONAL
FLEXIBILITY

The design of the welfare state coincided with the high noon of public sector planning. The methods of post-war reconstruction replicated many of the command economy features of public provision during the war years. It was thought that long standing issues of deprivation and unequal distribution could be resolved by the methods of supply side planning. This is what the English jurist, Albert Dicey, described as 'government for the good of the people by experts or officials who know or think they know what is good for the people better than any non-official person or than the mass of the people themselves'.[1] During an era of standardised work, male living wages and full employment, this model of planned provision was not without logic or success. Systems of public service delivery took on the features of Fordism, with long repetitive runs of production aimed at a standardised output. This is how governments, for instance, devised systems of comprehensive schooling and large-scale secondary health care. It reflects the way in which the mass production of standardised services relied on the functional specialisation of government departments and agencies.

Services were delivered through a production line approach, with a clear division of responsibility between specialised units of public administration, thus narrowing the role and skills of public officials to the equivalent of professional guilds. Students, for instance, are still expected to pass through differentiated phases of primary, secondary, technical and higher education in this way, even though changes in learning needs and technology have now blurred the institutional boundaries between each. The same tendency can be observed in the organisation of the health system, with its distinct stages of primary, secondary and tertiary care. A production line also emerged in systems of land use planning, with their separate zoning, development and building approval phases. Even in welfare services, functional specialisation has dominated the work of government, with the development of a separate category of administration, pastoral care and income support for each isolated episode of deprivation.

In this fashion, the welfare state followed the private sector into Fordist methods of hierarchical mass production. These principles of organisation—based on rigid systems of standardisation, specialisation and a hierarchical division of labour—represented a culture of producer sovereignty. Under the planning model, policy makers assumed that large-scale bureaucracies could not only anticipate the needs of the citizenry, but also could provide for a suitable supply of services. Not surprisingly, as the certainties of the old economy began to crumble, the effectiveness of supply side planning also declined. With the diversification of labour skills, working conditions and family types in a post-industrial society, the anticipation of public needs and the supply of matching services have become problematic.

As a result of these changes, social democracy has been forced to fundamentally rethink its methods. As noted in Part III, Rawlsian notions of social justice rely on the capacity of the public sector to adapt to changing social wants and needs. The planning model is not well suited to an era of rapid social and economic change. Through the post-war decades, left-of-centre thinking came to associate social equity with public ownership and monopoly service rights. These methods were seen as synonymous with social justice in practice. Inevitably, however, events have overtaken this static reform model, leaving a large gap between social democratic means and the emergence of a new generation of equity concerns.

The dynamic features of a post-industrial economy have undermined the effectiveness of most of the fixed asset strategies of government. In a closed, protected economy, governments could predict employment patterns with relative certainty. Land use, population settlement and transport links were planned accordingly. In an internationalised economy, however, the pace of economic restructuring far exceeds the rate of change in urban form. The age old demand for 'better planning' in itself can no longer narrow the gap between disadvantaged locations and the spread of socioeconomic opportunities. An example of this process can be found in the changing relevance of the fixed asset strategies of government in housing policy.

After the Second World War broadacre public housing estates were built on the edge of Australia's major cities to accommodate a blue collar workforce engaged in tariff protected manufacturing.

In the 1950s, 80 per cent of these households had at least one person in work. The figure is now 15 per cent, primarily as a result of economic restructuring and the growing gap between the location of new jobs and the labour market features of these housing estates. Governments now require greater flexibility to locate public housing tenants closer to employment and other social opportunities. This can best be achieved through the use of head leasing and lease back arrangements, involving a policy shift from publicly owned and managed housing to publicly subsidised and leased housing. Thus, the policy and resource allocation functions of government are separated from issues of fixed ownership, with both privately and publicly owned providers able to contest the new leasing arrangements.[2] During a time of rapid change, fixed asset strategies need to be replaced by flexible policy methods.

ACTIVE GOVERNMENT

This is an important agenda for the relevance of social democracy. Functional flexibility in the methods of the state public sector should not be seen as inconsistent with the active role of government. The satisfaction of social needs and wants now relies heavily on the capacity of the public sector to deal with diversity and the public demand for effective choice. Government has a renewed role to play in meeting the communal needs of citizens in an open society. It is important to recognise, however, that these needs are far from standardised. Their satisfaction relies on customised methods of delivery displaying the virtues of functional flexibility in the administration of government.

This is an agenda about the relevance and effectiveness of the state which supersedes questions as to whether we have too much or too little government. It is possible to be an effective advocate for government intervention without also having to defend the monopoly rights of the public sector to provide certain types of services. Functional flexibility relies on the separation of the role of government as a policy maker, regulator and funder of core services. This redefinition of the public sector as a purchaser of services, without having the provision of services expressed necessarily in the form of public ownership, can often lead to bigger government. The point is to maximise the flexibility of the public sector and the deployment of its resources in meeting diverse social needs.[3]

One of the reasons for the diminished reputation of government in recent decades has been its failure to match the gains in consumer sovereignty and responsiveness arising from the private sector. Post-Fordist production methods have been successful in providing specialised commodities and services at niche markets. As consumer demands have risen, the private system of production has responded with the diversification of its product types. Successful organisations, whether public or private, now need a high degree of adaptability to satisfy rapidly changing public demands. Flexibility and dexterity are essential: bringing together temporary alliances of personnel and know-how to address each market niche. Within this framework, the usefulness of a rigid approach to ownership issues, fixed capital assets and supply side planning has greatly diminished.

Some commentators have suggested, especially with advances in information technology, that the organisation of government will increasingly reflect these methods of post-Fordist production and service delivery. New forms of electronic communication offer greater flexibility in service delivery, and weaken the need for fixed forms of monopolistic government supply and ownership. They strengthen the capacity of the public sector to shift from the primacy of producer interests to the need for consumer sovereignty and customisation. The emergence of functional flexibility in the public sector is likely to dismantle conventional notions of state ownership, hierarchy and even nationality. As Gary Sturgess has forecast:

> The boundaries of government will become in time so blurred that we will have trouble knowing whether we are being served by a public servant or a private employee, whether we are dealing with national, state or local government or whether we are dealing with one of our own governments at all and what is more, increasingly we will not care. This is not about privatisation; it is not about making governments smaller, if by smaller government we mean stripping the public sector of its capacity to participate and intervene in society. It is about giving the state greater leverage in society, whatever the people through their elective representatives, decide that they want government to do.[4]

Logically, there is nothing in this paradigm which inherently places it outside the goals and policy interests of social democracy. Indeed, in most respects, it offers an important opportunity by which policy means and ends can be clearly distinguished. In the new paradigm, means and methods are given full flexibility. Owners and providers (public and private), competitors and regulators are arranged for specific tasks and purposes, each linked to the equity goals of government. At the point of service delivery it is difficult to distinguish between publicly and privately owned activities.

Thus, the functions of the public sector are seamless, blurring the traditional separation of public and private ownership. This creates some crucial opportunities for the active role of government. It should be evident enough that the success of the public sector relies on its capacity to adapt to changed circumstances and deal effectively with communal interests and needs.

BENEFITS OF FUNCTIONAL FLEXIBILITY

The shift from supply side planning to functional flexibility holds immense potential for rebuilding bonds of support between the citizenry and the public sector. First, by concentrating more on outcomes than methods, the responsibilities of the public sector are likely to be better understood and appreciated by the public. The one constant of government through the ages has been the impossibility of delivering enduring results without the trust and confidence of the people. This means much more than electoral survival, it goes to the heart of social democracy. Lasting progress relies on a partnership or synthesis between the public and the efforts of the public sector. It is the way of the conservative to undermine public faith in the virtues of collective solutions to social issues. Yet this faith now relies on the capacity of government to harvest results through a more flexible and responsive system of public administration.

Second, the seamlessness of government activity has the potential to ameliorate some unfortunate stereotypes about public sector waste and inefficiency. By focusing on outcomes, governments can foster the spread of effective freedoms across society. The traditional focus on means and methods has led to a perception that the public sector is insensitive to the preferences and aspirations of individuals. Generally, supply side planning and long chains of bureaucratic command have not shown themselves to be responsive to the rise of consumerism and the public's support for transactions of choice. This is where functional flexibility can enhance the standing and effectiveness of the state public sector. It provides a more responsive link between the diverse needs and preferences of citizens and the role of the state. Moreover, contestability between public and private owners for service provision can also secure important efficiency gains in the delivery of services to consumers.

Third, the flexibility of the new paradigm allows governments to respond more adeptly to new forms of social inequality. Rapid changes in technology, economic development and urban form in Australia are constantly opening up new issues of social injustice. The conventional style of government, with fixed assets and inflexible methods, has been ponderous in meeting these challenges. Adaptable methods are more likely to produce equitable outcomes. Matters of ownership, regulation and state control need to be considered solely for their responsiveness to the shifting sands of social capability. The welfare state will not survive by targeting issues and measures of equality now decades out of date. In particular, new systems of public administration are required to resolve the problems of entrenched exclusion in the new economy, especially on a locational scale. The next chapter demonstrates how the principles of functional flexibility can be applied to the public sector's management of disadvantaged people and places.

25

PLACE MANAGEMENT

There is a sound argument for rethinking from first principles the relationship between the organisational structure of the public sector and disadvantaged people. Since the days of Captain Phillip, government functions in Australia have structured themselves around professional groupings or guilds.[1] Consequently the public sector has focused more on inputs than outcomes. It has been organised through the eyes of producers, not consumers. Doctors run our hospitals, teachers run our schools, engineers control the roads system, town planners run urban affairs, and so on. The guilds determine the inputs to government but none regards itself as responsible for its outputs. They have created and preserved vertical structures of government unconnected to the integrated (horizontal) access and benefits most people seek from public services. This problem has led to the proliferation of inter-departmental and other 'coordinating committees', most of which are either powerless or degenerate into territorial struggles.

Government has been laid out like a series of stove-pipes or silos, with the public moving between each guild-based function to access services. This structure makes improbable the optimal allocation of public resources once departmental budgets have been allocated to a local level. This is how public housing estates can end up with wonderful community arts projects but no employment or transport services. Moreover, each silo or service provider is likely to allocate a share of its resources to special programs, ostensibly to assist the disadvantaged.[2] None of these measures, however, features the benefits of integrated service delivery. Unfortunately for disadvantaged people and suburbs, their problems do not easily fall into each segment of government. A poor education, unemployment, homelessness, drug reliance, domestic violence and other social problems often overlap with and reinforce each other.

Poverty and the elimination of welfare dependency need to be understood as a process, not an isolated or segmented event. Instead of managing people or places out of difficulty, governments have come to manage a heavily segmented and uncoordinated set of social and economic functions. The public sector has focused either on the symptoms of capability failure, such as income deprivation, or isolated events in the process of poverty, such as family counselling services. Departments and agencies deal with only part of each problem. None has the authority or resources to address, in its totality, the causes of capability failure, either among individuals or at a locational level. In a typical public housing estate in Sydney, for instance, there are 17 different agencies providing 23 different programs and support mechanisms—each of them important in its own right, but none of them properly linked to address the diverse needs and circumstances of recipient families.[3]

PLACE MATTERS

These methods can no longer cope with the spatial impact of the changing nature of work and issues of economic exclusion. The dynamic movement of capital has fostered greater economic competition between locations, based on their capacity to upgrade labour force and entrepreneurial skills. A large gap has emerged between these trends and the prospects of people and places rutted into a cycle of socioeconomic disadvantage. Governments are yet to respond in any meaningful way to this crisis of urban form and opportunity. Indeed, most of the administrative systems of the public sector were developed last century, at a time when urban areas and communities were more compact. The initial scale of public service provision responded to the limited geography of towns and suburbs. Sound arguments have now emerged for the public sector to disaggregate its organisational scale to better respond to the type of socioeconomic pressures impacting on neighbourhoods and regions.

The wealth of nations is primarily a function of the skills and capacity of their citizens. This is also true for areas and communities, where the substance of economic and social success relies heavily on the skills and insights of local residents. This link, however, flows two ways. Skills determine the socioeconomic features of places but so too do these features influence skill formation. Research by Bob Gregory and Boyd Hunter has shown that once personal characteristics are factored out of each Census Collector District, a significant residual remains in high unemployment areas which can only be explained in terms of a cycle of locational disadvantage. The general features and outcomes of the location cannot be explained solely in terms of the personal characteristics of those that live there. To be certain, place matters. From the analysis, it follows that governments need to develop a spatial policy approach. As Hunter writes:

> The asymmetry between low and high status regions provides direct evidence that regional policies may be appropriate in the worst regions. While policies directed at personal characteristics (for example, labour market programs based on duration of unemployment) may be appropriate to addressing inequality in middle and high status regions, it is likely that regional policies are needed to redress the disadvantage of low status regions.[4]

In the 1960s social democrats argued that universality in service provision would act as an equalising instrument in society. Three decades later it seems that this approach has done little to close the gap between social privilege and disadvantage on a locational scale. The social atlas of Australia's major cities shows that the most reliable guide to someone's employment, health and educational status is their postcode. The economic restructuring associated with globalisation has not only produced a new layer of income inequality, but also reinforced the tendency in urban form towards locational disadvantage and underclass. Areas like central western Sydney and the northern and western suburbs of Melbourne face a double jeopardy: postcodes, people and skills with poor access to internationally competitive industries and employment and, consequently, low incomes, low spending power and inadequate employment generation. For policy makers, this represents a deficiency in aggregate demand, a crisis in skills formation and the need for new forms of government intervention which break the cycle of locational disadvantage.

THE PLACE MANAGEMENT MODEL

The public sector needs to move into place management. It needs to cast its organisational methods at managing the problems of disadvantaged people and places, rather than a disparate set of functional responsibilities and inputs. The first step is to bundle together the public resources—in health, housing, education, training, employment initiatives and community services—of a selected suburb or local government area. These would then be managed by a place authority empowered to buy in the services best suited to meeting local needs. This structure represents a fundamental overhaul of the federal system of government in Australia. It necessitates, in neighbourhoods and areas of chronic need, the devolution of the functions and resources of large Federal and State departments to a local place manager. It also replicates at a local level the funder/purchaser/provider split which has worked effectively in other aspects of public sector reform. A guide to the organisational features of the place management model is presented in Figure 25.1.

The benefits of place management come from restructuring the public sector around our most serious social problems. It has the flexibility to create cross-sectoral solutions. It abolishes the guilds and relies on multi-disciplinary management teams and substantial community input. It levels the silos of government and pushes the allocation of public resources towards projects of greatest local benefit. It emphasises outcomes rather than self-serving and segmented administrative inputs. The equity in place management comes from targeting and redistributing resources on the basis of locational need. It also fosters a whole-of-government approach to the case management of disadvantaged citizens. This is a critical reform for the effectiveness of the welfare state. Disadvantaged people are not able to segment their problems into the discrete administrative units by which government has segmented its functions. Problems in employability, for instance, are invariably linked to family circumstances, educational opportunity, transport access, residential locational and health-related issues.

Just as poverty is a whole-of-life experience, the public sector needs to develop whole-of-government solutions. This means pursuing the benefits of universal case management. That is, a single case manager can take responsibility for moulding and customising each of the public services with which a client has contact. The success of labour market programs, for example, would be enhanced if training initiatives were linked to the tenancy decisions of public housing authorities (thereby matching new skills against the locational availability of employment). Equally, gains can be made in education from linking the home and school learning environments. Universal case management is made more feasible by the disaggregation of government scale implicit in the place management model. The place authority would employ a number of case managers (drawn from both the public and non-government sectors), each with the authority to customise and integrate services across the full range of government responsibilities.

This integration of the case and place management models is particularly beneficial. It facilitates the customisation of services for disadvantaged people and places. It also consolidates the notion of positive responsibilities within a single administrative system.

Figure 25.1 Place management model

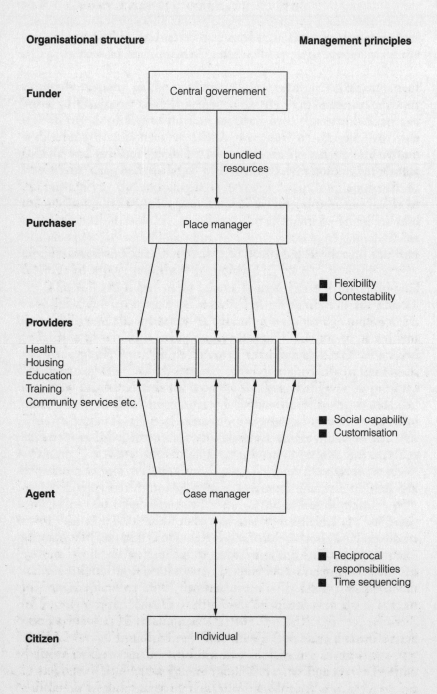

Case managers would be able to frame, in cooperation with welfare recipients, a clear set of reciprocal obligations across the range of public sector functions. This gives new meaning to the ideals of social contracting. Service recipients would commit themselves to agreed responsibilities in a single contract with their case manager. This might include responsibilities for training and skill development, improved personal health habits, the care and maintenance of public housing accommodation, and good parenting practices (such as undertaking courses to enhance the capability of parents in the home). Breaches of these responsibilities, as with Working Nation's Job Compact, would result in the application of income support sanctions. This system is similar to the public application of social responsibilities in some European nations. In Switzerland, for example, welfare recipients need to periodically present their credentials for good citizenship before their local canton board to justify the further payment of public income support.

AGENCY APPROACH

On a broader scale, place management adopts an agency approach to the work of the public sector among welfare dependent communities. The place authority would serve as an intermediary between the Federal/State governments and a specific location. Central governments (as a funder) would allocate bundled resources to a place manager (or purchaser) which would then buy in (from providers) a mix of services best suited to local needs and priorities. These funder/purchaser/provider arrangements break the supply side chain and open up contestability between government and non-government providers. This helps shift the focus of service provision from inputs (guilds and professions) to outcomes (upon which any competitive process must be based). This is one of the core benefits of the place management model. It fosters flexibility by directing the public sector at results, rather than simply complying with the departmental handbook. It demands performance and the satisfaction of public needs for the ongoing allocation of public resources.

This potential for contestability in the provision of place management services signifies an important break from the passive provision of public services in disadvantaged areas. It allows governments to provide a bundle of resources for competing agencies to solve social problems, for which they would be rewarded accordingly. A number of parish and charity-based organisations, for instance, would be well placed to apply for place management projects. They currently have, albeit operating under a diverse range of government and self-funded programs, the local infra-structure in place (schools, youth groups, family counsellors, welfare services, employment and training programs etc.) to fulfil the place management role. In particular, place managers would be able to broker many of the community-based employment functions outlined in chapter 13. These local authorities and agents would have the organisational flexibility to make best use of the public resources allocated for training, skill development, local infrastructure projects and civil sector and community services employment. This reflects the importance of the welfare functions of work and the desirability of whole-of-government solutions to the problems of economic exclusion.

Generally, governments have not pursued these principles due to the way in which they threaten the guild interests and supply side orthodoxy of Fordist government. The sheer size of the change process, no matter the pressing evidence of a welfare crisis in underclass neighbourhoods, has also been an obstacle to reform itself. Some reforms are so big that Ministers simply do not know where to commence. Some government departments have grown so large that nobody knows where to start in devolving their work to a local level. Our short, three or four year electoral cycle has made major reform of the welfare state an intimidating exercise for most politicians.

In this regard, place management presents reformers with a more manageable scale of change. It does not require the State-wide dismantling of departments or guild interests. It can be trialed at locations of critical need. In suburbs with unemployment rates of 30 per cent, and welfare dependency at 80 per cent (typical of public housing areas in Australia's major cities), little can be lost by way of public policy outcomes. Broken programs require new methods. Chronic problems require greenfield solutions. Indeed, place management offers a format within which each of the reforms advocated in this part of the book—especially in case management, reciprocal responsibilities and functional flexibility—can be developed. The organisational structure of the Australian public sector and its federal system requires no more pressing reform than the establishment of place management trials.

26

LIFELONG INCOME SUPPORT

Case and place management methods are required to deal with the problems of chronic economic exclusion and capability failure. For other citizens and their welfare interests, sitting beyond the formal safety net, a post-Fordist welfare state requires a different set of reforms. It needs to equip people with greater flexibility and security in the means by which they might deal with the remorseless spread of economic uncertainty. As noted in earlier chapters, the quality and availability of lifelong education is an essential part of this process. So, too, is the development of new systems of lifelong income support and provision. These are the basic tools of social capability in a post-industrial society: the benefits of employability security and active citizenship from an engagement in lifelong learning; a capacity to plan and save effectively against the contingencies of economic change through a lifelong process of income support.

THE NEED FOR REFORM

The Australian system of income support was designed to deal with vastly different economic and social circumstances to those arising in this era of globalisation and workplace change. The transfer payments system reflects a series of categories devised incrementally through the course of this century to deal with the emergence of new social problems and sources of economic exclusion. Governments responded to each of these issues with additional categories of payment. Despite the steady growth in the size and purpose of the welfare system, the allocation of transfer payments was still cast in official policy as nothing more substantial than a residual system of income support. Taken against the features of the new economy, however, these methods are in need of substantial reform. As Michael Jones has written:

> Australia has developed a reactive, ad hoc welfare state. Most programs still apply the selective means tested principles of the first age pensions established in 1901. This approach worked well enough when most dependants were aged and most households relied on wages. The protected economy and wage regulation supported high living standards, and intact families provided most social care. From 1970, Australian dependency levels began to rise rapidly, and the unemployed, families with children and the disabled became central groups in the new dependency . . . Ideally, Australian policy makers should have developed an entirely new system to cope with the rapidly changing dependency. This has not happened.[1]

The selective development of transfer payment categories has produced a number of structural weaknesses in the Australian welfare system. Most notably, given the rise in the income dependency ratio from 12 per cent to 27 per cent, incrementalism of this kind has progressively overloaded the fiscal carrying capacity of the public commons. The spread of economic insecurity and exclusion has strained the capacity of the tax/transfer system to adequately fund the welfare pool. The impact on the taxation system of economic internationalisation and the changing nature of production have not been compatible with the demands of an income transfer system supporting one in every four citizens. The weakening of the taxation net has coincided with the broadening of income support.

Attempts at targeting have only been able to marginally limit the growth in public welfare costs. For example, extensive targeting and means testing in the social security policies of the Hawke Government were only able to reduce the dependency ratio from 26 per cent in 1983 to 24.5 per cent in 1989. These gains were subsequently lost during the recession of the early 1990s and the rise of structural unemployment. It is now clear that the financial sustainability of Australia's income support system requires something more substantial than the immediate and direct provision of transfers from consolidated revenue. Just as the foundations of the tax system require fundamental reform, so too does the system of income transfers.

The incremental creation of categories, in tandem with the heavy targeting of benefits, has produced other difficulties in the structure of income support. The transfer payment system is now incredibly complex, both for clients to understand and for public servants to administer. The Department of Social Security *Hand-*

book, for example, now spans 150 pages and covers 34 categories of payment. These include transfers to the retired, disabled, sick, unemployed, families with children, housing assistance, widows, guardians, and child care users, as well as the parenting allowance and a maternity allowance. Each category has its own availability criteria and means testing methods, thereby creating a multitude of cut-in and cut-out points. In turn, these lead to 'border' problems, in which people with near-identical or only slightly changed circumstances end up with different eligibility outcomes. Members of the Federal Parliament daily encounter constituents in genuine need who have been disadvantaged by this system, either through the inability of the bureaucracy to administer its complexity, or by the way in which these applicants for income support have fallen between the cracks of its many categories and eligibility tests.

A selectivist or targeted welfare system also produces a range of incentive problems, especially in its interaction with the taxation system. High effective marginal tax rates (EMTR) occur when non-taxable transfer payments are withdrawn and replaced by taxable earnings. The Australian system features a number of these poverty traps. For example, if a family with one child aged under thirteen and without rent assistance increases its paid earnings from $417 to $485 per week (the range of the income test taper for Additional Family Payments), its disposable income increases by just $1.99. Further, a single unemployed person renting privately faces an EMTR of up to 140 per cent through the income range at which rent assistance is progressively withdrawn.[2]

Disincentives against improved earnings capacity, especially for two-income families with children, also occur in the income range within which most transfer payments and tax benefits are eliminated by means testing; that is, at around a combined earnings level of $62 000 per annum. Disincentives at both portions of the income scale have generated considerable public dissatisfaction with the transfer system, adding to the incidence of poverty traps among low income earners, plus the spread of downwards envy among the middle income group. It is simply untenable, especially during a time of economic change and insecurity, for the tax/transfer structure to provide disincentives to the pursuit of gainful work, earnings and personal capability.

REFORM GOALS

From these issues, a number of reform goals are apparent. Income support needs to be based on a simplified category structure which restores public confidence in the transfer system. It also needs to strongly reward individual effort aimed at work and earnings capacity, plus rebuild the financial sustainability and adequacy of the transfer net. Moreover, the welfare system needs to be able to explicitly respond to the contingencies, seemingly on a permanent basis, of economic change and uncertainty. This involves a major task in the flexibility of income support, with the establishment of a different timeframe over which the goals of income provision (public and private) might be cast. The Australian welfare system was never designed to cope with wide fluctuations in economic circumstances. By and large, it takes a 'snapshot' approach to income support, with its provision of single purpose payments at regular time intervals. It is without the capacity to bring forward or defer benefits according to personal need and changed economic circumstance and thus, is not able to deal adequately with the core features of a post-industrial economy.

The full employment of labour market participants, with full time jobs, can no longer be regarded as a sound basis for income security across the citizenry. A declining number of families seem to be able to rely on a living wage, through a lifetime of permanent full time work, with which to cover their housing, education and child rearing costs. Compared to the relative certainty of the 1960s, it is now estimated that the average working family is 50 per cent more likely to face an unexpected decline in its living standards.[3] This reflects the pace of economic restructuring and the rise of casual, part-time, temporary and contract employment in the new economy. Growing rates of long term unemployment and earnings dispersion have placed enormous pressure on the supposedly residual features of income support. Moreover, the use of multiple categories and eligibility criteria in the targeting of transfer payment has not been well suited to the dynamic nature of living standards in an open economy. The administration of this complex system is clearly struggling to cope with the fluctuating circumstances and needs of a substantial proportion of recipients. Between July and September 1995, for instance, 22 per cent of Department of Social Security clients of a workforce age moved from at least one payment type to another.[4]

An average working life is now likely to feature a considerable number of earnings fluctuations, as people move more frequently in and out of paid work; between full- and part-time earnings; from a different number of household income earners; and, even within the same form of employment, up and down the income scale. The Australian system of income support system (plus alternatives often advanced by way of private insurance) does not cope effectively with short term fluctuations of this kind. Both the targeted distribution of transfer payments and private systems of income insurance rely on a fairly flat and constant line of earnings capacity across a working life, with only occasional reliance—during times of sickness or temporary unemployment—on the welfare or insurance pool. This flat line has now been broken by the pace of economic change into a series of earnings oscillations.

In the experience of many nations overseas, especially in Western Europe, social insurance methods of income support are also struggling to cope with the welfare consequences of the new economy. They have found it difficult to meet the income support needs of the growing number of citizens permanently excluded from the economy. This problem, combined with society's ageing demographics, has meant that outlays from the common insurance pool have started to significantly exceed contributions. The absence of a sound actuarial relationship between contributions and benefits has led to a number of intergenerational inequities. That is, because these schemes are funded from pay-as-you-go contributions, while benefits are paid on a needs basis, one generation can end up covering the unfunded commitments of another. During a period of substantial economic and social change this is an undesirable, yet somewhat inevitable consequence of the social insurance approach.

There is, therefore, a need to consider the development of a vastly different system of income support in Australia. Internationally, the effectiveness of targeted transfer payments and systems of private and social insurance—each aimed at dealing with the welfare needs of the old economy—appears to be in irreversible decline. Social democracy needs to establish the principles and administrative methods by which the requirements of the new economy can be met. This involves the introduction of a flexible, lifelong structure of income support, based on elements of both public sector provision and self-provident savings. This system is best understood from its reliance on three aspects of welfare reform.

POLICY REFORM

The first is to simplify Australia's existing structure of transfer payments. During his time as Social Security Minister in the Keating Government, Peter Baldwin demonstrated the conceptual basis from which the transfer system could be reduced to 'a single generic payment for those of workforce age, subsuming the existing myriad of payments'.[5] It was proposed that the level and conditions of entitlement would vary with individual characteristics, such as age, workforce experience, parenting responsibilities, number of children, housing costs and disability-related issues. The Department of Social Security, especially with advances in information technology, should now be able to develop a thorough range of customised income support packages. In this manner, the current system of narrowly constructed categories can be replaced by a generic entitlement which recipients are then able to mould and customise according to their particular needs. As Baldwin has explained:

> It is envisaged that people will be able to select from a menu of products to produce a customised income support package, parallel with the revolution that has transformed financial markets—such that clients sit down in front of a computer terminal with a bank employee to work out what particular home loan package meets her/his needs most effectively. I would like to see DSS doing business in a similar way. This approach clearly has some profound implications, both legislative and administrative. It is not without risk, both to the customer and to the Department. But the experience of the financial sector shows that this kind of risk is manageable . . . Importantly, these flexible income support structures should greatly enhance people's capacity to exercise choice, to take control of their own lives. This takes us beyond the goal of simply providing a safety net to one of enhancing people's freedom to achieve—intrinsic to overcoming poverty viewed, in Sen's terms, as the loss of substantive freedom.[6]

This proposal represents a major advance in the capacity of public administration to deal with increasingly diverse social and economic circumstances. It bridges the concepts of simplification and customisation in service delivery though the use of actuarial risk management and new communications technology. Electronic forms of information, of course, not only offer the potential for greater public sector efficiency and flexibility, but also the potential for universality of service access. Through the development of telecottages and other information access points, a range of local, State and Federal services are likely to come on-line. This might involve functions as diverse as downloading personal and regulatory information, submitting building applications, enrolling in educational courses, completing taxation and other returns, communicating with parliamentarians and voting on local referendum questions. One of the most important uses of these new services undoubtedly lies in their potential for the customisation of income support.

The second stage of reform, closely linked to the principles of customised welfare, concerns the 'time sequencing' of income arrangements. Instead of providing a regular sequence of payments, the welfare system is given the flexibility by which, over time, citizens can adjust their entitlements against the contingencies of economic and lifestyle change. Let me give an example. It should be possible, under the payment system described above, to establish an 'income account' which would bring together the prospective entitlements of a family in child endowment, child care benefits and tax-related concessions. This would provide a consolidated package of financial resources, notionally held on behalf of a family by the Department of Social Security. The scope of family-related entitlements would be determined by calculating the benefits available per child over a period of several years. Within prudential limits, parents would be able to draw forward or defer their entitlements according to family circumstances. If one partner, for instance, suffered a reduction in earnings they might seek an advance on child care resources to allow the other parent to seek work. Or, if the parents were uncomfortable with out-of-home child care they might defer this part of their account to help cover the subsequent costs of schooling.

This proposal converts the snapshot method of single purpose payments into a flexible bundle of resources which recipients can then use and develop as a buffer against the consequences of social and economic change. In this fashion, time sequencing enhances the capability of income units to cope with the permanent threat of uncertainty in the new economy. It allows recipients to mould their entitlements according to personal need, judgments and circumstance, rather than being locked into a rigid set of departmental guidelines and categories. This sense of ownership and control has the potential to substantially improve public confidence in the effectiveness of the tax/transfer system. The legitimacy of the welfare state is enhanced whenever citizens are able to see its entitlements working directly towards the satisfaction of personal capability and socioeconomic security.

A leading objective of income support in a post-industrial economy is to smooth out, over time, the growing incidence of wide fluctuations in income capacity. Importantly, however, this smoothing process needs to operate with some degree of mutuality. While governments need to advance income support whenever its citizens are victim to economic uncertainty, they should also consider the equity features of a repayment scheme (similar to the principles underpinning HECS, the Higher Education Contribution Scheme) for recipients who subsequently benefit from economic change. This should be regarded as a key aspect of the development of reciprocal responsibilities in the welfare system. Those who benefit most from the discharge of public responsibilities have a moral obligation to replenish the common pool of public resources from which their improved circumstances, at least in part, originated. This concept also aids the inter-generational equity of the public commons by ensuring a reasonable balance of revenue contributions across all generations.

A third reform concerns the facilitation of a higher level of self-provision in the welfare system. Australia and New Zealand have been distinctive in the Western world for the general absence of contributory schemes. The economic uncertainties associated with globalisation offer sound reasons for rethinking this approach. After all, the best way for citizens to plan against change and economic insecurity is to enhance their future financial capacity through the habits of saving. Traditionally, Australians have made provision against the uncertainty of accidents and illness through public and private health insurance schemes. Variations in lifetime earning capacity, underscored by the fiscal crisis of the state, now warrant consideration of the personal contributions that might usefully be made to the provision of lifelong income support.

The Keating Government used this principle to overhaul Australia's retirement income system through the introduction of mandatory, occupational superannuation, with a mixture of employee, employer and government contributions (the latter having subsequently been abandoned in the second Costello Budget). One of the problems with this approach, however, was the way in which the scheme loaded the contributory income support of wage earners towards their retirement years, at the expense of pre-retirement income needs and security.[7] For most people, through the cycle of their active adult years, the critical lifestyle costs and financial pressures occur at a relatively early age, especially during the period of child rearing and home purchasing. There can be no resolution of the issue of income insecurity in Australia without addressing the shortcomings of the pre-retire-ment income system.

Inevitably this requires suitable regulations and incentives for self-providence and savings. The progressive expenditure tax system proposed in chapter 14 moves substantially in this direction. It breaks the tax regime into the downstream questions of con-sumption and savings, with tax deductibility taken in the form of registered savings and investment instruments. Under this system, personal contributions to a self-provident fund, such as superan-nuation or a new pre-retirement savings vehicle, would not be taxed until such time as they or their accumulated financial returns were actually spent. Governments could offer further incentives for savings of this kind by taxing at a concessional rate those forms of expenditure directly related to a specified self-provident purpose.

If, to take one example, policy makers wanted to encourage superannuants to plan and save for the costs of recreational learning in
their retirement years, then contributions and outlays identified for
this purpose would be taxed at a concessional PET rate.

INCOME SECURITY ACCOUNTS

Taken in combination, these key principles of income support
reform—simplification of the payment structure, time sequencing
of bundled accounts and the virtues of self providence—open
an opportunity for the development of a new structure of
pre-retirement income support in Australia. This scheme would act
as a bulwark against the uncertainties of economic change, with
the flexibility required to smooth out variations in earnings capacity
over the full period of labour force participation. It would shift the
resourcing of income dependency from a series of snapshot payments off consolidated revenue towards a lifelong structure of
income support, based on risk and need-rated public contributions
plus self-provident private funding. This is a critical response to
the declining legitimacy and sustainability of the public sector
commons. The foundations of a flexible, sustainable, lifelong
system of income support in Australia can be structured as follows:

- People would apply (upon leaving the education system and
  entering the labour market) to the Department of Social Security for the establishment of an Income Security Account (ISA).
  The account would be based on a generic payment structure,
  with payments varied according to identified need, changed
  circumstance and actuarial management issues. The accounts
  would thereby represent a consolidation of the existing 34
  payment categories, notionally held by DSS as a flexible bank
  of resources.
- ISA holders would then manage this bundle of entitlements
  (subject to prudential and risk assessment by DSS) to meet
  their own needs and aspirations. These principles of welfare
  customisation and time sequencing would place a great deal of
  effective choice and capability in the hands of recipients. The
  exercise of mutual responsibility would also ensure a two-way
  income smoothing process (whereby for the high income beneficiaries of economic change, a repayment scheme would
  apply).
- Citizens experiencing chronic problems of economic exclusion
  would have their ISA resources brought under the methods of

case management, with a clear social contract based on reciprocal responsibilities, skill development and employment goals.

- ISA holders would be encouraged to make financial contributions to their accounts on the basis of a concessional rate of
withdrawal under the PET system. That is, citizens who plan
and save against the contingencies of economic change would
not pay tax on these savings (either at the point of earnings or
their deposit in an ISA) and then only pay a concessional rate
(possibly zero) on the use of these savings for approved purposes. Such purposes would be based on the costs of economic
restructuring, including additional education qualifications,
labour market retraining, subsequent child care provision,
housing relocation and supplementary income support.[8]

- The interface between public entitlements and private contributions would need to be structured so as to avoid possible
disincentive effects for personal ISA contributions. If, after a
period of initial implementation, it were clear that the tax
concession approach was not sufficient to foster a strong level
of self-providence, policy makers would then need to develop
a mandated approach.

- The scheme would also need to establish a suitable interface
with the existing program of superannuation. This would
involve the capacity of wage earners, according to their personal needs and judgments, to bring forward part of their
employee superannuation contribution into the ISA system or
alternatively, defer some of their ISA resources for the benefit
of retirement income. At retirement age, of course, any remaining ISA balance would simply be rolled into the superannuation
pool.

This scheme has a number of clear advantages in the reform
of the welfare state. It recognises and rewards the virtues of savings
and self-providence during an era of permanent economic change,
while also removing the possibility of high EMTRs and disincentives against the enhancement of earnings capacity. It is simply not
possible for social democracy or, for that matter, the citizenry to
expect the open-ended allocation of public resources to be able to
meet every demand and need arising from the spread of insecurity.
This overload of government only adds to the incidence of downwards envy and the underlying weakness of the public sector
commons. The scheme developed above, importantly enough, helps
to enhance the public standing of income support. The bundling
of public and private ISA resources over time reduces the possibility of full income dependence on the public sector. Those

excluded from economic participation might just as likely be drawing on their own ISA contributions as on public sources of funding.

This self-provident aspect of the scheme helps to build the
intergenerational equity of lifelong income support, as well as
making it less vulnerable to the small government agenda of the
political Right. Moreover, an effective social safety net is able to
be maintained by combining the benefits of a simplified, generic
payment structure with elements of income targeting. This is made
feasible through Baldwin's proposal for the use of advanced information technology and actuarial management methods within the
Federal bureaucracy. The structure of the ISAs would always aim
to guarantee a basic threshold of income capability. For those
people, however, relying on this threshold and nothing else, case
and place management methods need to be used to break the cycle
of welfare dependency. Ultimately, the success of the welfare state
needs to be judged by the spread of earned contributions to the
ISA system.

Another feature of this approach to lifelong income support is
the way in which it creates—consistent with the principles of
functional flexibility—new demand side markets, especially in the
provision of child care services. This is a positive consequence of
the bundling of entitlements and facilitating their flexible use by
recipients. The ISA system allows, in the delivery of some social
goods, the weight of service control and choice to be shifted from
providers to consumers. This reflects how the attainment of complex equality requires more than the passive supply of government
services. The type of choices and skills exercised by individuals, in
combination with their access to essential social goods and a decent
threshold of primary goods, determines their capability set. Without a satisfactory level of personal responsibility and effort, an
individual's capacity to achieve effective freedoms is inevitably
restricted, both in the new economy and society.

Social democracy needs to be less dogmatic in the framing of
its equity goals. Simplistic forms and measures of equality, such as
arbitrary poverty lines, are a poor way of dealing with the diversity
of individual circumstance and need. This is why the capability
paradigm is so important. Rather than constructing an idealised
model of social equality, around which the state can centrally plan
its systems of provision, it emphasises the quality of a range of social
and economic interactions. Weight is given to items of particular
social need and merit, upon which one's freedom to achieve might
be based. This requires—in response to the uncertainty of the new
economy—flexible lifelong systems of income support. Moreover
and even more importantly, it necessitates new forms of state
intervention in the development of a learning society.

27

LIFELONG LEARNING

With the advent of knowledge as a core economic resource and the growing significance of cognitive skills, opportunities for lifelong learning have become the most important form of interaction between the state and its citizenry. Education has become the critical item of social capability in the post-industrial age. It serves not only as a catalyst for new forms of economic and technological progress, but is also the means by which each individual can develop the skills of adaptability. The capacity of the nation state and its governance to halt the spread of globalisation and the pace of social change is not strong (even if, indeed, this were desirable). The most effective form of collective action in an open economy and society now lies in ensuring that each of a nation's citizens can respond adeptly to the contingencies of change. This means using the learning process to empower people to act in new ways—to develop new skills and personal capacity, so that change can be treated more as an opportunity than a threat. It means teaching people, through the habits of lifelong learning, to fully develop their cognitive capacities and their understanding of themselves and the society in which they live.

PUBLIC UNIVERSALITY

The special status of education policy in a post-industrial society requires governments to develop new attitudes and systems of public resourcing. Education and research need to be seen not only as public goods and items of particular social merit, but also investments and functions servicing the national good. The new growth theorists have demonstrated how the public good qualities of knowledge result in its under-resourcing by the private sector.

As no single enterprise can capture the full gains of knowledge enhancement, a market system inevitably fails to invest to the full capacity and economic benefits of new forms of learning. Thus the education and research functions of the state have become a core source of national sovereignty in the new economy. So too, it is not possible to equip citizens with the skills of adaptability without recognising the social value of learning.

Nations are able to aspire to high skill-high wage production and work primarily through the success of their education systems. Countries which under-invest in the skills of their people make themselves more vulnerable to the movement of global capital. They also diminish the capacity of their citizens to deal with the incidence of social and economic change. This is why corporatist industry policies and segment-of-life programs represent such a damaging drain on the collective resources of the public sector. They divert scarce public resources away from the core functions of government in universally delivering the skills of adaptability and lifelong learning. They add to the fiscal crisis of the state and the inexorable spread of downwards envy without fostering new sources of socioeconomic security.

The principle of public universality in education is based on the way in which all citizens benefit from the development of a learning society—either in the direct use of learning services or in the indirect benefits of endogenous growth and social progress. This approach charters government with a strong set of responsibilities in the provision of educational opportunities. Unlike most inputs to the production process, knowledge is a self-replenishing resource. Its use, uniquely among items of economic and social merit, does not necessarily lead to its depletion or to a narrowing of its accessibility.[1] As the pool of knowledge can only increase over time, collective forms of service delivery are needed to foster this process and share its benefits. An effective economy of scale in the accumulation and transmission of knowledge can be created through a strong public investment in the formal institutions of a learning society.

Policy makers should be sceptical about the promise of the market system to deliver equity and effective choice in the processes of lifelong learning. Adam Smith was certainly correct in saying that when private markets work, they work exceptionally well. The problem for the advocates of commercialisation is that education services do not work well as open markets. Without the substantial involvement of the public sector they are subject to a series of market failures. If education is purchased and sold like any other market commodity, it is reduced solely to the status of a private good, denying society its opportunity to maximise the public good features of lifelong learning. Social democracy needs to fund education and research as items of unique national and public purpose.

In most Western nations, however, the debate about education funding has concentrated on the identification of private sources of revenue, corresponding with the type of economic benefits each individual might expect to derive from the education system. This has led to the development of quasi-markets in the delivery of learning services. User charges have been introduced, reflecting the balance of supply and demand for particular services, plus government estimates of the type of benefits that might accrue to individuals in their service consumption. Under circumstances of static economic output, where learning services were not able to impact on rates of national economic growth, this approach might have some conceptual appeal. It would allow governments to develop appropriate price signals in the rationing of the public's access to the finite benefits of education. For instance, scholarships would be developed to assist low income earners cover the expense of cost-recovery fees at the point of course entry. Governments would simply treat education as one of many services subject to the fiscal limits of the public sector, thereby requiring the targeting of cash transfers and service access.

The point of the new growth paradigm, however, is that national economies—particularly in the transition from an industrial to an information base—reflect dynamic patterns of economic growth, driven explicitly by the quality of the education and research system. This is why the debate about the relative share of public and private contributions to education funding is so narrow and self-defeating. It reflects an assumption of static national economic development, from which the chief purpose of public policy is to distribute or ration public access. This perspective overlooks the possibilities of new forms of knowledge, their creation and dissemination, driving the national economy to a new plane of growth and development. As the key public and national good of a post-industrial economy, education is likely to produce substantial economic gains from which each of a nation's citizens can derive lasting benefits (especially through the type of national gain sharing model developed in Part II). In this context, the public/private funding debate becomes superfluous, more the sign of a nation complacent about its economic interests than one willing to develop and drive a new growth agenda.

In the ongoing transition of the production base and the nature of work, all national economies, no matter how advanced and affluent by the standards of industrial production, need to be regarded as under-developed. A narrow focus on the private good features of education serves only to retard this transitional process

and the national benefits of knowledge-based economic development. Lifelong learning needs to be treated as an essential,
universally provided service of the nation state, both in its facilitation of public interests and social capability. All citizens need to
be able to draw on the learning process through all parts of their
life, without being impeded by financial or locational barriers to
service delivery. Active citizenship and capability now require a
range of adaptable skills with a lifetime commitment to education
and training. The pace of economic change is forcing participants
to the labour market to acquire a stronger and more diverse set of
skills. The rate of social change has also boosted the role of
education in assisting people to learn for life, both in terms of
good citizenship and their recreational pursuit of lifelong learning.

SOCIAL EQUITY

The core purpose of the public sector is in transition—most
notably, shedding its ownership of fixed industrial assets and investing ever more in the assets and capabilities of a learning society.
This, in turn, presents a critical opportunity for rejuvenating the
equity functions of government. The traditional methods of the
public sector—Fordist service delivery, passive transfer payments
and the planning strand—have not been able to counter the tendency of an open economy towards greater inequality. The
polarisation of incomes and lifestyles in most Western nations,
driven by the slow burning crisis of economic exclusion and underclass, reflect the shortcomings of the post-war welfare state. While
the reform of income support and service delivery methods can
make a constructive difference, the most substantial contribution
to social equity now lies in the universal spread of lifelong learning.

In particular, the public good features of knowledge have the
potential to alter the type of social relationship upon which economic inequality has conventionally been based. In the old
economy, the standard skills of labour were able to be exploited
by capital due to an imbalance in their supply and demand. The
relative scarcity of capital and abundance of labour transferred
market control and income premiums to the owners of industrial
investment. In a market system, economic power is primarily a
product of scarcity. As long as labour owned nothing more than a
standardised set of skills, and these skills were freely available in
the labour market, the income returns and market power of the
working class were inevitably diminished.

The advent of post-industrial production on a global scale,
however, has fundamentally altered this relationship. As nations

now have the capacity to trade in each other's savings, and as finance capital moves seamlessly across large parts of the international economy, the scarcity of capital has to some extent been ameliorated. With the emergence of new information-based industries and their endogenous boost to economic growth, knowledge skills have become the scarcest and most valuable type of production input. At a time in which unskilled labour remains plentiful across the global economy, and the footloose movement of capital investment has become widespread, economic premiums have started to flow decisively towards the value of highly skilled symbolic analysts. Clever nations have been able to succeed on a global scale, not by propping up routine production forms of work and slowing their economic development, but by increasing the proportion of their labour force engaged in knowledge work.

Given the role of government in resourcing and facilitating the learning process, these trends place additional weight on the equity functions of the public sector. The capacity of the citizenry to upgrade its knowledge skills and participate universally in the benefits of economic growth has a profound impact on the quality and equality of society. The purpose of education policy must be to allow each of a nation's citizens to harness and capture a strong share of these freshly formed knowledge skills. Importantly, this means providing something more substantial than a simple equality of opportunity in the public's access to educational services. Abstract rights of access are not sufficient to universally guarantee an effective freedom to achieve in education, by which all citizens can realise their personal potential for learning and skill enhancement. The role of the public sector needs to be framed such that it addresses issues of advantage and disadvantage in the range of learning capabilities each individual uniquely brings to the formal institutions of learning.

CUSTOMISED LEARNING

Far from treating people as if their circumstances and learning needs were identical, public policy should aim to compensate for the variations in learning potential that arise from factors outside the boundaries of what has conventionally been defined as the education sector. The freedom to achieve a good education needs to take account of capability parameters from all parts of an individual's learning experience, especially the interaction between the home learning environment, on-the-job learning and the formal institutions of the education system. Just as public policy needs to promote learning as a lifelong necessity, it also needs to cast the learning process as a whole-of-life experience. One of the critical aspects of schools policy, for instance, especially in dealing with intergenerational problems of educational disadvantage, is to establish a closer link between the quality of the home learning environment and school education.

These trends and policy goals reflect the unique nature of knowledge as an item of economic and social value. While the learning process carries many of the characteristics of a public good, in that access to the existing pool of knowledge cannot be restricted, it also displays some of the features of a private as well as developmental good. The creation of knowledge, especially in its original form, can be highly exclusive. It emerges and finds expression in different ways from each individual, thereby allowing some of its value to be captured as a private good. The subsequent transmission of new forms of knowledge throughout society, usually through the public institutions of learning, then gives the education system its public good qualities.

For each person, of course, the private good aspects of learning reflect the significance of innate cognitive skills. Given the extent of variations between people in this primary source of learning ability, it is plainly not possible for public policy to aim at equal outcomes in the spread of knowledge skills across society. Rather, the role of the public sector should be to facilitate an education environment within which the innate qualities of each individual are developed to their maximum skill and cognitive potential. The education process involves changing the way people behave and respond in their contact with new events and new forms of information. This means fostering the methods by which people can develop a clearer understanding of society and its relationship to their personal aspirations and fulfilment. The capability or effective freedom to learn is all important.

This goal also recognises the developmental or interactive nature of learning. The collective pool of knowledge and its transmission throughout society is never static, just as the personal skills of learning are always capable of further development. At each point in life, individuals have the capacity to grow their knowledge and understanding of society. Towards this end, the purpose of education policy should be to foster the most productive form of interaction between personalised learning needs and inclinations, and the formal institutions of the education system—that is, it should maximise the capacity of students to develop their innate ability into a higher plane of knowledge and learning skills. This again emphasises the importance of service customisation and flexibility. Unless the unique learning needs and habits of each person are catered for in their interaction with the learning process, it will not be possible to achieve the most effective form of educational outcomes.

THE GREAT DIVIDE

To be certain, the foundations of an equal society now depend heavily on the capacity of the public sector to convert the private and developmental good features of learning into a truly public good—universally delivering the benefits of personal adaptability and social capability. The freedom to achieve in a knowledge-based society has profound implications, not just for the work of the public sector, but also for the way in which the political system is structured and understood. For more than two centuries the politics of the Western world has been argued out through issues of ownership, the binary of industrial capital versus standard skill labour. In the old economy the entrenched, relatively fixed ownership of industrial capital stratified society on the basis of class. The intransigence of these ownership issues has been immensely frustrating for the politics of the old Left.

In the new economy, however, social mobility and opportunity rely more substantially on the dynamic possibilities and distribution of knowledge-based skills. Successful citizens are able to convert new forms of information into items of economic and social value. A key issue for social democracy, in the fulfilment of its equity functions, is not to allow the unequal distribution of primary goods from the industrial age to perpetuate itself, as society moves towards an information age, through the uneven distribution of learning capability. Policy makers need to be able to overcome the way in which problems of economic exclusion and disadvantage can lead to entrenched problems of educational disadvantage. This is why the principle of universality in the provision of education services is so important—guaranteeing all citizens a capacity to maximise their direct use of the learning process as well as enjoy the indirect benefits of new sources of national economic growth. It also means focusing the goals of education policy on issues of economic inclusion, as much as on the social benefits of learning.

Education and social progress have always gone together, in that the power of reason and knowledge exposes people to the virtues of rational thought and problem solving. The good society has always been an enlightened society, pushing the understanding and experience of its citizens towards the social habits of tolerance and cooperation. But now, in the new economy, education is much more than a tool for social enlightenment. It is, with the changing nature of work and production, the dividing line between the economic winners and losers in our society. The labour market has moved decisively in favour of highly skilled citizens and decisively against those without skills. In Reich's words:

> Gone forever are the assembly lines that used to provide lifetime jobs with rising wages and benefits to people straight out of high school, or even the good corporation that promised a lifetime of secure employment to the loyal white collar professional. Both are victims of the breaching of the tacit contract that promised a good life for employees so long as the company was making a healthy profit. The winners in this volatile, new globalised economy are those who can identify and solve problems, manipulate and analyse symbols, create and manage information. Those with a college degree are thus likely—not guaranteed, but likely—to end up on the happier side of the great divide.[2]

The only way of dealing equitably with this issue is to ensure that all citizens have the capability to benefit from new modes of learning and economic activity. The capability set of a learning society should not allow accumulated wealth and privilege to form the basis of educational attainment. The class structure of the industrial age should not be allowed to simply convert itself into a new system of social stratification between the information rich and the information poor. The public sector needs to be able to break, through new approaches to education policy, the intergenerational cycle of economic and educational disadvantage. It is plainly intolerable for a nation to have one-tenth or more of its citizens and neighbourhoods disenfranchised from the new economy, with this level of disadvantage then being conveyed to the next generation through the tragedy of educational under-achievement and skill exclusion. The first and most important step in building the national and public good features of a learning society involves overcoming the root causes of this type of capability failure.

In the new labour market, many of the characteristics of socio-economic disadvantage are now founded and expressed on a locational scale. In Australia the dual labour market has been associated with the polarisation of educational attainment. Gregory and Hunter's research has shown how, over the past two decades, the absolute gap in the distribution of tertiary qualifications between the wealthiest and poorest neighbourhoods has actually widened. In terms of their participation in the increased opportunities for a university education in Australia, 'neighbourhoods have not become more equal. For every ten new degree holders in the top five per cent of districts, there has been an additional three in low socio-economic status areas.'[3] While in the top neighbourhoods 1 in 5 adults possess degrees, this ratio falls to 1 in 33 in the bottom 5 per cent of districts.

These people and places face a doubly punishing dilemma: excluded from the economy during the transition from industrial to knowledge-based work; then further excluded, due to the inter-generational features of their disadvantage, from producing a strong number of school leavers with a decent set of tertiary qualifications. Residential location has become the most reliable indicator of a person's educational attainment and lifetime oppor-tunities. With the failure of the education system to fully adapt to these new causes of social and economic exclusion, a significant number of neighbourhoods, and even whole regions, in Australia are being left behind. The polarisation of the new labour market is being complemented and caused by the fragmentation of learning capability.

Unhappily, however, the growing problem of an educational underclass does not receive a great deal of attention in the public arena. Politicians and the media, with their interests fixed on the voting and buying habits of the stronger areas, have tended to focus on abstract notions of choice in the education debate. This is, for instance, a defining feature of the Howard Government's approach to schools policy. The absolute expression of choice in the education system, however, relies on a false assumption of socioeconomic neutrality. That is, all citizens are said to have an equal capacity to exercise choice and notional acts of choice them-selves are regarded as sufficient to satisfy need. There are, in fact, few absolute choices available to parents and students in the schools system. Choice in the selection of a particular school invariably carries a cost, either in terms of personal finance or travelling distance. In theory all families are free to undertake an education at the most privileged of private schools; in practice few can afford it.

The emergence of a dual labour market has added substantially to the number of Australian families for whom a school education means either a public education or the benevolence of the local parish. For another group of Australians, the poorest 5–10 per cent of neighbourhoods virtually excluded from economic participation, choice is again a relatively abstract notion. Their lifetime choices and effective freedoms have been broken by the spread of long term and intergenerational unemployment. This demonstrates that acts of choice in isolation are not able to universally satisfy social needs. Policy makers need to aim at the establishment of effective choices in education—allocating resources on the basis of learning needs and casting the purpose of policy at the attainment of effective freedoms and learning capability.

SCHOOLS POLICY

The foundations of an inclusive learning society, logically enough, lie in the type of outcomes achieved during the formative years of education. Every available report on the development of knowledge and personal skills highlights the significance of the early years of learning. Students who fall behind in their basic learning skills in the first few years of primary school are not likely, in the absence of early identification and remedial strategies, to overcome this initial source of disadvantage.[4] Equally, students who grow alienated from the learning process and their school and social environment through the teenage years are not likely to achieve the qualifications needed for workforce entry. This is what makes the nature of schools policy so important. Learning experiences through the school years have become the fulcrum upon which the possibilities of lifelong learning rest. At one end of the scale they can provide an effective platform for the knowledge skills of a post-industrial society, with a constant updating of the skills of active work and citizenship; at the other end, the likelihood of a lifetime of economic exclusion and capability failure.

Generally in Australia, public policy has not given sufficient weight to addressing this original source of educational advantage and disadvantage. The design and purpose of early education, in large part, still reflects a Fordist approach to service delivery framed to deal with the needs of the old economy. That is, there is an assumption that the needs and learning habits of students remain standardised, as does the purpose of skills development; and moreover, that these needs can be met within a comprehensive system of schooling under the control of large, centralised government departments. The failings of this system—its basic inability to cope with the growing diversity of student and locational needs—has pushed the focus of educational equity onto a range of post-secondary programs. These include labour market programs for the young unemployed, special student support payment categories and positive discrimination programs for tertiary entry. In practice, however, the best pathway to a post-secondary qualification lies in the successful school education of disadvantaged students and neighbourhoods. The inclusiveness of a learning society is inexorably founded on the quality of the educational experiences encountered by students during their early years of learning.

Social democracy needs to develop a new way of thinking about school education policy. The construction of a comprehensive system, while notionally providing an equality of opportunity between students, does not represent an effective way of dealing with the polarisation of learning needs and circumstances. The uniform construction of curricula, teaching methods, administrative systems and the other institutional features of schooling reflect a one-size-fits-all approach to learning needs. Within this system it is not possible to facilitate the benefits of customisation in the relationship between students and the schools system. The amelioration of educational disadvantage in our schools requires something more significant than the enhanced resourcing of schools in disadvantaged neighbourhoods, important as this may be for other reasons.[5]

Special needs require customised learning methods and particular attention to issues of institutional design. The reform of schools policy is not likely to succeed if it simply reflects a better resourced version of the comprehensive system. It is not likely that the adequate resourcing of schools, especially for students in disadvantaged areas, will ever be able to match the type of educational advantages students from affluent areas derive in the resourcing of their home learning environment. Public policy needs to be able to create additional learning value and capability for disadvantaged students and neighbourhoods, both in the school and home learning environment. In the first instance, this means advancing several aspects of learning customisation in the institutional features of schooling. One size no longer fits all in the construction of learning methods.

While the principles of customisation have been applied in some parts of the schools system, they do not appear to have influenced the formation of policies for disadvantaged schooling. In New South Wales, for instance, secondary school design has been tailored to assist the most gifted intellectually (via selective schools), artistically (performing arts schools), physically (special sports schools) and scientifically (technology schools). Yet the specialised needs of schools in disadvantaged neighbourhoods remain cast under the broad banner of the comprehensive system. In fact, more than any other part of the education system, these schools require customised methods of knowledge enhancement. Improved learning methods at a primary and secondary level—through smaller class sizes, enhanced pastoral care, the recruitment of the best available teachers and use of advanced learning technology—are an important part of this process. In the interactive nature of learning, students and parents must be willing to reciprocate the provision of these teaching resources by themselves working smarter and harder in their studies. There can be no end to entrenched disadvantage without ambition and hard work. Students in disadvantaged schools need to be prepared to undertake longer periods of classroom and home study than provided for under the comprehensive model.

Moreover, the place management model can be used to ensure that schools in disadvantaged neighbourhoods are able to break the comprehensive mould. The devolution of government authority provides an opportunity for schools to customise their methods and purpose to meet individualised and localised needs. Place managers would be able to fund and charter local schools in pursuit of certain educational outcomes, while leaving to the schools themselves the operational decisions upon which the satisfaction of their charter rests. It is desirable, indeed essential, in a system such as this to introduce strong elements of contestability. Social democracy cannot afford to tolerate failure in the processes of school education in poor neighbourhoods. There can be no more fundamental breach in the decency of our society to allow the cycle of educational and employment disadvantage to perpetuate itself on an intergenerational and locational scale.

Design principles which prove themselves in practice among place managed and chartered schools must be allowed to spread quickly to other disadvantaged areas, no matter how threatening this might appear to existing guild interests. Schools which fail to add value to the learning capabilities of their students should be closed down and replaced by a more successful schooling model. Education has become too precious a resource for the public sector to fund failure. Special funding should be provided to both the government and non-government school sectors to pioneer radical new solutions in this critical area of institutional design. No matter the cost, the slide of disadvantaged neighbourhoods in Australia towards an educational underclass must be decisively reversed.

Inevitably, this approach requires greater flexibility in the framing of teaching methods and curricula. The diverse learning skills and inclinations of students need to be matched by customised forms of education. Importantly, this approach does not require a streaming of students away from the basis of a strong general education. Schools and colleges need to engage their students in the processes of learning that best suit the circumstances of each student—teaching them how to adapt and constantly upgrade their skills. In a lifetime of learning, there should be scope aplenty for studying the best offerings of both general and vocational education. The most important aspect of education in a post-industrial society concerns the processes of learning. Studies show that few people remember a great deal of the content they were taught at school (or even university); the lasting significance is in acquiring a certain way of learning and thinking.

These strategies, of course, are most pressing in the early identification and amelioration of learning difficulties. For instance, it is estimated that, even with a satisfactory standard of teaching, up to 20 per cent of children in the early years of primary school in Australia will struggle to adequately develop their literacy skills. However, with specialised intervention strategies—often involving intensive, one-on-one tuition—these setbacks can be overcome, largely irrespective of variations in the innate cognitive skills of students. According to the Australian educationalist, Peter Hill, 'impressive empirical evidence is now available to support the notion that failure to make satisfactory progress in literacy is preventable for all except a very small proportion of children'.[6] Primary school skills-based testing and the resourcing of customised remedial teaching have become prerequisites for the success of a learning society.

Flexibility is also required in preparing students in the transition from education to employment. Teenagers are an exceptionally diverse group in their personal development, learning methods and career aspirations. A range of learning institutions and courses is needed to cope with this diversity. In particular, the senior years in some secondary schools should resemble a combination of what we now call school and TAFE. In some parts of Australia there are examples of how these vocational colleges—with a less structured learning environment, plus opportunities for applied as well as general education—have been able to overcome the alienation some students experience through their school years. Once placed in a different, more customised learning environment, these students have been able to establish effective pathways to the workforce, further TAFE studies and a university degree.[7]

PARENTS AS EDUCATORS

Another shortcoming in the effectiveness of the comprehensive system has been the way in which its involvement in the learning process has been restricted to the formal institutions of school. This silo method of service delivery has limited the capacity of the public sector to develop a whole-of-life approach to learning, especially in dealing with entrenched sources of learning disadvantage from outside the institutional framework of schooling. In this respect, the resources of a school education have become a fairly passive provider of learning services, contributing opportunities in just one portion of the learning environment. In many areas, especially those suffering from intergenerational unemployment, schools have not been able to break the cycle of disadvantage arising in the home. In the reform of schools policy, new measures are needed to address the variations in learning capability which students carry with them from the home learning environment.

Students do not pass through school with an equal set of opportunities in other parts of their life. Studies of educational outcomes in schools, both for the government and non-government sector, have shown how most of the observed differences in performance relate to the capabilities students bring to school, rather than 'value adding' by the school itself.[8] Policy makers need to recognise that education does not stop at the school gate each afternoon. A failure to receive adequate homework assistance, basic learning materials in the home, and parental support for the value of education can have a damaging impact on a student's learning capability—both directly in the quality of tuition and, more generally, in the importance of parents as role models. Public policy needs to take account of the strong correlation between parental involvement in school education and the academic performance of their children.[9]

Accordingly, educational services in disadvantaged areas need to provide the services by which parents can be trained as effective educators in the home. This might involve courses at the local school itself, whereby parents are able to enhance their literacy and numeracy skills, knowledge of the school curriculum and the general practices of good parenting. These programs should also serve as an opportunity for parents to maintain close contact with the school's teachers. Schools also need to consider, particularly as the technology further develops, the potential of the information highway as an interactive, daily link between the work of educators at school and in the home. Schools need to be developed as effective (and equal) partners with parents in improving the learning capacities of students. As stand-alone institutions, engaged in the passive delivery of services, they are not able to deal with the whole-of-life features of educational disadvantage.

These parental responsibilities form a logical part of the case management approach to socioeconomic disadvantage. For parents dependant on welfare support there can be no excuse for not upgrading their skills and effectiveness as educators in the home. This responsibility needs to be written into case management contracts, the fulfilment of which determines the ongoing allocation of income support. Sanctions should be applied to those transfer payment recipients unwilling to accept their proper responsibilities as home educators. Educational disadvantage cannot be resolved simply by providing better schools for the poor.

Parental responsibility and effort are all important. The whole environment of disadvantage must be confronted and overcome. This is a further reason why the place management model of service delivery makes so much sense. It allows the public sector to develop an integrated approach to the twin goals of employment creation and learning enhancement. It treats obstacles to learning capability as a process rather than an event, with a capacity to develop whole-of-government solutions to the basic sources of socioeconomic disadvantage.

POST-SECONDARY EDUCATION

Once a universal threshold of learning capability has been established through the school education process, public resources and policy need to be directed at the public good features of lifelong education. In Australia, this means substantially improving rates of post-secondary participation and establishing the most efficient means by which all adults, no matter their age or background, are able to periodically update their learning skills. The limited education system of the industrial age needs to be replaced by the flexible, lifelong learning of a post-industrial society. Through the early post-war decades, the school leaving certificate was regarded as sufficient to guarantee employability. Tertiary education access was effectively reserved for the professional and managerial classes. Across all parts of the workforce, education and training rarely extended beyond the teenage years.

In the new labour market, however, employability increasingly requires a post-secondary qualification. The highest rates of unemployment in Australia are heavily concentrated among labour force participants who did not complete their secondary schooling or pursue a skilled vocational qualification upon leaving school.[10] Strong senior school qualifications have become a prerequisite for workforce entry, with post-secondary education and training also emerging as an obligatory condition for finding employment. This confirms the way in which the institutions of post-secondary education in Australia—competency-based training, labour market programs, technical and further education and universities—need to be cast in the context of mass education. Despite the progress of the Hawke and Keating Governments in expanding each of these learning opportunities, Australia still lags behind international standards. In the OECD, for instance, Australia ranks in the bottom quarter of nations for post-secondary participation, with just 23 full-time students per thousand population. This compares unfavourably with Canada's 41 students, France's 36, Norway's 32, the United States' 31, Japan's 29 and New Zealand's 28.

In overcoming this deficiency, Australia needs to pursue a number of key national goals. A starting point lies in broadening the compulsory years of school education. In the new economy there are few, if any, jobs available for unskilled teenagers. It is pointless for young people to leave school without the support of a senior year qualification. This simply entrenches the problem of economic exclusion at an early and particularly vulnerable age. Australia needs to extend the number of compulsory years of education from eleven to thirteen.[11] Thereafter, in broadening the pathways from school to a skilled post-secondary qualification, it should establish the preconditions for a universal, open access regime to vocational and further education. No Australian school leaver should be discouraged, especially for financial reasons, from continuing their education past the secondary years. This means substantially increasing the number of post-secondary places, improving student income support and moderating the financial impact of HECS.

It needs to be recognised, however, even in a broadened system of post-secondary education, that the demand for some courses will always outstrip the supply of student places. This reflects labour market realities and the demand for many institutions and their courses, particularly at university, as positional goods (carrying a highly valued status and reputation). In a society wanting to reward effort and excellence, this rationing role in public policy needs to be undertaken by the principles of merit, rather than accumulated wealth and privilege. This is why the Howard Government's reintroduction of upfront university fees in Australia is so damaging. A two tier system of undergraduate entry undermines the basic ideals of meritocracy in our society. In particular, it sends an appalling message to a generation of young Australians. If their parents are wealthy, some students might think they do not have to study or work as hard at school. These under-performers can have a university place purchased for them by their parents.

All students in Australia need to be given the same rights of access in their application for post-secondary education and training; that is, on the basis of merit. The equity of a post-secondary system needs to be founded in the success of disadvantaged schooling, plus the broadening of service availability itself. One of the core purposes of education is to stimulate competition and striving between students, producing new standards of excellence and achievement. Nations which relaxed their grades and standards in the 1970s and 1980s are still struggling to recover from this loss of learning capability.[12] With the resourcing of lifelong learning as a public good, and the maintenance of high standards, equity and excellence in education policy can coexist.

LEARNING ACCOUNTS

Beyond the services school leavers require in the transition to this 'quasi-obligatory' round of post-secondary qualifications, education policy needs to establish two new systems of learning capability. First, as mentioned earlier, adults with chronic learning problems, leading to the problems of economic and social exclusion, require the customisation of service delivery through case management methods. Skills development is at the centre of this agenda. Second, for adults engaging in the benefits of lifelong learning, demand side flexibility and effective user choice are critical. Given the contingencies of economic and social change, the learning needs and circumstances of labour force participants have become incredibly diverse. The satisfaction of these diverse needs requires an extension of the Income Security Accounts system to cover the costs of adult, vocational and recreational learning.

This approach seeks to mould the delivery of educational services to suit the various needs of lifelong learning. One of the few certainties governments still have available to them in the planning of service delivery, concerns the growing need for school leavers to pursue post-secondary education. The existing system of supply side planning in tertiary education remains capable of meeting needs of this kind. The educational needs and resources of students preparing for labour market entry, however, are vastly different to those who have commenced a wage earning career. Adult learning needs, given the changing nature of work and society, have become too diverse for the rigidities of supply side planning. They require the benefits of functional flexibility, whereby skill recipients are able to pursue, according to their own needs and preferences, the most appropriate form of learning.

A number of British academics have developed this principle into the concept of 'learning accounts'.[13] These represent a flexible bundle of learning entitlements, allocated to individuals either in the form of cash transfers or course equivalents. Recipients are then able to use these resources to meet the costs of appropriate learning packages. This might involve under- or post-graduate university studies, vocational education at TAFE or from a private provider, undertaking a labour market program, accessing an adult and community education course, or any combination of these options, depending on need. Labour market participants are likely to benefit substantially from the provision of a universal learning entitlement, especially given the contingencies of economic restructuring and need for lifelong vocational education. One of the problems with the labour market programs established under Working Nation was their lack of flexibility and, for some recipients, their unsuitability.

The effective management of these learning accounts can be achieved by simply building them into the ISA structure. This would also allow other forms of education spending to be registered as a deductible PET item, thereby offering an incentive for private savings to supplement the national investment in lifelong learning. This demand side provision of learning entitlements represents an overhaul of the public sector's delivery of vocational and adult education. It has the potential to create the following advantages and feature of an advanced learning society:

- It forces educational institutions to accelerate the development of more flexible learning packages, particularly in the enhancement of interactive and distance learning technology. These have the potential to drive down, in appropriate courses, the unit costs of learning, thereby further enhancing the likelihood of universal access.

- The accelerated development of new learning technology in Australia also enhances the capacity of our education sector to cope with the emerging internationalisation of further education. Unless Australia develops its teaching and research capacity for interactive learning technology, we run the risk of turning our university and TAFE sectors from export earners into net importers.

- The learning accounts encourage greater cooperation and flexibility among the institutions of post-secondary education, especially in course provision and accreditation. The need for lifelong systems of vocational education has blurred forever the institutional boundaries between technical and higher education. The consumer sovereignty inherent in the learning accounts helps to address this supply side problem by promoting a seamless network of credit transfer and articulation.[14]

- The issue of sovereignty is also important in rectifying the deficiencies in Australia's training system. The rise of 'user choice', whereby employers determine the format and source of training packages (without the burden of 'user pays'), is not desirable. This represents the further socialisation of industry costs, and invariably leads to a narrow form of enterprise-applied training, contrary to the interests of employees. The learning accounts return the responsibility for selecting an appropriate form of training to the hands of trainees and apprentices.

- It is estimated that one in four Australian adults, primarily from weaker socioeconomic backgrounds, do not return to the education system upon leaving school. The creation of a specific learning entitlement for these Australians is a major equity initiative, fostering their re-engagement in the learning process. The learning accounts represent a way of improving public access to adult and community education, plus 'third age' learning—thereby emphasising the significance of lifelong education for social and recreational purposes.

SKILLED MIGRATION

Finally, the development of a learning society also relies on a carefully targeted migration program. At a time when knowledge has become a valuable economic resource, nations are only able to advance their interests by improving the skills of their people. Accordingly, the primary test for migration entry needs to be cast around the knowledge-based skills of prospective residents. Australia's recent experience, particularly through the large family reunion program in the late 1980s, has shown that poorly skilled migrants are unlikely to avoid the problems of economic exclusion and welfare dependency. For instance, five years after their arrival in Australia in 1989–90, one in four of the 58 000 settler migrants remained registered for unemployment benefits. The level of welfare dependency has, in some cases by place of origin, been even higher—such as a 71 per cent unemployment rate over the five year period for arrivals from Lebanon, and 79 per cent from Turkey.[15]

Migration policies such as these—which, perversely enough in the public arena, are often cast in the name of social justice—simply add to the extent of underclass neighbourhoods in Australia's major cities. In the new labour market there are virtually no jobs available for unskilled migrants. It is not wise, in the management of the public commons, to knowingly add to the demand for public resources without being able to simultaneously strengthen the carrying capacity of the commons. This approach inevitably builds resentment among those who have funded the commons for the way in which the new arrivals are able to draw on its resources. The recent history of unskilled migration to Australia has added considerably to the extent of downwards envy and the declining legitimacy of the public sector. The ALP, in advocating the policies of a learning society, needs to fundamentally alter its thinking on immigration.

Australia's post-war migration program was founded on two economic principles: that migrants could usefully add to the nation's pool of standard skill labour in routine production-type work; and that, in a relatively closed economy, Australia needed to increase the size of its consumer markets to provide a stronger economy of production scale. Both assumptions have now been made redundant with the emergence of an open, post-industrial economy. The labour market is demanding a strong base of knowledge skills for successful production, while competitive firms are capable of accessing markets worldwide. In this type of economy, the national purpose of migration policy lies in its capacity to attract the residency and skills of knowledge workers and entrepreneurs.[16]

In most aspects of public policy, governments need to adjust to the new geography of capital and its associated economic issues. The work of the nation state requires a spatial response to the growing influence of globalisation. Strategies framed solely around the benevolence of the modern state are not likely to satisfy the new tasks of national sovereignty and economic success. Likewise, it is undesirable to develop public policies—no matter how well intentioned—that add to the work of the public sector without also adding to the sustainability of the public commons. The facilitation of lifelong learning represents the most effective way by which the nation state can meet both these challenges. It forms the basis of a new expression of national economic sovereignty, plus—through the progressive spread of social capability—it significantly bolsters the fiscal carrying capacity of the public sector. It is the best investment any nation can make in the development of a competent and fair society.

28

CONCLUSION: MAKING WELFARE WORK

A learning society is able to provide its citizens with the security of lifelong education and training—the capacity to establish and renew the skills of adaptability through a lifetime of social change. Without constant attention to the enhancement of knowledge about one's self and the changing nature of society and its economy, the spread of insecurity becomes inevitable. New forms of learning security need to be complemented by the construction of lifelong income security. The role of the public sector is to assist each citizen in the development of a platform of primary goods and learning capability from which, in the exercise of personal responsibility and effort, social capability becomes possible. This form of social interdependence is best expressed through the devolution of welfare programs to the level of case and place management. Reciprocal responsibility, reward for effort, society's interdependence and the devolution of state programs—these are the recurring themes of social democracy's new radical centre.

In chapter 21 it was argued that quasi-market methods, both on the supply and demand side, have a role to play in the collective provision of services. This is reinforced by the need for functional flexibility in the work of the welfare state. It needs to be recognised, however, that this approach is not without its flaws. For instance, it cannot be assumed, especially in cases of chronic welfare dependency, that the foundations of effective choice are always available. Entrenched forms of disadvantage often erode the social and economic skills of participation and rationally constructed user choice. This is why the agency approach of case and place management is so important in assisting disadvantaged people and places with their use of publicly provided services.

Beyond the safety net, of course, these restrictions tend not to apply in the delivery of most forms of collective services.

Functional flexibility is achieved by placing individuals in a position where they can assess and act on their own social needs. This is a key feature of the ISA approach to income and learning security. In a diverse, post-industrial society, the attainment of a complex form of equality has become inconsistent with the planning strand of the post-war welfare state. Individuals, especially with a heightened base of cognitive skills and learning, are able to make the most appropriate judgment about their changing social needs and capability. The provision of early education services, of course, represents an exception to this principle.

The ISA system also delivers, among the criteria for restoring the sustainability of the welfare state, greater transparency and a more suitable scale for the public management of the commons. The capacity for account holders to mould their entitlements according to personal need, and thereby exercise greater control in their relationship with state institutions, helps to break down the problems of mass welfare. It creates a more active form of welfare and well-being—creating, for each person, a strong inter-action between effective choice, personal responsibility and the type of primary, social and public goods leading to social mobility. These themes of transparency and scale are further developed in Part V. In combination, the reforms leading to a post-Fordist welfare state build the basis of a new social contracting—a new relationship between citizen and state—founded on the following principles and programs of reform:

POST-WAR WELFARE STATE	POST-FORDIST WELFARE STATE
• poverty line measurement of material deprivation	• poverty as social capability failure
• passive systems of service delivery with a one way flow of social responsibility	• active programs with an emphasis on skills development and positive, reciprocated responsibilities
• reliance on supply side planning, fixed assets and a one-size-fits-all approach to service consumption	• customised systems of service delivery with greater functional flexibility
• a silo structure of public sector organisation, based on large centralised departments and agencies	• integrated place management and universal case management structure of service delivery

- a supposedly residual system of targeted transfer payments, paid off complex, multiple categories for 'snapshot' purposes
- a flexible, bundled and time sequenced system of lifelong income support, with elements of self-providence
- early life education producing standardised skills from a comprehensive schools system
- lifelong education as an essential public good, with strong elements of customised learning

An important part of this approach involves easing the fiscal crisis of the state. By offering incentives for greater self-providence it is possible to build effective systems of lifelong income support. By making welfare work it is possible to lower the rate of income dependency in society. This helps to demonstrate how good governance is not necessarily determined by the raw size of government. Breaking the cycle of socioeconomic disadvantage involves changing the functions and scale of government and, most critically, its relationship with disadvantaged people and places. This involves changing the nature of welfare, not the abolition of welfare itself.

To be certain, social capability does not require a rigid equality of all measures of life; nor the application of vertical equity principles (service means testing) to all parts of the public sector. The public good features of education are a case in point. The primary measure of social equality lies in the resolution of capability failure. To this end, it cannot be credibly argued that solutions to welfare dependency lie entirely outside the domain of the welfare state—in national rates of private sector growth, labour market deregulation and the rights of the individual. In practice, disadvantaged families and individuals can lose too many of the skills of social participation to be able to avoid perverse decisions about their well-being. Robust individualism and rational incentives only succeed if people see a link between their own circumstances and the incentives system. In this fashion, the effectiveness of the welfare policies of the political Right have collapsed. There is no way of breaking the entrenched features of the poverty cycle in the new economy without the active role of government.

This needs to be, however, a very different type of government to that envisaged and practised by the post-war welfare state. The days of social democracy's embrace of a centralised, over-administered, nanny state need to end. Through the 1950s and 1960s the welfare state fashioned a social contract based on the mass production by government of universal rights and entitlements. In the

1970s social democrats complacently assumed that systems of passive welfare still created the basis of active citizenship, despite evidence to the contrary in the emergence of long term and intergenerational poverty. Somewhere in the 1980s the ALP, for reasons not yet clear, appeared to allow issues of poverty and entrenched disadvantage to fall down its list of priorities. In the late 1990s we need to engage in the wholesale reform of the welfare state, aimed at breaking the cycle of educational and employment disadvantage. The immorality of a polarised society and entrenched underclass cannot be allowed to continue.

PART V

THE SEARCH FOR SOCIAL CAPITAL

Issues concerning the strength and composition of social capital are critical to the successful governance of society. Among the daily work and debates of national politics it is perhaps too easily forgotten that there are many forms of governance which do not directly involve the formal institutions of the state. This is the basis of civil society—the interaction of citizens through voluntary associations, networks and other forms of contact which, when regarded as a whole, constitute the self-governance of community life. One of the weaknesses of left-of-centre thinking, particularly in its attachment to the planning strand of the welfare state, has been its lack of interest in issues of non-state governance. State socialists and social democrats alike have concentrated their politics on the relationship between the state and its citizens. They have had little to contribute, either by way of ideology or policy, to the type of relations and interests people might usefully hold in common with their fellow citizens.

Yet rather self-evidently, the relations between people in any social setting—their level of cooperation, respect for each other and the strength of mutual trust and assistance—are important to the ideals of an inclusive and just society. This exposes one of the paradoxes of the modern welfare state. A decent safety net of transfer payments and service universality does not appear to have sustained a strong base of compassion and mutuality among society's values. With the overload of government, and severe rationing of social entitlements, welfare statism has added exponentially to the spread of downwards envy. By every measure of public opinion available to politicians in Australia—opinion polling, constituent work, talkback radio and the other forms of tabloid media—these views abound. The public's faith in open-ended transfer payments and passive welfare is in retreat. Social democracy's reform of the

260 THE SEARCH FOR SOCIAL CAPITAL

welfare state now needs to consider the possibility of non-state solutions to the welfare question.

The ALP's engagement in this type of approach has been limited. The Party's form response to social change has been to load ever more responsibilities onto the work of the state. In several areas, most notably the development of corporatist industry policies and segment-of-life programs, these additional outlays have not been able to counter the growing incidence of insecurity. In total, the overload of government demonstrates the way in which the social democratic method—its habit of addressing every new issue by further raising popular expectations about the role of the state public sector—ultimately devours its own programs. In its final logic, social democracy's misplaced faith in the primacy of the state has the potential to break the fiscal carrying capacity of the commons, and thereby erode the legitimacy of its own ideals and work. This is reason enough for turning to the value of collective institutions in the non-state public sector as an expression of social capability and complex equality. Just as social democracy needs to reclaim from the political Right an agenda for the exercise of social responsibility and effective choice, it should not regard non-state forms of collective action as antipathetic to its political purpose.

The capacity of each citizen to participate in our society—their freedom to achieve active citizenship—relies in good part on the way in which they are received and treated by other citizens. Without the freely formed bonds of mutual trust and cooperation—without these ingredients of social solidarity and connectedness—the effectiveness of social participation is substantially weakened. The security people find in sociability—their capacity to share interests and trust with others—is no less significant than any other type of security, social or economic. As they undertake new tasks in society, as they attempt to strengthen their relations with others, people need to know that their efforts—once discharged with responsibility and decency—will be received with respect and the prospect of mutuality. Otherwise, the likelihood of social contact and cooperation is much diminished.

Unhappily, the basis of social trust and mutuality appears everywhere to be in decline. In most Western nations, whether seen through the growth of walled housing estates, single resident households and individualised recreational pursuits or through falling rates of participation in most aspects of community life, the personal bonds of social capital are under pressure. In the political arena, this loss of community has expressed itself most explicitly through a range of law and order issues. It is now barely possible to switch on a radio or television news broadcast without encountering calls for tougher policing and harsher penalties. Australia's State and Territory election campaigns have been reduced to a bidding war as to which party's policies are likely to put the most people in gaol. The public has lost so much social trust and connectedness that it is overwhelmingly more interested in punishing lawlessness than addressing the social causes of crime.

For the ALP, of course, this is an unsatisfactory agenda. Surely it is possible to build a better society than one based on the constant spread of downwards envy and punishment. Surely it is still possible to value and foster the ideals of cooperation and mutual aid as inherent to the foundations of our society. Surely it is possible to reform the collective governance of society in a way that actively rebuilds the basis of society's connectedness and trust. These are matters for which this part of the book attempts to develop a new social democratic agenda. This involves an examination of the changing nature of social capital (especially among Australia's unique social and cultural institutions), as well as the development of a philosophy of social trust and recognition. It is argued that the social democratic project needs to embrace a radical program of devolution among the methods and institutions of public governance, thereby providing circumstances and opportunities by which citizens can mutually create the bonds of social capital and connectedness.

29

A QUESTION OF TRUST

Despite social democracy's preoccupation with the state-to-citizen relationship, social capital has remained an item of significant interest on the political agenda of most nations. Other strands of political thought have taken a strong interest in the social relations between citizens. Libertarian philosophy, for instance, has argued that the size and scope of the post-war welfare state has crowded out civil society; it maintains that, as governments have grown and taken on more functions, citizens have felt less inclined to engage themselves in the voluntary activities of civic life and community. From another perspective, futurists such as Alvin Toffler and Peter Drucker have suggested that the impact of globalisation has fundamentally weakened the logic of collective action, both for the state and non-state public sector. Still others, most notably the communitarians in the United States, have argued how effective national leadership, especially in the public's consideration of moral values, can play a role in strengthening the interdependence of government and community.[1] These ideologies and interests share a commitment to the means by which society might benefit from the enhancement of its stock of social capital: those elements of public interaction which generate trust and mutual gains between people. No such consensus exists, however, on how public policy might attain such goals.

Conversely, the social democratic project has aimed the decisions of central government at the material and lifestyle conditions of citizens, without necessarily considering the way in which the organisation of government also impacts on social trust and civil society. This mechanistic style of policy making, with its short term focus on the connection between public administration and social change, now needs to be broadened. Social democrats need to give stronger consideration to the relationship between government, globalisation and civil society. Australia's short, three-year electoral cycle should not preclude strategic thinking about the future of social capital. This is especially true for the ALP's commitment to social fairness and the virtues of collective action. It is difficult for any political party to define common interests and successfully manage the commons without strong elements of solidarity and trust in society—the type of relations between people which form the basis of public mutuality and collectivism. As Robert Putnam, whose work has led the research effort in this area, has written:

> For a variety of reasons, life is easier in a community blessed with a substantial stock of social capital. In the first place, networks of civic engagement foster sturdy norms of generalised reciprocity and encourage the emergence of social trust. Such networks facilitate coordination and communication, amplify reputations, and thus allow dilemmas of collective action to be resolved. When economic and political negotiation is embedded in dense networks of social interaction, incentives for opportunism are reduced. At the same time, networks of civic engagement embody past successes at collaboration, which can serve as a cultural template for future collaboration. Finally, dense networks of interaction probably broaden the participants' sense of self, enhancing the taste for collective benefits.[2]

The accumulated habits of trust allow a society, in the language of rational economics, to pursue first-best choices. Without reciprocated trust a family cannot reach its full potential for nurturing children and establishing systems of mutual support. Only with trust can people serve as good neighbours, with the mutual cooperation needed to care for each other's interests. Social trust allows a community to avoid the defensive actions otherwise required to combat public disorder and lawlessness. Without social capital it is difficult to define common interests in the public arena and act upon them in a sustainable way. In the workplace, mutual trust provides the foundation on which cooperation and innovation create a productive enterprise, especially with the reduction of checking and transaction costs. In any form of economic or social activity, risk taking relies heavily on the best efforts of others—their willingness to share the risks, the benefits of success, plus the consequences of failure.

Putnam's extensive study of the civic traditions of Italy has found that the positive aspects of civic engagement help to boost the performance of both the polity and its economy. 'Strong society, strong economy; strong society, strong state', he concludes.[3] This finding is supported by Francis Fukuyama's analysis

of the social virtues of trust and the creation of prosperity in each
of the advanced economies:

> rational utility maximisation is not enough to give a full or
> satisfying account of why successful economies prosper or unsuc-
> cessful ones stagnate and decline. The degree to which people
> value work over leisure, their respect for education, attitudes
> toward the family, and the degree of trust they show toward their
> fellows all have a direct impact on economic life and yet cannot
> be adequately explained in terms of the economists' basic model
> of man. Just as liberal democracy works best as a political system
> when its individualism is moderated by public spirit, so too is
> capitalism facilitated when its individualism is balanced by a
> readiness to associate.[4]

This suggests that, in answer to one of the oldest dilemmas of
social studies, by cause and effect, cultural conditions determine
economic and political outcomes more than the reverse sequence
does. More directly, for the cause of Labor, social trust can be
seen as a core precondition for the attainment of a social democracy. Interpersonal trust strikes an appropriate balance between
what would otherwise be the competing motivations of self-interest
and altruism. Altruism can be expressed in caring for the well-being
of others; self-interest in knowing that these feelings and actions
will be reciprocated. This is what de Tocqueville called 'self
interest properly understood'—enlightened self-interest by virtue
of being alive to the interests of others. In a similar fashion, John
Stuart Mill, in establishing the basis of public liberalism, noted the
distinction between self-regarding and other-regarding acts. Trust
between people is easily seen as the most basic of all other-regarding acts. Without it citizens can have so little regard for each other
that the very nature of social behaviour is placed in jeopardy.

Just as Sen's notion of social capability helps resolve the
philosophical tension between liberty and equality, an understanding of social trust helps reconcile the interests of personal
freedom with the necessity of collective action. Putnam's research
shows that citizens in highly civic communities, enjoying the benefits of social capital, also enjoy the greatest degree of personal
liberty. They are less hindered by the need for law and order and
less reliant on the coercive power of public law to maintain public
good.[5] Liberty and equality are thus reconciled—liberty in the free
associations of trust; equality in the needs-based nature of acts of
reciprocation. These principles are crucial to the successful management of the commons. High levels of mutual trust not only
make society and its economy more efficient, they are also an

important means by which a consensus can be constructed for the handling of collective interests.

This does not involve a consensus expressed through coercive enforcement or authoritarian government—which, once deployed, frequently involves high public costs and generally signifies the inherent weakness of social capital.[6] Rather, the consensus centres on the virtues of freely formed collective action. Successful social contracting relies on a mutual agreement to provide certain items across the citizenry for mutual benefit. The durability of this agreement and system of collective provision, in turn, relies on the capacity of public expressions of mutuality to reinforce themselves. If modes of mutual provision fail to produce further expressions of mutuality then inevitably, they will be replaced by individualised methods of provision. This is one of the chief problems of the modern welfare state, whereby, far from reinforcing the virtues of mutuality, it appears to be breeding mistrust.

The social norms of cooperation, supported by voluntary collectivism, are strongest in communities with a well-developed store of social capital and civic engagement. These norms arise because, through the exercise of social trust, citizens not only take responsibility for other-regarding acts or externalities (when their actions have negative or positive consequences for others) but also hold high expectations for reciprocity. As the US political scientist Michael Taylor has explained:

> Each individual act in a system of reciprocity is usually characterised by a combination of what one might call short term altruism and long term self-interest: I help you out now in the (possibly vague, uncertain and uncalculating) expectation that you will help me out in the future. Reciprocity is made up of a series of acts each of which is short run altruistic (benefiting others at a cost to the altruist) but which together typically make every participant better off.[7]

In this fashion the preconditions for the logic of collective action are established. When trust, responsibility and reciprocity come together citizens are most likely to see their own interests through the prism of social cooperation. This, of course, minimises the incentive for free riders: individuals who disregard the social norms of cooperation and ride on the efforts of others without reciprocation. When social trust and social capital are strongest, citizens are most likely to link their personal liberty and well-being to their participation in the common decisions and collective actions of society. 'Citizens in the civic community', by Putnam's assessment, 'deal fairly with one another and expect fair dealing in return'.[8] Relations such as these can only add to the strength of public mutuality and the political foundations of a truly social democracy.

TWO TYPES OF SOCIAL CAPITAL

A society of this kind, in which trust is widely exercised as an expression of freely formed mutuality, carries the characteristics of horizontal social capital. Herein lies an important distinction among the diverse features of social trust. Each of us tends to trust those in positions of authority—such as judges, teachers, police and doctors—for very different reasons and in very different ways to the sort of trust we might feel for friends, workmates and neighbours. Trust exercised through systems of hierarchy and authority is an expression of vertical social capital. This type of trust works by the threat of coercion, rather than the type of enlightened mutuality and reciprocation that characterises horizontal bonds of social capital.

All societies, no matter their culture, history, economic structures and systems of government, reflect a mix of horizontal and vertical social capital. The nature of the mix, of course, goes a long way to explaining the way in which a particular society might function and respond to a variety of social issues. Similarly, each of a society's institutions features varying elements of horizontal and vertical social capital. As Putnam notes, 'even bowling teams have captains, while prison guards occasionally fraternise with inmates'.[9] Consideration of this mix should be seen as a frontline issue for matters of public policy, particularly in the determination of institutional design. Successful institutions are able to nurture and maximise the flow of horizontal social capital, thereby sustaining the virtues of mutuality and cooperation.

Vertical social capital, by contrast, is sustained by the possession and exercise of coercive powers. Citizens have some of their rights of participation and choice replaced by the use of authority and control. This is the classic Hobbesian answer to the dilemma of collective action: obedience to the judgment of some greater source of decision and sanction making. The benevolent exercise of these powers tends to establish a formal patron/client relationship of dependency. The expression of power and authority is made lopsided by the improbability of reciprocation. Patrons exercise authority and dispense benefits according to their own judgment, without any reasonable expectation of reciprocity. Clients, by virtue of their dependency, are not able to engage in acts of mutual aid.

Vertical social capital thus represents a framework of inequality between citizens. The patron holds a status and authority on which the client must rely for progress and the satisfaction of self-interest. In search of greater equality the client may be forced towards opportunism, such as covertly storing resources and information. The patron, in search of personal benefits, may choose to exploit the client's dependency. In this fashion, despite the most forceful forms of coercion, the logic of collective action may dissolve. A common response to these dilemmas is to further strengthen the degree of vertical supplication and relationship inequality. Force is used, even more comprehensively, as a substitute for mutual trust. This is, for instance, an enduring feature of the law and order debate in societies featuring vertical networks of social capital. Yet Putnam has been able to argue persuasively that 'a very strong predictor of the crime rate in a neighbourhood is not how many cops there are on the beat, but how many neighbours know one another's first name'.[10]

A distinguishing feature between vertical and horizontal social capital is the question of ownership. Vertical relationships, by virtue of their essential inequality, are open to exclusive ownership. The patron—in most systems of modern governance this signifies the state—owns and controls the source of coercion. By contrast under horizontal structures, social capital cannot be appropriated as the exclusive property of any of its participants. It belongs to all and relies on the actions of all to sustain it. This means, of course, that horizontal social capital, unlike most things of value in a capitalist society, cannot be brought into the orbit of property rights. Most types of social capital are created or destroyed as a by-product of other activities. Horizontal forms of social capital tend to arise or disappear without anyone willing them into or out of existence. They are best understood, therefore, as a process rather than an event; and perhaps for this reason, social capital has been less recognised and studied in social research than the more tangible features of economic and human capital.[11]

Also unlike other forms of capital, horizontal social capital cannot be stocked. Either participants to its accumulation use it, or they will most certainly lose it. This demonstrates the essential civicness of social trust. While it may be held and nurtured in common, it cannot be satisfactorily subjected to third party direction or authority. Nor can it be institutionalised in the sense of having property rights or binding social obligations allocated to it. Horizontal social capital is a clear expression of what it means to engage in acts of self-governance, free from vertical systems of authority. This is why the state is not able to directly create social capital by means of its conventional legislative and welfare programs. It can only influence, indirectly and incrementally, the type of social relations which give rise to the formation of horizontal bonds and forms of trust.

The shared benefits of trust, social and economic, can only be enjoyed in their engagement between citizens. Hence horizontal social capital can be interpreted as an instance of equality in action. The equal rights and obligations of citizens are expressed through spontaneous acts of collective interest. This is an important departure from the practice of equal rights written into the rule of law. The impact of legislated rights relies heavily on the capacity of the state to effectively police and apply sanctions to cases where rights have been violated. The rights established through acts of inter-personal trust are mutually reinforcing (because my trust in another has been reciprocated, our equal status has been confirmed in practice).

Similar observations can be made with regard to the act of caring. In the human condition, altruism is reinforced by the practice of reciprocation. Clearly this is less likely under the vertical structures of a patron/client relationship than conditions of mutual trust. Especially when confronted by uncertain circumstances, people are more likely to care for others if they can trust in others doing the same. This shared, interactive experience helps establish the moral divide between giving and caring. While patrons can give, it may be that people only identify with a sense of caring through the accumulated experiences of mutuality and equality. Giving needs to arise from the virtues of mutuality. Political opinion polling, for instance, has identified a public belief that while governments may give transfer payments to clients they are not perceived as actually caring about welfare.

Putnam's research identifies positive externalities from horizontal networks of civic engagement: 'The more horizontally structured an organisation, the more it should foster institutional success in the broader community'.[12] In this respect, social capital developed among secondary associations—such as sports clubs, cooperatives, mutual aid societies and voluntary unions—has greater social utility than the popular engagement of primary associations like kinship and intimate friendship. It is the acquired habit of mutual trust expressed across society's boundaries—such as family, class and culture—which nourishes wider cooperation and collective action. While the sort of trust generated by family and friendship ties is undoubtedly important, it is not likely, in isolation, to establish the preconditions for broader forms of social trust. This is the critical test of horizontal social capital: to be able to trust another when the direct experiences of mutual aid are not necessarily deep and binding. Trust of this nature boosts the success of society's institutions because it provides the basis for easily establishing shared interests and pursuing the logic of collective action.

These findings are crucial to the reformulation of the role of the state. They point to the inherent weaknesses of mass welfare statism and the establishment of patron/client relationships. They expose the problems of supply side planning expressed through vertical structures of service delivery. They also highlight, with clarity and purpose, the dual features of economic management. It is likely that the success of an economy relies as much on social cooperation as transaction competition. That is, cooperation forms the basis of successful economic production while competition acts as a lever for efficiency at the point of economic exchange. Hence (as was argued in Parts I and II), collective arrangements in the workplace need to coexist with the rigorous application of competition policies to the private sector. The application of social capital theory to the structure and intent of public governance identifies a lodestar of policy reform.

THE BASIS OF SOCIAL CAPITAL

A shortcoming in Putnam's work is its lack of a philosophical setting. While exceptionally strong as a piece of social analysis, the research is more empirical than predictive. Putnam does not extend our knowledge of social capital to a theory of human behaviour. Accordingly, he is not able to explain or forecast changes in social capital beyond the movement in indicative variables such as institutional design, cultural habits and technology. To be certain, Putnam's research has been substantial by any measure of progress in the social sciences. The test for those wanting to take his work further is to give social capital roots in a philosophy of the human condition. What is it about mutual trust that seems so essential to the capacity of society to function and bond each of its members to a common set of values and interests?

A starting point is to understand how human behaviour has been set apart from the animal world by the yearning for recognition, the acknowledgement that each of our lives holds worth and value for others. While recognition can take several forms, none seems more fundamental than trust—that is, to not only be recognised by others as worthy of trust, but to have the depth of this recognition measured using the yardstick of one's self. As interpersonal trust functions by the principles of mutuality and equality, its value cannot be assessed in the abstract. The sense of dignity it brings to each participant constitutes a mode of recognition essential to the living of life itself: recognition of one's own worth. Whenever one trusts in another person and expects that trust to be reciprocated, an assessment is thereby made and reinforced about one's own worth.

This theory of recognition is drawn from Francis Fukuyama and his provocative book, *The End of History and the Last Man* (1992). Fukuyama picks up the Hegelian task of a universal theory of history. He advances his argument with the development of two universal truths. First, scientific methods and technological advances have a coherent impact on the direction of history. Second, human behaviour is primarily motivated by the need for recognition—a sense of worth and dignity, or what Plato in his *Republic* called 'thymos'. Fukuyama adds substantially to our understanding of society through the concept of recognition:

> human beings, like animals, have natural needs and desires for objects outside themselves such as food, drink, shelter and, above all, the preservation of their own bodies . . . but in addition, human beings seek recognition of their own worth, or of the people, things or principles that they invest with worth. The propensity to invest the self with a certain value and to demand recognition for that value, is what in today's popular language we would call self-esteem . . . It is like an innate human sense of justice.[13]

Fukuyama's work, in the way of these things, is derived from an interpretation of Hegel by the French philosopher, Alexander Kojeve. For Kojeve, only the desire for recognition can lead to self-consciousness:

> it is an animal desire which draws one to the body of another, but a human desire which is expressed as the wish to be desired, loved or recognised by another. The essential mark of human desire is that it does not consume its object. It is, in the presence of an absence, creative. To make the same point somewhat differently: the satisfaction of human desire requires some form of mutuality (the loved one returns the love) or social recognition of an object's value . . . The effort at satisfaction and conservation demands that this dialectic be linked with the development of self-consciousness.[14]

The concept of recognition passes a long way towards a comprehensive understanding of the human condition. It suggests that the search for recognition and self-esteem is fundamental to the participation of each person in society. It also explains why many aspects of economic behaviour are beyond the bounds of rationality, such as the accumulation of income and assets past the capacity of any individual to ever consume such wealth. It explains the sense of non-material loss people feel when they face unemployment. It explains why some young people, without the capacity or opportunity to excel by conventional means, seek recognition through various forms of negative behaviour. It helps to deepen our understanding of the full meaning of insecurity: the lack of dignity and worth in one's life which comes from a lack of recognition.

Moreover, it tells us that narrow individualism in society is not enough. Recognition can only come from an engagement in social activities. Without social connectedness none of us can attain recognition. Without such a thing as society there can be no value or purpose to any of our lives. The satisfaction we derive from interacting with others comes from our search for recognition. This framework leaves open the probability of altruistic as well as individualistic behaviour. Recognition can be obtained from assisting others in a range of social situations. The economic libertarian notion that rights and motives are directed solely for the purpose of self-interested materialism is misplaced. The concept of recognition directly challenges modes of liberal thought reliant on the ideals of self-preservation and boundless accumulation. It further punctures neoclassical notions of the rational economic man. As Fukuyama points out:

> What usually passes as economic motivation is in fact not a matter of rational desire but a manifestation of the desire for recognition. Natural wants and needs are few in number and rather easily satisfied, particularly in the context of a modern industrial economy. Our motivation in working and earning money is much more closely related to the recognition that such activity affords us, where money becomes a symbol not for material goods but for social status or recognition.[15]

This concept closely resembles Sen's notion of the 'freedom to achieve' in society. Primary goods cannot be regarded as an end in themselves but rather, the means by which individuals are able to seek other, more readily recognised, forms of well-being and self-esteem. This further explains, of course, the shortcomings of passive welfare, whereby citizens receive transfer payments without a matching transfer of social recognition and worth. The attainment of recognition in a diverse society, given the unique needs and priorities of each individual, is not something for which governments can simply legislate, plan or deliver through the conventional methods of the state public sector. It relies on the development of a certain type of citizen-to-citizen relationship, as well as a satisfactory link between the work of the state and the

needs of the citizenry. This argument again confirms the need for
social democracy to strengthen its appreciation of complex equality;
that is, the means by which each individual might exercise their
capability—through a particular set of primary goods, skills and
active social participation—to secure and enjoy recognition and
adequate self-esteem.

The forms of security, economic and social, addressed in this
book reflect the core requirements of personal recognition in a
post-industrial age. The value of work, earnings security, lifelong
learning and the skills of adaptability lie, first and foremost, in the
contribution they might make to a person's assessment of their
own worth and role in society. Outside a social setting none of
these items holds any lasting value or sense of personal satisfaction.
Yet in the framing of a relationship between people, they are
fundamental to securing peace of mind and certainty about the
value of one's place in society. In most respects, therefore, Sen's
capability set reflects an effective freedom to achieve personal
recognition. A good and equal society is based on the capacity of
its citizens to have the value and purpose of their life recognised.
This again reflects on the folly of social democracy in overlooking
the significance of social capital as a source of social equality. There
can be no proper understanding of the conditions giving rise to
self-esteem and worth in society without an appreciation of the
changing nature of interpersonal relations and the mutual trust
upon which they might be formed.

30

THE CHANGING NATURE OF TRUST

According to Hegel (followed by Kojeve and Fukuyama), the desire for recognition drives the whole historical process. It can also be used to explain the dynamic features of social capital. Trust is one of the means, certainly the most socially useful, by which people receive recognition. If trust were to be displaced by other forms of recognition in the normal course of social behaviour then, to be sure, social capital would be diminished. This replacement effect offers a sound explanation for how, over recent decades, social capital appears to have declined substantially in most Western nations. Moreover, it offers an opportunity for policy makers to consider the means by which the collective institutions of civil society might be strengthened.

Empirical support for the displacement of interpersonal trust as a primary source of social recognition can be found in Putnam's research. In a 1996 paper on the disappearance of civic America he examines a number of variables for their statistical correlation with patterns of social capital depletion.[1] Among these variables—including education levels, suburbanisation, work patterns, female labour force participation, the family unit, generational effects and the rise of the welfare state—Putnam finds just one valid relationship:

> It is as though the post-war generations were exposed to some mysterious x-ray that permanently and increasingly rendered them less likely to connect with the community. Whatever that force might have been, it—rather than anything that happened during the 1970s and 1980s—accounts for most of the civic disengagement. The culprit is television.[2]

TRUSTING TV

The advent of television in the 1950s seems to correspond with the general loss of civic engagement in the United States (with little reason to believe that other Western nations have been substantially different). For instance, the generation born in the early 1920s belonged to twice as many civic associations and were twice as likely to trust other people as the generation born in the 1960s. The amazing growth of television watching—to a point where it now occupies more than 50 per cent of the average American's free time—has shifted the point of social engagement from civic life to the lounge room. By time management alone, TV has depleted the opportunities citizens might take for inter-personal contact and group associations. Whereas family and community-based activities once dominated work-free time they now compete against a new generation of leisure alternatives, led by TV.

But what are the features of television, in terms of recognition theory, which have made it so attractive? What is it about TV that has caused so much of our social capital to be displaced and so much of our public culture to be absorbed? Unfortunately, the social study of television remains rudimentary. While the work of the state public sector has evoked endless inquiries and debates, the immersion of the non-state public sector in TV has passed without comprehensive public scrutiny. As social science advances its understanding of social capital, it will also have to more thoroughly analyse the power of television. A starting point is to understand the participatory nature of the medium.[3] While TV might commonly be regarded as a relatively passive form of recreation, it actually generates the basis of interactivity.

Television is entertaining because it presents an active flow of movement and events, stirring feelings and responses much more than simply conveying information. Whether we want it or not, each of us is a participant to the medium: either cheering for our favourite sporting team, answering the questions on quiz shows, stirred by the conflict and passion of news and current affairs, or relating our experiences and feelings to the ordinariness of soap operas and Oprah. We watch the show because in some way we are part of it. From participation flows recognition. Television has been able to simulate many of the everyday sources of life's worth. The commercial features of TV, particularly its paid advertisements, explicitly appeal to and recognise our behaviour as consumers. We commit ourselves to sporting events, political debates and special ceremonies on TV because of our search for recognition in group behaviour, especially nationalism.

Most of all, television has been able to create a comparative mode of recognition, measuring one's own worth through the experiences of those on TV. The medium has involved people in our lives like never before. A cast of people, characters and happenings pass through our lounge rooms day and night, each of them carrying potential for comparative recognition. Sometimes the comparison is downwards—characters and problems which give the worth and dignity of the viewer a more fortuitous perspective. More often the comparison is upwards—acts of imagination recognising the glorified lives of celebrities. This is why virtual reality has emerged as a natural spin-off from TV. Anyone can be recognised as a rock star at karaoke; anyone can beat Pete Sampras at tennis.

In this fashion, television is an appealing medium in the desire for recognition. It not only has the attraction of intimacy and variety, it is also convenient. If at any time recognition is diminished, the program can be changed or the machine turned off (especially when our identified sporting teams start to lose). Citizens who lack recognition in other parts of their life, such as work and social skills, can compensate through a continuous flow and growing number of program options. The difficulty arises, however, from the way in which comparative recognition, at best, provides only an ephemeral and superficial boost to one's worth and dignity. Television and its associated media, despite their entrenchment in popular culture, do not seem to have added to the depth of society's pool of interactive recognition.

Indeed, it may be that TV's comparative mode of recognition has contributed to the growth of anxiety and personal insecurity now remarked on by so many sociologists. Never before has society left it to a commercial market (and the mass media cannot be properly understood as anything but commerce) to fashion its norms, values and sources of social recognition. Young people in particular no longer take the bulk of their social atlas and role models from family life and community, but from television and other forms of electronic entertainment. The neighbours most commonly invited into Australian homes are from the fictitious Ramsay Street. In the United States it is estimated that the average teenager watches 21 hours of TV per week, while spending 5 minutes per week alone with his or her father, and 20 minutes alone with his or her mother.[4]

This reflects the paradox of the electronic media: how they seemingly carry so much potential for social enlightenment and learning, yet also seem to aggravate the weight of social anxiety. With the speculation surrounding the so-termed information superhighway, it is difficult to know whether it will be, as so many promise, a new tool of genuine progress or simply a more sophisticated mode of comparative recognition. Many people see something inherently worrying about a society which has lost so much of its personal interaction. A significant proportion of the things we now respond to as citizens are impersonal: concepts and images we shall never actually see, touch or experience at first hand. As a society we used to convey messages by language and personal contact. Now we seem to interact as much with electronic technology as with each other.[5] This poses a challenge to both the cognitive skills of each citizen, and to our most basic of instincts for sociability and recognition.

NEW FORMS OF SOCIAL CAPITAL

These trends have not only diminished the formation of social capital but also changed its format. Many of the acts of spontaneous civic life now find their expression in modern forms of technology. To give an example, each year many Sydney suburbs engage in the mass decoration of homes with Christmas lights. This is a spontaneous event in that the residents of these suburbs do not formally press each other to organise the lights, either with incentives or sanctions. Rather, they depend on horizontal sociability—with each resident equal in his or her actions and responsibilities; each relying on all others to reciprocate this effort and add to the suburb-wide impact and pleasure of the event. The level of community contact, however, does not appear to be substantial, as second party participation is mostly limited to driving or walking past to enjoy the lights on display.

Activities such as this signify a shift in social connectedness from the personal to the impersonal. Sociability has been maintained, but transmitted through new forms of technology instead of person-to-person contact. This is an interesting trend in our understanding of social capital. For instance, in what has become a leading symbol of the social capital issue, Putnam has asked why Americans are now more inclined to ten pin bowl alone rather than bowling in teams. The recognition in this particular game, as I understand it, can come just as readily from achieving perfect scores as actually defeating one's opponent. This is indicative of a new generation of recreational pursuits, including computer games and virtual reality, where people compete against machines instead of each other. The emergence of mail-based clubs and associations is another instance of the spread of impersonal sociability.

In charting the correlation between the growth of the popular media and decline of social capital, it is also important to make a distinction between vertical and horizontal systems of connectedness. It seems that organisations tending towards the vertical have declined most notably in their participation and relevance in recent decades. In the United States, Putnam has chronicled the loss of membership experienced by trade unions, political parties, churches, charities, the scouts and service clubs. Similar outcomes have been recorded in Australia.[6] Formally structured, intensely regulated, hierarchical organisations appear to have lost large slabs of public trust and involvement.[7] Conversely, some organisations displaying horizontal social capital and the virtues of mutual trust seem to have moved against the tide of social capital depletion.

While most of the evidence in Australia is only anecdotal, activities tending towards the casual and non-hierarchical—such as clean up campaigns, touch football, indoor cricket and netball, play groups and senior citizens' social clubs—have experienced strong levels of public participation. It is as if, as our communication networks have globalised and the popularity of TV has displaced some forms of social capital, society has found other ways in which to compensate through new, less hierarchical forms of participation. In the global village, hierarchy is having far less success in telling people what to do. This is not surprising given the lift in educational standards and cognitive skills in most Western nations. It seems evident, therefore, from the scattered success of some horizontal networks, that the virtues of mutual trust may not be as endangered as the direction of society otherwise suggests.

POSSIBLE EXPLANATIONS

History tells us that the best features of the human condition have generally held the habits of resilience, no matter the technology, no matter the circumstances. Further empirical study is required to establish whether mutual trust has a way of creating its own history; whether people, in response to social change, are explicitly substituting horizontal for vertical forms of social capital. Nonetheless, one argument can be identified as particularly unsatisfactory: the way in which economic libertarians believe that the establishment of welfare rights and entitlements have caused citizens to lose the habits of social and economic connectedness. This view sets human behaviour in the context of self-interested material accumulation, arguing that the organised provision of welfare crowds out personal incentives for economic and civic effort. This thesis has two significant deficiencies.

First, it frequently confuses self-interested economic behaviour with the social significance of recognition. For instance, it is maintained that the pension for single parents encourages teenage girls to have children. A more likely explanation, if indeed such actions are planned, is that teenagers lacking a sense of worth and dignity in their studies and social relations might seek recognition from the status of parenthood. Second, the crowding out thesis does not square with much of the empirical evidence concerning public attitudes to the state public sector. For several decades opinion polls throughout the Western world have consistently shown a solid decline in the public's trust and confidence in the institutions of government. Given the way in which economic libertarians cast the success of the state and civil society as mutually exclusive, one would reasonably expect the failings of the state to have produced a surge in non-state activity.

Clearly, however, this has not been the case. Factors external to the provision of welfare seem to have eroded the public's confidence in the value of personal interaction and collective activity, whether expressed through the institutions of the state or civil society. Confirmation of this view can be found in Putnam's research. His data shows that 'indicators of social capital are, if anything, positively correlated with the size of the state'. While not claiming a causal relationship between social connectedness and the strength of the welfare safety net, he nonetheless notes that 'this simple finding is not easily reconciled with the notion that big government undermines social capital'.[8] Hence the crowding out thesis, with its focus on economic liberty, underestimates the way in which economic relations themselves—impacting under the banner of globalisation—have most likely placed new pressures on the cohesiveness of civil society.

Indeed, a practical argument can be put such that the same economic and social changes which have weakened the effectiveness of government have also eroded the strength of social capital. Globalisation appears to be associated with new pressures on the sustainability of social connectedness. The weight of life's responsibilities has lifted to the global arena, with a growing number of citizens devoting themselves to international communications, employment and travel. For other citizens, without these opportunities and horizons, the strain of economic and social change has become more acute. In aggregate, these trends have loosened the glue of localism, making it harder to hold communities, families and civil society together.

Since the time of the Industrial Revolution the role of the family unit in society has been in decline. Last century work moved from the home to the factory, health and aged care became the responsibility of the state, while education moved to the local school. It seems that in a post-industrial society the mass media have displaced part of the traditional role of parenting in information sharing and the formation of social values and morality. From this perspective it is not difficult to understand the evolutionary passage of social capital. As citizens we do not have as many activities to undertake within civil society. With the diversification of work and social values we do not seem to share the same depth of mutual interests upon which voluntary associations might be formed. The fundamentals of social connectedness and contact have loosened.

In its various forms, globalisation has uprooted many of the mechanisms for recognition upon which the strength and cohesiveness of civil society has traditionally relied. For instance, the internationalisation of the economy has weakened the competitiveness of the type of producer and consumer cooperatives which flourished in most nations during the first part of this century. A similar process has taken place among our social institutions. When social contact was structured on a local scale, people tended to be recognised for their contribution to civic endeavours—the success of local enterprises, contributions to the parish, achievements at the local school, the town's sports people, and the recognition and support of family members. Voluntary effort and cooperation through civic associations were regarded as being of lasting social worth. Now, with a global system of communications, the bar has been lifted on what constitutes a recognisable contribution to society.

By and large, people have come to judge and acknowledge each other's worth on a scale well beyond civic life. Even though the mass media carries only a small proportion of information of any practical use in our lives, it has become the yardstick by which society measures success. This is what gives the media its mass: a feeling of everyone knowing what others are doing. This knowledge can convey an idealised standard of social worth and dignity. Recognition now sits on a global scale—the business tycoons, sports heroes and movie stars: anyone important enough to appear on TV. When civil society was strong there was no such thing as a celebrity.

Not surprisingly, the value of civic effort has been downgraded, more so given the way in which the visual media rely more on themes of conflict than cooperation. Western society has come to feature a growing gap between the expectations and achievements of its citizenry. This is a defining aspect of youth culture: high expectations for personal worth and social recognition, followed by large slabs of disappointment and alienation. In this fashion, globalisation has created new forms of social unease, in addition to economic uncertainty. This is an unease not directly linked to prejudice or material deprivation, but to the apparent complexity of an open society: the time management of work, leisure and family responsibilities; the overload of available information; the lack of recognition; the loss of social capital and civic certainty. Many people increasingly see civic effort and an involvement with voluntary associations as something which would further complicate their lives. Hence they find a certain comfort in bowling alone.

IN SUMMARY

It is necessary, at this point in the analysis of social capital, to try to bring together its disparate themes: the inexorable search for social recognition; the popularity of the visual media; the decline in vertical social capital; signs of a shift from personal to impersonal relations; the popularity of several loose, horizontal forms of social capital; and, from globalisation, the spread of life's responsibilities and expectations. It is possible, taken as a whole, that these trends feed off and reinforce each other. People not only seem to be doing more in our open society but also struggling for more recognition. The time intensity of a modern life seems to have fostered more intimate and less formal types of sociability, such as TV watching and other unstructured forms of recreation. Citizens have registered a diminishing sense of reward and recognition in vertical systems of coercion. The hierarchy of patron/client relationships has fallen off the meter of public trust.

Yet a problem is immediately clear. The modern search for recognition has been intensely frustrating. Television, in particular, has presented a false dawn. It creates false expectations and delivers, at best, ephemeral satisfaction and recognition. It fosters a form of social interaction without the lasting benefits of social connectedness. It is not able to create the depth of dignity and worth founded in interpersonal trust and mutuality. It simply encourages, through the additional weight of anxiety and comparativity, a further retreat from the common, especially from the most hierarchical parts of the public sector, state and non-state. Television, despite its immense popularity and appeal, has not been able to compensate for the loss of social recognition and connectedness arising from other aspects of globalisation.

This is where the reform of public policy and the work of the state might have a role to play. With the upward shift of capital and many forms of social activity to an international arena, there may be a compensatory role for the state public sector in devolving some of its functions closer to a local scale of self-governance. The durability of social capital relies on people having interests to pursue and things to do in common. Without the interpersonal contact arising from mutual self-governance, it is difficult to create the basis of social trust. This again exposes the shortcomings of the libertarian analysis. It is not welfare *per se*, or even the absolute size of the state, which has undermined social capital. Rather, the upward shift of life's responsibilities to a global scale, unchecked by the centralised scale of most forms of government, has most likely weakened the bonds of social connectedness and mutuality. The global spread of electronic information and other forms of economic and social activity has weakened the basis of interpersonal contact and trust.

In Australia, of course, these issues carry a particular significance, given the fragile nature of the nation's social capital. The way of the social reformer has become doubly difficult. Policy makers not only need to counter the decline of social trust and connectedness being experienced generally in Western nations, but also Australia's ingrained tendency—in most parts of its culture and politics—for centralised, state-led forms of development. Without a strong history of freely formed, cooperative organisations at the centre of our society, the tasks of public mutuality in Australian politics, especially in response to the rise of globalisation, have become quite acute. These are issues to which the next chapter turns.

31

AUSTRALIAN SOCIAL CAPITAL

In 1996 Liverpool City Council in Sydney's south west undertook a survey of the social values and lifestyle interests of residents in one of its new housing estates. This was a snapshot of middle Australia—over-geared mortgages, hand-to-mouth living standards and a disengagement from formally organised institutions. One of the councillors described the results as reflecting a 'do not disturb' generation: young families generally distanced from civil society. Their social capital extended no further than immediate family contact, Saturday sport with the children and a Sunday BBQ with friends. Surveys such as these are often taken as reflecting unfavourably on the state of social connectedness in Australia. Undoubtedly our nation has not been immune from the influences straining social capital across the Western world. It may be, however, from the accumulated habits of public culture, that social capital in Australia has been particularly vulnerable to these more universal trends.

The nation's cultural history has featured a distinctive combination of vertical and horizontal structures. The circumstances of Australia's settlement fostered elements of both state-led development and interpersonal bonding through the institution of mateship. Not so well developed, however, have been organisations in the middle, the voluntary networks of civic life which help to spread the radius of trust beyond the bonds of family and friendship. These organisations, if densely formed and popular, also serve to influence the work of the state, shifting its methods from the vertical to horizontal.

Hence Australian social capital is best understood as bi-polar: lifting most forms of governance to the tier of the state, while pushing down most forms of civic life to the level of friendship networks. State paternalism and mateship bonding have dominated the cultural norms of Australian public life. From this construction of Australian history, with its special origins and terms of settlement, unique modes of social capital have also emerged. This confirms our understanding of social capital as a matter of historical accumulation. It cannot be formed or reinvented overnight. It represents, inevitably enough, the accumulation of social and cultural habits acquired from circumstance.

AUSTRALIAN STATISM

From the time of European settlement, the Australian state was born modern. Nation states had been forming in Europe through the aggregation of public functions previously discharged at a local level. While the nation emerged as the dominant form of state activity, the civic associations of parish and village life remained intact. Australia, however, never experienced effective local governance, in the sense of an active tier of intermediary organisations filling the civic gap between the individual and central power. Our system of formal local government was established on the delegated authority of the colonies to undertake a range of property-related functions. Today it still lacks constitutional recognition and the range of financial and functional responsibilities common in most parts of Europe.

The great Australian achievement of the nineteenth century was to settle and develop the largest and driest continent on earth. Under these conditions, strong state action carried with it the force of logic and need. As W. K. Hancock recorded in 1930:

> Collective action is indispensable if an obstinate environment is to be mastered. But how can this scattered and shifting aggregate of uprooted units (pioneer settlers) act collectively except through the state? They look to the government to help them because they have nowhere else to look . . . The greater part of Australia can only be opened for settlement by heavy initial expenditure. Who is to undertake it? About the middle of the nineteenth century there were some experiments in railway construction by private companies, but the conditions of Australia's economic geography made the land-grant railway, save in exceptional cases, an impossibility. English investors themselves insisted upon having the guarantee of the state.[1]

Sturgess has elsewhere chronicled how, contrary to the body of official history, Australia's colonial development did not rely solely on public ownership. Privately funded infrastructure, service delivery and joint ventures were common enough.[2] Yet the central point concerning state-led development remains. New countries tend to turn to the nation-building power of the state. Hancock accordingly described 'the prevailing ideology of Australian democracy [as featuring] the appeal to government as the instrument of self-realisation'.[3]

Even though the First Fleeters carried with them British ideas about private property rights, it was soon clear that all of the general resources of the colony belonged to the government. This established in Australian politics an enduring pattern of land tenure struggle—from the first land grants and pastoral leases, through the Gold Rush controversies and post-war dream of urban home ownership, to contemporary debates about the land rights of those Australians, poignantly enough, whose ancestors at one time possessed it all. These struggles, so important to Australian public life, have essentially centred on the rights of the individual against the rights of the state. Organisations at the middle have again been absent.

Many of the characteristics of social capital in Australia have been carried forward from the circumstances of the penal colony. The vertical structures of the state were reinforced by its control over the labour market (convict labour) and the reliance of the emerging private sector on state patronage. These trends provided the cultural preconditions by which centralised wage fixing, business welfare and trade protectionism emerged as key features of Australia's economic policy. While many aspects of these policies have changed in recent decades, strong expectations remain in the public arena for the role of the state as a protector of both labour and capital interests.

AUSTRALIAN MATESHIP

The circumstances of the convicts and early free settlers also help explain the emergence of mateship as the most identifiable form of horizontal social capital in Australia. The frontier settlement of the colony was primarily undertaken by men working in small groups. In his epic, *The Fatal Shore* (1988), Robert Hughes brings together accounts of how:

> One would imagine that a residence in such a lone place would be liable to cause a change of some consequence in the minds and habits of any person; and it would be an interesting point to ascertain the effect on the convict stock-keepers who, for weeks together, can have no opportunity of conversing with a

white man, except their sole companion; for there are always two
to a hut. And it did affect them. It promoted the pair-bonding,
the feeling of reliance on one's mate, that would lie forever at
the heart of masculine social behaviour in Australia.[4]

Hughes goes on to describe how the ties of mutual recognition,
forged through the unhappy shared interests of repression, bound
the convicts together in friendship. Visitors to Australia noted the
'mutual regard and trust engendered by two men working together
in the otherwise solitary bush. Men under these circumstances
often stand by one another through thick and thin; in fact it is a
universal feeling that a man ought to be able to trust his mate in
anything.'[5] This feeling of mateship-based trust has carried forward
to the present, finding broader cultural expression in national icons
such as the Anzac tradition and sporting triumphs.

The cultural aspects of social capital are proof of its evolutionary features.[6] The work of a public culture is to encourage society
to value past experiences and find solidarity in past traditions.
Culture effectively comprises the stories we tell ourselves about
ourselves. The creation of culture is invariably followed by the
collective invention of social traditions (and people are often busi-
est fortifying their traditions when the cultural narratives of the
present are most acutely feeling the strain of economic and social
change). In Australia's history this has meant a special attachment
to the horizontal features of mateship and the expectation of
client/patron relations with government.

Not surprisingly by the theory of social capital, this has engendered a strong sense of mutuality and equality among mates as well
as public scepticism about the performance of government. Indeed,
mateship has formed the basis of the Australian claim to egalitarianism: as mates know and treat each other as equals, it is assumed
that in all other parts of society, Jack is as good as his master.[7] It
is problematic, however, to gauge the manner in which these values
of mutual trust and cultural egalitarianism have influenced the
performance of other institutions. For instance, trust in the production process has the positive impact of lowering transaction
costs and lifting productivity. Yet these are not generally regarded
as best practice features in the Australian workplace. It may be that
the habits of risk taking and cooperation have not extended beyond
the small group institution of mateship.

This seems to provide an explanation for what Hughes has
described as the 'defensive optimism' of the Australian character;
that is, a capacity for confident and gregarious social behaviour,
yet a poor reputation for business risk taking and assertiveness.
The features of friendship trust in Australia do not seem to have

flowed on to a broader scale of civic life and the creation of organisations in the middle. Certainly the relationship between the citizenry and state public sector has not been representative of mutual trust. Despite the state's active role in the settlement and servicing of the nation, it is not generally respected in the public arena. From the colonial period, Australians have not been comfortable, as clients, with the exercise of central authority. In part, this comes from the indiscriminate use of authority in the convict era. This early scepticism, regarded by many as a healthy part of the Australian character, has not been dissolved by the subsequent work of the state public sector.

A common factor in the formation of horizontal and vertical structures in Australian society has been the role of geography and space. The scale, harshness and isolation of the decades of frontier settlement appear to have been fundamental to both the establishment of mateship and the structure of the central patron state. The most enduring impact of the tyranny of distance, properly understood, has been its influence on social capital. If high density living and large group interaction are assessed as preconditions for viable civic life (a notion supported by Putnam's study of the city states in Italy) then Australian conditions—from the isolation of both the bush frontier and urban fringe—have not been conducive to the spread of horizontal social capital.

CIVIC ASSOCIATIONS

None of this is to suggest, however, that Australian history has been devoid of civic associations. It needs to be acknowledged that nothing could be more civic than Aboriginal tribal life. Through the first century or so of European settlement in Australia, church-based benevolent societies, member-run libraries, mechanics institutes, bush nursing auxiliaries and self-provident friendly societies were an important part of public life. In this century trade unionism, service clubs, the scouts and girl guide movements, local sporting associations, environmental action groups, agricultural and housing cooperatives, credit unions, progress associations, bush fire brigades, the Country Women's Association and other civic groups have constituted an active, non-state, public sector.

The point to be confirmed, especially by the standards of social capital studies internationally, is that Australia cannot be regarded as a high trust, densely civic society. We do not have a strong proportion of horizontal organisations at the middle. Many of the associations listed above rely more on vertical structures than horizontal. Still others have experienced a secular decline in membership and participation in recent decades. The anecdotal evidence of new sources of horizontal social capital is yet to be verified or fully understood through rigorous empirical study. Generally, history tells us that Australians have been more inclined to pursue the logic of collective action through personal networks of mateship and/or the patronage of the central state than by spontaneously civic means at the middle.

By the compelling rationale of circumstance, Australia has not accumulated a tradition of intermediary organisations bridging the work of citizenry and state. A big, isolated country identified an economy of scale and settlement in state-led development and infrastructure. In the provision of basic human services, central authority was an inexorable feature of the governance of the penal colony. From the beginning, the principles of a command state applied to the notion of social welfare. Australia's first benevolent societies used government as virtually the sole source of running cost and capital funds. The Elizabethan poor law ideals of civic benevolence were not applicable to Australia's circumstances. As the historian Brian Dickey records:

> There were no paupers aboard the First Fleet, nor any poor laws. There were paid officials of the central state under the direction of the Home Office; there was a military force of marines, some with their families; and there were convicts, state dependants who legally were no longer the responsibility of a parish but were under the control of the Home Office. The labour of the convicts, but not their persons, was assigned to Governor Phillip, who in turn would assign that labour as he thought fit in the colony. Who needed a poor law in a jail? . . . The central fact of welfare provision in Australia was that the colonial governments were indeed the principal subscribers and providers.[8]

In a young society like ours, barely two centuries in the making, many of the habits of culture and social capital remain substantially unaltered from their point of origin. One of the curious debates of modern Australian politics has been the notion that State Governments represent a tier of devolution in the administration of public responsibilities. In truth, most States still run their chief departments—police, education, hospitals and transport—with a central authority and command ethos little diminished from the days of Phillip. A defining aspect of vertical systems of organisation is their centralisation of authority. An ethos of decentralisation is better expressed through horizontal structures which disperse control and decision making equally across networks of mutual trust. Instances of mass movements at the middle of Australian society have been rare. The most significant appears to have been the friendly societies which served as self-provident welfare and health providers from the 1830s through to the Great Depression. By the eve of the First World War, 46 per cent of all Australians were benefiting from friendly society services. At the heart of their creed was a commitment to male fraternity, suggesting that the societies carried with them the social capital of mateship. This meant the creation of distinctly horizontal structures. As David Green has chronicled:

> Membership of a friendly society gave the industrial worker a status his working life failed to offer. He might have to sell his labour to earn a living, but in the lodge room the member was much more than a mere wage labourer. He was a member of a fraternity committed to high ideals, and ideals which were blatantly superior to those espoused by many of his employers. In the lodge room there were no bosses. More than this, the lodge member did not just accept a given code of rules, he participated freely and fully in the process of making, amending or rescinding the rules.[9]

The societies were based on voluntary partnership through subscription, autonomy in the allocation of benefits to members in need and careful rules for risk selection. Candidates for the membership of the sick and funeral funds had to comply with three requirements—prescribed age, good health and good character (which normally required employment). The societies contracted with local doctors for the provision of medical services to members on the basis of an annual capitation fee.[10] The problem of free riders, known as 'bludgers' in the Australian language, was dealt with by internal systems of detection and sanction.

It is sometimes argued that the friendly societies and like systems of mutual aid were dissolved by the weight of the emerging welfare state. This view mistakes the proper sequence of cause and effect. Any system of self-provident insurance pooling is vulnerable to instances of actuarial overload. Green himself records how, 'the Depression years took a heavy toll on friendly society membership and many societies never fully recovered'.[11] In these circumstances government transfer payments emerged as a social insurer of last resort—able to cope with, in terms of pooled risk and universal coverage, a sudden downturn in economic conditions. Compulsory taxation effectively replaced voluntary contributions, while the capacity of each citizen for earnings and hence premiums no longer determined their eligibility for safety net benefits. The authority of the state provided a scale of actuarial smoothing beyond the scope of the friendly societies. Moreover, Green's research shows how the consumer sovereignty of the friendly societies in the mutual organisation of health services was destroyed, not by the welfare state as such, but by the producer sovereignty of Australia's most militant trade union, the AMA.[12]

The experience of the friendly societies leads to a broader set of issues in the framing of public policy. One cannot reasonably expect, as some libertarians might, that the abandonment of the welfare state will be replaced by the mass formation of intermediary associations if, as appears plain, the social capital for such a task is insufficient. The friendly societies cannot spontaneously re-emerge because, just as their role dissolved earlier this century, so too did the social capital upon which they relied. Similarly, it cannot be reasonably assumed (as social democrats might) that the vertical structures of the welfare state are sustainable either in their social legitimacy or the effectiveness of their outcomes.

This suggests the desirability of a middle way: a system maintaining the actuarial strengths and universal coverage of the welfare state, yet also contributing to gains in the level of mutual trust and horizontal social capital—that is, one preserving the immutable safety net of a civilised society while also turning the vertical, patron/client characteristics of the state towards the virtues of horizontal social capital at the middle. The next two chapters deal with the feasibility of this approach as a program of Labor reform. They examine, in turn, the use of social capital in the contemporary political debate; the reformulation of the social democratic method; and specific reforms aimed at the devolution of the organisational scale and transparency of the state public sector.

32

POLITICAL CAPITAL

In advocating public policies in this field, one needs to be careful about some of the mythology associated with the concept of social capital. For some time public opinion has expressed a concern about the apparent loss of traditional values. It has become convenient for a generation of politicians—confronted by the problem of managing a dynamic period of economic and social change—to appeal to these traditions as a definitive source of security against change. Social capital has been used as a rhetorical tool to convey a nostalgic sense of family and community values. As a new concept in social studies, social capital is somewhat malleable. This has allowed it to be used in the political debate for presentational purposes alone, without the backing of substantive policy reform. As a rule, the fewer answers politicians have about the future the more inclined they are to talk about the past.

As a piece of nostalgia, however, social capital has no practical use. It cannot be revived simply by talking about the past. Only from fresh questions concerning institutional design and the possible reform of public policy, properly defined, can it be relevant for the future. As ever, one needs to be careful about the nature of reminiscences. As outlined earlier, it is difficult to identify a golden age of community values and horizontal social capital in Australia. Further, it cannot be assumed that all expressions of social capital, past and present, are socially useful. It is not uncommon for vertically structured community organisations to have a negative impact on the spread of social trust. So too, highly isolated and inward looking communities are rarely trustful of outsiders. A range of rights and freedoms are required to safeguard instances when civil society might drift towards bigotry and oppression. Social capital cannot be regarded as an end in itself. Issues of institutional design are all important among those entities with the potential to create social connectedness.

Unhappily, much of the current debate about social capital also reflects old ideological struggles. It is as if the dogmatic Right and Left have simply transposed their long standing views on ownership issues to this fresh, substantially unformed, issue. The Right has argued, under the banner of economic libertarianism, that the strength of social capital is inversely proportional to the size of government. The unreconstructed Left in Australia, most notably Eva Cox in the ABC's 1995 Boyer Lecture series, has sought to use social capital as an alibi for extending the supply side methods of the state public sector.[1] It is, of course, absurd to argue, as Cox does, that 'increasing the functions and visibility of government' can rebuild social capital, unless government can first demonstrate a capacity to foster the interdependence of civic effort. More likely, passive welfarism generates elements of dependence between governments and citizens, rather than interdependence within civil society.

A different set of organisational principles—emphasising horizontal devolution, mutual aid and active welfare—offer greater potential for the enhancement of social trust. Yet these initiatives are anathema to Cox's preference for a command economy in the social sector. Cox also argues that competition in society inexorably breaks down the strength of social capital. This view ignores the way in which most forms of competition, be they economic or social, are underpinned by active cooperation and social interdependence. As enterprises compete against each other their success relies fundamentally on the extent of cooperation in their workplace. As sporting teams compete, team mates rely on each other for their collective success. The success of a society relies on an appropriate balance between competition and cooperation in its values and institutions—competition to foster innovation and creativity; cooperation to build social trust and inclusiveness.

A leading task of successful governance is to guide and foster this balance. During Labor's time in office the Australian economy was increasingly exposed to market competition. The role of the state shifted from protecting capital to making it compete: dismantling tariff protection, liberalising the financial sector and exchange rate, plus reforming product markets and public utilities. Little attention, however, was given to developing a strategy by which these policies might be complemented by the facilitation of social capital. An important task for Labor's time out of office is to establish a policy framework which strengthens the underpinnings of cooperation and mutuality in Australian society.

REFORM TECHNIQUE

A starting point is to rethink the social democratic technique. The role of policy reformers in the decades following the Second World War was to argue that Keynesian economic management, service planning and welfare statism could mould society towards new standards of equality and opportunity. The preconditions of this model, continuous economic growth and stable social conditions, have now clearly dissolved with the onset of globalisation and all it denotes. While some may judge this as simply a problem of circumstance—if the times have changed then so too can the social democratic mould—a more serious problem of technique remains. Civil society has a way of its own, not always suited to the ethical judgments and methods of social democracy. The British social thinker, David Marquand, has described the problem neatly:

> Despite the humanity and generosity of its founders, [social democracy] degenerated, in practice, into a system of social engineering. The engineers could pull the levers in the knowledge that the machine would respond as they wished. Social democrats wanted to do good, but they were more anxious to do good to others than to help others do good to themselves. As they saw it, the role of public intervention was to provide, to manipulate, or to instruct, rather than to empower . . . Hand in hand with all this went a curiously simplistic attitude to the state and to the relationship between the state and the web of intermediate institutions and voluntary associations which make up a civil society. The state was seen as an instrument (or set of instruments) which social democratic ministers could use as they wished. Civil society was seen, all too often, not as an agent but as a patient: as an inert body, lying on an operating table, undergoing social democratic surgery.[2]

Far from taking the role of an inert body, civil society, through the possibilities of horizontal social capital, has devised its own prescription for equality and mutual aid. It makes little sense, of course, to frame the hopes and standards of social democracy (or any other political doctrine) in a manner divorced from these social relations. Indeed, it might be argued that social reformers have for centuries been engaged in acts of political folly by seeking to direct rather than facilitate the type of equality found in civil society. The exercise of mutual trust appears to reflect the oldest and perhaps wisest of socialist traditions: from each according to one's ability, to each according to one's needs. Yet far from nurturing these tendencies as the basis of the good society, the parliamentary and extra-parliamentary Left alike have pursued values framed more at the abstract level and relied on methods drawn more from the technique of top–down reform.

The cause of Australian Labor, perhaps more than ever in recent practice, has fallen prone to these errors. These have been sins of commission as much as omission—committing ourselves to techniques divorced from social practice; omitting to factor the strength and composition of social capital into our approach to social justice. Given that Labor's hopes for a more equal and just society have always relied on a certain judgment about human values—a belief that while people will always defend their own interests, they are also likely to care enough about the society in which they live to advance the interests of others—then social capital theory seems integral to Labor ideology. It is not possible to breed mutuality and maintain the collective expression of common needs in society without facilitating the strength of social capital.

Left-of-centre thinking needs to broaden its political goals beyond the state-to-citizen relationship. This requires a new sensitivity among the reform techniques of the social democratic project. Social trust cannot be legislated into existence the way a government might seek to create new economic regulations and institutions. Social capital does not lie motionless, awaiting some form of social democratic surgery to give it new life and purpose. It has a way of making its own history and habits. The composition of social trust and connectedness, forming and changing across generations, arises from the influence of society's culture and values. 'The civic community has deep historical roots', Putnam confirms, and hence, 'social context and history profoundly condition the effectiveness of institutions'.[3] Those attached to a mechanistic view of social democracy—its capacity to pull the levers of social change and produce immediate outcomes—may be unimpressed by conclusions of this kind. It might be argued that the cause of Labor, set within the context of parliamentary reform and short term electoral cycles, requires more tangible and immediate goals. Such a perspective, however, sells short both the critical features of social capital and the prospects of social change from a fresh approach to institutional reform.

Indeed, Putnam does not regard his research findings as 'an invitation to quietism'. Rather, the reform of society's institutions, especially those concerning the nature of public governance, is likely to alter social values and practices.[4] Culture, while impacting powerfully on the methods of social and political organisation, should not be regarded as immutable. History records the frequency of cultural change and the influence of political acts. This century, for instance, the Catholic Church, along with several other social institutions, managed to transform its cultural relationship with capitalism.[5] Economic acts, particularly in the change from a Fordist mode of production to post-Fordist work, have helped to remake the cultural habits of most workplaces. The transformation from an industrial to information-based society is undoubtedly having a profound impact on most aspects of our public culture. To be certain, cultures have the capacity to adapt and progress by way of gradualist reform. While this process is rarely, if ever, pronounced across the short to medium term, it nonetheless confirms the evolutionary nature of cultural change and the means by which it impacts on social capital.

The relationship between culture and public governance reflects an interactive flow of cause and effect. Acts of institutional change and redesign influence the habits of culture, just as culture impacts on the nature of governance. Institutional reform helps to foster social learning, 'learning by doing'.[6] Changes of this kind have the capacity to alter the way in which people think about and respond to public affairs. The interaction between the state and citizenry, with its influence on the cultural habits of governance, also impacts on the relationship people hold with each other. Civil society cannot be quarantined from the social values and habits that inevitably emerge from the formal organisation of government. This confirms the essential flaw in the social democratic technique: assuming that the structure of government is somehow removed from the formation of public culture. According to Putnam, 'linear causal questions must not crowd out equilibrium analysis. In this context, the culture versus structure, chicken-and-egg debate is ultimately fruitless. More important is to understand how history smoothes some paths and closes off others.'[7] Social democracy needs to embrace this compelling conclusion. The strength of social capital profoundly influences the type of society in which we live and—among the policy options available to government—the design and functioning of public institutions can have a lasting impact on the formation and composition of social capital.

INSTITUTIONAL DESIGN

Public policy has a role to play in smoothing the path to social trust. Governments have the capacity, through their design of public institutions, to create an environment within which citizens are able to find and foster mutuality. This means devolving the structures of governance such that people are able to establish commonality in their interests and, in acting to advance these shared goals, are in a position to build the habits of reciprocated trust. It is not possible to create social connectedness unless people are able to interact in a way that exposes them to the logic of mutuality. Cooperation is always more likely if people expect to be involved with each other again and they regard this future interaction as important. Social capital is created as a by-product of this recurring pattern of shared interests and interaction. The formation of social trust and mutuality relies, therefore, on a certain type of institutional design. People need to be able to interact on an organisational scale within which they can constantly assess the behaviour of others and find reasons for the creation of trust.

In Part III of the book it was argued that the successful management of the commons requires a smaller and more transparent scale of governance. If people are not able to see the boundaries of the commons and monitor the behaviour of others then the basis of commonality is not likely to be sustained. This is also true of the processes leading to the formation of social capital. Individuals need to be able to feel that their personal contribution makes a substantive difference to the management of the group; and moreover, that these efforts are likely to be reciprocated. The viability of the public commons, therefore, rests on a scale best measured by the transparency of individual and group behaviour. The raw size of an organisation is not as important as the level of visibility in the interaction between its members. Without the constant flow of mutual interest and effort between people it is not possible to strengthen the bonds of interpersonal trust and recognition.

Like so many other parts of our political system, issues of administrative scale and manageability tend to be judged in the public arena through the Right/Left binary. This positions individuals and economic markets—purportedly representing the virtues of small, freely formed networks—at the opposite end of the organisational spectrum to the state public sector, which is usually identified with large, centralised organisations operating on a national scale. In practice, however, many participants to the market, particularly large multinational corporations and trade unions, operate on the same mass scale and with the same lack of behavioural transparency as the state public sector. Equally, not all forms of governance need to reflect the Fordist methods of the modern state. It is possible for public policy to devolve a substantial part of the functions and organisational features of the state to smaller, more virtual units of public mutuality.

A better understanding of these questions of size and scale lies outside the traditional binary. Small-scale groups, whether in the market or various forms of social governance, tend to have highly visible and decentralised forms of interaction. Conversely, large-scale units are characterised by their opaqueness and top-down systems of control. Issues of scale within a particular group are best determined by the density and visibility of interaction between its members, rather than the size of its membership or financial turnover. Consider, for instance, two diverse types of group behaviour drawn from the world of sport. A Mexican wave of some 40 000 spectators might be judged as carrying the features of a small-scale group, given its high level of behavioural transparency and group interaction. By contrast, a professional sporting team, perhaps with no more than twenty members, yet managed with a strong sense of hierarchy and centralised decision making, reflects a mass scale of organisation.

Driven by the conventional binary, politics in most nations has been reduced to a struggle about the raw size of government. The Left has tended to advocate more money for more programs, without necessarily ensuring that the organisational principles and scale of the public sector reflect a high level of public interaction and mutuality. The political Right has attempted to decrease the size of government, virtually as an end in itself, without necessarily considering the type and quality of the citizen-to-citizen relationship that might replace the role of the state. This relatively barren, big versus small government debate has overlooked the possibility of a different form of collective action in the public arena—the devolution of public governance to a more transparent and horizontal scale of public organisation. It has failed to consider the means by which the state might foster new forms of social interaction and connectedness through the transfer of some of its decision-making powers to organisations at the middle of society. In no other policy area has the Right/Left binary become more dated and worn than its inability to cope with the theory and practice of social capital.

The devolution of public governance also helps to reposition our understanding of social equality. It aims to transfer some of the responsibilities of governance from the state-to-citizen relationships in the hope of creating equality in the relations between citizens. While this does not necessarily involve bigger or smaller government, gauged by the conventional wisdom, it certainly requires governance of a different type and scale to that promulgated by the post-war welfare state. The shortcomings of the modern state have been exposed in the centralised scale of its planning and provision, much more than the ideals of welfare itself. Top–down bureaucracies have obscured the transparency and sense of active participation needed to sustain the sound management of the public commons. The creation of patron/client relationships in most parts of the public sector has reduced the capacity of public welfare to breed mutuality and the benefits of social trust and connectedness.

In an information-based society, where a substantial proportion of the citizenry carries a well-developed set of knowledge skills, the hierarchical features of the patron/client relationship seem increasingly at odds with the identification of personal preferences and needs. People with the cognitive capacity to creatively use and adapt new sources of information, naturally enough, want to be able to maximise their input and control over the processes of public governance, especially on those issues and decisions which impact directly on their lives. During an era of globalisation, when the tasks of social recognition appear more difficult, this trend has become particularly significant. Even though improved standards of educational access have provided a greater number of citizens with the skills of adaptation and social participation, there also appears to be a declining number of public forums within which these skills might be applied. As globalisation continues to erode the foundations of social connectedness, an important compensatory role has emerged for public policy in opening up new opportunities for mutuality and self-governing interaction. Appropriate forums need to be provided within which people are able to define common interests and, in the satisfaction of common needs, build the bonds of social recognition.

This means creating a new generation of public sector reforms, advancing beyond the post-Fordist trend towards functional flexibility and its reliance on quasi-markets. Reforms of this kind, while welcome in their capacity to customise service delivery and address the requirements of complex equality, still reflect some of the hierarchical features of the patron/client relationship. The interaction between the state and the citizenry remains lopsided because of the improbability of reciprocation. Even in the most decentralised type of quasi-market arrangements, the chief organisational principles remain top-down in their focus, with few incentives for citizens to embrace the benefits of mutuality. The strengthening of state hierarchies and the establishment of quasi-markets should not be perceived as the only valid alternatives in the development of new systems of public governance.

Social democratic reform needs to embrace a third way, contrary to the vertical structures of both state coercion and market simulation. As Taylor has argued, 'hierarchy is not the only form of governance, not the only remedy of market failure (which is general, not exceptional) and not our only defence against the many destructive effects of the market'.[8] The ideals of social trust can help to create the ethical basis of a form of governance beyond the rigid hierarchies of the state public sector and the shortcomings of the market system. This means establishing an organisational format by which citizens can interact as equals in the satisfaction of needs and interests held in common, rather than as clients to the bureaucracy or quasi-markets.

In this fashion, the devolution paradigm helps to downgrade the role of both statism and individualism in our society. It recognises the limits of state control and coercion, while also rejecting the primacy of the individual as an answer to social needs and the logic of collective action. It declares a preference for the type of social trust and connectedness arising from the formation of self-governing organisations at the middle of society; preferable indeed to the vertical structures of state provision and the anti-social consequences of narrow individualism. Devolution strikes something of a new radical centre in public governance, moving beyond the dichotomy between the state and open markets. It represents not only the hope of a better form of public governance, but also an immense challenge to social democracy in the creation of the type of reforms by which devolution might succeed in practice.

33

DEVOLUTION IN PRACTICE

The devolution of governance requires a fundamental restructuring of the work of the state public sector. The rise of the welfare state was based on an assumption that government needed to act as both a funder and provider of public services. The coercive powers of the state in taxation were used to fund large, top-down bureaucracies and Fordist systems of service delivery. The machinery of government left few opportunities for the development of forms of governance outside the welfare and planning strands of social provision. Within this framework, debates about the role of the state have been limited to questions of size. In response to new social issues, left-of-centre parties have argued for an expansion of both the funder and provider functions of government, while the Right has consistently sought to wind back the size and significance of these two roles.

In all likelihood, the most appropriate form of public governance now lies beyond the traditional binary. In the organisation of collective activity, the funder and provider functions do not, in all circumstances, need to be discharged concurrently by government. In most, if not all, areas of public responsibility, the state has an important role to play in resourcing and regulating systems of social provision. It does not necessarily follow, however, that the state public sector represents, in all cases, the most appropriate means by which the process of service delivery should be discharged. In some instances, depending on the nature of the particular form of collective activity, the best way of building new forms of social equality and connectedness lies in fostering the role of non-state, mutual organisations at the middle of society. That is, government should continue to fulfil its traditional role as a funder and regulator of service provision, while ensuring that part of its functions as a service provider is devolved to the non-state public sector.

This approach relies on two related organisational principles. First, the vertical, coercive structures of the state are deployed in the collection of resource inputs, thereby establishing the actuarial basis of a social safety net. This positions the role of government as a social insurer, without necessarily requiring from it the conventional top–down method of service delivery. Taxes and other forms of revenue would continue to be collected by central government, but instead of then being distributed to service providers within the state sector, they would be allocated directly among the citizenry. Within this system of demand side entitlements, government agencies would be required to undertake an assessment, according to the principles of equity and universality, of the amount and type of resources that need to be made available to each citizen. This approach to public sector management is similar to the proposals outlined earlier in this book for the establishment of a customised system of Income Security Accounts.

Second, the methods of horizontal social capital are used for determining the means by which these resources can be deployed and distributed for the purpose of service outputs. Citizens would be able to aggregate their entitlements into self-governing units of public administration, within which they would be able to interact and build the bonds of public mutuality and cooperation. Government would need to fulfil its role as a regulator by establishing sound guidelines, prudential and administrative, by which these mutual bodies might operate. Internationally, the cooperatives movement has provided a useful model for this type of public governance—based on the benefits of common ownership and control, strong standards of accountability and a record of democratic administration. While the cooperatives structure in Australia has been used mainly for the purpose of economic production and marketing, its ethos and methods are just as relevant to the task of social provision. It reflects, in the facilitation of common interests and social connectedness, the virtues of governance without government.

Significantly, these principles mirror the methods by which civil society has structured most of its new forms of casual, non-hierarchical organisation. To use another example from the sporting world: the proliferation of relatively informal activities, such as indoor cricket and netball, reflects a concentration of organisational effort on service outputs, rather than inputs—that is, participants spend a minimum amount of time involved in the collection of financial capitations, while maximising their time and effort in the game itself. This reflects the benefits of what I would term 'thin input coercion' and 'thick output mutuality'—allowing people, in the design of the public institutions with which they have contact, to maximise their interaction with freely formed horizontal structures, and minimise the role of vertically structured coercion. There appears to be no sound reason why other, more substantial, forms of public provision cannot be organised in this fashion.

These principles also reflect a different way of thinking about the scale of public administration—using the nation state as the most appropriate scale and unit for raising public resources; and using freely formed, small-scale units of self-governance as the most appropriate means of organising the provision of public services. In this fashion, they address many of the difficulties now facing the welfare state. As the British sociologist, Anthony Giddens, has written:

> The welfare state is a passive risk system—it isn't designed to encourage people to make active investment decisions with their lives. It only reacts to things when they go wrong: it takes care of you when you are ill, it puts you on the dole when you are unemployed. But it has been ineffective in actually countering poverty or redistributing wealth in the long term. Think of the welfare state not as the Left has traditionally thought of it—as a mechanism to alleviate inequality—but as a kind of insurance system that allows people to take risks. We must provide people with the resources they require to be active investors, as it were, but at the same time we must provide security mechanisms which protect them.[1]

At logic, governments do not always need to act as service providers to fulfil their role as social insurers. The provision of demand side entitlements helps to discharge the social protection functions of the state, while also allowing policy makers to encourage the exercise of personal effort and risk. This relies, of course, on an active welfare approach, with the provision of entitlements according to the principles of customisation and reciprocated responsibility. Acts of self-governance in the delivery of public services are also an important means by which the exercise of personal risk and effort in society can be maximised. Self-governance helps to build the skills and practice of social participation and commonality. It forces citizens to take and manage risks in the realisation of their needs and interests. It engages them in the possibilities of cooperation—trusting in others to meet common needs; and working collectively towards the satisfaction of mutual interests.

A smaller scale of public organisation also helps to address the two policy dilemmas normally associated with a social insurance approach to governance. The first issue concerns the problem of 'adverse selection'—when the insurer is not able to distinguish between good and bad insurance risks and accordingly, sets an inappropriate rate of premium. Small-scale groups, with their strong levels of behavioural transparency and sanction-making powers, are well placed to identify and deal with the problem of unanticipated risk. This means either recommending to central government a suitable adjustment in the level of individual entitlement, or themselves taking action to overcome the causes of bad risk behaviour. A second issue relates to the possibility of 'moral hazard'—when the nature of the insurance contract adversely alters the behaviour of the insured person. Again, small-scale, mutual organisations are well situated to deal with the behavioural issues arising from the free rider problem. They offer a clear direction and set of organisational principles by which public sector reform can proceed in practice.

REFORM IN PRACTICE

Devolution represents a major reform to the social democratic technique; a reform so vast that, inevitably enough, it will be prone to error and substantial revision. This is why it is important to adopt an empirical approach to policy making in this area. While social democracy can draw on decades of theory and practice in the state-to-citizen relationship, its application of devolution policies remains relatively untested and unformed. Policy makers will need to learn by doing; to revise and reconstruct policy according to events and empirical observation; to establish from experience the type of reforms that work in practice and those that do not. Hence the policy changes advocated below—preliminary and rudimentary as they stand—need to be taken with some caution. In many cases, their full implementation will depend on the success of pilot schemes and trials.

Caution also needs to be taken with proposals for devolution which, in practice, do not shift the structure of governance from vertical to horizontal forms of social capital. In Britain, for instance, the Blair Government has used devolution as a way of establishing a new set of parliaments. While reforms of this nature may be beneficial in fostering greater regional autonomy, they are not likely to impact on society in a way that builds new sources of interpersonal trust. Likewise in Australia, while gains can be made in the rationalisation of responsibilities between the Commonwealth and the States and Territories, the most beneficial change in the format of government is likely to arise from a genuine program of devolution from the state to the non-state public sector. The transfer of responsibilities among the formal tiers of the federal system can have only a limited impact on the quality of governance if the hierarchical nature of client/patron relationships remains unaltered. After all, in the creation of public trust and mutuality, the difference between being a client to the large-scale bureaucracies of the States and Territories, compared to the top–down structures of the Commonwealth, is not great. Devolution is not likely to be achieved through the creation of more government of the old kind. It relies, first and foremost, on the possibility of new forms of commonality in the public arena.

An important part of the creation of public mutuality, of course, lies in the identification of mutual interests. This book has argued that the concept of public universality is now best understood and expressed through forms of public governance which address the core insecurities of life—in employment, income support, lifelong learning, health care, personal safety and social connectedness. These responsibilities provide an appropriate charter from which social democracy can consider a program of devolution in the administration of the public sector. They hold potential, through the facilitation of self-governance, for rebuilding the citizenry's faith in the logic of collective action. They help to accommodate the diversity of a post-industrial society by allowing people with like interests and inclinations to realise the benefits of public mutuality. The following reform proposals offer a guide to this particular approach to public policy.

An obvious starting point lies in more thoroughly resourcing the work of the non-state public sector. With the advent of globalisation, most of our society's problems have deepened and become more complex. The conventional methods of government are struggling to deal with the entrenched problems of economic and social exclusion. Social problems are not being solved by the old formula of providing more money for more programs. Without effort, risk and innovation at a community level—without solutions from the bottom–upwards as well as top–down—there can be no resolution of the issues facing our open society and economy. In this age of immense social change—a time when the challenges and choices in our lives have never been so great—the state needs to establish a new relationship with its citizens. It needs to get out of the habit of telling people what to do, of always trying to plan and control society's direction, and allow more of society's answers to come from community and civic life.

In Part II of the book, for instance, it was argued that solutions to the problem of unemployment now rely on the creation of new forms of work in the non-state public sector. Civic associations should be able to access public resources to sponsor projects and employment, especially in dealing with the spatial features of the new labour market. This does not mean using the authority of the state to direct changes in civil society, but turning over a share of its resources for genuinely civic purposes; that is, preferring solutions which reflect a strengthening of social capital to those devised by law makers; and preferring outcomes arrived at by participants in civil society to the supply side methods of conventional government. Too often it is assumed that law making in itself remakes values and outcomes across society. Often better results arise from placing people and organisations in a position where they can freely and mutually arrive at solutions themselves.

The provision of health care and other forms of welfare support are also conducive to this type of policy devolution. Improvements in health and information technology now make it possible for governments to move towards a system of demand side entitlements in the provision of health services. This approach, often described as 'demand side socialism', relies on the payment of a risk-rated capitation amount to each citizen, covering the estimated cost of their service needs and circumstances. For instance, high-risk groups, such as the elderly and chronic health care users, would receive a larger capitation payment than low-risk health consumers. Citizens would then be free to use their capitation amount to form mutual health care organisations, much in the style of health consumer cooperatives. These self-governing groups would be chartered with identifying and meeting the health care needs of their members, specifically through the purchase of an appropriate set of health services and insurance arrangements.

Within this framework, the direct role of government is limited to the funding of demand side entitlements, along with the regulation of the administrative and prudential standards of the cooperatives system. Governments would also continue to discharge their responsibilities as a service provider; although in this instance, as a response to the purchasing decisions of mutual bodies, rather than the conventional methods of supply side provision. Privately owned health providers would operate in a similar fashion. Public goals for service universality and access would be factored into the calculation of the entitlement paid to each consumer. The establishment of a demand side market for health care—albeit a market with strong elements of government resourcing and regulation—opens up the potential for public mutuality. Consumer cooperatives have the capacity to provide for health care interests held in common; to monitor the needs and service utilisation of their members; plus, through the processes of self-governance, to build new forms of social trust and connectedness. A detailed program of health care reform, expanding on this concept of demand side mutuality within the Australian health system, is set out in Appendix IV.

Similar principles of devolution can be applied to the management of public needs in income support and associated welfare purposes. With advances in the application of information technology, it is now possible to administer flexible systems of income support through a network of small-scale, mutually formed organisations. This requires, further to the welfare reforms advocated in chapter 26, a capacity for recipients to transfer their ISA entitlements to a cooperatives structure. This positions the income support system along the lines of a federation, with the state resourcing and supervising an acceptable standard of resource input, while a range of welfare cooperatives determines the distribution and delivery of welfare support. Given the potential of these mutual bodies to assist the formation of social capital and thereby lower a range of other social costs, it is appropriate for central government to offer financial incentives (most likely through the tax system) to encourage the growth and success of the cooperatives system. Trust and mutuality in society should be rewarded no less than effort and performance in the market economy.

In all aspects of policy devolution, the balance of public governance needs to shift, as much as possible, from vertical to horizontal relationships. Even in areas of public responsibility where it is not feasible to create the administrative basis of self-governance—such as public good services in law and order—the nexus between horizontal and vertical forms of social capital still matters. It is commonly thought, for instance, that the success of the Japanese police force comes from the high level of trust established between its officers and the public. This has emerged from a close and responsive relationship between the police and the communities they seek to serve, both by way of a localised system of police posts and high levels of public interaction. As Taylor has noted:

> Crime control, insofar as it involves specialised policing, will be more effective as well as more democratic to the degree that the hierarchical relation between police and people approximates a cooperative model of hierarchy, rather than a coercive one. The police must not only devolve to the people as much as possible of the work of monitoring and sanctioning and socialising, making use of whatever embeddedness in community or social networks is available; they must also relate to these communities

in ways which build and sustain social capital. This, too, is what happens in Japan.[2]

In this fashion, community services need to be judged and supported, not just for their frontline role in service provision, but for the potential facilitation of social capital. In particular, with the development of lifelong learning, the education system is emerging as society's most prominent forum for public interaction. Learning opportunities need to be developed, not just as institutions discharging certain curriculum requirements, but as places where people can learn for life by learning from each other. People are more likely to develop a moral sense of right and wrong from various forms of public interaction than the top–down creation of public laws. In Switzerland, for instance, this approach has guided the development of a system of 'learning circles' in adult and community education. These involve a discussion group format within which citizens are encouraged to share their experiences and knowledge, thereby helping to build the bonds of both applied learning and social connectedness. Similar practices, valuing the importance of social learning, can be applied to most other parts of the education system.[3]

Finally, the formation of social capital should not be seen as outside the domain of economic policy. Putnam's research has shown that in highly civic societies, solidarity in the workplace is one of the preconditions of social trust.[4] In public policy, this means supporting the role of organised labour, as well as enacting industrial laws that facilitate the spread of collective bargaining ahead of individualised employment contracts. Importantly, the type of worker-owned cooperatives advocated in chapter 13 can also assist in the creation of trust and mutuality in the workplace. These strategies, in the framing of economic policy, help to strike an appropriate balance between competition at the point of market exchange and cooperation in the production of goods and services. They recognise the importance of social capital in the workplace as much as in any other part of society.

These proposals for devolution represent the type of agenda by which Australian Labor can more effectively engage itself in issues of community and social capital. They help to distinguish social democratic thinking from the type of 'moral leadership' practised by the political Right, with its conservative emphasis on nostalgia and the need for more social punishment. It is simply not possible to create social capital and connectedness with leadership of the talking kind. Nor is it possible to create a stronger society by seeking, in answer to all social issues, to strengthen the vertical supplication of the state. The search for social capital requires a different approach to social reform, based on a different type of social organisation to that offered by contemporary government. It requires basic changes to the institutional design of the public sector, changes that give people things to do and interests to build in common.

34

CONCLUSION: REBUILDING PUBLIC MUTUALITY

Without widespread trust in the processes of public governance, it is simply not possible to build the basis of public mutuality. Passive systems of welfare and governance are a poor way of creating commonality and trust in a post-industrial society. Social democracy has no greater shortcoming than this flaw in its management of the public commons. In the design of the post-war welfare state, with the primacy of the state public sector as an expression of collective action, the strength of public commonality has been allowed to decline. Especially with the spread of social and economic insecurity, a substantial proportion of the citizenry is now pursuing answers to the welfare question in the politics of downwards envy and vertical supplication. The aspirations of the social democratic project for the redistribution of public resources appears to be in jeopardy in most parts of the public arena. Marquand has exposed this flaw in the prospects of public sector redistribution as follows:

> A redistributionist must be able to answer the question, why should I make sacrifices for others? The answer 'because it is in your interests' is unlikely to carry much conviction for long, while the answer 'because you are a kindly altruist, who feels compassion for those less fortunate than yourself' dodges the real problem. However emollient the language in which it is put, the answer has to be, 'because it is your duty, because you are part of a community which helped to make you what you are' . . . Redistribution can be justified only by some notion of fraternity (or mutuality), for only a notion of fraternity can make it a duty as opposed to a compassionate whim to help one's fellows.[1]

Social democracy without mutuality represents a fading political cause. Reformers need to recognise, particularly given the

309

dilemmas of overloaded government, the limited scope of collectivism expressed through the vertical structures of the state. The
attainment of social equality does not lie in straining the carrying
capacity of the public commons. Nor does it lie in perceiving the
state as the only legitimate expression of collective interest and
action. Indeed, in our type of society, it can be argued that active
forms of democracy and social provision are more likely to be
developed from a certain form of interaction between citizens than
the relationship between citizens and state hierarchies. Social
democracy, in the satisfaction of its political purpose, needs to
examine and foster new sources of public mutuality outside the
formal boundaries of government.

This means shifting from a public sector based on the coercive
and vertical systems of the state to one structured around the
horizontal features of civil society. In an era of globalised economic
and social relations, the viability of collective action relies on a
smaller, more interactive scale of mutuality. Shared interests and
provision can only be maintained if people are able to interact with
each other in a manner that actively develops the habits of reciprocated trust and connectedness. As Michael Walzer has written,
'mutual respect and a shared self-respect are the deep strengths of
complex equality, and together they are the source of its possible
endurance'.[2] They are also, crucially enough, the key to holding
together the cohesiveness of a post-industrial society.

In the 1970s it was fashionable to talk of the future of Western
civilisation as pivoting on a choice between socialism and barbarism. This proposition may not be as improbable as it once looked,
particularly if one adopts Tony Blair's use of the term 'social-ism',
meaning an equality of social relations, much more than economic.[3]
There are undoubtedly dangers in a society which loses too much
of its social capital. Its members start to see self-preservation and
their relations with other people as mutually exclusive. As Hugh
Mackay has written from his Australian research:

> We are social creatures and we thrive socially, intellectually,
> culturally and morally on our personal connections with each
> other. We are at our best when we are fully integrated with the
> herd; we are at our worst when we are isolated, anonymous and
> alienated. We might as well acknowledge that the savage lurks
> within even the most civilised breast. When we loosen our social
> connections, we increase the risk that the savage will break the
> leash.[4]

The suppression of this kind of barbarism requires a strengthening of the citizen-to-citizen relationship in society, much more

than the state-to-citizen relationship. This exposes a basic flaw in the way in which ideologies across the political spectrum have approached the bundle of issues connected with social cohesiveness. On the political Right, libertarians have sought to weaken the functions and significance of the state, purportedly to strengthen the nature of civil society. It is difficult, however, to envisage how Australia's store of social capital can replenish itself sufficiently to replace each of the primary functions of the state in public provision. A crippled state sector is not likely to be able to protect even the most basic of rights and liberties in our society.

History shows that weak states often seek to exert themselves through a greater level of social control and coercion. This reflects, among other parts of the political Right, the folly of populist calls for further vertical supplication. At a time when a large part of the citizenry appears agitated by a sense of insecurity—in their work, on their streets, for their children's future—appeals to order and authority can carry popular weight. In practice, however, such policies serve only to further erode the basis of social trust and connectedness. They shift society further away from horizontal systems of trust to vertical structures of authority and coercion. In seeking answers to social anxiety—what Durkheim described as anomie, a sense of normlessness—the further fragmentation of relations between people, with a narrow agenda of distrust and punishment, represents a self-defeating agenda.

Likewise, social democrats have erred in their assumption that the strength of the state corresponds with its raw size and the spread of government power. Strong states require the trust of their citizens. They require popular recognition of the sustainable management of the commons and the strength of public mutuality. In a post-industrial society this requires a smaller and more thoroughly devolved scale of social governance—combining vertical statism in the arrangement of inputs for public purposes with horizontal systems of self-governance and devolution in the determination of outputs. Only when the public comes to fully trust in the legitimacy and effectiveness of collective institutions, state and non-state, will social democracy be able to realise its goals for social mutuality and equality in practice. Now, more than ever, it needs to embrace the goals, values and policies of public devolution.

The pulse readers of public opinion are constantly reporting the way in which people want more connectedness, more contact, more of the things we might hold in common as a society. This is, in its desire, a yell for recognition—a boost to the self-esteem and worth people naturally seek from their interaction with others—but which, during this era of permanent change and uncertainty, they are struggling to secure. Public commonality of this kind, logically enough, requires a measure of equality: the things we do, value and share as citizens and ultimately, are willing to reciprocate. Historically, the cause of socialism and like movements has left itself short in the theory and practice of this form of social equality. The politics of the Left has tended to pursue equality through reforms aimed at the distribution of primary goods, rather than the type of citizen-to-citizen relations held throughout society.

This part of the book has advocated a different strategy and understanding of equality—that is, a set of social principles and political goals primarily about the quality and equality of relations between people, not just about the ownership and distribution of economic resources. Through policies of devolution and the consequent creation of social trust, it is entirely possible for market systems, carrying the benefits of economic effort and growth, to coexist with conditions of social mutuality and equality. The human traits of cooperation and competition, once expressed within an appropriate framework of public institutions and social relations, need not be regarded as incompatible. Much can be achieved through a reform agenda aimed at the creation of social capital. To be certain, social trust and connectedness matter; and through the devolution of social control and governance so too, once more, might social democracy.

PART VI

CONCLUSION

35

SOCIAL DEMOCRACY
IN TRANSITION

Pragmatism is not enough—we also need argument. Or, to put it another way, compromise can only emerge from disputation . . . We can argue over ends and means, but without some larger awareness of the cause in whose name the compromises are made, without the energy of doctrinal zeal, the cause withers. Politics without principles becomes a mere exercise in the pursuit of power. Politics without memory—a living, vital memory, that resists the temptations of celebration of nostalgia—becomes empty and cynical. To celebrate the Labor Party as a cause for power is not enough. True believers need beliefs.

Stuart Macintyre, Manning Clark Lecture,
ALP National Conference, September 1994.

In many respects the social democratic project has been a victim of its own success. By the 1970s it had achieved most of its goals for the active role of the state in society, primarily through the spread of Keynesian economics, welfare statism and service planning. The exhaustion of this agenda, however, produced something of a vacuum within left-of-centre thinking and policy making. In most nations throughout the 1980s this policy void was filled by the deregulation of product and capital markets, plus the commercialisation of a wide range of public services. The rise of globalisation forced nations to pursue new forms of competitive economic advantage, often by reducing the size and scope of the public sector. Policies such as these, however, have not been able to overcome the entrenched problems of economic and social exclusion. Simply winding back the role of government, without the creation of new forms of collective action and responsibility, has not been an effective response to globalisation. From this perspective, the 1990s have produced a policy hiatus on both sides of the conventional binary. The political Right has had to deal with the failings of its economic libertarian agenda, plus public concerns about the spread of narrow individualism in society. Likewise, the Left has had to confront the declining relevance of old statism and the perception, in most parts of the public arena, that the system of government has fundamentally broken down.

Both sides of politics have been unable to resolve these dilemmas of policy and public governance. With an absence of clear answers, the political debate has tended to deteriorate into sloganeering and electoral opportunism. More than ever, politicians are trying to give the impression that they can halt the change process when, in fact, the tasks of good governance lie in helping society adapt to the inevitability of economic and social change. This approach has served primarily to aggravate the strained relationship between the governed and the institutions of government. The problems of a post-industrial society cannot be overcome by engaging in acts of political nostalgia, either through so-called traditional social values or interventionist economics. Policies such as these build up public expectations about the political process beyond the capacity of governments to deliver. Just as the rhetorical embrace of the popular values of the 1950s cannot make society relaxed and comfortable, old types of industry policy are no longer able to generate employment growth and security. Politicians who follow these paths are simply adding to the public's distrust of modern democracy—creating a cycle of false promises and failed expectations from which other, relevant types of reform are made more difficult to achieve.

In truth, a new bundle of policy issues now dominates the public agenda. Nations are struggling to reassert their economic sovereignty in the face of the massive mobility and footloose features of global capital. Old policies—active macroeconomics, crude protectionism and open-ended subsidies for the corporate sector—are not likely to succeed in the new economy. In the global marketplace, economic problems will not be solved by the systematic restraint of economic freedoms. Likewise, the legitimacy and effectiveness of the post-war welfare state is in retreat. The planning strand of government, with its reliance on rigid systems of service delivery, has shown itself to be an inadequate way of handling the diversity of modern society. The old Left formula of allocating more resources for more programs, thereby perpetuating the failings of passive welfare, has fallen well short of the attainment of public commonality and equality in practice. In most parts of the public arena, the overload of government has sullied the sound management of the commons and encouraged the spread of downwards envy. Society appears to have lost too much faith in the processes of public governance to truly maintain the benefits of public mutuality.

Parties and politicians interested in a more just society are being called on to develop new expressions of national economic sovereignty, in tandem with the creation of new forms of social trust and commonality. They face two exceptionally difficult tasks: in economic policy, reconciling the international sphere of capital with the localised nature of democratic politics; and in social policy, offsetting the impact of globalisation through new modes of inter-personal trust and social solidarity. The success of this project—and with it, the rejuvenation of social democracy—relies on overhauling the basic purposes and organisational methods of public gover-nance. This means, above all else, transforming the relationship between the state and its citizens such that the logic of collective action in society can be reaffirmed and strengthened. It means creating a new form of collectivism by which the shared interests and needs of a post-industrial society can be effectively expressed and maintained.

NEW COLLECTIVISM

In an era of permanent economic and social change, the work of government should not be taken as immutable. There can be no sound reason for tolerating the failings of the modern state. As the British social democrat, Harold Laski, wrote earlier this century, 'the state is not an end, but merely the means to an end, which is realised only in the enrichment of human lives. The power and allegiance it can win depend upon what it achieves for that enrich-ment.'[1] This notion, of course, reflects one of the paradoxes of the recent period of social change. While insecurity and anxiety abound in the public arena, and people everywhere claim to be wanting to do more in common, the state public sector is not perceived as a credible way of addressing these issues. In fact, the bonds of collectivism appear to have weakened, as a growing number of citizens look to government as one of the causes of social insecur-ity, rather than a possible remedy. By this test alone, major reform of our system of government has become inevitable.

History tells us that whenever society has faced widespread insecurity and rapid economic change, lasting answers have only ever been found in the logic of collective action. This is just as likely to be true during the current era of change and uncertainty. Individuals acting in isolation cannot overcome the lifestyle and economic pressures of globalisation. Even the most skilled and privileged of citizens need to rely on some element of collective provision, if only to insure themselves against the possibilities of failure in a dynamic business and social environment. Herein lies the central purpose and legitimacy of public governance: finding collective remedies to fresh forms of social and economic insecurity. Indeed, the reformulation of the social democratic project has no higher purpose than restoring this simple sense of public mutuality.

This book has identified three measures by which the logic of collective action might be strengthened in the public arena. The first is to define the type of social provision and interests likely to be held in common in a post-industrial society. This needs to be taken as an essential part of the social democratic purpose: adjusting the role of collective institutions to cope with the changing nature of social wants and needs. Citizens are most likely to pool their resources and recognise the value of collectivism if they are able to identify shared interests. Mutual needs and mutual membership reinforce the sense and sustainability of mutual provision. This is why, during an era of permanent social change, the comprehensive reform of government should be regarded as unavoidable. Without reform there can be no redefinition of the processes of public mutuality.

In the post-war period, with its relative certainty and standardised patterns of production and work, the collective system of provision involved direct state interventions in most parts of society. The Keynesian, planning and welfare strands of social democracy were entrenched in the public policies of Western nations. Redistributive goals were pursued through the work of the tax/transfer system. Attempts were made to engineer a type of equality in each of the quantities, qualities and behavioural character'stics of life. This book has argued that the rise of economic globalisation and the advent of a post-industrial society have diminished the effectiveness of these methods. The policies and ideology of social democracy have been placed in transition, as they seek to adjust to the demands of the new economy and emergence of a new set of social needs.

This process, of course, has invoked a reassessment of the foundations of public mutuality. For several decades, left-of-centre causes have engaged themselves in a debate about the appropriate role of government. The debate has centred on controversies about the asset holdings of the state—whether governments should continue to invest in old forms of industrial and financial capital, or transfer public assets to the creation of human capital through increased education and health expenditure. Important as this debate may be, further steps are still required to comprehensively redefine the purposes of public governance. Consideration needs to be given to the means by which systems of common provision can be more closely aligned with the needs of the citizenry held in common. This involves not just a fundamental change in the methods of government, but also a fresh evaluation of its purpose. It has been maintained throughout this book that the processes of public provision need to address, first and foremost, the core insecurities of an open society and economy—in the universal creation of employability, job replacement, income security, life-long learning, personal well-being and sociability.

In an era of permanent change, the capacity to adapt and deal with social uncertainty has become a critical item of social need. Without this form of security—the peace of mind and confidence that comes from being able to engage constructively in the change process—it is not possible to achieve other forms of social progress. If citizens do not feel secure about their circumstances in society then their capacity to care and provide for the interests of others is much diminished. This sense of security tends to serve as a precondition for acts of public mutuality. It is, therefore, prudent for governments committed to strengthening the logic of collective action to concentrate their responsibilities and resources on issues of socioeconomic security. Social needs and services that cannot be accommodated within this framework are more appropriately discharged by individual systems and means of provision. In an era of widespread insecurity, public functions applicable to just a fraction of society or, worse still, those that create zero-sum choices in the public arena, stand well outside the sound management of the public commons.

A second step in the creation of public mutuality lies in addressing the overload of modern government and attendant fiscal crisis of the state. It is not possible to satisfy mutual interests in society unless systems of mutual provision are shown to be sustainable. Social democracy has normally tried to protect those citizens vulnerable to the changing nature of a market economy by boosting the level of public expenditure. It is clear, however, especially with the exposure of national economies to internationalisation, that this approach is now limited by the fiscal carrying capacity of the state. Under conditions of fiscal crisis, policies need to be judged by more than their positive intentions. Bigger government in the traditional sense, with the allocation of extra resources and programs, is not likely to produce greater equity, especially when it adds to the overload of government and problem of downwards envy. It is no longer sufficient to grow the role of the state public sector without first considering its impact on the sustainability of the commons.

Social democracy needs to get out of the habit of loading additional responsibilities onto the state. It needs to rationalise its equity goals and program outlays and produce a more durable notion of public commonality. This is where the capability paradigm and its conceptualisation of complex equality has such a valuable role to play. Over time, left-of-centre thinking has accumulated a vast range of goals and values: material equality, classlessness, democratic socialism, state ownership, social justice, equality of opportunity, gender equity, social tolerance, national identity, international cooperation and so forth. Each has been associated with new layers of state activism and the growth of public outlays. Taken as a whole, the social democratic project has become unsustainable, given the rationing of scarce public resources and the spread of public resentment about the role of government.

The attainment of public mutuality now requires the rationalisation of publicly funded forms of social provision. While national circumstances are bound to vary, a number of conclusions can be drawn about this process. This book has attempted to draw attention to the principles and proposals by which the fiscal crisis of the state might be addressed. These can be summarised as follows:

- strengthening the effectiveness and fairness of the taxation system through the implementation of a progressive expenditure tax regime;
- providing appropriate rewards and responsibilities within the welfare system for the spread of self-providence, especially with the development of new systems of lifelong income support;
- limiting service universality to those areas of social provision where benefits—direct and indirect—are enjoyed in common. This focuses the role of the state on securing for its citizens greater social and economic certainty;
- facilitating, through policies of devolution, the strength of social capital and public mutuality, thereby enhancing the viability of non-state solutions to public issues;
- reducing outlays on industry welfare, given the folly of political jurisdictions engaging in bidding wars for the locational decisions of footloose capital;
- abolishing outlays on positive discrimination programs and other segment-of-life measures, given that this approach to social justice forces zero-sum choices in the public arena.

These reforms do not signify an end to state activism but rather, a recognition of its limits. They do not rule out the possibility of new state programs but rather, seek to link their costs and implementation to the fiscal restrictions of the modern state. In fact, there may be a need, in selected areas of public responsibility, for greater state intervention. Public funding of civil sector employment and the education and research functions of the state offer two examples of this approach. In general, however, the overriding test of the effectiveness of state provision lies in its public sustainability. No one should—or for that matter, really does—question the need for the state to take some responsibility for addressing social needs as they arise, especially when other forms of social provision have shown themselves to be inadequate. What tends to be questioned, particularly under conditions of overloaded government, is who will fund these responsibilities and why. Social democrats can only answer these issues through the potency of public mutuality—satisfactorily defining mutual interests; financially sustaining mutual provision; and ultimately, strengthening the basis of mutual membership.

It is only right and proper for people to regard their commitment to collective institutions as a function of the effectiveness of public governance. If taxes could be regarded as the price of making welfare work or improving society's connectedness then they could be levied, or even increased, without public disquiet. This is why issues of institutional design are so important to the future of social democracy. Without an institutional framework of governance capable of promoting the virtues of mutual membership, the prospects of social equality are diminished. Unfortunately, too much of the work of the state public sector has resembled an open access regime, creating the problem—or at least the widespread public perception—of free riding. Large-scale service providers and bureaucracies have lacked the transparency and behavioural sanctions needed to generate public trust and mutuality.

The answer to this difficulty lies in the devolution of public governance. Small-scale units of public administration, especially when freely formed and mutual, have the capacity to generate a positive sense of participation and behavioural transparency among their membership. They help to expose citizens to the benefits of public cooperation, thereby building the ideals and practice of common membership. At a time when most forms of information and economic interaction have moved to the global arena, this type of social provision has the potential to create new communities of interest and social interaction. This is particularly important in an information-rich society where, more than ever, people are looking to use their skills in a relevant way. It is not possible to establish the preconditions of mutual membership unless people are given an outlet for the expression of their interests and capacities.

Goals such as these challenge the passive systems of public provision and democracy now dominant among the governance of Western nations. Democracy was originally premised on a high level and quality of interaction between citizens and their government. The rise throughout this century, of a centralised scale of state provision, however, has encouraged the growth of sectional interest politics. The citizenry has been excluded from the corporatist dealings of cabinet ministers, captains of industry, so-called ethnic leaders and the professional representatives of the social sector. Even backbench members of parliament, especially given the concentration of political power in the executive wing of government, are likely to feel marginalised in the decision-making process. In practice, corporatist government has become far more accountable to the public forums of the electronic media than the parliamentary process. This process, however, is also unsatisfactory given the way it concentrates political influence with a narrow band of commercial interests and opinionated talkback hosts.

Accordingly, the public arena is dominated by perceptions that the political process has become external to the needs and interests of ordinary people. The public's distrust of politicians appears to be matched only by its dissatisfaction with the media. Corporatist government, with its passive form of democracy, has added to the erosion of social trust and connectedness. Citizens have lost the personal recognition and sense of worth arising from a genuinely interactive form of democracy. This is why the possibilities of self-governing, mutual forms of social provision have become doubly significant: devolving the power of public decision making into the hands of citizens; allowing mutual interests in society to be expressed and developed through the bonds of interpersonal trust and cooperation. Unless the state is willing to recognise the skills and diverse interests of its citizens, thereby facilitating forums and acts of self-governance, it is difficult to perceive how the declining legitimacy of the public sector can be reversed. As ever, real power in public life comes from giving power away.

For social democracy, of course, issues of this kind raise a more basic question of methodology. It is not accustomed, in its programs and policies, to the transfer of political power to the institutions of the non-state public sector. One of the problems with left-of-centre thinking has been the way in which it has tended to treat state action as an end in itself. Political issues and reform goals have been considered as if the work of state and non-state institutions are incompatible. As a matter of reform technique, the growth of the state public sector has been taken as synonymous with the creation of social equality, while activities outside the domain of the state have been regarded as damaging social justice.

This interpretation, of course, sells short the role of social capital in fostering social equality in practice.

Non-state institutions are fundamentally diverse in their organisational features and impact on society. While, for instance, market-based transactions are likely to promote aspects of individualism and economic competition, civil society has the potential to create the virtues of freely formed collective action. For this reason, social democracy needs to rethink its positioning of non-state institutions on the political spectrum. It is more productive, in this respect, to develop a binary based on the role of collective institutions in society, whether from the state or non-state public sector, as against the tendency of economic markets to foster individualism. The ownership features of the state—with their artificial link between the public interest and public ownership—can no longer be taken as a reliable guide to the attainment of social justice. Collectivism of any kind, whether notionally held in public or private hands, needs to be valued for the contribution it might make to the processes of public commonality.

The resolution of most social and economic issues now requires a higher degree of cooperation between state and non-state forms of collective action. For instance, the spatial features of the new labour market require governments to pursue solutions to the problem of unemployment by resourcing a new generation of civil sector work. In other aspects of devolution, the state needs to assist the role of self-governing mutual organisations in the tasks of service provision. This can be achieved by restricting the work of government to service funding and regulation, with the implementation of social provision undertaken by non-state institutions. Policy makers are not likely to overcome the problems of economic and social exclusion without an active partnership between the state and civil society. Social democracy needs to foster every available opportunity by which, irrespective of issues of ownership and control, people can be exposed to the logic and necessity of collective action. Through this revised approach to collectivism, with its offering of a new ideology for social democracy, the foundations of public mutuality can be substantially enhanced.

NEW IDEOLOGY

Unlike many parts of the political Left, social democracy has never stood for the creation of a new system of economic production. Rather, it has attempted to ameliorate the impact of the market on society. It has maintained that a healthy range of economic freedoms can coexist with the foundations of a good and decent society. Indeed, social democracy's acceptance of the capitalist economy has been fundamental to its political success. Without the growth horizons of an economy based on incentives and rewards for effort, it is not possible to sustain and resource an effective system of social provision. In this manner, social democracy has traditionally positioned the civilising role of the state public sector and the productivity of a market-led economy as symbiotic.

The rise of globalisation and spread of social insecurity, however, have forced a reassessment of this approach. It is no longer clear that the traditional methods of government are consistent with the demands and consequences of an open economy. Most forms of state activism appear to be in retreat. Even the keenest advocates of state intervention have had to question whether governments can achieve anything more substantial than compliance to the international market. They are having to wonder why, at a time in which the collective need for social and economic security appears so pronounced, so many people have identified government as part of the problem, rather than the solution. This is the paradox of how a significant portion of the citizenry have come to dislike the work of the state even though, in its origins and theory, it is supposed to be theirs.

The decline of state activism, however, does not signify the end of left-of-centre ideology. It is important to recognise that the erosion of state power in the last part of this century simply reflects the reversal of a trend which commenced in the final decades of last century. At that time, following the consolidation of the powers of the nation state, government started to assume several of the social functions previously discharged by private capital. Now, with the shift of capital to global arenas, many of the functions and powers of the state are being dispersed. New centres of economic and political power are being created as a consequence of globalisation. Social reformers are being challenged to devise the means by which this process might be influenced, consistent with long standing goals for a stronger and fairer society.

Social democracy can no longer afford to stridently defend state interventions of the old kind. Indeed, the failings of the post-war welfare state—unless repaired by new forms of collective governance and social provision—are likely to mean that the new centres of political power will be based on the spread of individualism. This prospect gives a hard edge of urgency to the tasks of public sector reform. Social democrats need to embrace a new set of political goals—one seeking equality in the relations between people, no less than in the relationship between citizens and the state. This means resolving the tension in left-of-centre thinking, now spanning two centuries, between the ideologies of state activism and social devolution by decisively moving in support of the latter. The inexorable dispersion of state power needs to be directed at the creation of new forms of mutuality and common trust in the non-state public sector. This is the most effective means by which social democracy can counter the prospects of social fragmentation.

This approach to policy reform reflects a number of important principles from the origins of Left politics last century. It is now too readily forgotten that the socialist cause commenced as a social creed in search of mutuality and self-sufficiency. It was not necessarily assumed, however, that the achievement of these goals required a large and centralised scale of state provision. This only arose as a consequence of state socialist ideology and, particularly after the Second World War, the expansion of Fordist government and state planning. Early Left thinking, such as the ideals of guild socialism,[2] was heavily influenced by the possibilities of a smaller scale of public mutuality. This ideology was expressed through attempts to create a new type of production system: the development of self-governing guilds in the workplace, similar to what we would now think of as industrial democracy. The task for social democrats now lies in applying these ideals to the work of the social sector.

Left-of-centre causes have not been successful in securing social equity by means of economic reform. Attempts to transform the production system on the basis of public ownership and control have struggled to maintain a high productivity, high growth economy. They have also reflected a narrow understanding of equity issues, with an assumption that the equal distribution of material items in society is sufficient to secure social participation for all. Just as much, however, the effectiveness of centralised systems of social provision has declined. The welfare state has not been able to overcome new, entrenched forms of economic and social exclusion. The path to social equity no longer lies in the dogma of state planning and control, whether economic or social.

These issues point to the need for a third way: beyond state ownership of the means of production; beyond the Fordist organisation of social provision. A reformed social democratic project needs to create the means by which capitalist markets and social mutuality might coexist. It needs to square the benefits of market-led economic growth with the possibilities of personal liberty and social capability. It needs to position capitalism as the means by which the material base of society can be expanded, while ensuring—through new forms of non-state mutuality—that the relations between people represent an expanding circle of social connectedness and recognition. This approach—in its reconciliation of the benefits of economic competition with the virtues of social cooperation—brings the citizenry closer to the values and interaction of a truly social democracy; that is, to a form of social participation in which the dignity and capability of each individual is defined and nurtured by the bonds of mutual provision and mutual trust.

NEW RESPONSIBILITIES

The recasting of social democratic ideology draws from the most attractive aspects of liberalism and socialism: liberal in the sense of selectively pursuing state powers for the creation of social and economic freedoms; socialist in the sense of wanting to foster a dense web of social responsibility and respect for the common good.[3] The shortcomings of the traditional binary are replaced by the politics of the new radical centre. Its key purpose is to accommodate the processes of social change without diminishing the prospects of personal liberty and social harmony. Governments need to respond to the unsettling impact of globalisation by developing fresh sources of social opportunity and solidarity. One of the themes of this book has been to reconcile the widening spread of life's responsibilities and loyalties with the need for social cohesiveness.

As citizens, each of us has an instinctive attachment to the benefits of social contact—whether expressed through family, community, national or international bonds. The purpose of governance, at least in its idealised form, is to give public expression to the type of contact and cooperation that might help to bond society and its interests. The advent of globalisation has strained many of society's traditional relationships, forcing the need for major reform to the public sector. Citizens are having to deal with new responsibilities and loyalties, especially in their engagement with global forms of economic activity, social contact and information access. People are having to stretch and harmonise their activities at each of the local, national and international spheres of life's interests. This is, significantly enough, an event rare in history—an era in which the organisation of society is being remade. Inevitably, one of the victims of this process has been the politics of the industrial age.

The broadening of life's responsibilities has deepened the complexity of the political debate. The relative simplicity of industrial society, with its focus on the capital/labour binary, is in retreat. Public governance now needs to be able to cope with the emergence of a four-plane matrix of political issues and values. It is no longer sufficient for social democracy to take a position on one or any combination of these planes—capital and labour, international and national, the information rich and poor, and issues of commonality and community—and assume that it has fulfilled its political objectives. New types of public mutuality need to be established which supersede the four planes and, in their implementation, reinforce the logic of collective action. The tensions and inequities of a post-industrial society can only be overcome by fundamentally altering the structure of public governance.

A starting point is to respond to the way in which, more than ever, people are working and communicating at a global level, yet also continuing to interact in local communities. A territorial gap has opened up between the level at which most political and economic issues are determined and the way in which most people organise their daily lives.[4] The horizons of social recognition have lifted towards national and global arenas, thereby placing pressure on the strength of community life. Social democrats need to adapt to these trends, not waste their efforts in trying to reverse them. As economic and political space moves upwards to supra-national forums there is a need to reform the governance of nations, regions and communities. This is not only an important part of making the transition costs of change more acceptable; it is also a logical way of strengthening the spread of life's responsibilities. It ensures that, even though many of us are finding new responsibilities as international citizens, we can also find new relevance and identity in our national citizenship and participation in our local community.

This is not to suggest, of course, that these layers of responsibility will never come into conflict. Through an intense period of social change, political tensions are inevitable. The point of public sector reform is to harmonise, as much as possible, the institutions of governance with the various tiers of spatial and economic activity. With the advent of national economic activity last century, political power and decision making became concentrated in the forums of the nation state. The rise of nationalist feeling promised to answer the public's interest in new forms of community and social interdependence. For a considerable time, nations coped well with this process—adding to social recognition through the creation of citizenship rights and a safety net of social provision. With the passing of the industrial age, however, the nation state—especially when governed by large, centralised bureaucracies—has struggled to establish and express a strong sense of collective interests. National sovereignty has been eroded by the internationalisation of economic activity, while the fragmentation of social capital has undermined the bonds of localism. To paraphrase Daniel Bell, the nation state now appears too small for the big responsibilities of government, yet too big to create a new, smaller scale of public mutuality.

Nations, in recognition of these trends, need to engage in the dispersal of political power. In the words of Michael Sandel:

> If the nation cannot summon more than a minimal commonality, it is unlikely that the global community can do better, at least on its own. A more promising basis for a democratic politics that reaches beyond nations is a revitalised civic life nourished in the more particular communities we inhabit. In the age of NAFTA (or APEC) the politics of neighbourhood matters more, not less. People will not pledge allegiance to vast and distant entities, whatever their importance, unless those institutions are somehow connected to political arrangements that reflect the identity of the participants . . . Since the days of Aristotle's polis, the republican tradition has viewed self-government as an activity rooted in a particular place, carried out by citizens loyal to that place and the way of life it embodies. Self-government today, however, requires a politics that plays itself out in a multiplicity of settings, from neighbourhoods to nations to the world as a whole. Such a politics requires citizens who can abide the ambiguity associated with divided sovereignty, who can think and act as multiply-situated selves. The civic virtue distinctive to our time is the capacity to negotiate our way among the sometimes overlapping and sometimes conflicting obligations that claim us, and to live with the tension to which multiple loyalties give rise.[5]

The ideals of supra-national governance are based on bringing order and cooperation to the upward movement of economic space and activity. It is hardly surprising that, as capital has globalised, so too might a number of political institutions. In this process, logically enough, the responsibilities of other layers of public administration also need to be reformed and re-ordered. In particular, this means repairing the civic life upon which democracy depends. The revenue raising functions of the nation state need to coexist with a smaller scale of social governance. The state needs to maintain its role as a funder and regulator of services, while facilitating the discharge of service provision at a level much closer to civil society. This reflects the politics of paradox—how the creation of a more equal and mutual society now depends on the dispersal of political power away from traditional forms of statism.

During a time of perpetual change, the restoration of civic life is an important stabiliser for society. It allows citizens to develop new types of social recognition as a way of compensating for the impact of internationalisation. It also demonstrates the fluid nature

of sovereignty. Even though nations have lost part of their economic sovereignty to the global arena, it is still possible to build
new forms of social sovereignty and identity at a local level. In this
way, citizens can find the type of security that helps build the bonds
of social solidarity. Otherwise, they may turn—in trying to cope
with the challenges of uncertainty—to the worst features of tribalism: regarding members of their social unit as inherently superior
to outsiders; seeking confirmation of their value to society by
refusing to tolerate the diverse values and habits of other people.
It is from these feelings that social reaction and conservatism
inevitably arise.

These issues are particularly significant in Australia's circumstances. As a young nation, questions of identity and social
cohesiveness remain relatively unformed in the public arena. Most
issues of national concern now lie balanced between the competing
interests of globalism and parochialism. This is new Australia—
outward looking, globally integrated, cosmopolitan and
confident—struggling against old Australia: parochial, insecure,
even isolationist in its instincts. This tension reflects the politics
of a society in transition; especially in the need to reconcile
traditional institutions and values with the emergence of globalisation and an information-rich citizenry. Some of Australia's oldest
views about the meaning of social fairness have fallen into conflict
with the recent period of social change.

Australia's national ethos and cultural traits have tended to
project a unique interpretation of fairness. For most of our history,
fairness has, in fact, meant sameness—not the fairness that might
be meant by class analysis or redistributive politics, but the idea
that all Australians should be the same and be treated the same
way. This ethos of sameness provided the foundation for the
post-Federation settlement of national policies. White Australia
was framed to keep Australians looking the same; the basic wage
was designed to ensure workers were paid the same; tariff protection was maintained to provide the same access to work; while state
utilities were developed to give all parts of Australia the same access
to services and economic opportunities.

An insightful reading of the cultural implications of the Australian sense of sameness can be found in Elaine Thompson's *Fair
Enough* (1994). She presents egalitarianism as a social mannerism.
In this respect, a popular belief in the essential fairness of society
is at the core of Australian egalitarianism, more so than the type
of judgment about equality that might be made from class analysis
and other forms of social theory. Cultural practices matter more
than the construction of theory. Australian egalitarianism reflects
a belief that each of us is equal in status and equally able to get

ahead in society, thereby implying that the public sector should treat all Australians the same way. These cultural traits, however, are not without their contradictions. Thompson notes how—for the great bulk of our history since European settlement—this form of egalitarianism did not extend beyond a white, male-dominated culture; the part of Australia best understood by the ethos of mateship. Hence, Thompson identifies the paradox of how:

> Australia was egalitarian because it was xenophobic and sexist. White Australia was the direct product of an Australian egalitarianism based around the central egalitarian idea of sameness—that its society was socially and culturally homogeneous and that such homogeneity was an indispensable precondition of democracy. Australian democrats asserted that a society with more than one race could not have equality of those races. Non-Anglo white immigration was tolerated because it was believed that such immigrants could be assimilated and that the democratic base of a culturally homogeneous society could be maintained. Moreover such immigration was necessary to create a strong, prosperous Australia which could remain white . . . It meant that all those defined as Australians fell within the 'community of egalitarians' and must be treated equally.[6]

For much of this century, of course, the ALP gave political expression to the cultural values of sameness. The Party helped to develop and maintain the post-Federation social settlement. Over time, however, portions of Labor policy—especially the embrace of a social democratic 'rights' agenda—fell into conflict with the politics of sameness. Whenever governments engage in the rationing of scarce public resources they are susceptible to claims of unfair treatment from those who lose out in the allocation of entitlements. Australians appear to be sceptical about the value of abstract rights, particularly when expressed in the form of positive discrimination. Zero-sum choices undermine the public's support for social justice. These tensions were revealed at the last Federal election; to use the words of the ALP national president, Barry Jones:

> losing the election was the second worst consequence of 2 March. The worst was the realisation that we deluded ourselves that there was a natural consensus on issues of race, sexuality, gender and tolerance, and acted accordingly. Regrettably, this was not the case.[7]

Long held views and values, the core of Australia's cultural heritage, are not likely to change overnight or even over decades.

Indeed, the ALP in government was foolish to think otherwise. The challenge for policy reformers now lies in determining whether or not, following a period of massive change, it is possible to arrive at a new social settlement about the meaning of Australian egalitarianism. For the ALP, this means embellishing those aspects of sameness that remain consistent with the Party's goals for social capability. Policies aimed at denying social diversity—the hope that all Australians might look and act the same way—need to be rejected. Protection against negative forms of discrimination is an important part of the work of the state. In other aspects of policy, however, sameness can be embraced as a positive force for social equity.

One of our strongest feelings as a nation is that all Australians should have the same access to basic services, just as their earnings should be underpinned by a basic living wage. Now is not the time, as our national economy takes its place on global markets, for Australia to lose this sense of sameness. In a nation culturally weaned on an ethos of sameness, the virtues of diversity and openness need to be supplemented by new types of social assurance. This is why the nation, region and community building efforts of government are so important. They help build a sense of common purpose and the common good at each tier of political activity. They are an essential part of strengthening social cohesiveness at a time when other changes are creating new distributional questions and sources of insecurity.

Policy makers also need to develop a strong set of guarantees in the relationship between the state and its citizens. This book has argued that in an open society and economy, public policy needs to provide a guaranteed share of national income growth for all workers; a guaranteed level of infrastructure and employment for all regions; and guaranteed public utilisation of lifelong learning, income support and health care. In as much as these goals are consistent with the politics of sameness, they provide the basis of a successful social democratic program in Australia. They also serve to reconcile the broadening of life's responsibilities and challenges. In particular, they help to close the gap between the values and aspirations of the information rich and the information poor in society. Whereas old models of education assumed that only a small proportion of the population was capable of cognitive excellence, the advent of mass education has now made it possible for society to enhance the cognitive skills of most, if not all, of its citizens.[8] The power of lifelong education, in tandem with the guarantees listed above, provide society with the ballast it requires to cope with the dislocation costs of change.

NEW STRANDS

The renewal of the social democratic project relies on comprehensive changes to its ideology and technique. It needs to identify the type of collective action and governance best suited to a post-industrial society. This means replacing the Keynesian, planning and welfare methods of government with five new strands of public policy:

Equality strand

The needs and diversity of our society are now best handled through the conceptualisation of a complex form of equality. Unlike earlier Left thinking, this does not require a rigid equality between citizens across all items of economic and social value. It allows people to identify the particular combination of primary and social goods and interpersonal relations most likely to satisfy their needs and aspirations. While each individual needs to be in a position to drive this process, their capability set still relies, in large part, on the logic of collective action. Items of social merit are only likely to be made available across the citizenry through various forms of social interdependence. This is particularly true of the attainment of minimum living standards, the possibilities of lifelong learning and the foundations of interpersonal trust and recognition. In this fashion, notions of complex equality represent something more valuable than a political theory of the individual.

In a society based on the values and practice of equality, each citizen is able to use these merit items to achieve social competence—their personal freedom to achieve. Poverty is defined as a form of capability failure, demonstrating the way in which social participation now relies on skills and capacities beyond the material safety net. This process reflects the means by which different social resources hold a different value and deliver different benefits to each individual. This is why the work of government needs to concentrate on items of universal need and security. It needs to assist the citizenry as it copes with the inevitability of change, therein fostering an appropriate balance and interaction between the role of collective governance and the exercise of personal responsibility.

In its most basic form, complex equality represents a certain kind of relationship between people—mediated by certain social goods and public institutions. It rejects the remedies of the traditional political binary by placing equal weight, in the attainment of social competence, on the role of the individual, the significance of free market forces and the civilising role of collective action. It regards the good society as offering something more substantial than the extremes of the new Right and the old Left; that is, either an identity of material possessions determined by *laissez-faire* economics, or a type of governance where most forms of social responsibility and authority have been transferred to the hands of the state. Ultimately, it calls forth a different set of principles to guide the work of social democracy, founded on the values of social responsibility, incentives, interdependence and devolution.

Sovereignty strand

The internationalisation of economic activity has created a significant gap between the global sphere of capital and the local arena of democratic politics. Nations can only counter the footloose features of capital by developing spatial strategies based on other, less mobile forms of economic activity. This means investing heavily in those inputs to the production process anchored within the boundaries of the nation state—in education and training, infrastructure development and the public sector's role as an employer of last resort. In particular, this approach recognises the importance of knowledge as an economic input. By developing the public good features of education and research—effectively socialising the public's access to knowledge—nations can realise the benefits of new, endogenous sources of economic growth. This is the most effective means by which the citizenry can assert its economic sovereignty over global capital.

Social democracy needs to expose the myths and tensions underpinning the competitive advantage paradigm. It needs to demonstrate how the economic interests of the nation state and multinational capital are by no means synonymous. It needs a higher purpose in public policy than merely papering over the failings of business management through the allocation of public subsidies to the corporate sector. Faster economic growth will not be achieved by dedicating scarce public resources to bidding wars aimed at the locational decisions of footloose capital. In an open economy, answers to the entrenched problems of unemployment lie in the pursuit of new sources of growth, plus new forms of public sector intervention in training and employment creation. Conventional notions of productivity and competitiveness are not sufficient to clear the spatial features of the new labour market.

Gain sharing strand

National economic policies need to be directed at the failings of the profit system—not by shielding capital from market competition but by superseding the market through new systems of employment creation and income distribution. In the new economy, this approach relies on the transfer of economic resources from the traded to the non-traded sector. Protectionist measures are no longer an effective means by which social democracy can engage in acts of economic redistribution. The split geography of economic activity, plus the tendency towards income and employment dispersion in the new labour market, have altered the basis of national gain sharing.

As the concentration of wealth and income continues to grow, more active forms of redistribution are required to maintain society's inclusiveness. This is particularly reflected in the need for publicly funded forms of employment creation. More than ever, society's most privileged citizens will need to support the creation of economic opportunities for the less privileged. This again emphasises the need for methods of governance that enhance the strength of public mutuality. It is not possible to create the foundations of social equality without a substantial transfer of resources from those internationally competitive citizens to the middle and bottom tiers of a 30/40/30 society. Hence, national gain sharing requires:

- policies to repair the effectiveness of the tax/transfer system, especially through the introduction of a progressive expenditure tax regime;
- income and employment transfers through the functioning of an upstairs/downstairs labour market, with the use of publicly funded forms of civil sector employment to overcome spatial and skill imbalances; and
- the establishment of a living wage model of earnings growth at the bottom of the labour market.

Policies such as these are critical to the effectiveness of Australian Labor, especially its aspirations for providing security against the contingencies of globalisation. As the 1996 Federal election demonstrated, the spread of economic insecurity has unsettled the traditional pattern of party alignment. In an internationalised economy, many workers face levels of uncertainty and income instability no less severe than those excluded from the production process. Labor needs to look above as well as below the safety net for a full understanding of social inclusiveness. It needs to ensure that the wages, employment and education systems deliver new forms of employability, earnings and job replacement security. Without a sustainable structure of national gain sharing, it is not possible to address the economic needs of the newly insecure, middle group in the Australian electorate.

New welfare strand

In its current form, the welfare state reflects the thinking of the post-war decades of economic boom. It is without solutions to the problems of entrenched exclusion and inequality in a post-industrial society. Without the dismantling of old forms of welfare and their replacement with the tools of social capability, there can be no renewal of the social democratic project. The only worthwhile form of welfare is that which improves the skills and social participation of its recipients. The development of new skills, of course, requires a strong set of reciprocal responsibilities and rewards for effort. Passive programs need to be replaced by interventions which actively case manage the needs of each individual. Segment-of-life programs need to be abandoned in favour of this customised approach to public assistance. For disadvantaged communities, customisation is most likely to be achieved through place management reforms. One size no longer fits all in the design of welfare policy.

The changing nature of work and its relationship with leisure time and family responsibilities have also challenged the effectiveness of traditional methods of service delivery. There is a clear tension between the lifestyle pressures and diversity of society and the rigid supply side methods of the state public sector. Social democracy needs to embrace flexible demand side entitlements to overcome this dilemma. Moreover, these entitlements need to be set within the context of lifelong systems of income support and education. The advent of structural unemployment, part-time and casual work, zero- and two-income families, and widely fluctuating income levels means that fewer citizens can now look forward to any form of economic certainty. The welfare state reform needs to focus on the possibilities of income smoothing and lifelong learning. This requires the establishment, from cradle to grave, of bold new systems of public resource pooling, personal savings effort and educational opportunity.

Devolution strand

These new strands of social democracy are not likely to be achieved, however, without the restoration of mutuality in the public arena. Unless social democrats can prove the need for systems of common provision and redistribution, social equality becomes unobtainable. These issues are particularly significant in

Australia, given the way in which the Coalition parties have sought to exploit, through the politics of wedge issues, the growth of downwards envy. The ALP can no longer pretend that traditional forms of statism—in which governments progressively overload the fiscal carrying capacity of the state—are able to resolve this dilemma. Government of the old kind lacks the transparency and participation needed to build public confidence in the processes of common provision. It needs to be replaced, through the wholesale devolution of public governance, with a smaller, more interactive scale of public mutuality.

Devolution, of course, does not mean transferring power to new types of parliaments or departments. It involves the replacement of vertical systems of state control with the possibilities of horizontal social capital. This is an important task in Australia, given the nation's historic attachment to state-led development and low level forms of mateship trust. Governments need to create room at the middle of society for the formation of self-governing mutual bodies. The devolution of public functions in health care, welfare and civil sector employment are well suited to this purpose. They allow citizens to define and act on their common interests through the logic of collective action. The dignity and recognition arising from interpersonal trust needs to be regarded as an essential part of each citizen's freedom to achieve in society.

New Labor

The challenge for political parties now lies in adapting to the new politics of globalisation while still maintaining a broad base of electoral appeal. Parties that cling to old constituencies and old ways are not likely to survive. Australian Labor needs to keep the policy wheel turning with new, more effective measures of social reform. The Party's tradition, properly understood and celebrated, does not reflect the politics of conformity and caution. Indeed, the most successful periods in Labor's recent history—the great era of Gough Whitlam's reforms and the triumphs of the Hawke and Keating Governments—showed how reformers need to confront weaknesses in the structure of policy, rather than pursue the comfort of the status quo. Labor is at its best when it mixes its passion for causes with its natural larrikin streak; at its worst when our policy makers are too scared to put a foot forward for fear of putting a foot wrong.

Danger also lies in the way in which Labor might be tempted—in response to the growing diversity of social needs and ideals—to allow its electoral base to fragment into a loose coalition of sectional interests. Coalition-building is not an effective way of dealing with the four planes of the new political spectrum. Values and policies need to be cast with a strong sense of universality—the means by which diverse social interests can be reconciled during an era of perpetual change and uncertainty. One of the disappointing aspects of the Federal Labor Government 1983–96 was the way in which its values, over time, lost a broad sense of public appeal. It is now too readily forgotten that Labor was elected to office in 1983 on the basis of a universal set of values—Bob Hawke's program of reconciliation, recovery and reconstruction. By 1996, however, the Keating Government was decisively defeated amid public perceptions that its policies had become exclusive in their focus. Labor was perceived to be supporting the allocation of public resources on the basis of segment-of-life categories, at the expense of broader programs of socioeconomic security. This led to a view in the electorate that Labor's values and ideals applied only to a minority of citizens.

This remains a critical lesson for the modernisation of the Party. It is only possible to deal with so-termed wedge issues and the politics of downwards envy by pursuing national interests and broadly framed values. In its transition from the old to new strands of social democracy, Labor needs to avoid the segmentation of policies and constituencies. It cannot afford to restrict its base to those interest groups associated with each of the layers of post-war social democratic reform—such as protectionists concerned solely with the scale of trade unionism in manufacturing industries; feminists arguing for social justice solely through the prism of gender equity; and multiculturalists concerned solely with the maintenance of segment-of-life programs.[9] To maintain a broad base of electoral support, Labor needs to appeal to citizens and concerns beyond the politics of segmentation and sectional interests.

This is why the values of the new radical centre have become so important. In an open society and economy, each of us needs to do more to counter insecurity. Individual effort needs to be maximised through a strong set of incentives and rewards in the relationship between citizens and the state. People are more likely to support the need for collective action if it is associated with the exercise of individual responsibility. Governments need to foster this process, acting as a fulcrum between the spread of individual and collective effort in society. In this manner, society's interdependence is fortified by the seamless interaction of personal liberties, mutual responsibility and common provision. The strength of society needs to be based on more than expectations about the innate goodness of human kind. The design of public institutions needs to facilitate an environment in which citizens are able to enjoy the virtues of social equality and solidarity.

These values position Labor as a broad-based yet progressive cause for change—in the old language, the great centre–left party in Australian politics. That is, a party with a soft heart but a hard head: one interested in the scale and quality of government interventions, not dated debates about their size; one committed to the logic of collective solutions in response to globalisation, rather than the folly of narrow individualism; one pursuing a redefinition of economic sovereignty around the fixed assets of the nation state, rather than the crude subsidisation of footloose capital; one overcoming the social trauma of unemployment through policies aimed at the spatial features of the new labour market; one rewarding work and ensuring a decent distribution of national economic gains through the establishment of a living wage system; one repairing the effectiveness of the tax/transfer system through the progressive taxation of expenditure; one committed to the sound management of the public commons and maintenance of public mutuality; one determined to reform and strengthen the welfare state, not dismantle it; one willing to develop new systems of public support, such as place management, to overcome the problems of underclass; one engaging in the devolution of public governance, thereby correcting the shortcomings of the Fordist state; one defining the decency and equality of our society as much in the relationship between people as through the work of government; one giving to all citizens a platform of social capability and recognition on which to base their participation in society; and—as a consequence of these values and policies—a party capable of civilising global capital.

APPENDICES

APPENDIX I
NEW
MACROECONOMICS

Changes in the mode of production have inevitably led to changes in the way in which economic events are interpreted. Most notably, economists in most Western nations are trying to comprehend the way in which the business cycle has flattened and moved with relative stability throughout the 1990s. It appears that the new system of production has narrowed the time horizon between production and consumption, and thereby reduced the likelihood of extreme peaks and troughs in economic activity. This is not to suggest, of course, that the profit system has found a way to end macroeconomic uncertainties. Rather, the narrowing of the time lag between economic judgments and economic events has eased the impact of uncertainty on the business cycle, nationally and internationally.

Commonsense tells us that businesses need to make decisions about their investment and output before they can know the actual state of consumer demand. If they overestimate the level of demand then they will be left with surplus production capacity. If they underestimate demand then prices and activity will need to accelerate to make up for the shortfall. This is the simple reason why all advanced economies have a clearly defined business cycle. It stands to reason that smaller, more virtual and flexible systems of production have shortened the time horizons on cycles of production and allowed businesses to adjust more adeptly to movements in demand.

The emergence of just-in-time manufacturing has been complemented by the growth of the services sector which, by its nature, must function on a just-in-time basis. With more open international trade and product competition, the international business cycle has moved into a relatively stable period of low inflationary growth. This does not, however, eliminate the possibility of economic boom and bust. It simply implies that post-industrial production can be judged as more inherently stable in the macroeconomics of the business cycle than the Fordist long-lead-time features of the old economy. In future, sources of economic instability are more likely to arise from wide variations in consumer spending—especially in an era of international capital markets and easier finance—than the methods by which production decisions are formulated.

The new economy has also eroded the relevance of traditional methods of economic measurement. Most of the national economic debate follows the monthly or quarterly release of various forms of macroeconomic data. These are consistent with the high expectations associated with short term demand management. They are also a legacy of Keynesian economics, which monitors macroeconomic flows off the national accounts. There are, however, two fundamental flaws in the usefulness of this framework as a way of understanding the Australian economy. First is a series of measurement issues. For a start, the national accounts measure macroeconomic flows rather than stocks; hence they are incomplete. The economic decisions of individuals and companies are guided not just by their annual income, but also by the value of their net assets. So too for a nation: movements in national wealth, especially from changed expectations about the future income generating capacity of existing capital stock, impact heavily on the business cycle and its management.

Even in the measurement of macroeconomic flows the statistician faces a number of problems. Most notably, it is almost impossible to measure the features of services sector activity, especially labour productivity. The national accounts were designed for an economy based on mining, agriculture and manufacturing (goods not services), and infrastructure based on transport, construction and public utilities (physical capital not human capital). These industries now represent less than 30 per cent of the workforce, whereas in the 1950s they covered more than one-half. Moreover, economic forecasting is made much harder by the way in which statisticians can barely understand the past let alone the future. For instance, the short term reporting of changes in economic activity usually reflects a snapshot of changes in stocks and inventories, not actual output. Inventory investment in Australia between 1965 and 1995 represented only a small proportion of national output, yet quarterly changes in inventories through this period accounted for 59 per cent of the change in measured GDP.

Second, while the Keynesian style of aggregating national data was well suited to the closed Australian economy up to the 1980s, it is of limited use in an internationalised trading environment. Over the past decade the scale of Australia's traded sector (export plus import competing production) has doubled from 20 per cent to 40 per cent of GDP. This international competition has substantially increased the complexity of the so-called national economy. Aggregated data are no longer a reliable guide to the Australian economy given the disaggregation of economic activity.

In an internationalised economy employment growth is spatially dispersed and diverse. Not all regions are able to share in the success of the traded sector. Equally, national income growth tends to be distributed unevenly across the workforce. The changing nature of work, with the specialisation of production skills, has divided the labour market into hundreds of segments. The implications of these changes for the political process in Australia are immense. As the Keating Government found, sustained periods of national economic growth do not necessarily guarantee electoral success. Aggregated figures offer little guide to the complex and increasingly disparate manner in which income and employment are distributed in an open economy.

APPENDIX II
TWIN DEFICITS
THEORY

The Howard Government has based its entire budget strategy on a single, essentially flawed, economic theory—the twin deficits theory. This argues that a reduction in the Federal budget deficit will automatically reduce the current account deficit (CAD). It relies on an assumption that an increase in public savings will increase national savings (S) which will, in turn, close the gap between national savings and national investment (I), thereby lowering the current account deficit. This follows the accounting identity whereby CAD = I – S. It is further assumed that with a lower structural CAD, Australia can sustain a higher rate of economic growth—lifting the so-called speed limit on growth.

There are three basic flaws in the government's twin deficits theory. First, recent history in Australia has shown that it does not automatically work. In the late 1980s the Treasury elevated the twin deficits to the Holy Grail of economic policy. Yet deep cuts to Federal spending were associated with increases in the current account deficit. Internationally, the same problem has arisen. New Zealand, for instance, forecast a budget operating surplus of 2.9 per cent in 1996–97 yet a CAD of 5.1 per cent of GDP. In Malaysia, a comfortable budget surplus and national savings rate of 32 per cent has produced a CAD of 8.8 per cent of GDP.

This empirical evidence, of course, highlights the second flaw in the twin deficits theory; that is, it makes no allowance for a surge in national investment. This is the key contradiction in the 1996–97 budget strategy: saying that the core objective of policy is to reduce the CAD, yet talking up confidence effects (from a cut in Commonwealth outlays) as the basis for a surge in business investment. Even if fiscal consolidation produced a gain in national savings, a comparable increase in national investment would leave the CAD unaltered. This is simply repeating the experience of the 1980s when net public sector borrowing was replaced by higher private borrowing, leaving the underlying trend in the CAD and foreign debt unaltered.

The third flaw in the twin deficits theory concerns the high substitution effects in Australia between public savings and private savings. In a developed nation such as ours, with a strong culture of consumption, improvements in public savings are often associated with a decline in private savings. Even the Treasury in 1996 Budget Paper No. 1 (at page 1.30) notes that, 'both the IMF and OECD have recently published reports which suggest that the private sector tends to compensate, in part, for changes to public sector saving'. The 1996 Budget was rife with substitution effects of this kind. Most of the $2 billion revenue gains reflected a straight transfer from private savings to public savings, without any net gain in national savings.

On the outlays side, Australians are unlikely to lower their consumption of basic education, child care, health, pharmaceutical and nursing home services solely on the basis that the Federal Government has made them more expensive. In a nation accustomed to First World services, these items form part of the essentials of family life. As such, they are price inelastic and subject to substitution effects between public and private expenditure. Other Budget cuts simply reflected public-to-public outlay shuffling, especially the cuts to the States (which lead either to a reduction in State savings or further cuts to essential public services).

APPENDIX III
THE KALDOR
TAX—ISSUES AND
SOLUTIONS

Ian Hinckfuss, from the University of Queensland, has presented the following guide as to how a range of issues might be dealt with in the implementation of a Kaldor tax in Australia:

ISSUE NO. 1   People occasionally have years of large expenditure when they purchase a car, for example. The progressive expenditure tax may yield a massive tax for those years despite the fact that one's usual expenditure is modest. To illustrate this, assume we had a progressive tax on expenditure as follows:

Taxable Expenditure	Marginal Tax Rate (%)
$0–$10,000	0
$10 000–$20 000	50
$20 000–$30 000	100
$30 000–$40 000	200
$40 000–$50 000	400

Assume also that somebody had an income of $20 000 per annum and spent $10 000 of that per annum and saved the rest. They would pay no tax. But after three years they withdraw their savings of $30 000 and spend the money on a car. As well, in that year, they spend their normal $10 000, making a total expenditure of $40 000. The tax on that would be $35 000, well in excess of their annual income.

Solution   Allow people the option of averaging their expenditure over several (say five) years. In the above example, that would entail taxing the person for five years as if he or she were spending $16 000 per year for each of the five years. That would result in tax payments of $3000 per year, a total of $15 000 over five years.

ISSUE NO. 2   In most families there is a considerable disparity in income between different members of the family. Without some compensating mechanism, a progressive tax would hit the highest earner in the family hard. Individuals who were not part of an economic unit such as a family, and who spent at the average rate of expenditure for a one-income family, would be taxed less than the average rate per person in the family group. This is an inequitable result, both for families and for other groups with shared consumption.

Solution   This problem exists within the present progressive income tax system as well. The solution is the same. Deem each person in an economic group with x members to have spent one xth of the total family or group expenditure for the purposes of the tax. In that way, for example, a family of two adults and three children which spent $50 000 would pay five times the tax payable on $10 000; that is, five times $0 equals $0 on the above scale. Without income sharing of this kind, the tax would have been $75 000.

ISSUE NO. 3   Gifts will be taxed twice. Without some adjustment, a donor's gift would be regarded as expenditure. The gift, if subsequently expended, would attract tax again. This would discourage people from spreading their wealth and so be a discouragement to material equity.

Solution   Acknowledge gifts to anybody as a tax deduction for the donor, provided the recipient is willing to acknowledge the gift as income for taxation purposes.

ISSUE NO. 4   Traditionally, home ownership has been encouraged in Australia. Usually, this involves a large amount of borrowing or disinvestment. This would, in turn, engender an even more massive tax impost, given the progressive Kaldor system. For most people, therefore, it would be impossible for them to purchase their own homes.

Solution   Count investment in one's primary residence (up to some reasonable market amount) as a tax deductible investment and the proceeds from the sale of one's home as income. Home improvements over this investment limit would count as personal expenditure. Taxable expenditure on the purchase of a new home, or other acceptable investments after the sale of a previous dwelling would be calculated by subtracting the sale price of the previous dwelling from the purchase price of the new dwelling or investment.

ISSUE NO. 5   Such a tax would be difficult to administer, or at least would involve massive and confusing changes to the existing tax system.

Solution   The current administrative machinery for taxation in Australia, with its tax file numbers and annual tax accounting, is eminently suited to a Kaldor tax scheme. The basic system of tax gathering, including provision for 'paying as you go', would remain as it is. The investment and disinvestment data which would be required by the Taxation Commissioner are already required for the purposes of the existing capital gains tax. An administrative simplification would involve the abolition of the capital gains tax as a separate tax. Capital gains would automatically be taxed as part of the Kaldor tax. Bank investment or withdrawals would easily be registered as the difference between the balance at the end of the taxation year and the balance at the beginning.

ISSUE NO. 6   Even if some form of Kaldor tax were optimal in the long run, there would be problems for the government in its introduction. How would a government know what its revenue was going to be in the first year of its operation? How would it know what rates of taxation to set?

Solution   To the extent that there was a perceived need to overcome these difficulties, the tax could be introduced piecemeal, with subsequent adjustments to the tax rate, if necessary, ensuring that there were no vast unforeseen deficits in government revenue. A first step would be to take the tax off superannuation contributions. It is only recently that superannuation contributions have been taxed. Before that, the tax on superannuation was effectively a Kaldor tax. The investment was not taxed, but the pension or the lump sum disinvestment was taxed. That is the way it should have been left. Having dealt with superannuation, the government could then begin to treat business investments as a tax deduction and to treat disinvestment of those same investments as taxable income. Finally, the government could introduce a tax on the difference between bank withdrawals (including borrowings) and bank deposits. Any deficit in the Federal budget would only be as a result of a shift towards investment.

ISSUE NO. 7   What of death duties and inheritance?

Solution   One of the objections to death duties is the inequity of a tax on the inheritors, especially where the inheritance is a family farm or other business at which the inheritor has worked most of his or her adult life. To pay the death duties, the inheritor may have to sell the farm and go out of business, losing this source of income. With a Kaldor tax there would be no tax on such an inheritance, provided that the inheritance were not sold off, or if it were, that the money obtained was appropriately reinvested. Otherwise, an inheritance could be treated as income and taxed in the same way as other income. Kaldor taxation, therefore, automatically sorts out the death duties dilemma.

Source: Ian Hinckfuss, Progressive Taxation on Personal Expenditure, unpublished paper, University of Queensland, 1996.

[Author's note: this material is an indicative guide only, the consequences of which, in terms of detailed policy making, the author does not necessarily endorse.]

APPENDIX IV
HEALTH REFORM IN
AUSTRALIA

It is now more than 30 years since Gough Whitlam first met John Deeble and Dick Scotton to set down plans for universal public health insurance in Australia. Medibank and its successor, Medicare, represent the last major change in the structure of the national health system. Since then the horizons of health administration have changed fundamentally, driven by new health technology and practices, higher public demand and expectations and advances in health data assessment. Quite plainly, the development of public policy has not kept pace with these changes. Health delivery has fallen into a pattern of incremental reform.

Too much of the health debate in Australia is bogged down in a struggle between free markets and public providers. Ownership issues have obscured the importance of outcomes. In truth, a free market cannot work in health care. It departs too substantially from basic goals of access and equity. Just as much, public monopolies suffer from a lack of responsiveness to consumer preferences and efficiency goals. There is much to commend a third way in health policy, featuring regionally integrated services, rationalised Federal–State relations, greater supply side contestability and enhanced consumer sovereignty on the demand side of the health economy. This package of reforms has the potential to establish a network of consumer cooperatives, featuring elements of public mutuality and self-governance.

HEALTH CARE GOALS

Health should no longer be set solely in a social welfare framework; that is, it should not be perceived as good people doing good things in a way which cannot be measured in economic terms. While health care can be classified as a social good, its outcomes, like any other good, are bound by the successes and failures of quasi-markets and government regulation. It involves, albeit for an essential public purpose, an active system of production and distribution. The mystique of health as an item of public merit should not act as an alibi for avoiding structural change.

Indeed, health's role as a social good makes efficiency gains all the more significant. Any worthwhile social justice strategy is dependent on the efficiency of the social and welfare sectors. Whenever government programs by-pass their intended beneficiaries or waste financial resources, they represent an opportunity cost for those most in need. While the lost opportunities of government barely impact on the wealthy, they entrench the disadvantages of the poor. Health and welfare outlays in Australia are approximately equal to the output of all public utilities, yet health and welfare have largely avoided the rigour of efficiency gains.

Structural reform, however, should only proceed on the basis of satisfying Labor's goals for access, equity and efficiency in health care. Barriers to health access may be financial or locational. The purpose of universal health insurance is to reduce or eliminate out-of-pocket costs, especially for low income earners, which would otherwise prohibit the purchase of health care services. This remains the great strength of the universality principles pursued by successive Labor Governments.

Conversely, issues of locational access have not been prominent in the national debate. The distribution of secondary care services has been left as a State responsibility, administered with uneven results. The Hawke and Keating Governments were not able to progress the intention of Chifley's *National Health Services Act 1948* or Whitlam's national hospitals plan for a national health system based on locational equity. This remains a serious shortcoming in Federal responsibilities for health. All Australians, no matter their income, no matter their location, should have equal access to essential health services under the universal coverage of health entitlements.

Efficiency considerations can be split into allocative and cost goals. Allocative efficiency seeks to define the combination of health interventions that make the greatest contribution to the preservation and quality of life. Health economists are now able to produce cost/benefit analyses on various treatment types, maximising community gains for a fixed outlay of health expenditure. This is known as the Oregon model, where the people of that US State produced a list of 700 categories of illnesses and treatment of which the government funds 568 for low income Medicaid beneficiaries. This represents a form of health care rationing. Public funds are limited to certain types of illnesses, the treatment of which maximises quality-adjusted life years (QALYs) for the community. The ultimate objective is to facilitate the redistribution of resources across the health system, between stages of care and disease categories, so that the marginal cost-effectiveness ratio is equal for all health interventions.

This approach, however, has little acceptance among public opinion in Australia. Australian views about health care are strongly egalitarian, as a 1994 study concluded: 'a policy of health benefit maximisation (simple utility) received very limited support when the consequence is a loss of equity and access for the elderly and for people with a limited potential for improving their health'.[1] National values have rejected the explicit rationing of health care and full allocative efficiency, giving higher priority to the full treatment of life-threatening episodes and access for the elderly and low income groups. These values, in turn, should form the basis of the social premium used by governments to establish an appropriate social safety net in health.

The leading efficiency goal for policy makers, therefore, concerns cost or technical efficiency. That is, minimising the unit costs of production and making room for new or expanded programs. The potential for large efficiency gains has generally been overlooked in the public consideration of health reform in Australia. This deficiency can now be overcome through the emerging focus on integrated health systems and benefits of structural reform.

STRUCTURAL EFFICIENCY AND ACCESS

Increases in the range, expense and demand for medical treatments have forced most developed nations to seek supply side efficiencies. While changes in work practices, technology and demographics have increasingly blurred the distinction between hospital and community care, Australia's health system has maintained an archaic and overlapping set of Federal and State responsibilities. The key to structural reform is to organise hospitals, general practitioners and community-based services in a way that best satisfies the changing nature of health consumer demand.

Australia has one of the most complex health systems in the world. It is a plainly illogical structure of health financing, production and distribution. The Federal Government alone has established 60 separate health programs, each with its own statutory base, eligibility rules and funding arrangements. The States and Territories have layered onto this structure their own programs and initiatives, thereby producing a myriad of uncoordinated and unfocused health outlays. In John Paterson's words:

> There is little structural connection between most of the programs. The specific providers will be paid regardless of how they fit in with the rest of Australian health care. For the small proportion of Australians who at any one time need intensive and continuing services from multiple programs, the burden of putting a package of coordinated care together is enormous, and in the end, chancy. Yet the 10 per cent of people needing on-going 'multi-program' services consume 50 per cent of Australian health care outlays.[2]

This basic inefficiency is aggravated by the disparate treatment of public and private services by both the Federal and State Governments. The distinction between public and private health activities in Australia cannot be made by ownership and funding sources, but by methods of reimbursement. Private activities—such as medical services, pharmaceutical and private hospitals—are funded on an uncapped, fee-for-service basis at above average cost prices. Public services, such as nursing homes and public hospitals are funded on the basis of capped annual grants with insufficient recognition of service demand and volumes. These arrangements inhibit the movement of resources from less efficient to more efficient health programs. They also impose an artificial set of market shares for the public and private sectors. International experience shows that it is impossible to establish a natural balance or market equilibrium between public and private sources of health care.

The complexity and inconsistency of the health system has produced five basic efficiency flaws: segmented services, mismatched responsibilities for service funding and delivery, location inequities, financially restricted services and a range of market perversions. First, it is impossible under current arrangements to effectively integrate the health care needs and demands of the community. Most forms of health care, especially with advances in technology, can now be substituted in appropriate cases for a range of other strategies and treatments. Substitutability in Australia, however, is severely restricted by the segmented and diverse nature of government responsibilities and provider and funding arrangements. This has produced a heavy reliance on relatively expensive forms of secondary care. Without coordinating strategies between hospitals and the various forms of primary and community care, too many patients are forced into unnecessary hospital admissions.

Second, funding responsibilities among the three tiers of   government do not correspond to logical levels of service delivery on the hierarchy of health treatment. Through Medicare the Federal Government controls the direct funding of primary or local health care, at the bottom of the treatment hierarchy. Paradoxically, State Governments have retained responsibilities for secondary and tertiary level facilities. Medicare, at least in the form originally proposed by Deeble and Scotton, was intended for integration with other parts of the health system. It was also proposed to establish a degree of fiscal equivalence between tax collections and Federal outlays on health. Scotton has placed these issues back on the national agenda:

> The most obvious result has been that the structure and levels of health benefits are increasingly driven by the exigencies of annual Commonwealth budgets rather than by any consideration of broader social costs and benefits—or by analysis of equity and efficiency criteria applicable to the many different components of health care financing. The overriding issue of how to incorporate incentives into the funding side remains not so much unsolved as forgotten. Furthermore, the lack of any relationship between the Medicare levy and the Medicare outlays, which in effect has turned the levy into a component of income tax, has obscured the potential for substitution between public charges and private insurance premiums and contributed to illogical policy choices.[3]

Third, health in Australia is without national standards for service delivery and an equitable distribution of resources. This is a major deficiency in Labor's goals for locational access to health care. There are significant variations in resource allocations across States and between regions. These inequities are felt most acutely on the edge of Australia's major cities, with their suburban corridors of population growth. In particular, the distribution of health services in Sydney and Melbourne reflects historical rather than contemporary patterns of urban settlement. This lag means that most beds and services are where the people used to live, not where they live now. In Melbourne, for instance, there are 6.1 hospital beds per thousand people in the inner metropolitan area and 1.3 in the outer area. The health status and needs of Australians are linked not just to how they live, but where they live.

Fourth, the differential system of financial reimbursement promotes the possibility of public squalor and private affluence in health. The fiscal crisis of the States has prompted some limited micro reforms on public hospitals while the greatest source of rising health costs, uncapped medical and pharmaceutical benefits, has avoided any lasting reform. In particular, over-servicing problems remain unresolved. It is, of course, irrational to manage any form of economic rationing in a manner unrelated to legitimate consumer preferences and opportunity cost assessments.

Fifth, the basic structural flaws in Australian health care produce a series of market perversions. These include different pricing rules for close substitutes, collusive practices on the private supply side and incentives for cost shifting. For example, the privatisation of outpatient clinics shifts costs from State Governments to the direct billing of Medicare. Across the board, the cost of services has shifted from the financially capped public hospital sector into the uncapped Medicare and Pharmaceutical Benefit schemes—in accident and emergency departments, pharmaceutical, radiology and pathology services. The privatisation of public services has become an unintended consequence of Medicare.

REGIONALLY INTEGRATED HEALTH

A starting point for health reform lies in the integration of services on a regional scale. In an integrated system, the planning and resource allocation of all forms of substitutable health care are drawn together into a single organisational structure. This objective and the concurrent goal of locational access can only be achieved through regional or area health management. Regional authorities are able to comprehend the health needs of their community. They have the flexibility to improve patient outcomes, adopt a community health outlook and secure the substitutability of services.

The proposal is to bring together the various programs and services of the Federal and State Governments into a single pool of health resources. Although representing a major shift in Federal–State relations, technically it is not difficult to pool the health resources of all levels of government. It simply means bundling together all Federal allocations including the Medicare Agreements, general purpose grants spent on health, and State funding raised from State revenue sources. The resource pool could be totally funded by the Commonwealth through an appropriate adjustment to the general purpose grants spent on purposes other than health. This could then establish a link, for cost control reasons, between public sector health outlays and an adjustable proportion of Federal income tax revenue.

The Federal–State pool of health funds would be distributed to regional authorities on the basis of resource allocation formulas agreed to by the Commonwealth and each State. These formulas are currently in place in several State health systems. They have been developed to achieve a more geographically equitable distribution of resources compared to the concentration of facilities which resulted from allocations on the basis of past expenditure. Labor's goals for locational access are best achieved through formulas based on adjusted population data, locational and socioeconomic factors and special allocations for the construction of tertiary services in fast-growing regions.

Regionally integrated health plans represent a substantial change in Federal–State relations. The Commonwealth would shed direct service responsibilities but take on an important equity role in the distribution of health resources between regions. The States, through regional management, would assume responsibility for the delivery of all health services. This approach has benefits for both levels of government. In particular, it is more appropriate for the Federal Government to concentrate on national policy objectives (such as service universality, access and equity) than the detail of service delivery. National goals can be met by monitoring the performance of regional authorities.

Integrated health management has the advantage of not only breaking down parochial behaviour between service providers, but also provoking more rational Federal and State responsibilities. It represents an outstanding opportunity to overcome the outdated dogma of Australian politics about centralism and States' rights. The founding arguments for federalism in 1901, about State rivalries and the tyranny of distance, now appear archaic. Real geographic distinctions in Australia are regional, and even at a neighbourhood level, not between the States and Territories. State boundaries—lines drawn in at Whitehall last century—have shown themselves to be an irrelevant guide to locational inequality.

The ALP, at least since the advent of Whitlam's leadership in the 1960s, has argued for the regionalisation of basic services. Virtually without public comment or recognition, regions have become a feature of State administrative arrangements. A range of State services are now administered by regional authorities—in school education, electricity and water distribution, public housing, economic development boards, road funding and the police. In one of the striking ironies of Australian politics, the advocates of States' rights are actually running their States through regional structures of bureaucracy.

This opens up an important chance for the rationalisation of Federal–State relations in Australia. Our federal system would be made more effective if the Commonwealth took responsibility for economic institutions and national infrastructure, with the States transferring their powers in industrial relations, business regulation and consumer affairs. Likewise, the States and their local government authorities should be encouraged to administer the delivery of human services, with the Commonwealth establishing and monitoring effective national standards in service access and equity.

HEALTHY COMPETITION

Too often in the Labor movement it is assumed that social goods and services can only be delivered in the public interest by government monopoly outlets. This ignores the immense contribution to the social sector of privately owned, especially not-for-profit, service providers. Ownership does not matter as much as outcomes. Significant gains can be made from the introduction of quasi-market competition. This approach seeks to lower unit costs and improve the allocation of public resources by stimulating competitive forces on the supply and/or demand side of the social sector.

Health care markets have traditionally featured three main blemishes: limited consumer knowledge and choice of service types; diminution of the pricing mechanism through insurance arrangements; and an historic difficulty with the quantification of costs and prices. It is a necessary condition for allocative efficiency that the prices of substitutable products reflect production costs. At least with this requirement, substantial progress has been made through the introduction of diagnosis-related groups (categories of treatment types to which costings can be applied) and casemix funding.

Casemix or output-related payments involve complex aspects of data collection which have only become feasible in the last decade through advances in health information technology. They are based on the commonsense proposition that efficient production is achieved by paying producers for their output rather than inputs. Producers respond to a fixed price on output by trying to meet client demand at the lowest cost. While case payments are best known for their transformation of hospital budgets and management, they are just as applicable and useful in other parts of the health system.

Casemix represents a simple but effective change in the financing of hospitals. The traditional method of funding—fixed annual allocations unrelated to output—simply institutionalises hospital inefficiency. Hospitals invariably increase their waiting lists as a means of attracting additional government funding. Casemix funding, which pays hospitals according to the services they perform, provides a strong incentive to increase activity and cut waiting lists. The introduction of case payments should not be a matter of partisan politics. It is a practical measure to provide the necessary incentive and management motivation for improved hospital efficiency. This approach will inevitably be developed in other health services, such as general and geriatric rehabilitation, palliative care and psychiatric treatment; building on the establishment of output-based Federal funding for nursing homes and hostels.

The most effective system of health financing offers a reconciliation between the interests of needs-based funding (to achieve equity goals) and casemix (as an efficiency measure). Federal–State payments to regions supplemented by the use of case payments by regional authorities establish a desirable funding mix. The availability of case payments also enables regional authorities to develop a clear separation between purchasers and providers of services. This purchaser/provider split can be an important source of competition on the supply or production side of the health market.

In many public authorities a single administrative unit is both the purchaser and provider of services to consumers. That is, the same managers who allocate or purchase resources (to meet public demand) are also responsible for the production of the service being purchased. This can lead to conflicting objectives and inefficiencies. Through the separation of purchaser and provider functions, governments can use competition between service providers—no matter their ownership—to improve outcomes for the public. The purchaser function, therefore, becomes a clearing house for the allocation of resources to those providers best able to satisfy the service goals of regional health authorities.

Under this system, the role of purchasers or regional authorities would be to assess the health needs of their client populations and arrange contracts with providers to deliver high quality services as efficiently and effectively as possible. The service provider role would involve competition to secure performance-based contracts specifying appropriate price, quantity and quality arrangements. Contracts would be on the basis of output payments, with flexibility to reflect capital costs and facilitate capital investment decisions by providers. These arrangements involve a fundamental shift in health funding in Australia: moving from priorities set around inputs, ownership and tradition to a system based on outputs, contestability and flexibility.

DEMAND SIDE SOCIALISM

Competition policies on the demand or distribution side of the health market involve a model of managed insurance competition initially developed by the US health economist, Alain Enthoven. This model aims to facilitate consumer choice between competing health insurance plans. Enthoven has summarised his scheme as follows:

> Experience with successful models of competition among health plans suggests that tools are available to enable sponsors to use competition to achieve a reasonable degree of efficiency and equity for their sponsored populations. Sponsors are active collective agents [governments or some other form of pooled resources] on the demand side of the market who contract with the competing health [insurance] plans and continuously structure and adjust the market to overcome its tendency to fail. A sponsor assures each eligible

beneficiary of financial coverage of health care expenses at a reasonable price. The sponsor is the ultimate guarantor of coverage,
though it may share risk with health plans. In a competitive model,
the sponsor serves as the broker that structures the coverages,
contracts with the beneficiaries and health plans regarding the rules
of participation, manages the enrolment process, collects premium
contributions from beneficiaries, pays premiums to health plans and
administers cross subsidies among beneficiaries and subsidies available to the whole group.[4]

With the establishment of consumer–sponsor–insurance plan relationships, sponsors (holding budgets on behalf of a particular group of health
consumers) would then make appropriate arrangements with service providers to fulfil the coverage requirements of consumers (representing a
purchaser/provider split on the demand side of the market). This model
seeks to overcome the problem of limited consumer choice and knowledge
by developing an agency approach. This is based on the capacity of budget
holding sponsors to act on behalf of customers and use their countervailing market power to purchase wisely and efficiently from both public and
private service providers.

Much as travel agents shop around the travel industry to bring
together the best package for their customers, it is intended for budget
holders to secure the best deal for their members. Choice would be
maximised through a large number of competing sponsors. Governments
would fulfil their obligations for service universality and access through
a risk-rated capitation payment for each consumer. These payments, with
the option of privately funded supplements, would be used to purchase
the health plan best suited to the needs of each consumer.

Scotton and Paterson have demonstrated the feasibility of this model
under Australian circumstances. It relies on what can be termed demand
side socialism—providing equity in health care access and coverage by
funding entitlements on the demand side of the health economy. This
approach becomes viable through the bundling of health resources, integration of service delivery and development of a national network of
patient information.[5] Rules would need to be established to prevent the
possibility of deliberate risk selection or cream skimming by sponsors,
plus any cost shifting practices. Scotton has proposed that registered
government and non-government organisations would be eligible to act
as budget holders and provide access for a national standard of health
care access, 'with one exception: in-hospital treatment as a private patient
would be available under private plans, as at present'.[6]

The establishment of this system of demand side socialism also opens
up the possibility of greater consumer sovereignty and self-governance.
Paterson has pointed out that an agency or managed care approach best
suits the needs of chronic users of the health system (the 10 per cent of
the population—the disabled, mentally ill, chronically aged, drug dependant and other permanent users of health care—that absorbs one-half of
all health expenditure). These citizens require intensive contact with their

agents to help guide them through the complexity of the health system and satisfy their chronic needs. Governments should establish a pooled global budget to support these services through the work of one-on-one agent–client relationships.

The remaining 90 per cent of the population, whose health needs lie in occasional episodes of general and acute care, require sponsors for the establishment of an appropriate health access plan. It is possible for these citizens to form not-for-profit health consumer groups with strong elements of self-governance and mutuality. These could be structured on a cooperatives model, featuring:

- payment by the Federal Government of a risk-rated (and in some cases, location-rated) capitation amount for each member of the cooperative. Risk rating would proceed according to standard guidelines for the likely incidence of health care. These funds would help address actuarial issues within the cooperative structure and provide a permanent safety net of health resourcing, consistent with national standards for universality, access and equity. Cooperatives would either be freely formed by people with mutual health care interests, or around existing non-state institutions, such as churches and other voluntary associations.
- capacity for each cooperative—within prudential guidelines—to establish its own health care contracts. This might involve, for instance, salary employment of a general practitioner, access to dental services and community health centres, availability of a range of preventive and allied health programs and separate insurance arrangements for acute care. Cooperatives would be in a position to identify their own needs and arrange for service provision accordingly. Salaried GPs would be able to act as a cooperative's agent for insurance and contracting purposes.
- State Governments and regional health authorities, under these arrangements, are allocated a service provider function, in tandem with non-government health organisations. Each cooperative would negotiate service contracts and insurance packages to suit its particular needs.
- the determination of health needs, service availability and the general administration of the cooperatives offer scope for the development of self-governance. This is consistent with the principles of small-scale, transparent and horizontally structured organisations. Members would have clear rights of entry to and exit from the cooperative, along with the capacity to develop rules, administrative and monitoring systems and service provision of mutual interest. A cooperative structure entrusts control and democratic governance in the hands of participating members, giving rise to a consumer focus in health care.

This structure combines the benefits of self-governance with national standards for resource inputs. It demonstrates how, with advances in information technology, it is technically possible for the revenue raising functions of the nation state to coexist with a smaller and more effective scale of governance. Self-governance, of course, has the capacity to breed further mutuality. In the case of the health cooperatives, this might mean the raising of financial contributions beyond the standard government capitation and the further development of collective service provision. In this fashion, the cooperative would be able to avoid the type of patron/client relationship somewhat implicit in the Enthoven/Scotton model of demand side socialism.

It should be noted that this proposal also revives some of the features and functions of the Friendly Societies in Australia. It demonstrates the utility of a form of social provision beyond the binary of state and market. It shows how the Fordist organisation of government—in this case, the heavy segmentation and centralised control of health services—can be disaggregated without losing the equity features implicit in national standards of service provision. It reflects an important division of public responsibility in the organisation of governance: vertical state control of the inputs to the process of public provision; horizontal, non-state governance of the outputs to public provision which, in turn, offer the potential for public mutuality.

Importantly, the proposal revisits, also from the time of the Friendly Societies, the relationship between producer sovereignty, consumer sovereignty and the role of the state in the Australian health sector. Part of the reason for the demise of the Friendly Societies earlier this century was the decision of various Federal and State Governments to support the (then) British Medical Association in its campaign to abolish the salaried employment of GPs by the societies. The health budgets of governments, Federal and State, in Australia are yet to recover from this act of folly. The public sector has consistently failed to restrict the producer sovereignty and market strength of the medical profession and its union. The establishment of fee-for-service funding, plus the intensification of collusive practices in the supply of specialist doctors,[7] have undermined the efficiency and integrity of the Australian health system. The rights and needs of health care consumers have been treated as a second and third order concern.

In particular, since the 1940s, Labor Governments have been frustrated by their inability to regulate the public cost of the medical profession. This feeling has been aggravated by the way in which the public sector subsidises the training and facilities from which doctors draw a substantial part of their income. For historical and constitutional reasons in Australia doctors have held strong bargaining and market powers. In 1949 the High Court interpreted Section 51 (23A) of the Constitution to mean that the prohibition of civil conscription in medical services precludes the Commonwealth from directly controlling medical fees.[8]

An answer to this issue of cost control and health sector efficiency lies in the enhancement of consumer sovereignty. The reform path leading to demand side socialism serves to contain health costs by forcing the medical profession, on the basis of need and merit, to contest service contracts and employment from both managed care budget holders and health consumer cooperatives. Hence, by every test of Labor's goals in social policy—the creation of equity, service efficiency and public mutuality—there is much to acclaim in a third way to health policy, especially in the advancement of demand side socialism.

SUMMARY

The proposals developed above, of course, cannot be implemented in their entirety through the short term. They require progressive implementation over a number of years, based on the following five steps:

1 pooling the health resources of the Federal Government and each State, with fiscal equivalence between public sector health outlays and Federal revenue, plus the development of new patient information systems;
2 implementation of regional health management with fully integrated service provision and the establishment of national access and equity standards;
3 payment to service providers on an output basis through pricing mechanisms such as casemix;
4 phased introduction of purchaser/provider arrangements, establishing contestability between public and private providers for performance-based service contracts from regional authorities;
5 finally, the introduction of demand side socialism, through the establishment of managed care agents for chronic users of the health system and health consumer cooperatives for the remainder of the population.

NOTES

INTRODUCTION

1 Barbara Tuchman, *The March of Folly*, Abacus, London, 1985, p. 480.
2 As quoted in D. Green and L. Cromwell, *Mutual Aid or Welfare State: Australia's Friendly Societies*, Allen & Unwin, Sydney, 1984, p. xviii.
3 As quoted in Bob Catley, *Globalising Australian Capitalism*, Cambridge University Press, 1996, p. 1. There is, of course, an active debate as to the extent and meaning of globalisation—see, for instance, Paul Hirst and Grahame Thompson, *Globalization in Question*, Polity Press, Cambridge, 1996. In the book at hand, globalisation is described and used as a tendency—towards the freer flow of information, finance, production and trade between nations—not as a finished process. The economic controls and influence of the nation state have not been completely resolved; rather, they are passing through a period of fundamental transition. These matters are dealt with at greater length in Part I.
4 See *The Australian*, 23 November 1996.
5 Larry Letich, 'Is Life Outsmarting Us?', *The Washington Post*, 2 April 1995, p. C5.
6 After the 1996 New Zealand election, conducted for the first time under a proportional representation voting system, the National Party and New Zealand First formed a coalition government.
7 The clearest expression of these views lies in Christopher Lasch's *The Revolt of the Elites*, W. W. Norton and Co., New York, 1995.
8 James S. Coleman, 'Social Capital in the Creation of Human Capital', *American Journal of Sociology*, vol. 94, 1988, supplement p. 100.
9 For instance, the campaign for the 1997 British election, which resulted in a Labour landslide victory, prominently featured issues as diverse as street crime and European monetary union.
10 Tony Blair, *Socialism*, British Fabian Society pamphlet 565, 1994, p. 7.
11 Dick Morris, *Behind the Oval Office*, Random House, New York, 1997, p. 92.

12 ibid., p. 86. In Bill Clinton's last campaign, for instance, his tax policy was based on assisting families that were struggling to meet the costs of post-secondary education.

13 ibid., p. 211.

14 For a guide to some of the multi-plane features of Australian electoral behaviour, see Simon Jackman, Racial Attitudes in Australian Political Ideology: Political Elites Verus the Mainstream, unpublished paper, Department of Political Science, Research School of the Social Sciences, Australian National University, Canberra, 13 January 1997.

15 See Guy Rundle, 'The Good Society', *Australian Book Review*, June 1997, pp. 29–30.

16 John Gray, 'Is Equality a Lost Cause?', *New Statesman*, 28 February 1997, pp. 44–45.

17 See David Marquand, *The Unprincipled Society*, Jonathan Cape, London, 1988, pp. 28–37.

18 Anthony Crosland, *The Future of Socialism*, Jonathan Cape, London, 1956, p. 22.

19 See Gray, 'Is Equality a Lost Cause?', 1997, reflecting on Crosland's philosophy of equality.

20 Michael Walzer, *Spheres of Justice*, Martin Robertson, Oxford, 1983, p. 18.

21 Amartya Sen, *Inequality Reexamined*, Clarendon Press, Oxford, 1992, p. 150.

22 See Peter Baldwin, *Beyond the Safety Net*, Department of Social Security, Canberra, March 1995.

23 ibid., p. 39.

24 Walzer, *Spheres of Justice*, 1983, p. 66.

CHAPTER 1   NATIONAL CAPITAL

1 In 1870 output per man-hour (standard unit) for Australia was 1.30, compared to 0.43 Austria, 0.64 Canada, 0.44 Denmark, 0.42 France, 0.43 Germany, 0.44 Italy, 0.31 Sweden, 0.55 Switzerland, 0.80 United Kingdom and 0.70 United States. See Robert J Barro, *Modern Business Cycle Theory*, Harvard University Press, Cambridge Mass., 1989, p. 56.

2 In 1979 output per man-hour for Australia was 6.5, compared to 5.9 Austria, 7.0 Canada, 5.3 Denmark, 7.1 France, 6.9 Germany, 5.8 Italy, 6.7 Sweden, 5.1 Switzerland, 5.5 United Kingdom and 8.3 United States. ibid.

3 Anthony Crosland, *The Future of Socialism*, Jonathan Cape, London, 1956.

4 Francis Castles, *Australian Public Policy and Economic Vulnerability*, Allen & Unwin, Sydney, 1988, p. 21.

CHAPTER 2   GLOBAL CAPITAL

1 Delegates from 44 nations met at Bretton Woods, New Hampshire, in 1944 to establish the International Monetary Fund. This new set of rules included stable exchange rates based on the relationship between $US and gold. The system broke down in the early 1970s when the value of $US could no longer be sustained.

2 See paper by Ian Manning to the Economic Planning Advisory Council (EPAC) seminar on 'Globalisation: Issues for Australia', Canberra, 15 September 1994.

3 Fred Argy 'The Integration of World Capital Markets: Some Economic and Social Implications', in *Economic Papers*, vol. 15, no. 2, June 1996, p. 2.

4 During 1996, for instance, the Reserve Bank of Australia held foreign exchange reserves of between $17.1 billion and $22.5 billion, while the *daily average* of foreign exchange turnover against Australian dollars, measured on a monthly basis, ranged between $24.9 billion and $33.1 billion.

5 For further analysis see 'A Survey of the World Economy', *The Economist*, 7 October 1995.

6 This approach was set out by Treasurer Paul Keating in his 1989/90 Budget speech:

    Last financial year national spending increased by nearly 8 per cent in real terms. Yet gross domestic product—the measure of everything we produce in Australia—grew by under 4 per cent. That big gap, spending at 8 per cent and production at 4 per cent, sums up our trade problem. It is a gap which must be closed. In the short term that can only be done by bringing that high demand down to a more realistic level. This is where interest rates have played an appropriate role.

7 Tony Makin in *Agenda*, vol. 1, no. 2, 1994, pp. 152–3.

8 See Will Hutton, 'Remove the Villain of Free Finance', *The Australian*, 29 November 1996.

9 Named after James Tobin, a Nobel Prize winning economist, who first proposed this tax in 1978 as a way of 'throwing sand in the wheels of international finance'.

10 A sustainable financial position is benchmarked by budget deficits at no more than 3 per cent of GDP and public sector debt at no more than 60 per cent of GDP.

CHAPTER 3   COMPETITIVE ADVANTAGE

1 Robert Reich, *The Work of Nations*, Simon & Schuster, London, 1991, p. 3.

2 For a more detailed analysis of this phenomenon from a neo-Marxist perspective, see Dick Bryan, 'International Competitiveness: National

and Class Agendas', *Journal of Australian Political Economy*, no. 35, June 1995, pp. 1–23.

3 See *The Australian Financial Review*, 9 June 1993.

4 See Paul Romer, 'Increasing Returns and Long-Run Growth', *Journal of Political Economy*, vol. 94, no. 5, 1986, pp. 1002–17. These new growth theories are dealt with in greater length in chapter 7.

5 Robert Putnam, *Making Democracy Work: Civic Traditions in Modern Italy*, Princeton University Press, Princeton, 1993.

CHAPTER 4   NEW POLITICAL ECONOMY

1 James O'Connor, *The Fiscal Crisis of the State*, St Martin's Press, New York, 1973.

2 In the narrowing of the State tax base, for instance, combined State government assistance in payroll tax concessions to industry total $4.8 billion—$1.7 billion in NSW, $1.2 billion Victoria, $620 million Queensland, $580 million Western Australia and $700 million in the remaining two States and two Territories. See the draft Industry Commission report, *State, Territory and Local Government Assistance to Industry*, Canberra, July 1996, page xii.

3 Unfortunately the Commonwealth Department of Finance has only been able to access underlying outlays data on a consistent basis since 1976/77, thus making difficult a detailed statistical analysis for the full period under consideration. The descriptive analysis provided in the main text, however, is certainly consistent with fiscal trends from 1976/77 to date.

4 James O'Connor, *The Fiscal Crisis of the State*, 1973, p. 40.

5 For a fuller explanation of strategies of domestic defence and domestic compensation, see Francis Castles, *Australian Public Policy and Economic Vulnerability*, Allen & Unwin, Sydney, 1988.

CHAPTER 5   ECONOMIC RATIONALISM

1 See Michael Pusey, *Economic Rationalism in Canberra*, Cambridge University Press, Melbourne, 1991.

2 See, for instance, Peter Love, *Labor and the Money Power*, Melbourne University Press, Melbourne, 1984.

3 Peter Sheehan in 'Economics and the National Interest', *Dialogues on Australia's Future*, Victoria University of Technology, Melbourne, 1996, p. 388, lists the six main assumptions of the neoclassical framework as follows:

• The existence of complete markets and a finite economy, and assumptions concerning expectations and perfect information.
• The existence of independent, utility or profit maximising agents.

- The assumption that firms have no sunk costs, no market power and convex production functions.
- The assumption that all firms and consumers are price-takers, interacting only through markets.
- The assumption that technological change is external to the economic system, and determined by factors outside the economy.
- The assumption that the structure of the economy (e.g. the number and nature of firms and the preferences of consumers) can be treated as given and fixed, and hence as independent of developments within the economy.

4 David Burchell, 'The Curious Career of Economic Rationalism: Government and Economy in the Current Policy Debate', *Australian and New Zealand Journal of Sociology*, vol. 30, no. 3, November 1994, p. 328.
5 This appears to be a characteristic, for instance, of the supporters of Pauline Hanson's One Nation Party. The use of the critique of economic rationalism as a way of arguing for economic isolation demonstrates how questions of economic nationalism and internationalism have blurred the traditional Left/Right divide. For an analysis of these issues, see Lindsay Tanner's celebrated paper, 'Populism and Rationalism', submission to ALP Living Standards and Employment Policy Committee, May 1997.

CHAPTER 6   ECONOMIC NATIONALISM

1 Dick Bryan, *The Chase Across the Globe, International Accumulation and the Contradictions for Nation States*, Westview Press, Boulder, CO, 1995, p. 183.
2 ibid., p. 191.
3 Especially in non-metropolitan Australia, public complaints about issues such as the anti-competitive pricing policies of the multinational petrol companies, and poor corporate morality of the big banks, are widespread. A number of recent studies have also highlighted the public distrust of large corporations; see, for instance, 'Middle Class Reports Lifestyle Slide', *The Sydney Morning Herald*, 5 July 1997, p. 2.

CHAPTER 7   NEW GROWTH POLICIES

1 See David Aschauer, *Public Investment and Private Sector Growth*, Economic Policy Institute, Washington, 1990, p. 11.
2 Paul Romer, 'Beyond Classical and Keynesian Macroeconomic Policy', *Policy Options*, vol. 15, no. 6, July–August 1994, p. 16.
3 An excellent summary of the new growth theories can be found in Steve Dowrick, 'A Review of New Theories and Evidence on Eco-

nomic Growth: Their Implications for Australian Policy', ANU
Centre for Economic Policy Research, Discussion Paper No. 275,
October 1992.
4 Peter Drucker, *Post-capitalist Society*, Butterworth Heinemann,
Oxford, 1993, p. 167.
5 Report by the House of Representatives Standing Committee for
Long Term Strategies, *The Workforce of the Future*, Australian Government Publishing Service (AGPS), Canberra, June 1995, p. 52.
6 Brian Toohey, 'The Knowledge-based Road to Growth', *The Australian Financial Review*, 22 July 1997, p. 17.
7 See Dowrick, 'A Review of New Theories and Evidence on Economic
Growth: Their Implications for Australian Policy', 1992, pp. 9–11.
8 Industry assistance figures are taken from the draft report of the
Industry Commission, *State, Territory and Local Government Assistance
to Industry*, AGPS, Canberra, July 1996.

CHAPTER 8   INDUSTRY POLICY

1 See reports from *The Australian*, 6 and 7 June 1997.
2 See William Mitchell, 'Business Welfare—A Legitimate Role for
Government?', *Current Affairs Bulletin*, April/May 1995, pp. 4–13;
and Ian Henderson, 'Industry Subsidy Must Not Be a Lucky Dip',
The Australian, 11 June 1997.
3 See reports from *The Australian Financial Review*, 10 June 1997, p. 18.
4 Gough Whitlam, *The Whitlam Government 1972–1975*, Viking, Melbourne, 1985, pp. 188–96.
5 See Paul Kelly, 'Tariffs: A Tax on All Our Houses', *The Australian*,
12 March 1997. Internationally, studies by the World Bank and
OECD have chronicled the costs to consumers of trade controls:
sugar in the United States, $735 million in 1983; shoes in Britain,
$170 million in 1979; Japanese cars in the US, $2.3 billion in 1983;
farming in all OECD nations, $200 billion in 1991—the equivalent
of $230 per capita (all amounts in $US). See *The Economist*, 27 March
1993, p. 18.
6 Paul Hirst and Grahame Thompson, *Globalization in Question*, Polity
Press, Cambridge, 1996, p. 144.
7 See House of Representatives Hansard, *Parliamentary Debates*, Answer
to Question No. 1029, 5 February 1997, p. 281.
8 Ironically, the advocates of industry protection and sector planning
tend to argue that their policies are aimed at assisting, in the words
of John McEwen, 'efficient and economic industry'. It is never
explained, however, why efficient and supposedly competitive corporations require assistance at public expense, especially when the act
of assistance itself is likely over time to make them less efficient. See
Peter Walsh, 'Govt Assistance or Extortion?', *The Australian Financial
Review*, 1 August 1995.

CHAPTER 9   CONCLUSION: RESPONDING TO
GLOBALISATION

1 An argument developed by Robert Reich, 'Bidding Against the Future?',
address to the Conference on the Economic War Among the States,
National Academy of Sciences, Washington DC, 22 May 1996.

CHAPTER 10   THE NEW ECONOMY

1 Australian Bureau of Statistics, *Australian Social Trends 1997*, cata-
logue no. 4102.0, ABS, Canberra.
2 ibid.
3 See *Australian Accountant*, vol. 66, no. 8, September 1996, p. 32.
4 Vince Fitzgerald, *Australia's Capital Market (Summary)*, The Allen
Consulting Group, Sydney, June 1996, p. 9.
5 Robert Reich, *The Work of Nations*, Simon & Schuster, London, 1991.
6 ibid., p. 178.
7 House of Representatives Standing Committee for Long Term Strategies, *The Workforce of the Future*, Report, AGPS, Canberra, June
1995.
8 Figures for services sector employment are drawn from ABS, *Australian Social Trends 1997*; and Phil Ruthven, 'New Growth', *The
Australian Financial Review*, 5 January 1995.
9 ABS, *Australian Social Trends 1997*.
10 This analysis is adapted from Will Hutton, 'High-risk Strategy is Not
Paying Off', *Guardian Weekly*, 12 November 1995, p. 13.

CHAPTER 11   INCOME INEQUALITY

1 Jeff Borland and Keith Norris, 'Equity', in *The Changing Australian
Labour Market*, EPAC Paper No. 11, March 1996, p. 88.
2 John Buchanan and Toni O'Loughlin, 'Reforms No Solution for the
Unemployed', *The Australian*, 24 May 1996.
3 Jeff Borland, 'Education and the Structure of Earnings in Australia',
The Economic Record, vol. 72, no. 219, December 1996, p. 379.
4 Borland and Norris, 'Equity', March 1996, p. 91.
5 Jeff Borland and Roger Wilkins, 'Earning Inequality in Australia',
The Economic Record, vol. 72, no. 216, March 1996, p. 23.
6 See *The Sydney Morning Herald*, 15 January 1997, p. 15.
7 Bob Gregory has also argued against the usefulness of real wage
overhang theories, especially in their practical consequences:

The argument is that in a deregulated labour market the wage of
the long term unemployed will fall and as a result jobs will be created
for them. The issue is what is the empirical magnitude of the
elasticity of demand for labour? The greater the elasticity the less

the wage need fall and the greater the number of jobs created. There is an older econometric literature which suggests that the elasticity might be 0.3. That is, to increase employment by ten per cent wages need to fall by 33 per cent. To estimate the proportionate increase in the number of jobs needed is not easy but suppose the 300 000 long term unemployed effectively compete with a group of workers that number about one million. If this was a reasonable estimate then to create 300 000 jobs would require a 30 per cent increase in employment and therefore a 90 per cent wage reduction (if the elasticity were 0.3). This is a very large wage reduction indeed. Perhaps the long term unemployed compete with two million workers, if so the wage would need to fall by 45 per cent. These are very large wage falls.

See Bob Gregory, 'Unemployment: What to Do?', *The Sydney Papers*, The Sydney Institute, Spring 1994, p. 109.

8 David Card and Alan Krueger, *Myth and Measurement: The New Economics of the Minimum Wage*, Princeton University Press, New Jersey, 1995, p. 1.

9 Buchanan and O'Loughlin, *The Australian*, 24 May 1996.

10 Card and Krueger, *Myth and Measurement*, 1995, p. 3.

11 ibid., pages 394–5. AWE minus X reflects full indexation to movements in average weekly earnings minus some other (subjectively determined) amount. In the alternative method, the living wage would be fully indexed to movements in wages around the 30th–40th percentile of earnings.

12 Bernie Fraser, 'Some Observations on Current Economic Developments', speech to the 500 Club Luncheon, Perth, 16 July 1996.

13 Australian Industrial Relations Commission, *Safety Net Review— Wages*, April 1997, pp. 70–1.

CHAPTER 12   ECONOMIC EXCLUSION

1 Bob Gregory and Boyd Hunter, 'The Spatial Structure of the Labour Market', paper presented to the Metropolitan Round Table, Canberra, 17–18 March 1994, p. 32.

2 Bob Gregory, 'Unemployment: What to Do?', *The Sydney Papers*, The Sydney Institute, Spring 1994, p. 111.

3 See Gregory and Hunter, 'The Spatial Structure of the Labour Market', March 1994.

4 Bob Gregory and Boyd Hunter, 'The Macro Economy and the Growth of Ghettos and Urban Poverty in Australia', ANU Centre for Economic Policy Research, Discussion Paper No. 325, April 1995, p. 28.

5 ibid., pp. 31–2.

6 Bob Gregory, 'Disappearing Middle or Vanishing Bottom? A Reply', *The Economic Record*, vol. 72, no. 218, September 1996, p. 296.

7 Bob Gregory, 'Wage Deregulation, Low Paid Workers and Full Employment' in *Dialogues on Australia's Future*, eds Peter Sheehan,

Bhajan Grewal and Margarita Kumnick, Centre for Strategic Economic Studies, Victoria University, 1996, pp. 81–101.

8 Gregory and Hunter, 'The Macro Economy and the Growth of Ghettos and Urban Poverty in Australia', April 1995, pp. 22.

9 ibid., p. 26

10 Peter McDonald, 'Creating Jobs', *Australian Urban and Regional Development Review*, Discussion Paper No. 3, 1994, pp. 20–1.

11 See Schools Council, National Board Of Employment, Education and Training, *Locational Disadvantage in Educational Outcomes*, Report, AGPS, Canberra, 1994.

12 McDonald, 'Creating Jobs', 1994, p. 21.

13 The Working Nation and Job Compact programs did not feature a strong spatial dimension. That is, they concentrated more on supply side interventions directed at the duration of unemployment than demand side policies targeted on the location of unemployment. For instance, the forward budget estimates for 1995/96 reflected outlays of $1886 million for supply side labour market programs (primarily training and wage subsidies) compared to $410 million for regionally targeted employment initiatives ($46.5 million Regional Development Program and $363.5 million New Work Opportunities).

   Importantly, NWO focused on the provision of relatively labour intensive employment in the services sector. These are the jobs required in disadvantaged regions to offset the loss of manufacturing employment. However, given the program's reliance on applications from sponsor organisations, it was not possible to guarantee a close correlation between job placements and high unemployment locations. For instance, of the 6700 approved and pending NWO places as at February 1995, less than 100 were located in the depressed regional labour markets of mid-west Sydney and northern and western Melbourne. Moreover, the limited duration of placements (6–12 months) did not reflect a long term basis for public sector employment creation.

CHAPTER 13   EMPLOYMENT CREATION

1 Bob Gregory and Boyd Hunter, 'The Macro Economy and the Growth of Ghettos and Urban Poverty in Australia', ANU Centre for Economic Policy Research, Discussion Paper No. 325, April 1995, pp. 27–8.

2 McKinsey and Company, *Lead Local Compete Global*, Report for the Department of Housing and Regional Development, Canberra, July 1994.

3 See Glenn Otto and Graham Voss, 'Public Infrastructure and Private Production', *Agenda*, vol.2, no.2, 1995, pp. 181–9.

4 David Aschauer, *Public Investment and Private Sector Growth*, Economic Policy Institute, Washington, 1990.

5 Steve Dowrick, 'Assessing the Economic Value of Infrastructure

Investment', paper presented to an Australian Urban and Regional Development Review Seminar, Canberra, 24 August 1994.

6 Lindsay Tanner, 'A Role Best Left to Government', *The Australian*, 24 February, 1997.

7 Inequities in the distribution of health resources are set out in Appendix IV. Moreover, the Government's 1992–96 National Child Care Strategy did not apply socioeconomic indicators to the distribution of funding for outside school hours care, long day care, occasional care and family day care programs. The Minister for Family Services explained how 'socioeconomic status is not used in arriving at recommendations on areas to be targeted for new places. Places are allocated to levels of unmet demand in an area'. See Answer to Question No. 1247, *House of Representatives Hansard*, 23 August 1994, p. 129.

8 As quoted in Jeremy Rifkin, *The End of Work*, G. P. Putnam's Sons, New York, 1995, p. 37.

9 ibid., p. 249.

10 ibid., p. 266.

11 See Race Mathews, 'The Mondragon Phenomenon', *The Australian Financial Review*, 25 September 1996.

12 These principles apply in the author's Private Member's Bill, the Trade Practices Amendment (Petroleum Access Regime) Bill 1997; see *House of Representatives Hansard*, 10 February 1997, p. 447.

13 William Mitchell, 'Business Welfare—a Legitimate Role for Government?', *Current Affairs Bulletin*, April/May 1995, p. 7.

CHAPTER 14   FINANCING GOVERNMENT

1 See Vince Fitzgerald, *National Savings*, Report to the Federal Treasurer, AGPS, Canberra, 1993, p. 76.

2 See Answer to Question No. 1285, *House of Representatives Hansard*, 15 May 1997, p. 3875.

3 Peter Costello and John Fahey, *Budget Statements 1996–97*, Paper No.1, AGPS, Canberra, 20 August 1997, pp. 2.35–2.36.

4 ibid., p. 1.29.

5 ibid.

6 Fred Argy, 'A Review of the National Saving Debate', *Business Council Bulletin*, April 1996, p. 25.

7 Take, for instance, the development of taxation policies for the farm sector, as set out by Dr Ken Henry, First Assistant Secretary, Taxation Policy Division, The Treasury, at the National Rural Finance Summit, 3 July, 1996:

> Farmers have access to numerous special tax provisions. Indeed, there are more special tax provisions for farmers than for any other sector of the economy. These include generous livestock valuation provisions; a drought investment allowance; generous provisions for viticulture; accelerated write-off for expenditure on water conveyance and conservation; immediate tax write-off for landcare expenses;

accelerated depreciation for horticulture plantings; tax write-off for telephone and electricity lines; special tax provisions for Income Equalisation Deposits and Farm Management Bonds; income tax averaging; exemption for farm income from quarterly payments of provisional tax; income deferral where there is a forced sale of livestock or where there is a second wool clip; and zone rebates. Many of these concessions permit tax to be reduced even where there is no economic cost incurred by the farmer. This is what makes 'farming' especially attractive on Pitt Street and Collins Street. For example, over the last three years a total of $73 million of land degradation claims have been made, of which $34 million has been claimed by taxpayers who describe their main occupation as other than farming . . . The tax provisions available for farming activity are neither equitable nor efficient. Nor do they advantage all farmers; indeed, in many cases farmers are clearly disadvantaged.

To this end, Dr Henry points out that:

an industry with many tax concessions is likely to have structural adjustment problems. Put bluntly as one example of this, Pitt Street and Collins Street farmers push up rural property prices and depress pre-tax returns—to the cost of fulltime farmers, particularly low income farmers . . . A sector 'favoured' by many tax concessions relative to other sectors is likely to have high asset prices, yet low pre-tax returns on investment, and constant pressure for low income participants to leave the sector. Farming [in Australia] has the symptoms of just such a sector.

8 See Brian Toohey, 'Rich Pickings', *The Australian Financial Review*, 3 July 1997, p. 12.
9 See Brian Toohey, 'Tax—It's Flatter Than You Think', *The Australian Financial Review*, 10 February 1997, p. 14.
10 See letters to the editor, *The Australian Financial Review*, 10 December 1991.
11 Report of a Committee (Chaired by Professor Meade), *The Structure and Reform of Direct Taxation*, The Institute for Fiscal Studies, London, 1978.
12 Martin Feldstein, 'A New Route to Reform: Taxing Consumption', *The New Republic*, vol. 174, no. 9, February 1976, pp. 14–17.
13 Jeremy Rifkin, *The End of Work*, G.P. Putnam's Sons, New York, 1995, pp. 272.
14 Under the PET

the after-tax return to the saver from a dollar saved is equal to the full return yielded on the underlying investments in the economy which are financed by the saving. That is, savers are presented with the full rate of trade off between consumption now and consumption in the future that the economy can actually deliver using the real resources involved. Inter-temporal choices are completely undistorted, and the incentive to save kept strong.

See Vince Fitzgerald's advocacy of the Kaldor system in *Reform of Australia's Taxation System*, CEDA Information Paper No. 46, October 1996, p. 23.
15 ibid.
16 ibid.

CHAPTER 15   CONCLUSION:
SUPERSEDING THE MARKET

1 See Alan Ramsey, 'Jobs Policy—a Matter of Opinion', *The Sydney Morning Herald*, 7 June 1997, p. 41.
2 Paul Romer, 'Beyond Classical and Keynesian Macroeconomic Policy', *Policy Options*, vol. 15, no. 6, July–August 1994, p. 20.
3 For a more thorough examination of these expenditure switching effects, using variations on the Salter–Swan model of economic growth, see John Quiggan, Managing the Australian Economy in 1995 and Beyond: Full Employment verus Monetary Contraction, unpublished paper, ANU Centre for Economic Policy Research, November 1994.
4 Francis Castles, *Australian Public Policy and Economic Vulnerability*, Allen & Unwin, Sydney, 1988, p. 161.

CHAPTER 16   THE THEORY AND PRACTICE
OF SOCIAL JUSTICE

1 John Rawls, *A Theory of Justice*, Harvard University Press, 1971.
2 ibid., p. 12.
3 ibid., p. 14.
4 ibid., p. 62.
5 ibid.
6 ibid., p, 13.
7 ibid., p. 584.

CHAPTER 17   QUESTIONS OF LEGITIMACY

1 Quoted in Jeremy Rifkin, *The End of Work*, G. P. Putnam's Sons, New York, 1995, p. 180.
2 John Kenneth Galbraith, *The Culture of Contentment*, Penguin Books, 1992.
3 The binary approach of the commercial media reflects the priority it provides to popular entertainment ahead of strict news value. Quite simply, the promotion of interests associated with those excluded from the production process, the bottom 30 per cent of social interests, is not regarded as compatible with the profitability of media corporations. As John Alexander, editor-in-chief of *The Sydney Morning Herald*, is fond of telling his editorial meetings, 'we must appeal to those who read newspapers, not sleep under them'.
4 William Safire, *Before the Fall*, Belmont Tower Books, New York, 1975.

CHAPTER 18   OVERLOADED GOVERNMENT

1 John Stuart Mill, *On Liberty and Representative Government*, Everymans Library, London, 1962, p. 68.
2 For an outline of this approach to social justice, see Andrew Theophanous, *Understanding Social Justice: An Australian Perspective*, Elikia Books, Melbourne, 1994.

CHAPTER 19   FIRST PRINCIPLES

1 The Australian, 26 October 1996.
2 See I. Dobson, B. Birrell and V. Rapson, 'The Participation of Non-English-speaking Background Persons in Higher Education', *People and Place*, vol. 4, no. 1, pp. 46–54.
3 See *People and Place*, vol. 3, no. 4, pp. 5–12.

CHAPTER 20   THE PUBLIC COMMONS

1 This analysis is drawn from David Thomson, *Welfare States and the Problem of the Common*, CIS Occasional Papers 43, 1992.
2 Garrett Hardin and John Baden, *Managing the Commons*, W. H. Freeman and Company, San Francisco, 1977, p. 20.
3 Thomson, *Welfare States and the Problem of the Common*, 1992, p. 2.
4 ibid., p. 3.
5 Thomson notes how:

> Modern states maintain accounts of their transactions of the moment, but seldom relate these measures through time. The records of each year remain discrete, so that we do not know what experiences individuals or generations are amassing. The person who is 60 at this moment is treated as little but a person of 60: she is not someone with a history, a record of six decades of interaction with others . . . Successful commons cannot operate under such determined opacity.

ibid., p. 14.
6 ibid., p. 28.
7 Mancur Olson, *The Logic of Collective Action*, Harvard University Press, 1965, p. 2.
8 Thomson, *Welfare States and the Problem of the Common*, 1992, p. 16.
9 See Mancur Olson, *The Rise and Decline of Nations*, Yale University Press, New Haven, 1982.
10 See Elinor Ostrom, *Governing the Commons: The Evolution of Institutions for Collective Action*, Cambridge University Press, 1990, pp. 88–102.
11 ibid., p. 89.
12 Thomson, *Welfare States and the Problem of the Common*, 1992, pp. 13, 29 and 30.

CHAPTER 21   A ROLE FOR GOVERNMENT

1 Graham Freudenberg, *William McKell Lecture*, NSW Branch ALP, Sydney, 21 December 1988.
2 See Saul Estrin and Julian Le Grand, *Market Socialism*, Clarendon Press, Oxford, 1989, p. 2.
3 Kenneth Arrow and Robert Lind set out this argument as follows:

> when risks are publicly borne, the costs of risk-bearing are negligible; therefore, a public investment with an expected return which is less than that of a given private investment may nevertheless be superior to the private alternative. Therefore, the fact that public investments with lower expected return may replace private investment is not necessarily cause for concern.

See 'Uncertainty and the Evaluation of Public Investment Decisions', *American Economic Review*, 60, p. 375.
4 These points are drawn from Tom Valentine, 'Economic Rationalism Versus the Entitlement Consensus', *Policy*, Centre for Independent Studies, Spring 1996, pp. 3–10.
5 David Thomson, *Welfare States and the Problem of the Common*, CIS Occasional Papers 43, 1992, p. 29.

CHAPTER 23   SHIFTING SANDS

1 Taken from various ABS sources. The income dependency figures relate to four benefit types: the aged pension, unemployment benefits, the disability pension and sole parent pension.
2 For a critique of the relevance of the Henderson approach, see Peter Baldwin, *Beyond the Safety Net*, Department of Social Security, Canberra, March 1995.
3 Geoff Mulgan, 'Think Well-being, not Welfare', *New Statesman*, 17 January 1997, p. 29.

CHAPTER 24   FUNCTIONAL FLEXIBILITY

1 As quoted in Robert Skidelsky, *The World After Communism*, Macmillan, London, 1995, p. 17.
2 The planning model, with its focus on public ownership and monopoly service rights, also struggles to deal effectively with horizontal equity issues. For instance, private rental housing in Australia receives the smallest amount of government support per household even though it has the greatest number of households in poverty. On the annual value of subsidies and tax concessions, owners receive approximately $1200 per household, purchasers $1330, public rental households $1800 and private rental households $300. The Commonwealth–State Housing Agreement needs to develop a funding mechanism by which, on the

basis of means testing, private rental housing receives as much government support as public housing.

3 See Ross Gittins, 'A Policy Speech for Voters with Brains', *The Sydney Morning Herald*, 20 March 1995.

4 Gary Sturgess, 'Virtual Government—the Public Sector of the Future', Address to the Public Service Commission's Lunchtime Seminar, Canberra, 25 July 1994.

CHAPTER 25   PLACE MANAGEMENT

1 This is an analysis which the urban policy consultants, John Mant and Martin Stewart-Weeks, have placed before local and State government forums in recent years. I am indebted to both for assisting the development of my thinking in this area.

2 A good summary of the silo approach of service delivery can be found in the NSW Government's Social Justice Budget Statement (1995–96). It lists a series of supply side initiatives without any attempt to integrate their impact on disadvantaged people or communities (or with similar Federal and local government measures). The statement's index offers an accurate guide to the complexity of 'segmented social justice': health care, education and training, youth, initiatives for women, children and family services, ageing initiatives, disability initiatives, the justice system, Aboriginal affairs, ethnic affairs, regional and rural communities, urban development, public transport and housing.

3 Figures presented by Craig Knowles, NSW Minister for Planning and Urban Affairs, at a WSROC local government conference, Merrylands, 22 November 1996.

4 See Boyd Hunter, 'Is there an Australian Underclass?', *Urban Futures*, 1995, no. 18, p. 20.

CHAPTER 26   LIFELONG INCOME SUPPORT

1 Michael Jones, *The Australian Welfare State*, Allen & Unwin, Sydney, 1996, p. 1.

2 See Ann Harding and Josh Polette, 'The Price of Means-tested Transfers: Effective Marginal Tax Rates in Australia in 1994', *Australian Economic Review*, no. 111, July–September 1995, p. 100.

3 Will Hutton, 'High-risk Strategy is not Paying Off', *Guardian Weekly*, 12 November 1995, p. 13.

4 See National Commission of Audit, *Report to the Commonwealth Government*, AGPS, Canberra, 1996, p. 112.

5 Peter Baldwin, *Beyond the Safety Net*, Department of Social Security, Canberra, 1995, p. 52.

6 ibid., pp. 51 & 53. In other parts of his paper Baldwin outlines the technical means by which this scheme, its risks and information processing, can be soundly managed. See pp. 55–62.

7 For the original scheme, it was estimated that someone on 75 per cent of average weekly earnings, with contributions at 15 per cent of earnings (comprised of a 9 per cent employer contribution, 3 per cent employee contribution and 3 per cent government co-contribution), would generate a disposable retirement income of almost 120 per cent of their pre-retirement earnings. Contributors on $30 000 per annum over a working life of 40 years would have received a standard of retirement income more than three times their pre-retirement earnings capacity. See Brian Toohey, 'Super Plan Tramples Over our Freedom', *The Australian Financial Review*, 6 August 1997.

8 Prescribing a particular set of approved uses for self-provident contributions to the ISAs also acts as a guarantee against their exploitation in the minimisation of tax. In this part of the scheme, government would also need to devise an appropriate method of funds management to maximise returns on self-provident contributions.

CHAPTER 27   LIFELONG LEARNING

1 Knowledge-based industries avoid the use of depletable raw materials, giving them the virtue of environmental sustainability. The portability of knowledge work, expressed through the growth of telecommuting, also offers benefits in the management of urban environmental issues.

2 Robert Reich, 'Secession of the Successful', *National Policy*, Spring 1996, p. 18.

3 Bob Gregory and Boyd Hunter, 'The Macro Economy and the Growth of Ghettos and Urban Poverty in Australia', ANU Centre for Economic Policy Research, Discussion Paper No. 325, Canberra, April 1995, p. 27.

4 See Peter Baldwin, The Lighthouse: Towards a Labor Vision for the Learning Society, unpublished discussion paper, Canberra, April 1997, p. 55.

5 Around Australia, government and non-government schools alike are struggling to provide an adequate base of educational resources in disadvantaged areas. The additional unit costs involved in vocational education, limited private resources of school communities and emphasis given in government funding to issues of notional choice have placed immense strain on the capacity of these schools to keep pace with advances in learning opportunities.

6 As quoted in Baldwin, The Lighthouse, April 1997, p. 55.

7 Examples of these colleges can be found in the ACT and there is

Bradfield College at North Sydney. Customised learning packages in the transition from school to work should include any suitable combination of apprenticeship, traineeship, TAFE and school courses.

8 See address by the Federal Minister for Schools, David Kemp (in the 'Issues in Public Sector Change' Lecture Series), 'Is there a Crisis in Government Schools?' at the Centre for Public Policy, University of Melbourne, 21 April 1997.

9 See the 'Finn Report' of the Australian Education Council Review Committee, *Young People's Participation in Post-compulsory Education and Training*, AGPS, Canberra, July 1991, p. 151.

10 The overall proportion of employees in Australia with post-secondary qualifications rose from 38 per cent in 1980 to 52 per cent in 1993, with increases in every industry sector. See Peter Costello and John Fahey, *Budget Strategy and Outlook 1997–98*, Budget Paper No. 1, AGPS, Canberra, 1997, p. 3.10.

11 This represents the equivalent of a Year 12 school leaver or competency-based vocational qualification. It matches a similar goal established by President Clinton in the United States.

12 Michael Porter, *The Competitive Advantage of Nations*, Macmillan Press, London, 1990, p. 628. Porter's work also demonstrates how quality education is not possible without quality teaching. Australia has consistently under-resourced the training, remuneration and public standing of its teaching profession at all levels of the education system.

13 At the last British election the Labour Party promised to establish 250 000 learning accounts as a form of labour market adjustment program. In Australia, Peter Baldwin has produced a comprehensive version of this concept in his monograph, The Lighthouse, April 1997.

14 By and large, our secondary schools, TAFE system and universities have been organised like a series of silos, each structured on assumptions formed from the old economy. Inevitably a new funding and administrative system will emerge: an integrated, multi-purpose system, serving as a single resource for learning needs across all vocational callings. This is the institutional design most likely to minimise pathway blockages and create greater service flexibility, especially on a regional scale.

15 See Ernest Healey, 'Unemployment Dependency Rates Amongst Recently Arrived Migrants: An Update', *People and Place*, vol. 2, no. 3, 1994, pp. 47–54.

16 There are also sound reasons for limiting the scope of Australia's migration program, due to its adverse impact on the sustainability of the urban environment, particularly in Sydney. See, for instance, Katharine Betts, 'Growth Crisis a Family Affair', *The Sydney Morning Herald*, 2 July 1996, and Mark Latham, 'Urban Policy and the Environment in Western Sydney', *Australian Quarterly*, Autumn 1992, vol. 64, no.1, pp. 71–82.

CHAPTER 29   A QUESTION OF TRUST

1 For an outline of the libertarian position, see F. A. Hayek, *The Road to Serfdom*, Routledge & Kegan, London, 1944; for the post-industrial futurists, see Peter Drucker, *Post-Capitalist Society*, Butterworth-Heinemann, Oxford, 1993 and Alvin Toffler, *Powershift*, Bantam Books, New York, 1991; for the communitarian position, see Amitai Etzioni, *The Spirit of Community*, Crown Publishers, New York, 1993.

2 Robert Putnam, 'Bowling Alone: America's Declining Social Capital', in *Journal of Democracy*, vol. 6, 1995, p. 67.

3 Robert Putnam, *Making Democracy Work: Civic Traditions in Modern Italy*, Princeton University Press, 1993, p. 176.

4 Francis Fukuyama, *Trust: The Social Virtues and the Creation of Prosperity*, Penguin Books, London, 1995, p. 351.

5 See Putnam, *Making Democracy Work*, 1993, p. 113:

> Yet the vicious circle winds tighter still. In the civic regions even a heavy-handed government—the agent for law enforcement—is itself enfeebled by the uncivic social context. The very character of the community that leads citizens to demand stronger government makes it less likely that any government can be strong, at least if it remains democratic. (This is a reasonable interpretation, for example, of the Italian state's futile anti-Mafia efforts in Sicily over the last half century.) In civic regions, by contrast, light-touch government is effortlessly stronger because it can count on more willing cooperation and self-enforcement among the citizenry.

6 See Fukuyama, *Trust*, 1995, p. 11:

> Already the United States pays significantly more than other industrialised countries for police protection and keeps more than one percent of its total population in prison. The United States also pays substantially more than does Europe or Japan to its lawyers, so that its citizens can sue one another. Both of these costs, which amount to a measurable percentage of gross domestic product annually, constitute a direct tax imposed by the breakdown of trust in the society.

7 Michael Taylor, *Community, Anarchy and Liberty*, Cambridge University Press, 1982, pp. 28–9.

8 Putnam, *Making Democracy Work*, 1993, p. 111.

9 ibid., p. 173.

10 Robert Putnam interviewed on the ABC Lateline program. 'Costing the Community', 8 November 1995.

11 See James Coleman, *Foundations of Social Theory*, Havard University Press, 1990, pp. 317–18.

12 Putnam, *Making Democracy Work*, 1993, p. 175.

13 Francis Fukuyama, *The End of History and the Last Man*, Hamish Hamilton, London, 1992, pp. xvi–xvii.

14 As quoted in Michael Roth, 'A Problem of Recognition: Alexander

Kojeve and the End of History', *History and Theory*, vol. 24, no. 3, pp. 295–6.

15 Fukuyama, *Trust*, 1995, p. 359.

CHAPTER 30   THE CHANGING NATURE OF TRUST

1 Robert Putnam, 'The Strange Disappearance of Civic America', *Policy*, vol. 12, no. 1, Autumn 1996, pp. 3–15.

2 ibid., p. 12.

3 See Marshall McLuhan, *Understanding Media: The Extensions of Man*, McGraw-Hill, New York, 1964.

4 Lester Thurow, *The Future of Capitalism*, Allen & Unwin, Sydney, 1996, p. 82.

5 Hugh Mackay, 'Can We Know Too Much—Information and Morality', *LASIE*, vol. 26, no. 1–3, 1995, pp. 6–17.

6 Robert Putnam in 'Bowling Alone: America's Declining Social Capital', *Journal of Democracy*, vol. 6, 1995 records from the United States:

- the fall in weekly churchgoing from 48 per cent of citizens in the late 1950s to less than 40 per cent now
- the decline in union membership from 33 per cent in 1953 to 16 per cent in 1992
- the fall in participation in parent–teacher organisations from 12 million in 1964 to seven million now
- a fall in the membership of women's clubs by around one-half
- the decline in civic volunteerism, such as the boy scouts (down by 26 per cent since 1970) and Red Cross (down by 61 per cent since 1970)
- a general decline in fraternal club membership, such as the Lions (down 12 per cent since 1983), Jaycees (down 44 per cent since 1979) and Masons (down 39 per cent since 1959)

A survey of similar organisations in Australia was presented in the *IPA Review*, vol. 48, no. 2, 1995, showing:

- that only 17 per cent of Australians are now reported as weekly churchgoers
- there are one-third fewer scouts since the 1960s
- the Masons have shrunk by more than two-thirds since the Second World War
- Country Women's Association membership has fallen from 110 000 in 1954 to 48 000 now
- the general decline in political party, trade union and service club membership

7 This has even occurred with a number of prominent charities. It is important to recognise that the role of charities is somewhat different to the functions of organisations at the middle of society (horizontally framed and intermediary between the state and citizenry). As David

Green has written: 'Charities pick up the conspicuous victims and dust them off. The business of charities is more salvation than mitigation. By the time charity finds its wards they have fallen right through the economic system. It is mutual aid that mitigates the rigours for those still in the economic system.' D. Green & L. Cromwell, *Mutual Aid or Welfare State: Australia's Friendly Societies*, Allen & Unwin, Sydney, 1984, p. xv.

8 Putnam, 'The Strange Disappearance of Civic America', 1996, p. 9.

CHAPTER 31   AUSTRALIAN SOCIAL CAPITAL

1 W. K. Hancock, *Australia*, Ernest Benn, London, 1930, p. 70.
2 Gary L. Sturgess, The Decline and Fall of the Industrial State, unpublished paper (Sturgess Australia), pp. 3–4:

> It has often been said that Australia by-passed this era of private government, progressing from colonial socialism to state socialism in the early decades of the twentieth century. Of course, the ideology of the industrial state arose out of the new paradigms generated by the Industrial Revolution and it is unsurprising that Australia, which only began to form its public institutions in the early nineteenth century, came under its sway. But the story is much more complex. The first bridge built across the Nepean River in the 1850s was a private tollbridge. So, too, was the bridge across Darling Harbour built in 1859. Until recent years, the main road down the Great Dividing Range from Toowoomba to Brisbane was known as the Toll Bar. It was constructed in 1846 by local landowners and operated as a tollroad, replacing a track which had been known as 'Hell Hole Road'. The Hornibrook Highway at Redcliffe on the outskirts of Brisbane, for many years the longest bridge in the southern hemisphere, was built during the depression by the famous Queensland builder, Manuel Hornibrook. It operated successfully as a private tollbridge for forty years, until 1975.
>
> The first steam railway in this country was privately-owned and ran from Melbourne to Port Melbourne. Private electricity suppliers operated until as late as the 1940s. It was 1946 when a Liberal Premier, Tom Playford, nationalised the Adelaide Electric Supply Company, and Joe Cahill took over the Electric Light and Power Corporation in Sydney in 1950. The origins of Australia's overseas telecommunications industry also lie in the private sector. In 1854, shortly after the opening of the nation's first telegraph line, the colonial governments were approached by an English company, the General Oceanic Telegraph Company, seeking a contract to connect Australia to Europe by cable. Australia's overseas telecommunications services were operated by a substantially private company, AWA, until as late as 1946.
>
> In NSW, gas supply remained in the hands of a private utility, the Australian Gaslight Company, a business that has been operating since 1837. To the people of NSW, there is nothing anomalous about this. In the other Australian States, governments nationalised their gas industries decades ago and the people have long since come to

think of them as public utilities. But the people of Sydney find nothing strange about buying their gas from a private company. Some of these enterprises, of course, were short-lived. Others survived for more than a century. Some survive to this day.

3 Hancock, *Australia*, 1930, p. 75.
4 Robert Hughes, *The Fatal Shore*, Pan Books, London, 1988, p. 320.
5 ibid., p. 353.
6 Just a small example of the stickiness of cultural habits: during my time as Mayor of Liverpool (1991–94) I noticed vastly different attitudes to civic process among the city's group of Italian builders and developers. Those who had migrated from the South expected a mayor to exercise authority and act as a patron of their cause; those from the North were much more tolerant of the ideals of public participation and civicness. Looking back, it was like observing Putnam's book in practice.
7 Just as the Australian state was born modern, there is evidence to suggest that Australian society was born classless, or as Lachlan Macquarie wrote to the Home Secretary, Lord Bathurst, in 1822: 'There are only two classes of person in New South Wales. Those who have been convicted and those who ought to have been.'
8 Brian Dickey, 'Why Were There No Poor Laws in Australia?', *Journal of Policy History*, vol. 4, no. 2, 1992, pp. 111 and 130.
9 D. Green & L. Cromwell, *Mutual Aid or Welfare State: Australia's Friendly Societies*, Allen & Unwin, Sydney, 1984, p. 20.
10 See Vern Hughes, 'Between Individual and State', *IPA Review*, vol. 48, no. 2, 1995, pp. 32–8.
11 Green & Cromwell, *Mutual Aid or Welfare State*, 1984, p. 14.
12 ibid., pp. 75–131.

CHAPTER 32   POLITICAL CAPITAL

1 Eva Cox, *A Truly Civil Society*, ABC Books, Sydney, 1995.
2 As quoted by David Burchell, 'After Social Democracy', *Australian Left Review*, September 1992, p. 27. Burchell's analysis has also been relied on here.
3 Robert Putnam, *Making Democracy Work: Civic Traditions in Modern Italy*, Princeton University Press, 1993, pp. 182–3.
4 ibid., p. 184.
5 Francis Fukuyama, *Trust: The Social Virtues and the Creation of Prosperity*, Penguin Books, London, 1995, pp. 40–1.
6 Putnam, *Making Democracy Work*, 1993, p. 184.
7 ibid., p. 181.
8 Michael Taylor, 'Good Government: On Hierarchy, Social Capital and the Limitations of Rational Choice Theory', *Journal of Political Philosophy*, vol. 4, no. 1, 1996, p. 2.

CHAPTER 33   DEVOLUTION IN PRACTICE

1 As quoted in Robert Boynton, 'The Two Tonys', *The New Yorker*, 6 October 1997, p. 69.
2 Michael Taylor, 'Good Government: On Hierarchy, Social Capital and the Limitations of Rational Choice Theory', *Journal of Political Philosophy*, vol. 4, no. 1, 1996, p. 10.
3 See Tom Bentley, 'Learning Beyond the Classroom', *Demos Quarterly*, issue 9, Demos Centre, London, 1996, pp. 44–5.
4 Robert Putnam, *Making Democracy Work: Civic Traditions in Modern Italy*, Princeton University Press, 1993, p. 107.

CHAPTER 34   CONCLUSION: REBUILDING PUBLIC MUTUALITY

1 David Marquand, *The Unprincipled Society*, Jonathan Cape, London, 1988, p. 226.
2 Michael Walzer, *Spheres of Justice*, Martin Robertson, Oxford, 1983.
3 Tony Blair, *Socialism*, British Fabian Society Pamphlet 565, July 1994.
4 Hugh Mackay, 'Can We Know Too Much—Information and Morality', *LASIE*, vol. 26, no. 1–3, 1995, p. 15.

CHAPTER 35   SOCIAL DEMOCRACY IN TRANSITION

1 Harold Laski, *A Grammar of Politics*, Allen & Unwin, London, 1925, p. 88.
2 See G. D. H. Cole, *Guild Socialism Re-stated*, Leonard Parsons, London, 1920.
3 For an explanation of earlier forms of liberal socialist ideology, see Leonard Hobhouse, *Liberalism*, Oxford University Press, London, 1964 (originally published in 1911).
4 See Gary Sturgess, *The Boundaries of Life's Responsibilities: Community and Nation in a Global Environment*, Centre for Independent Studies, Occasional Paper No. 57, 1996.
5 Michael Sandel, 'America's Search for a New Public Philosophy', *Atlantic Monthly*, March 1996, p. 74.
6 Elaine Thompson, *Fair Enough: Egalitarianism in Australia*, UNSW Press, 1994, p. 252.
7 Barry Jones, *Work in Progress*, Victorian Branch ALP, Melbourne, 1996, p. 3.
8 See address by Don Aitkin, 'Educating for the Future', The Chief of Army Exercise, Canberra, 16 July 1997.
9 In the words of the Federal ALP frontbencher, Laurie Ferguson, 'Two big negatives for the Keating Government were the question

of migration and multiculturalism. Unfortunately the Party became convinced that dancing polkas and going to the mosque mean that some Iman can deliver 20 000 votes to you tomorrow morning.' See *The 1996 Federal Election Symposium*, The Centre for Corporate Public Affairs, 15 April 1996, p. 36.

APPENDIX IV   HEALTH REFORM IN AUSTRALIA

1 E. Nord, J. Richardson, A. Street, H. Kuhse and P. Singer, 'Do Australians Want Their Health System to Maximise Health?', Paper presented to the Conference of Australian Health Economists, ANU, 7–8 July 1994, p. i.

2 John Paterson, *National Healthcare Reform—The Last Picture Show*, Victorian Department of Human Services, Melbourne, April 1996, p. 14.

3 R. B. Scotton and C. R. Macdonald, *The Making of Medibank*, UNSW Press, 1993, p. 273.

4 Alain Enthoven, 'Managed Competition: An Agenda for Action', *Health Affairs*, vol. 7, no. 3, Summer 1988, p. 28.

5 See Paterson, *National Healthcare Reform*, April 1996.

6 R. B. Scotton, 'Managed Competition: The Scotton Model', *Healthcover*, June–July 1997, p. 28.

7 Paterson's research has detailed the over-supply of GPs and under-supply of specialists in Australia. Medical colleges are able to restrict the supply of specialists and increase copayment prices through their control of post-graduate training. Cardio-thoracic surgeons have the most imbalanced market conditions, with the top 25 per cent earning around $700 000 per annum, of which approximately one-half is in the form of patient copayments. The supply of these surgeons, 0.56 per 100 000 population, is well below the 0.85 target set by government reports. Specialists such as these are among the highest income earners drawing on the public purse in Australia. See John Paterson, 'A New Look at National Medical Workforce Strategy', *Australian Health Review*, vol. 17, no. 1, 1994, pp. 5–42.

8 See *BMA v. Commonwealth*, (1949), 79 CLR 201.

INDEX

385